Horizons

Mathematics 5

Teacher's Guide

Authors:

Cindi Mitchell & Lori Fowler

Editor:

Alan Christopherson

Graphic Design:

Chris Burkholder
Mark Aguilar
Brian Ring

JoAnn Cumming
Keith Piccolo
Marybeth Graville

Annette Walker
Lisa Kelly

Alpha Omega Publications, Inc. • Rock Rapids, IA

Horizons Mathematics 5 Teacher's Guide
© MCMXCVIII by Alpha Omega Publications, Inc.® All rights reserved.
804 N. 2nd Ave. E., Rock Rapids, IA 51246-1759

Printed in the United States of America
ISBN 978-1-58095-899-8

Contents

Section One   **Page**

Introduction

    Before You Start 5

    Readiness Evaluation 7

    Preparing a Lesson 13

    Scope & Sequence 17

    Where to Use Mathematics Worksheets 20

    Appearance of Concepts 22

Section Two

Teacher's Lessons (1–160) 37

Section Three

Answer Keys (Lessons 1–160) 227

Test Keys (Tests 1–16) 295

Section Four

Worksheets (1–80) 305

Worksheet Answer Keys 387

Section Five

Quarter Tests 405

Final Exam 424

Test Keys 431

Introduction

Before You Start ...

THE CHALLENGE

Today's average high school graduate knows and can do less math than their counterpart of ten, fifteen, or twenty years ago. Basic math skills have deteriorated to the point that many wonder if this country can continue to be a leader in shaping the technology of the future. Unfortunately, the general trend of modern education of all types is downward. Students in private education, while they score higher overall than public school students, still do poorly in math computation skills.

THE GOAL

The goal of this curriculum is to provide the parent and teacher with a tool that will help them effectively combat this deterioration of math skills by raising the level of student performance. Research of the content and methods of other existing curriculums, the concepts evaluated by achievement tests, and typical courses of study resulted in selection of the *Scope and Sequence* starting on page 17. This curriculum was not planned around any particular group of students. Rather, it was determined that the material in this curriculum constituted a reasonable level of performance for fifth grade students. The curriculum is designed so that the teacher can adapt its use to student(s) of widely varying ability. In other words, the curriculum is a tool that is capable of performing well over a broad range of student ability to help them achieve a higher minimum level of proficiency. The two major components of the curriculum are the student text (in two volumes) and the *Teacher's Guide*. These are the absolute minimum components for accomplishing the objective of teaching the concepts in the *Scope and Sequence*. Since this book was designed as an integral part of the curriculum, it is absolutely necessary to use the Teacher's Guide. It contains activities not found in the student texts that are essential to the accomplishment of the curriculum objectives. As you will see in the following sections, this *Teacher's Guide* contains a significant number of suggestions and helps for the teacher.

THE DESIGN

Take a moment to look at the sample chart entitled, *Appearance of Concepts*, on page 22. Take note of how the curriculum concepts are developed. The first presentation is usually a brief familiarization. Then the basic teaching is accomplished as part of three to five lessons. The thoroughness of a presentation depends on how new and how important the concept is to the student's academic development.

The Development

Each concept will be reviewed for three to five lessons after the complete presentation. For the next two months the concept will be presented every two weeks as a part of two or three lessons. After a break in presentation of a few weeks, the concept will be thoroughly reviewed as part of the lesson for three to five days. This will be followed by a period where the concept will be reviewed every two weeks as part of two or three lessons. This progression continues until the student(s) have had the opportunity to thoroughly master the concept.

An Example

Some mathematics curriculums might teach *division* for two months and not go back to it again. In this curriculum it will be introduced and practiced for two weeks. For the next two months, *division* will be presented every two weeks as a part of two or three lessons to give the student(s) continual practice to develop mastery of the concept. The third month will be considered a break from presenting the concept. In the fourth month, *division* will first be thoroughly reviewed and again practiced every two weeks as a part of two or three lessons. By having a series of practices every two weeks, the student(s) will retain what they have learned to a greater degree. Short periods of exposure repeated many times is much more effective than long periods with fewer exposures. Review the chart on page 22 to see how the concepts are developed.

Readiness Evaluation

WHY EVALUATE READINESS?
Teaching could be defined as the process of starting with what a student knows and guiding him to added knowledge with new material. While this may not be a dictionary definition of teaching, it is descriptive of the processes involved. Determining a student's readiness for fifth grade mathematics is the first step to successful teaching.

TYPES OF READINESS
True readiness has little to do with chronological age. Emotional maturity and mental preparation are the main components of academic readiness. The teacher who is dealing directly with the student is best able to determine a child's emotional maturity. All emotionally immature students may need special student training in their problem areas. A child's mental *preparation* can be more easily discerned with a simple diagnostic evaluation. Observing the child's attitude of confidence or insecurity while taking the evaluation may help determine emotional readiness.

DETERMINING READINESS
The fifth grade *Readiness Evaluation* on pages 8–12 helps the teacher to determine if student(s) are ready to begin studying math at the fifth grade level. Complete this evaluation the first or second day of school.

The evaluation should take 45-60 minutes. It would be helpful to evaluate all of the students to determine what each student knows. However, you may want to evaluate only those student(s) who have not had a thorough fourth grade program. It is especially important to evaluate any student who is using this curriculum for the first time. The student(s) should be able to complete the test on their own with the teacher making sure they understand the directions for each individual activity.

The answer key is on page 8. Count each individual answer as a separate point. The total for the test is 81 points. The student(s) should achieve a score of 57 or more points to be ready to begin fifth grade. Be sure to note the areas of weakness of each student, even those who have scored over 57 points. If the student(s) scored under 57 points, they may need to repeat fourth grade math or do some refresher work in their areas of weakness. For possible review of the identified areas of weakness, refer to the chart *Appearance of Concepts* on page 22 of the *Horizons Math 4 Teacher's Guide*. It will locate lessons where the concepts were taught.

Count each individual answer as a separate point. The total for the test is 81 points. The student should achieve a score of 57 or more points to be ready to begin fifth grade. Be sure to note the areas of weakness even for those who score over 57 points.

1. \$6.02; \$1.19; \$7.89; \$2.37; \$5.18

2. 70; 90; 10; 20; 40

3. Tami

4. 1. j
   2. i
   3. b
   4. h
   5. m
   6. g
   7. c
   8. l
   9. d
   10. a
   11. k
   12. o
   13. e
   14. f
   15. n

5. 1. ∠RXS, ∠ XSQ
   2. ∠ RXQ, ∠ RXP
   3. $\overleftrightarrow{PQ}$ and $\overleftrightarrow{AB}$
   4. $\overleftrightarrow{AB}$ and $\overleftrightarrow{CD}$ or $\overleftrightarrow{PQ}$ and $\overleftrightarrow{RX}$

6. 1. Circle X
   2. 2 cm
   3. 2 cm
   4. CD
   5. 8 cm

7.

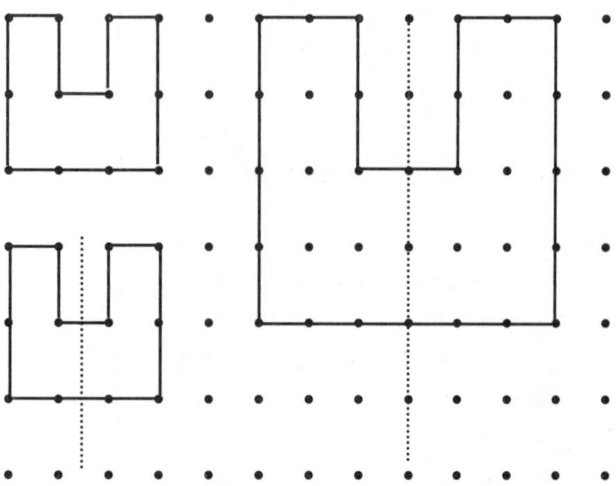

8. Figure A – perimeter 60 in; area 200 in^2
   Figure B – 24 cm^3

9. 27; 42; 48; 81

10. $\frac{3}{3} = 1$; $\frac{4}{10} = \frac{2}{5}$; $\frac{6}{12} = \frac{1}{2}$
    $\frac{6}{7}$; $\frac{13}{14}$; $\frac{13}{9} = 1\frac{4}{9}$

11. $\frac{4}{8} = \frac{1}{2}$; $\frac{10}{15} = \frac{2}{3}$; $\frac{8}{10} = \frac{4}{5}$
    $\frac{8}{12} = \frac{2}{3}$; $\frac{9}{12} = \frac{3}{4}$; $\frac{11}{15}$

12. $8\frac{3}{6} = 8\frac{1}{2}$; $28\frac{5}{7}$; $\frac{3}{6} = \frac{1}{2}$;
    $10\frac{4}{12} = 10\frac{1}{3}$; 16

13. $>$ $=$ $<$ $=$

14. 53.244; 698.022; 1.132; 6.82

15. 89.0; 7,889
    0.587; 85,400
    656,000; 700.1

Preparing a Lesson

GENERAL INFORMATION

There is some room on the teacher lessons for you to write your own notes. The more you personalize your Teacher's Guide in this way, the more useful it will be to you.

You will notice that there are 160 student lessons in the curriculum. This allows for the inevitable interruptions to the school year like holidays, test days, inclement weather days, and those unexpected interruptions. It also allows the teacher the opportunity to spend more time teaching any concept that the student(s) may have difficulty with. Or, you might wish to spend a day doing some of the fun activities mentioned in the Teaching Tips. If you find that the student(s) need extra drill, use the worksheets as extra lessons.

STUDENT'S LESSONS
ORGANIZATION

The lessons are designed to be completed in forty-five to sixty minutes a day. If extra manipulatives or worksheets are utilized, you will need to allow more time for teaching. Each lesson consists of a major concept and practice of previously taught concepts. If the student(s) find the presence of four or five different activities in one lesson a little overwhelming at the beginning, start guiding the student(s) through each activity. By the end of two weeks, they should be able to work more independently as they adjust to the format. Mastery of a new concept is not necessary the first time it is presented. Complete understanding of a new concept will come as the concept is approached from different views using different methods at different intervals. Directions to the student(s) are given and examples or explanations are presented.

Tests

Starting with Lesson 10, tests are included in every tenth lesson. They should require approximately forty minutes to administer. If your daily schedule time is a major factor, the student lesson may be completed the following day. This will require efficient scheduling of the lessons throughout the year to complete the program by the end of the school year. The 16 tests, 4 quarter tests, 1 final exam and 160 lessons each administered or taught on separate days would bring the scheduled curriculum days to a total of 181.

Do not make the test a special lesson. Allow the student(s) to perceive the test as a regular lesson with no undue pressure. The purpose of testing is not just to measure student progress, although that is an important consideration. A test is also an important teaching tool. It should be returned to the student and any missed items discussed so that it is a true learning experience. For this reason, it is important to grade and return the tests as soon as possible while the material is fresh in the student's mind.

The test structure is such that the student(s) will have had sufficient practice with a concept to have learned it before being tested. Therefore, no concept is tested until the initial presentation has been completed. For example, Test 2 in Lesson 20 covers concepts completed in Lessons 6–15. Lessons 16–19 may include the introduction of some new material which will not be covered in Test 2. Test 8 in Lesson 80 will cover Lessons 66–75. The new material from Lessons 76–79 will not be covered in Test 8.

TEACHER'S LESSONS
ORGANIZATION

Each lesson is organized into the following sections: **Concepts**; **Objectives**; **Teaching Tips**; **Materials, Supplies**, and **Equipment; Activities**; and a maxim or proverb. Each of the sections have a distinct symbol to help you locate them on the page of the teacher's lesson. To be a master teacher you will need to prepare each lesson well in advance.

Concepts

Concepts are listed at the beginning of each lesson. New concepts are listed first followed by concepts that are practiced from previous lessons. Fifth grade math has twenty-one major concepts. These are developed in a progression that is designed to give the student(s) a solid foundation in the basic math skills while providing enough variety to hold the student's interest.

Objectives

The Objectives list criteria for the student's performance. They state what the student should be able to do at the completion of the lesson. You will find objectives helpful in determining the student's progress, the need for remedial work, and readiness for more advanced information. Objectives are stated in terms of measurable student performance. The teacher then has a fixed level of performance to be attained before the student(s) are ready to progress to the next level.

Teaching Tips

Each tip is related to one of the Activities in the lesson. Some Teaching Tips require the teacher to make a manipulative needed to complete the activity. Teaching Tips are activities that the teacher can do to enhance the teaching process. You will find them useful for helping the student who needs additional practice to master the concepts or for the student who needs to be challenged by extra work.

Materials, Supplies, and Equipment

Materials, Supplies, and Equipment lists the things you'll need to find before you teach each lesson. Sometimes you will also find instructions on how to make your own materials, supplies, and equipment. This section also lists the worksheets. There is approximately one worksheet for every two lessons. If worksheets are suggested in a particular lesson you will find them listed. Each worksheet has a worksheet number. The chart on pages 20-21 gives the number of the lesson with which it is associated. The Teacher's Guide identifies where these resource worksheets are essential to the lessons. The worksheets will be handy for many purposes. You might use them for extra work for student(s) who demonstrate extra aptitude or ability or as remedial work for the student(s) who demonstrate a lack of aptitude or ability. You may also make your own worksheets and note where you would use them in the materials section on the teacher's lesson. Some of the worksheets become manipulative aids for specific concepts.

Activities

The teacher's greatest concentration should be on the **Activities** section. Here the teacher will find directions for teaching each lesson. All activities are designed to be teacher directed both in the student lesson and in the Teacher's Guide. You will need to use your own judgement concerning how much time is necessary to carry out the activities. Each activity is important to the over all scope of the lesson and must be completed. Do not omit any portion of the activities, particularly the multiplication and division drill with flashcards, unless the student(s) have thoroughly mastered the concept being presented. Please do not put off looking at the activities in the lesson until you are actually teaching. Taking time to preview what you will be teaching is essential. Choose the manipulatives that fit your program best.

Each lesson starts with an **Explanation** section that discusses the new material being introduced in the lesson. Sample problems are often included in this section. Some students will be able to read and comprehend the information on their own. Other students need to be guided through this section for complete understanding. Following the **Explanation** of each lesson are the numbered **Practice** problems for the lesson. Number 1 of the **Practice** section always applies the skills learned in the **Explanation** box. Exercises from 2 on, review previously taught concepts.

Maxims

You will find a short maxim or proverb at the bottom of each lesson. These maxims provide a collection of various wise and pithy sayings that deal with character. They are intended for the teacher to share and discuss with the student(s). Ask the student(s) to suggest ways that they could apply the maxim to their day-to-day activities of life. Have them think of a time when their friends may have put the maxim into practice. Tell them to watch for opportunities to practice the maxim in the next week and report the incident to you. You may use or not use them as you wish.

ANSWER KEYS

The answer keys section of the Teacher's Guide provides answers to the student lessons. It is suggested that you give the student(s) a grade for tests only. Daily work is to be a learning experience for the student, so do not put unnecessary pressure on them. You should correct every paper, but you should not grade every paper. This means that each lesson should be marked for correct and incorrect answers, but it is not necessary to record a letter or percentage grade on every lesson. The lessons should then be returned to the student(s) so that they have the opportunity to learn from their mistakes.

WORKSHEETS

The next section contains the worksheets. They are reproducible and can be copied freely. These worksheets have been developed for reinforcement and drill. You will find a complete listing of worksheets and where they might best be used on pages 20 and 21. Separate packets of all the necessary worksheets for an individual student are also available. Answer keys to the worksheets are provided in the same manner as for the student lessons.

UNIT TESTS

Quarter, Semester and Final Exam tests are provided to evaluate overall student progress. They can be administered after Lesson 40, Lesson 80, Lesson 120, and Lesson 160. Answer keys are provided for these tests.

Fifth Grade Mathematics
SCOPE & SEQUENCE

1. NUMBER THEORY
word numbers through hundred billion
(review) expanded form through hundred billion
(review) Roman numerals
divisibility
prime and composite
prime factorization
*factor trees (slight introduction before)
*exponents (slight introduction before)

2. PLACE VALUE
ones, tens, hundreds
thousands, ten thousands, hundred thousands
millions, ten millions, hundred millions
billions, ten billions, hundred billions

3. NUMBER ORDER
*rounding to the nearest 10
*rounding to the nearest 100
*rounding to the nearest 1,000
*greater than and less than
*equal and not equal

4. ADDITION
*addition properties
*addition terms
*addition facts
*addition with two-, three-, four-, five-, and six-digit numbers
equations
column addition
missing addends
estimating
adding money
more than one operation

*new concepts

5. SUBTRACTION
*subtraction properties
*subtraction terms
*basic facts
*subtraction with two-, three-, four-, five-, and six-digit numbers
equations
estimating
subtracting money
more than one operation

6. MULTIPLICATION
*multiplication terms
*multiplication facts
*multiplication properties
two-digit times two-digit numbers
triple digit times a single-digit number
*three digit times three-digit numbers
multiplying by 10, 100, and 1000
money by two-digit number
missing factors
estimating products
*exponents

7. DIVISION
*division terms
*division facts
*division properties
one-digit dividend by one-digit divisor with remainders
two-digit dividend by one-digit divisor
dividing money
zeros in the quotient
two-digit divisors that are multiples of ten
two-digit divisors with one-digit quotients
two-digit divisors when the guess is incorrect
two-digit divisors with two-digit quotients
estimating quotients
*three-digit quotients with remainders
*averaging with remainders

8. TIME

terms
A.M., P.M.
century
time equivalents
elapsed time
calendar
time zones

9. MONEY

money will be covered under addition,
subtraction, multiplication, and division
counting change

10. GEOMETRY

shapes, solids and diagonals
symmetry
*congruent and similar figures
*congruent segments and angles
line, line segment, ray, endpoint, plane
parallel, intersecting, perpendicular lines
angles—rays, vertex, acute, obtuse, right
*circles: diameter, radius, and chord
*compass
*protractor
*types of triangles
*classifying polygons

11. PERIMETER, AREA, AND VOLUME

perimeter
area
volume
*surface area

12. FRACTIONS

equivalent fractions
greatest common factor
reducing fractions
comparing and ordering fractions
adding and subtracting fractions with
common denominators
mixed numbers
improper fractions
*least common multiples
*adding and subtracting fractions with
    unlike denominators

*adding and subtracting mixed numbers
    without regrouping
*renaming mixed numbers
*adding mixed numbers, renaming fractions
*more renaming
*subtracting mixed numbers with common
    denominators—borrowing from whole
    numbers
*subtracting mixed numbers with unlike
    denominators—borrowing from whole
    numbers
*multiplying fractions with whole numbers
*multiplying two fractions together
*multiplying mixed numbers together
*dividing whole numbers by fractions
*dividing fractions by whole numbers
*dividing fractions by fractions

13. DECIMALS

fractions to decimals
*word numbers to thousandths
*comparing decimals
*ordering decimals
add decimals (horizontally and vertically)
subtracting decimals
estimating decimals
estimating decimals with money
*multiplying decimals by whole numbers
*multiplying decimals by decimals
*dividing decimals by whole numbers

14. RATIO

writing simple ratios
multiplying to find equal ratios
dividing to find equal ratios
*cross products

15. MEASUREMENT

standard and metric linear equivalent
standard and metric liquid equivalent
standard and metric weight equivalent
temperature reading and understanding
Fahrenheit and Celsius
millimeter, centimeter, decimeter, meter
decameter, hectometer, kilometer

*new concepts

16. GRAPHS
bar
line
pictographs
circle
coordinate graphs
comparing graphs
*mean, mode, median

17. EQUATIONS
addition
subtraction
multiplication
division

18. PERCENT
*understanding the concept
*finding the percent of a number
*percent and decimals
*percent and fractions
*discount and sales tax
*fractions as percent

19. PROBLEM SOLVING
Four-step method
understanding the question
choosing an operation
reasonable or unreasonable
too much/too little information
Guess and Check
understanding remainders
making organized lists
working backwards
Make it Simpler
logical reasoning
drawing a picture

20. PROBABILITY
one variable

21. CALCULATOR MATH
problem solving with calculators

*new concepts

Where To Use
Mathematics Worksheets

*In this guide you will find eighty worksheets to be used as **Duplication Masters**.*

This chart shows where worksheets may be used for *Horizons Math 5*.
You will need to **duplicate** any worksheet that you plan to use more than once.

No.	Concept	Lessons Where Worksheets Are Used
1	Addition facts	1
2	Subtraction facts	2
3	Multiplication facts	3
4	Division facts	4
5	Using more than 1 operation working in the parentheses first	6
6	Addition of equations	7
7	Subtraction of equations	8
8	Place value to the hundred billions	11-13
9	Expanded form	14
10	Rounding to the 10, 100, 1,000	18
11	Addition with 4, 5, and 6 digits	22
12	Column addition with 2- and 3-digit numbers	23
13	Subtraction with 4, 5, and 6 digits	26
14	Estimate subtraction	27
15	Add and subtract money	28
16	Factor trees	32
17	Prime and composite numbers	33
18	Multiply by 10, 100, 1,000	35
19	Multiplication (2-digit x 2-digit)	36
20	Multiplication (3-digit x 3-digit)	37
21	Multiplication of equations	39
22	Exponents	40
23	Multiply and divide money (1-digit divisor, no remainder)	43 and 29
24	Dividing Equations	44
25	Averaging with remainders	49
26	Divide by 10, 100	51
27	Division (2-digit divisor/2-digit quotient)	53
28	Division (2-digit divisor/2-digit quotient with zeros in the quotient)	56
29	Divisibility 2, 3, 5, 10	59
30	A.M. and P.M.	62 and 65
31	Time equivalents	64
32	Time Zones	67
33	Counting money	68
34	Giving change	69
35	Points, lines, line segments, rays, and angles	71 and 73
36	Parallel, intersecting, perpendicular	72
37	Protractors	74

Where To Use Mathematics Worksheets, continued:

No.	Concept	Lessons Where Worksheets Are Used
38	Types of triangles: isosceles, equilateral, scalene	75
39	Quadrilaterals	76
40	Other types of polygons	77
41	Circles and compass	78
42	Graphing ordered pairs	79
43	Congruent segments, angles and polygons	82
44	Similar figures	83
45	Space figures	84
46	Perimeter	85
47	Area	86
48	Volume	87
49	Surface area	88
50	Fractions	91
51	Equivalent fractions	92
52	Reducing (Lowest Terms)	94
53	Adding and subtracting fractions with common denominator	96
54	Converting from mixed number to improper fraction & vice-versa	98
55	Adding and subtracting fractions with unlike denominators	102
56	Adding and subtracting mixed numbers	104
57	Renaming mixed numbers	105
58	Adding and subtracting mixed numbers and renaming sums	106
59	Adding and subtracting mixed numbers and renaming sums	107
60	Adding, subtracting mixed numbers, fractions with like and unlike denominators, and whole numbers	110
61	Multiplication of fractions	112
62	Multiplication of mixed numbers	113
63	Division of fractions and whole numbers	115
64	Reading/writing ratios	117
65	Finding a percent of a ratio	119
66	Place Value - decimals through the ten thousandths	123
67	Comparing/ordering decimals, rounding decimals	124 and 125
68	Adding/subtracting decimals	128
69	Multiplication of decimals by whole numbers	131
70	Multiplication of decimals	132
71	Division of decimals with zeros	134
72	Percents to decimals, and decimals to fractions	138
73	Finding the percent of a number	139
74	Standard measurement, weight, and liquid measure	143
75	Metric measure, weight and liquid measure	147
76	Standard and metric temperature	148
77	Bar and line graphs	152
78	Pictographs and circle graphs	154
79	Mean, median and mode	158
80	Probability	160

Appearance of Concepts

Lesson 1
addition terms
addition properties
addition of fractions
geometric terms
place value

Lesson 2
subtraction properties
subtraction terms
subtraction problems
addition of fractions
place value
written and number fractions
geometric terms

Lesson 3
multiplication properties
multiplication terms
multiplication problems
geometric terms
liquid equivalent
addition problems
subtraction problems
even numbers

Lesson 4
division terms
division properties
division problems
subtraction of fractions
geometric terms
odd numbers

Lesson 5
missing addends
addition problems
subtraction problems
multiplication problems
value of money
division problems
missing numerator and
   denominator
identify polygons

Lesson 6
order of operations
missing addends
multiplication problems
division problems
missing numerator and
   denominator
label polygons
geometric terms

Lesson 7
addition equations
order of operations
missing addends
division problems
rename fractions
similar and congruent shapes
liquid measure

Lesson 8
subtraction equations
addition problems
order of operations
missing addends
rename fractions
similar and congruent shapes
linear measure

Lesson 9
word problems for calculators
addition equations
subtraction equations
number patterns
order fractions — least to greatest
symmetry

Lesson 10
problem solving (4 step plan)
addition equations
subtraction equations
word problems for calculators
symmetry
number patterns
order fractions—least to greatest

Lesson 11
place value
missing subtrahends
problem solving
calculator
mixed to improper fractions
circles
addition of decimals

Lesson 12
place value
problem solving
calculator
mixed to improper fractions
circles
addition of decimals
value of money

Lesson 13
place value
problem solving
calculator
mixed to improper fractions
space figures
subtraction of decimals
money
even and odd numbers

Lesson 14
standard, written, expanded form
place value
improper to mixed fractions
space figures
temperature
addition terms and facts
multiplication facts

Lesson 15
Roman numerals
place value
addition of mixed numbers
perimeter
addition terms and facts
comparing decimals

Appearance of Concepts

Lesson 16
order numbers
Roman numerals
place value
addition of mixed numbers
perimeter
subtraction terms and facts

Lesson 17
rounding numbers
order numbers
Roman numerals
place value
subtraction of mixed numbers
area
bar graphs
subtraction terms and facts

Lesson 18
rounding numbers
comparing numbers
Roman numerals
subtract mixed numbers
writing a check
area
circle graph
multiplication terms

Lesson 19
problem solving
rounding numbers
comparing numbers
renaming fractions
line graphs
word problems
multiplication terms and facts

Lesson 20
calculator
problem solving
rounding numbers
comparing numbers
pictograph
missing minuends or subtrahends
division terms and facts

Lesson 21
2- and 3-digit addition
addition of fractions
value of money
problem solving
volume
place value
missing addends

Lesson 22
4-, 5-, and 6-digit addition
2- and 3-digit addition
value of money
problem solving
volume
place value
missing addends

Lesson 23
column addition
4-, 5-, and 6-digit addition
2- and 3-digit addition
mixed to improper fractions
problem solving
compare and order
geometric shapes

Lesson 24
estimating sums
regrouping process
2-, 3-, 4-, 5-, and 6-digit addition
column addition
problem solving
compare and order
order of operations
geometric shapes

Lesson 25
2- and 3-digit subtraction
regrouping process
estimating sums
column addition
4-, 5-, and 6-digit addition
rounding numbers
addition terms and facts
addition equations

Lesson 26
2-, 3-, 4-, 5-, and 6-digit subtraction
regrouping process
estimating sums
column addition
rounding numbers
addition terms and facts
addition equations

Lesson 27
estimating differences
2-, 3-, 4-, 5-, and 6-digit subtraction
regrouping process
estimating sums
subtraction equations
subtraction terms and facts
space figures

Lesson 28
addition and subtraction of money
estimating differences
2-, 3-, 4-, 5-, and 6-digit subtraction
regrouping process
subtraction equations
subtraction terms and facts
space figures

Lesson 29
word problems
money
estimating differences
4-, 5-, and 6-digit subtraction
dividing ratios
geometric figures

Lesson 30
problem solving
money
estimating differences
even and odd numbers
number recognition
multiplication terms and facts
geometric figures

Appearance of Concepts

Lesson 31
multiplication table
convert fractions to decimals
column addition
division with 1-digit divisors
word problems
five-digit addition

Lesson 32
factoring
multiplication tables
2- and 3-digit addition
mystery numbers
division with 1-digit divisors
5-digit addition

Lesson 33
prime/composite numbers
multiplication tables
liters, meters, and grams
4-digit addition
missing addends
place value

Lesson 34
2- and 3-digit multiplication
ratios
four-digit subtraction
divisibility
place value
prime numbers

Lesson 35
multiply by 10, 100, 1000
multiplication problems
ratio
place value
prime numbers
factor trees

Lesson 36
2-digit multiplication
subtraction problems
two operations
multiplication by multiples of 10
factor trees
prime numbers
1-digit multiplication

Lesson 37
3-digit multiplication
multiplication by multiples of 10
5- and 6-digit addition
prime factors
1-digit multiplication

Lesson 38
estimating products
2-digit multiplication
multiplication by factors of 10
subtraction problems
addition equations

Lesson 39
multiplication equations
estimating products
polygons
2-digit multiplication
subtraction equations

Lesson 40
exponents
multiplication equations
estimating products
geometric shapes
2-digit multiplication
multiplication tables
prime numbers

Lesson 41
1-digit quotient division
2- and 3-digit addition
factor trees
customary units of measure
temperature (Fahrenheit)
century
multiplication terms

Lesson 42
1- and 2-digit quotient division
2- and 3-digit addition
factor trees
customary units of measure
time measurement definitions
division terms

Lesson 43
1- and 2-digit quotient division
division of money
4-, 5-, and 6-digit addition
prime/composite
customary units of measure
missing addends

Lesson 44
division equations
1- and 2-digit quotient division
division of money
4-, 5-, and 6-digit addition
place value
missing addends

Lesson 45
2- and 3-digit quotient division
division of money
3-digit multiplication
2- and 3-digit subtraction
place value
multiple operations

Appearance of Concepts

Lesson 46
division with zeros in quotient
3-digit quotient division
division of money
2-digit multiplication
compare/order whole numbers
addition problems
multiple operations

Lesson 47
estimating quotients
division with zeros in quotient
2-digit multiplication
2- and 3-digit subtraction
compare/order whole numbers
addition terms
addition equations

Lesson 48
averaging
estimating quotients
division problems
4-, 5-, and 6-digit subtraction
3-digit multiplication
subtraction terms and facts
addition equations

Lesson 49
averaging
estimating quotients
division with zeros in quotient
4-, 5-, and 6-digit subtraction
rounding to 10, 100 and 1,000
subtraction terms
subtraction equations

Lesson 50
interpreting answers
averaging
estimating quotients
division
exponents
multiplication equations
subtraction equations

Lesson 51
division by multiples of 10
factor trees
solid figures
metric definitions
geometric figures
multiplication
2-digit divisor division

Lesson 52
2-digit divisor division
factor trees
solid figures
divisibility
measurement
division problems

Lesson 53
2-digit quotient division
prime numbers
divisibility
measurement
simple division

Lesson 54
division and estimation
divide by multiples of 10
prime and composite
missing addends
bar graphs
magic squares

Lesson 55
3-digit quotient division
2-digit quotient division
multiplication
logical reasoning
missing addends
place value
subtraction problems

Lesson 56
division with zeros in quotient
multiplication
2-digit quotient division
column addition
place value
problems with two operations
multiplication

Lesson 57
division to estimate quotients
simple addition
2-digit divisor division
ordering numbers
2- and 3-digit quotient division
problems with two operations
multiplication equations

Lesson 58
divide money
exponents
addition equations
addition
place value
magic squares

Lesson 59
divisibility
dividing money
addition
addition equations
averaging
3-digit addition

Lesson 60
problem solving
dividing money
subtraction
divisibility
subtraction equations
averaging with decimal remainders
averaging with fractional
  remainders

Appearance of Concepts

Lesson 61
time definitions
polygons
number identification
1-digit quotient division
factor trees
multiplication facts and terms
addition equations

Lesson 62
A.M. & P.M.
3-D figures: faces, edges, vertices
line graphs
2-digit quotient division
factor trees
problem solving
multiplication terms and facts

Lesson 63
centuries
types of angles
pie graphs
3-digit quotient division
prime and composite numbers
division terms and facts

Lesson 64
time equivalents
perimeter
division terms and facts
division with zeros in quotient
prime and composite numbers
geometric figures

Lesson 65
elapsed time
time equivalents
area
averaging
3-digit multiplication
2- and 3-digit subtraction
problem solving
more than one operation

Lesson 66
calendar
elapsed time
time equivalents
averaging with a remainder
3-digit multiplication
4-, 5-, and 6-digit multiplication
missing addends

Lesson 67
time zones
calendar
elapsed time
time equivalents
2-digit divisor division
3-digit multiplication
2- and 3-digit subtraction
more than one operation

Lesson 68
counting money
time zones
calendar
elapsed time
2-digit divisor division
multiplication equations
more than one operation
4-, 5-, and 6-digit multiplication

Lesson 69
giving change
counting money
time zones
calendar
2-digit divisor division
exponents
addition and subtraction of money
addition equations

Lesson 70
problem solving
reasonable answers
giving change
counting money
time zones
divisibility
exponents
subtraction equations

Lesson 71
points, lines, segments
mystery numbers
subtraction of fractions
liquid measures
time definitions
division by multiples of 10

Lesson 72
intersecting, parallel, and
  perpendicular lines
points, lines, segments
adding fractions
A.M. & P.M.
linear measure
2-digit divisor division

Lesson 73
angles
types of lines
intersecting, parallel and
  perpendicular lines
equivalent fractions
century
time equivalents

Lesson 74
protractor
intersecting, parallel, and
  perpendicular lines
types of lines
time equivalents
factor trees
1-digit divisor division
missing addends

Lesson 75
types of triangles
protractor
types of angles
word problems
2-digit divisor division

© MCMXCVIII Alpha Omega Publications, Inc.

Appearance of Concepts

Lesson 76
quadrilaterals
triangles
multiplication problems
place value

Lesson 77
polygons
quadrilaterals
triangles
protractor
angles
A.M. & P.M.
multiplication problems

Lesson 78
circles
polygons
quadrilaterals
triangles
averaging
multiplication problems
place value
mystery number

Lesson 79
graphing
circles
polygons
multiplication of equations
place value
addition problems

Lesson 80
guess and check
circles
polygons
more polygons
exponents
subtraction problems
rounding

Lesson 81
symmetry
geometric terms
time definitions
division problems
rounding numbers
subtraction problems

Lesson 82
congruent
geometric terms
symmetry
angles
time definitions
word problems
logical reasoning

Lesson 83
similar figures
symmetry
types of triangles
division problems
word problems
multiplication problems

Lesson 84
space figures
faces, edges, vertices
congruent
types of triangles
symmetry
century
rounding numbers
division problems

Lesson 85
perimeter
space figures
quadrilaterals
elapsed time
division problems
similar figures

Lesson 86
area
perimeter
space figures
faces, edges, vertices
similar figures
addition problems
division problems

Lesson 87
volume
perimeter
area
addition problems
divisibility
missing addends

Lesson 88
surface area
volume
area
circles
column addition
dividing money
mystery number

Lesson 89
word problems
surface area
perimeter
area
money
subtraction problems
more than one operation

Lesson 90
problem solving
word problems
surface area
volume
area
perimeter
subtraction problems
ordering numbers

Appearance of Concepts

Lesson 91
fractions
symmetry
division problems
rounding numbers
geometric terms

Lesson 92
equivalent fractions
congruent figures
angles
A.M. & P.M.
rounding numbers
division problems

Lesson 93
greatest common factors
equivalent fractions
measuring with a protractor
perimeter
division problems
time equivalents
similar figures

Lesson 94
lowest term fractions
greatest common factors
equivalent fractions
volume
space figures
division problems
time equivalents
logical reasoning

Lesson 95
compare and order fractions
lowest term fractions
greatest common factor
equivalent fractions
quadrilaterals
perimeter and area
division of decimals

Lesson 96
add and subtract fractions
compare and order fractions
lowest term fractions
define polygons
mystery numbers
addition problems
rounding numbers

Lesson 97
mixed number to
  improper fractions
add and subtract fractions
order fractions
renaming fractions
prime numbers
divisibility
time zones

Lesson 98
improper fractions to
  mixed numbers
add and subtract fractions
comparing fractions
prime and composite numbers
subtraction problems

Lesson 99
least common multiple and
  least common denominator
add and subtract fractions
improper fractions to mixed
  numbers and mixed numbers
  to improper fractions
multiplication problems
subtraction problems
place value

Lesson 100
problem solving
least common multiple and
  least common denominator
improper fractions to
  mixed numbers
add and subtract fractions
multiplication equations
coordinate graphs

Lesson 101
add fractions
addition terms and facts
symmetry
perimeter
area
volume
multiplication by 10, 100, 1,000
compare and order whole numbers
geometric terms

Lesson 102
subtract fractions
add fractions
least common multiple
geometric terms
using a protractor
2-digit multiplication
rounding numbers
subtraction terms and facts

Lesson 103
addition of mixed numbers
subtraction of mixed numbers
addition of fractions
subtraction of fractions
triangles
3-digit multiplication
rounding numbers
subtraction terms and facts

Lesson 104
addition of mixed numbers
subtraction of mixed numbers
addition of fractions
subtraction of fractions
estimating products
problem solving
multiplication terms and facts
quadrilaterals
bar graphs

Lesson 105
renaming improper fractions
addition of mixed numbers
subtraction of mixed numbers
addition of fractions
subtraction of fractions
multiplication equations
problem solving
multiplication terms and facts
circles

Appearance of Concepts

Lesson 106
addition of mixed numbers
converting improper fractions
addition of mixed numbers
subtraction of mixed numbers
1-digit divisor division
exponents
division terms and facts
capacity

Lesson 107
addition of mixed numbers
converting improper fractions
addition of mixed numbers
subtraction of mixed numbers
least common multiple
1-digit divisor division

Lesson 108
subtraction of mixed numbers
renaming improper fractions
addition of mixed numbers
subtraction of mixed numbers
dividing money
factor trees
2- and 3-digit addition
missing addends

Lesson 109
subtraction of mixed numbers
renaming improper fractions
prime and composite numbers
4-, 5-, and 6-digit addition
place value
missing addends

Lesson 110
adding and subtracting of
  whole numbers, mixed numbers
  and fractions
rename mixed numbers
column addition
place value
more than one operation

Lesson 111
fraction of a number
subtraction of fractions
least common denominator
addition of fractions
two operations
calculator division

Lesson 112
multiplying fractions
fraction of a number
adding and subtracting fractions
division problems
triangles
5-digit subtraction
place value

Lesson 113
multiplying mixed numbers
multiplying fractions
making change
fraction of a number
subtraction of equations
rounding to 100
protractors

Lesson 114
dividing fractions
multiplying mixed numbers
multiplying fractions
averaging
multiplication problems
rounding to 1,000
fraction of a number

Lesson 115
dividing a fraction by a
  whole number
dividing a whole number by
  a fraction
multiplying fractions
averaging
2-digit multiplication
word problems

Lesson 116
dividing two fractions
divide a fraction by a
  whole number
word problems
adding fractions
division problems
2-digit multiplication
missing digits

Lesson 117
reading and writing ratios
dividing a whole number by
  a fraction
dividing a fraction by a
  whole number
dividing two fractions
3-digit multiplication
division problems

Lesson 118
multiplying to find equal ratios
reading and writing ratios
dividing two fractions
dividing a whole number by
  a fraction
multiplication equations

Lesson 119
dividing to find equal ratios
multiplying to find equal ratios
word problems with ratios
ordering fractions
2-digit multiplication
division problems
mystery number

Lesson 120
ratios and the calculator
finding equal ratios
exponents
4-digit addition
comparing fractions
equations

Appearance of Concepts

Lesson 121
decimals–tenths
mystery number
time equivalents
2-digit divisor division
addition of mixed numbers
 with renamed sums

Lesson 122
decimals–hundredths, tenths
A.M./P.M./century
2-digit divisor division
prime and composite numbers
4-, 5-, and 6-digit subtraction
subtraction of mixed numbers
 with common denominators

Lesson 123
decimals–thousandths, hundredths
 tenths
mystery number
least common multiple
subtraction of mixed numbers
 with unlike denominators
addition and subtraction of money
subtraction problems
factor trees

Lesson 124
compare and order decimals
decimals–tenths, hundredths,
 and thousandths
mystery number
division of money
fraction of a number
multiplication terms and facts

Lesson 125
rounding decimals
comparing and ordering decimals
decimals–thousandths, hundredths,
 and tenths
1-digit divisor division
2-digit multiplication
multiplication of fractions
addition problems

Lesson 126
estimation of decimals
rounding decimals
comparing and ordering
 decimals–thousandths
multiplication of mixed numbers
3-digit multiplication
division terms and facts

Lesson 127
addition of decimals
estimation of decimals
rounding decimals
comparing and ordering decimals
division of money
estimating quotients
estimating products
multiplication of mixed and
 whole numbers

Lesson 128
subtraction of decimals
addition of decimals
estimation of decimals
rounding decimals
divisibility
multiplication equations
division of fractions

Lesson 129
decimals in word problems
subtraction of decimals
addition of decimals
estimation of decimals
time equivalents
averaging with remainders
exponents
missing addends

Lesson 130
problem solving–working
 backwards
decimals in word problems
subtraction of decimals
addition of decimals
giving change
triangles
problem solving using more than
 one operation

Lesson 131
decimal times a whole number
subtracting decimals
word problems with decimals
adding decimals
triangles
least common denominator

Lesson 132
multiplying two decimals
decimal times a whole number
subtracting decimals
protractor
place value
multiplying mixed numbers
addition of equations

Lesson 133
dividing decimals
dividing fractions
quadrilaterals
parallelograms and polygons
multiplying two decimals
decimal times a whole number
place value

Lesson 134
dividing decimals with zeros
dividing decimals
decimals times whole numbers
2-digit divisor division
ordering whole numbers

Lesson 135
understanding percent
dividing decimals
decimal times a whole number
multiplying fractions
ordering decimals

Appearance of Concepts

Lesson 136
percents and decimals
understanding percent
ratios
dividing decimals
multiplying decimals
ordering decimals
rounding to thousands'
finding products by estimating

Lesson 137
percent as a fraction
percent as a decimal
ratio as a percent
percent as a ratio
dividing decimals
rounding to the nearest 100
dividing money

Lesson 138
fraction as a percent
percent as a fraction
percent as a decimal
percent as a ratio
adding mixed numbers
adding decimals

Lesson 139
finding a percent of a number
changing fractions into percents
   using a calculator
finding equivalent fractions
percents
decimals and ratios
adding mixed numbers
ordering fractions and decimals
divisibility

Lesson 140
problem solving using decimals
percent of a number
fractions to percents
percents to fractions
divisibility
comparing decimals

Lesson 141
standard measure to ⅛ inch
addition of decimals
multiplication of fractions
addition of fractions with unlike
   denominators
2-digit divisor division
4-, 5-, and 6-digit addition
addition terms and facts

Lesson 142
standard weight
standard measure to ⅛ inch
subtraction of decimals
2-digit divisor division
subtraction of fractions with
   unlike denominators
addition terms and facts

Lesson 143
standard liquid measure
standard weight
standard measure to feet
multiplication of decimals
addition of mixed numbers
place value through billions' place
subtraction problems

Lesson 144
standard (Fahrenheit) temperature
standard liquid measure
standard weight
standard measure to inch
division of decimals
place value through billions' place
subtraction of mixed numbers

Lesson 145
metric measurement
standard (Fahrenheit) temperature
standard liquid measure
standard weight
4-, 5-, and 6-digit subtraction
renaming mixed numbers

Lesson 146
metric weight
metric measurement
standard (Fahrenheit) temperature
standard measure
addition of mixed numbers and
   renaming their sums
decimal place value through
   thousandths
multiplication terms and facts

Lesson 147
metric liquid measure
metric weight
metric measurement
standard (Fahrenheit) and
   metric (Celsius) temperature
2-digit divisor division
subtraction of mixed numbers with
   unlike denominators
division terms and facts

Lesson 148
metric (Celsius) temperature
metric liquid measure
metric weight
metric measurement
2-digit divisor division
1-digit divisor division
least common multiple
division terms and facts

Lesson 149
problem solving with
   measurement data
metric (Celsius) temperature
metric liquid measure
triangles
divisibility of money
multiplication of larger decimal
   numbers
missing addends

Lesson 150
problem solving – drawing pictures
problem solving with
   measurement data
using a compass to draw circles
metric liquid measurement
1-digit divisor division
division of larger decimal numbers
using data contained in a chart
identifying Celsius and Fahrenheit
   temperatures

Appearance of Concepts

Lesson 151
bar graphs
multiplication of decimals
fractional portion of a number
averaging without remainders
factor trees
4-, 5-, and 6-digit addition
problem solving using more than
  one operation

Lesson 152
line graphs
bar graphs
multiplication of larger decimals
averaging with remainders
prime and composite numbers
multiplication of fractions
addition equations

Lesson 153
pictographs
line graphs
division of decimals
multiplication of mixed numbers
multiplication problems
column additions
subtraction equations

Lesson 154
circle (pie) graphs
pictographs
cross products
multiplication of mixed and
  whole numbers
multiplication by 10, 100 and 1,000
subtraction problems
place value through billions'

Lesson 155
coordinate graphs
circle (pie) graphs
decimal place value through
  thousandths'
division of fractions
multiplication problems
subtraction problems
place value through billions'

Lesson 156
range and mean
coordinate graphs
calculating the percent of a number
subtraction of mixed numbers with
  common denominators
multiplication problems
addition and subtraction of money
compare and order whole numbers

Lesson 157
range, mode and mean
converting percents to decimals
subtraction of mixed numbers
  with unlike denominators
parallel, perpendicular, and
  intersecting lines
space figures
estimating products
compare and order whole numbers

Lesson 158
range, median, mode, and mean
converting percents to fractions
addition and subtraction of whole
  numbers and mixed numbers
rays and angles
multiplication equations
rounding to the nearest 10, 100
  and 1,000

Lesson 159
probability
range, median, mode and mean
discounts and sales tax
addition of fractions with unlike
  denominators
exponents
rounding to the nearest 10, 100
  and 1,000

Lesson 160
probability
median, mode and mean
triangles
estimating quotients with
  a one-digit divisor
problem solving

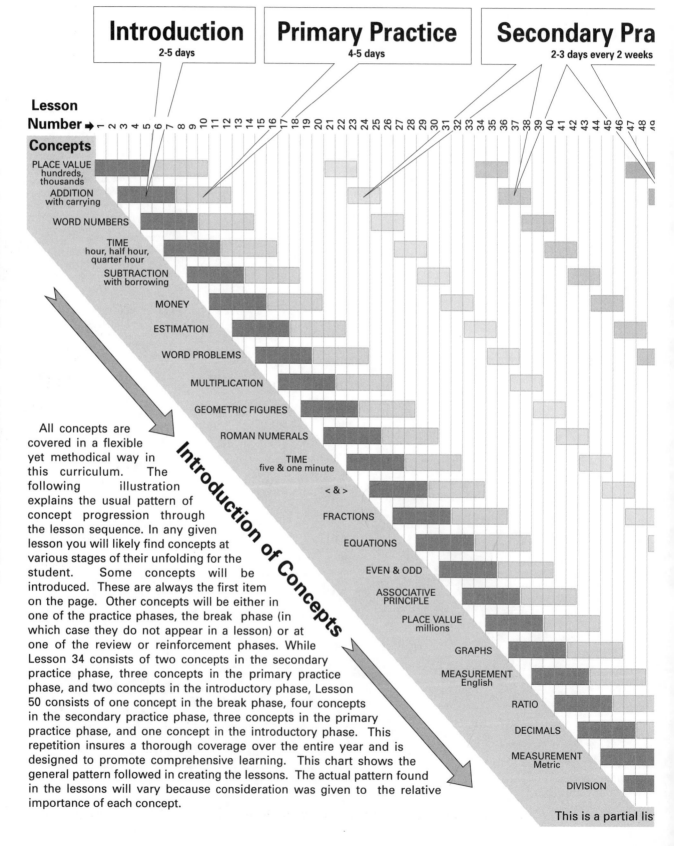

Developme

Grades

GENERAL PATTERN:

Introduction	Primary Practice	Secondary Pra
2-5 days	4-5 days	2-3 days every 2 weeks

Lesson Number → 1 2 3 4 5 6 7 8 9 10 11 12 13 14 15 16 17 18 19 20 21 22 23 24 25 26 27 28 29 30 31 32 33 34 35 36 37 38 39 40 41 42 43 44 45 46 47 48 49

Concepts

- PLACE VALUE hundreds, thousands
- ADDITION with carrying
- WORD NUMBERS
- TIME hour, half hour, quarter hour
- SUBTRACTION with borrowing
- MONEY
- ESTIMATION
- WORD PROBLEMS
- MULTIPLICATION
- GEOMETRIC FIGURES
- ROMAN NUMERALS
- TIME five & one minute
- < & >
- FRACTIONS
- EQUATIONS
- EVEN & ODD
- ASSOCIATIVE PRINCIPLE
- PLACE VALUE millions
- GRAPHS
- MEASUREMENT English
- RATIO
- DECIMALS
- MEASUREMENT Metric
- DIVISION

Introduction of Concepts

All concepts are covered in a flexible yet methodical way in this curriculum. The following illustration explains the usual pattern of concept progression through the lesson sequence. In any given lesson you will likely find concepts at various stages of their unfolding for the student. Some concepts will be introduced. These are always the first item on the page. Other concepts will be either in one of the practice phases, the break phase (in which case they do not appear in a lesson) or at one of the review or reinforcement phases. While Lesson 34 consists of two concepts in the secondary practice phase, three concepts in the primary practice phase, and two concepts in the introductory phase, Lesson 50 consists of one concept in the break phase, four concepts in the secondary practice phase, three concepts in the primary practice phase, and one concept in the introductory phase. This repetition insures a thorough coverage over the entire year and is designed to promote comprehensive learning. This chart shows the general pattern followed in creating the lessons. The actual pattern found in the lessons will vary because consideration was given to the relative importance of each concept.

This is a partial lis

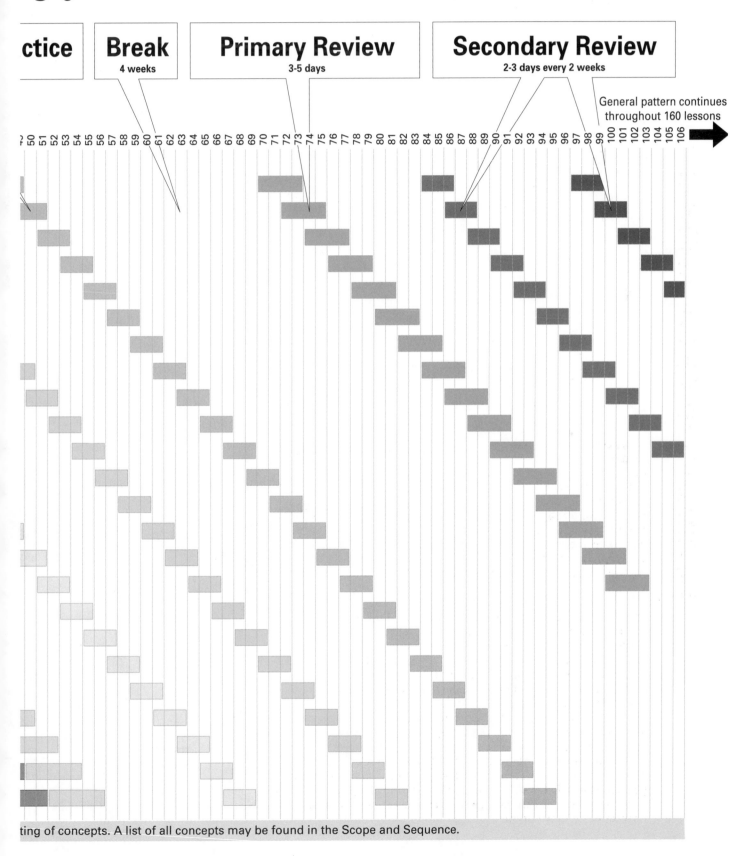

ctice

Break
4 weeks

Primary Review
3-5 days

Secondary Review
2-3 days every 2 weeks

General pattern continues
throughout 160 lessons

ting of concepts. A list of all concepts may be found in the Scope and Sequence.

Lessons

Lesson 1

Concepts:
 Addition, addition properties, addition terms, fractions, geometric terms, place value

Objectives:
 1. The student will be able to write the names of the addition terms.
 2. The student will be able to apply the addition properties to mathematical statements.
 3. The student will be able to add fractions with common denominators and rename in lowest terms.
 4. Given pictorial representations, the student will be able to identify lines that are parallel, intersecting, and perpendicular.
 5. The student will be able to arrange numbers to find the largest decimal possible.

Teaching Tips:
 Give the students addition drill sheets until they can add problems quickly.

Materials, Supplies, and Equipment:
 1. Counters, beans, or anything that can be grouped
 2. Chart paper and markers
 3. *Worksheet 1*

Activities:
 1. After reviewing the addition terms, write each of the addition properties on the board. Challenge the students to prove the properties are true using counters. Demonstrate the Order Property of Addition.

   $4 + 6 = 10$ $6 + 4 = 10$

   ☆☆☆☆ + ☆☆☆☆☆☆ = 10   ☆☆☆☆☆☆ + ☆☆☆☆ = 10

 2. The students might prove the Zero Property of Addition as follows:

   $8 + 0 = 8$

   ☆☆☆☆☆☆☆☆ + (no counters) = 8

 3. The students might prove the Grouping Property of Addition as follows:

   $(5 + 2) + 1 = 8$ $5 + (2 + 1) = 8$

   (☆☆☆☆☆ + ☆☆) + ☆ = 8   ☆☆☆☆☆ + (☆☆ + ☆) = 8

        7   + 1 = 8   5   +   3   = 8

 4. Have the students restate the addition properties in their own words and write them on the chart paper.
 5. The students should be able to complete **Lesson 1-Explanation** and **Lesson 1-Practice** independently.
 6. **Lessons 1-10** review many of the skills covered in previous *Horizons Math* workbooks. Any students new to the *Horizons Math* program can be helped through these review exercises by discussing the **Explanations** for these problems that appear later in the student book. For example, an explanation for the geometry terms reviewed in **Lesson 1** can be found in **Lesson 72 Explanation**.

 Those who are wise will shine like the brightness of the heavens, and those who lead many to righteousness, like the stars for ever and ever.
 Daniel 12:3

Lesson 2

Concepts:
Subtraction, subtraction properties, subtraction terms, fractions, place value, geometric terms

Objectives:
1. The student will be able to write the names of the subtraction terms.
2. The student will be able to apply the subtraction properties to mathematical statements.
3. The student will be able to solve basic subtraction problems.
4. The student will be able to add fractions with common denominators and rename in lowest terms.
5. The student will be able to arrange numbers to find the smallest decimal possible.
6. The student will be able to match written fractions with number fractions.
7. Given pictorial representations, the student will be able to identify lines that are parallel, intersecting, and perpendicular.

Teaching Tips:
Give the students subtraction drill sheets until they can subtract problems quickly.

Materials, Supplies, and Equipment:
1. Counters, beans, or anything that can be grouped
2. Chart paper and markers
3. *Worksheet 2*

Activities:
1. After reviewing the subtraction terms, write each of the subtraction properties on the board. Challenge the students to prove the properties are true using counters. Demonstrate the Zero Property of Subtraction.
   $8 - 0 = 8$
   ☆☆☆☆☆☆☆ – (take away none) = 8
2. The students might demonstrate the Opposites Property as follows:
   $7 + 2 = 9$ so, $9 - 2 = 7$
   ☆☆☆☆☆☆☆ + ☆☆ = 9,   ☆☆☆☆☆☆☆☆☆ – ☆☆ = 7.
3. Challenge the students to demonstrate why the Order Property of Addition does not apply to subtraction.
   The students might demonstrate as follows:
   $5 - 2 = 3$ $2 - 5 \neq 3$
   ☆☆☆☆☆ – ☆☆ = 3   ☆☆ – ☆☆☆☆☆ ≠ 3
4. Have the students restate the subtraction properties in their own words and write them on the chart paper.
5. The students should be able to complete **Lesson 2-Explanation** and **Lesson 2-Practice** independently.
6. **Lessons 1-10** review many of the skills covered in previous *Horizons Math* workbooks. Any students new to the *Horizons Math* program can be helped through these review exercises by discussing the **Explanations** for these problems that appear later in the student book. For example, an explanation for the geometry terms reviewed in **Lesson 2** can be found in the **Lesson 72 Explanation**.

Everyone who listens to these words of mine and acts on them will be like a wise man who built his house on rock. The rain fell, the floods came, and the winds blew and buffeted the house. But it did not collapse; it had been set solidly on rock.
Matthew 7:24-25

Lesson 3

Concepts:

Multiplication, multiplication properties, geometric terms, liquid measure, addition, even numbers

Objectives:

1. The student will be able to write the names of the multiplication terms.
2. The student will be able to apply the multiplication properties to mathematical statements.
3. The student will be able to solve basic multiplication problems.
4. The student will be able to draw and label the following: ray, right angle, acute angle, obtuse angle.
5. The student will be able to find liquid equivalents.
6. The student will be able to solve basic addition and subtraction problems.
7. Given a set of numbers, the student will be able to find even numbers.

Teaching Tips:

Give the students multiplication drill sheets until they can multiply problems quickly.

Materials, Supplies, and Equipment:

1. Counters, beans, or anything that can be grouped
2. Chart paper and markers
3. *Worksheet 3*

Activities:

1. After reviewing the multiplication terms, write each of the multiplication properties on the board. Challenge the students to prove that each property is true using counters. Demonstrate with the Order Property of Multiplication.

   3 x 2 = 6   2 x 3 = 6
   ☆☆   ☆☆☆
   ☆☆   ☆☆☆
   ☆☆

2. The students might prove the Grouping Property of Multiplication as follows:

   a. Work *inside* the parentheses first.

        (2 x 4) x 3 = 24   2 x (4 x 3) = 24
        ☆☆☆☆   ☆☆☆ ☆☆☆
        ☆☆☆☆   ☆☆☆ ☆☆☆
          8   12

   b. Work *outside* the parentheses next.

        (2 x 4) x 3 = 24   2 x (4 x 3) = 24
          8 x 3   2 x 12
   ☆☆☆☆ ☆☆☆☆ ☆☆☆☆   ☆☆☆☆☆☆☆☆☆☆☆☆
   ☆☆☆☆ ☆☆☆☆ ☆☆☆☆   ☆☆☆☆☆☆☆☆☆☆☆☆
         24   24

3. The students might prove the One Property of Multiplication as follows:

   5 x 1 = 5 (five groups of one)   ☆ ☆ ☆ ☆ ☆ = 5
   7 x 1 = 7 (seven groups of one)   ☆ ☆ ☆ ☆ ☆ ☆ ☆ = 7

4. The students might prove the Zero Property of Multiplication as follows:

   5 x 0 = 0 (five sets of zero). You have no counters to use, so the answer is 0.

5. Have the students restate the multiplication properties in their own words and write them on the chart paper.

6. The students should be able to complete **Lesson 3-Explanation** and **Lesson 3-Practice** independently.

7. **Lessons 1-10** review many of the skills covered in previous *Horizons Math* workbooks. Any students new to the *Horizons Math* program can be helped through these review exercises by discussing the **Explanations** for these problems that appear later in the student book. For example, an explanation for the geometry terms reviewed in **Lesson 3** can be found in the **Lesson 71 Explanation**.

And behold, I am with you always, until the end of the age.
Matthew 28:20

Lesson 4

Concepts:
Division, division properties, fractions, geometric terms, addition, odd numbers

Objectives:

1. The student will be able to write the names of the division terms.
2. The student will be able to apply the division properties to mathematical statements.
3. The student will be able to solve basic division problems.
4. The student will be able to subtract fractions with common denominators.
5. The student will be able to draw and label the following: ray, right angle, acute angle, obtuse angle.
6. Given a set of numbers, the student will be able to find odd numbers.

Teaching Tips:
Give the students division drill sheets until they can divide problems quickly.

Materials, Supplies, and Equipment:
1. Beans, pennies, counters, or similar items that can be easily counted and grouped
2. Overhead projector, transparent counters (for group instruction)
3. *Worksheet 4*

Activities:
1. Review division terms. Place ten counters randomly on the desk or overhead. Ask the students to rearrange the counters so that they are in even groups with none left over. Encourage them to discover all of the possible answers as follows:
   ☆☆ ☆☆ ☆☆ ☆☆ ☆☆   ☆☆☆☆☆ ☆☆☆☆☆   ☆☆☆☆☆☆☆☆☆☆
2. Have the students say the division fact represented in each array as follows:
   ☆☆ ☆☆ ☆☆ ☆☆ ☆☆ $(10 \div 2 = 5)$ ☆☆☆☆☆ ☆☆☆☆☆ $(10 \div 5 = 2)$
   ☆☆☆☆☆☆☆☆☆☆ $(10 \div 1 = 10)$
3. Give each student 20 counters and have them solve each division problem using the manipulatives.

   $20 \div 5=$ ☆☆☆☆☆ ☆☆☆☆☆ ☆☆☆☆☆ ☆☆☆☆☆ $20 \div 5 = 4$
          1   2   3   4

   $20 \div 10 =$ ☆☆☆☆☆☆☆☆☆☆ ☆☆☆☆☆☆☆☆☆☆ $20 \div 10 = 2$
           1   2

   $15 \div 3 =$ ☆☆☆ ☆☆☆ ☆☆☆ ☆☆☆ ☆☆☆ $15 \div 3 = 5$
        1   2   3   4   5

   $12 \div 4 =$ ☆☆☆☆ ☆☆☆☆ ☆☆☆☆ $12 \div 4 = 3$
        1   2   3
4. The students should be able to complete **Lesson 4-Explanation** and **Lesson 4-Practice** independently. They may use counters to help them visualize each process.
5. **Lessons 1-10** review many of the skills covered in previous *Horizons Math* workbooks. Any students new to the *Horizons Math* program can be helped through these review exercises by discussing the **Explanations** for these problems that appear later in the student book. For example, an explanation for the geometry terms reviewed in **Lesson 4** can be found in the **Lesson 73 Explanation**.

Anyone can eat an elephant if you cut it up in small enough pieces.
Author Unknown

Lesson 5

Concepts:
Missing addends, multiplication, money, division, addition, fractions, polygons

Objectives:
1. Given known addends and the sum, the student will be able to find the missing addend.
2. The student will be able to solve basic addition and subtraction problems.
3. The student will be able to solve basic multiplication problems.
4. The student will be able to find the value of money.
5. The student will be able to solve basic division problems.
6. Given equivalent fractions, the student will be able to find the missing numerator or denominator.
7. The student will be able to identify the following: triangle, decagon, square, pentagon, hexagon.

Teaching Tips:
Continue to give students drill sheets.

Materials, Supplies, and Equipment:
1. Beans, pennies, counters, or similar items that can be easily counted and grouped
2. Overhead projector, transparent counters (for group instruction)

Activities:
1. Read **Lesson 5 Explanation** with the students.
2. Demonstrate sample problems using the overhead projector as follows:
   Place counters in the following groups   2   5   8   ?   = 19
   Have a student count the counters and determine the missing addend.   4
3. Choose a student to come to the overhead and create their own problem with a missing addend. Have a student count the counters and determine the missing addend.
4. Continue with concrete examples until the students grasp each concept.
5. The students should be able to complete **Lesson 5-Practice** independently.
6. **Lessons 1-10** review many of the skills covered in previous *Horizons Math* workbooks. Any students new to the *Horizons Math* program can be helped through these review exercises by discussing the **Explanations** for these problems that appear later in the student book. For example, an explanation for the geometry terms reviewed in **Lesson 5** can be found in the **Lesson 76 & 77 Explanation**.

God's hand reaches us, even in the disasters of life, and draws us to Himself–and home!
Margaret Jensen

© MCMXCVIII Alpha Omega Publications, Inc.

Lesson 6

Concepts:

More than one operation, missing addends, division, multiplication, equivalent fractions, polygons, geometric terms

Objectives:

1. The student will be able to solve problems that have more than one operation.
2. Given known addends and the sum, the student will be able to find the missing addend.
3. The student will be able to solve basic multiplication problems.
4. The student will be able to solve basic division problems.
5. Given equivalent fractions, the student will be able to find the missing numerator or denominator.
6. The student will be able to label the following: decagon, square, pentagon, hexagon, octagon.
7. The student will be able to match the geometric symbols with the corresponding picture for the following: line, line segment, and ray.

Teaching Tips:

Continue to give students drill sheets.

Materials, Supplies, and Equipment:

1. *Worksheet 5*

Activities:

1. Read **Lesson 6 Explanation** with the students.
2. Write the following problem on the board. 2 + 6 x 8 = 50 Ask the students to put the parentheses in the proper place to make the problem true. **2 + (6 x 8) = 50**
3. Have the students create their own problem with more than one operation. Tell them not to place the parentheses in the problem and be sure and write the answer.
4. Have some students put their problems on the board. Ask the other students to determine where the parentheses should go.
5. The students should be able to complete **Lesson 6 Explanation** and **Lesson 6 Practice** independently.
6. **Lessons 1-10** review many of the skills covered in previous *Horizons Math* workbooks. Any students new to the *Horizons Math* program can be helped through these review exercises by discussing the **Explanations** for these problems that appear later in the student book.

Think before you do anything–hold on to what is good
and avoid every form of evil.
1 Thessalonians 5:21-22

Lesson 7

Concepts:

Addition equations, more than one operation, missing addends, division, fractions, similar and congruent, liquid measure

Objectives:

1. The student will be able to solve addition equations.
2. The student will be able to solve problems that have more than one operation.
3. Given known addends and the sum, the students will be able to find the missing addend.
4. The student will be able to solve basic division problems.
5. The student will be able to rename fractions in lowest terms.
6. The student will be able to find shapes that are similar and congruent.
7. The student will be able to find liquid equivalents.

Teaching Tips:

Allow the students the opportunity to work equations at the concrete level first. Emphasize that both sides of the equation are always equal.

Materials, Supplies, and Equipment:

1. Beans, counters, or any item that is easy to count
2. *Worksheet 6*

Activities:

1. Tell the students, **"An equation is a number sentence where both sides are equal. A variable is a letter that stands for a number."**
2. Have the students work the problems at their desks with counters as you demonstrate at the board. Use the following examples:

1. ********	=	***** + n
2. *************	=	** + n
3. *** + n	=	*******
4. *** + n	=	*****************

Ask the students, **"If n is the variable, how many stars would we need to put in its place to make the equation equal?"** (1. 3, 2. 12, 3. 4, 4. 15)

3. Demonstrate that it is easy to check to see if an equation is correct. Replace n with the stars and show that both sides are equal.
4. Direct the students' attention to **Lesson 7 Explanation**. Read orally. Emphasize that an equation is a number sentence where both sides are equal.
5. The students should be able to complete **Lesson 7 Practice** independently.
6. **Lessons 1-10** review many of the skills covered in previous *Horizons Math* workbooks. Any students new to the *Horizons Math* program can be helped through these review exercises by discussing the **Explanations** for these problems that appear later in the student book.

Do you not know that your body is a temple of the Holy Spirit within you...?
1 Corinthians 6:19

Lesson 8

Concepts:

Subtraction equations, addition, more than one operation, missing addends, fractions, similar and congruent, linear measure

Objectives:

1. The student will be able to solve subtraction equations.
2. The student will be able to solve basic addition problems.
3. The student will be able to solve problems that have more than one operation.
4. Given known addends and the sum, the students will be able to find the missing addend.
5. The student will be able to rename fractions in lowest terms.
6. Given a figure, the student will be able to draw similar and congruent figures.
7. The student will be able to find linear equivalents.

Teaching Tips:

Allow the students the opportunity to work equations at the concrete level first. Emphasize that both sides of the equation are *always* equal.

Materials, Supplies, and Equipment:

1. *Worksheet 7*

Activities:

1. Direct the students' attention to **Lesson 8 Explanation**. Read orally.
2. Use the following problem for additional practice. Work each step slowly.

$$
\begin{aligned}
n - 13 &= 46 \\
+\ 13 &= 46 + 13 \\
\hline
n &= 59
\end{aligned}
$$

Check: $59 - 13 = 46$

3. The students should be able to complete **Lesson 8 Practice** independently.
4. **Lessons 1-10** review many of the skills covered in previous *Horizons Math* workbooks. Any students new to the *Horizons Math* program can be helped through these review exercises by discussing the **Explanations** for these problems that appear later in the student book.

> *Where two or three are gathered together in my*
> *name, there am I in the midst of them.*
> **Matthew 18:20**

Lesson 9

Concepts:

Calculator, addition equations, subtraction equations, number patterns, fractions, symmetry

Objectives:

1. The student will use a calculator to solve problems with large numbers.
2. The student will be able to solve addition equations.
3. The student will be able to solve subtraction equations.
4. Given a numeric pattern, the student will be able to determine which numbers come next.
5. The student will be able to order fractions with common denominators from least to greatest.
6. The student will be able to draw a symmetrical shape.

Teaching Tips:

Emphasize that calculators are useful tools to help us solve problems quickly, but they are *never* a substitute for learning basic math facts.

Materials, Supplies, and Equipment:

1. Calculator (1 per student)

Activities:

1. Pass out calculators and allow students to experiment with them for a few minutes.
2. Direct students' attention to **Lesson 9 Explanation**.
   Read orally using the calculators to solve.
3. The students should be able to complete **Lesson 9 Practice** independently.
4. **Lessons 1-10** review many of the skills covered in previous *Horizons Math* workbooks. Any students new to the *Horizons Math* program can be helped through these review exercises by discussing the **Explanations** for these problems that appear later in the student book.

> *It's a fine thing to have ability, but the ability to discover*
> *ability in others is the true test.*
> **Elbert Hubbard**

Lesson 10

Concepts:
>   Problem solving, addition and subtraction equations, word problems for calculators, symmetry, number patterns, fractions

Objectives:
1.   The student will be able to use the Four Step Method to solve word problems.
2.   The student will be able to solve addition and subtraction equations.
3.   The student will be able to solve word problems using a calculator.
4.   Given numbers, the student will be able to find lines of symmetry.
5.   Given a numeric pattern, the student will be able to determine which numbers come next.
6.   The student will be able to write fractions given pictorial representations.
7.   The student will be able to order fractions with common denominators from least to greatest.

Teaching Tips:
>   Allow the children many opportunities to solve word problems that relate to other subject areas.

Materials, Supplies, and Equipment:

Activities:
1.   Direct students' attention to **Lesson 10 Explanation**. Read orally.
2.   Encourage students to make their own word problems.
     Post them for other students to solve.
3.   The students should be able to complete **Lesson 10 Practice** independently.
4.   **Lessons 1-10** review many of the skills covered in previous *Horizons Math* workbooks. Any students new to the *Horizons Math* program can be helped through these review exercises by discussing the **Explanations** for these problems that appear later in the student book.

Test:
1.   Test 1 covers Lessons 1-5.
2.   Administer Test 1, allowing the students 30-40 minutes to complete the test.

>   *I will praise the name of God with a song, and will magnify him with thanksgiving.*
>   **Psalms 69:30**

Centimeter Graph Paper

Lesson 11

Concepts:

Place value, subtraction, problem solving, mixed fractions to improper fractions, circles, addition of decimals

Objectives:

1. The student will be able to read and write written numbers which contain place value through the thousands' place.
2. The student will be able to solve for missing subtrahends.
3. The student will be able to use the four-step problem solving process to solve problems.
4. The student will be able to use a calculator to perform operations and solve problems.
5. The student will be able to convert mixed fractions to improper fractions.
6. The student will be able to identify and label the following items when given a diagram of a circle: radius, diameter, and chord.
7. The student will be able to add decimals.

Teaching Tips:

Give the students the opportunity to make their own place value chart which they can keep for easy reference. Allow enough room for additional columns, which will be discussed in **Lessons 12** and **13**.

Materials, Supplies, and Equipment:

1. Centimeter graph paper
2. *Worksheet 8*

Activities:

1. The students may need a quick review of the place value chart before beginning into the lesson. Use the centimeter graph paper to illustrate the lower levels of the place value chart. Cut the graph paper into several individual squares, strips of 10, and squares containing 100 individual squares. Demonstrate the relationship between each of the three items by having the student illustrate a 3-digit number on the place value chart.   Look at the example below:

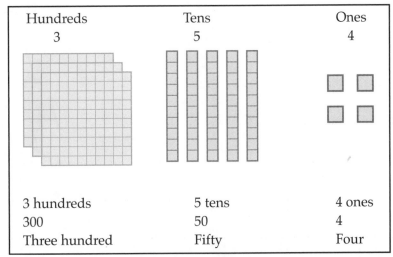

Write several three-, two-, and one-digit numbers and have the students illustrate them with the place value pieces. Gradually move to the larger columns.

2. Remind the students the proper way to read a number. Move to the writing stage where the students write the number in written form, just as it is pronounced. **Hint: Remember not to use the word "and." This means "decimal" in mathematical terms and is only used when a decimal is present.**

3. Read **Lesson 11 Explanation** together. Complete the example problems.

4. The student should be able to complete **Lesson 11 Practice** independently.

For I live in eager expectation and hope that I will never do anything that will cause me to be ashamed of myself, but that I will always be ready to speak out boldly for Christ while I am going through all these trials here, just as I have in the past; and that I will always be an honor to Christ, whether I live or whether I must die.
Philippians 1:20

© MCMXCVIII Alpha Omega Publications, Inc.

Lesson 12

Concepts:

Place value, problem solving, calculator, mixed fractions to improper fractions, circles, addition of decimals, value of money

Objectives:

1. The student will be able to read and write written numbers which contain place value through the millions' place.
2. The student will be able to use the four-step problem solving process to solve problems.
3. The student will be able to use a calculator to perform operations and solve problems.
4. The student will be able to convert mixed fractions to improper fractions.
5. The student will be able to identify and label the following items when given a diagram of a circle: radius, diameter, and chord.
6. The student will be able to add decimals.
7. The student will be able to identify and label the value of a sum of money.

Teaching Tips:

Review **Lesson 11** before beginning today's lesson.

Materials, Supplies, and Equipment:

1. Student place value charts
2. Large instructional place value chart
3. *Worksheet 8*

Activities:

1. Prior to the lesson, make a large place value chart on posterboard. Show place value through the 100 billions column. Have these sheets laminated, if possible, so that you may write on them with an overhead marker and reuse them each day. Review the basic place value chart together while reviewing **Lesson 11**.
2. Read **Lesson 12 Explanation** together and complete the example problem together. Have the students make up several numbers, write them on the place value chart and practice reading them. Also have the students read several numbers which you make up and write (in both standard and written form) on the chalkboard, or a dry erase board. Practice writing and reading numbers with and without the place value chart. The students need to get use to reading larger numbers without the aid of the chart. Using the written form and the standard form without the chart will help them master this task.
3. The student should be able to complete **Lesson 12 Practice** independently.

> *I have been crucified with Christ; and I myself no longer live, but Christ lives in me. And the real life I now have within this body is a result of my trusting in the Son of God, who loved me and gave himself for me.*
> **Galatians 2:20**

Lesson 13

Concepts:

Place value, problem solving, improper to mixed fractions, space figures, subtract decimals, money, even and odd numbers

Objectives:

1. The student will be able to read and write written numbers which contain place value through the billions' place.
2. The student will be able to use the four-step problem solving process to solve problems.
3. The student will be able to convert an improper fraction to a mixed number.
4. The student will be able to correctly identify, label, and draw specified space figures.
5. The student will be able to subtract decimal numbers.
6. The student will be able to identify and label a sum of money.
7. The student will be able to identify even and odd numbers.

Teaching Tips:

Review **Lesson 12** before beginning the lesson. The students should be able to function without the aid of the place value chart. Use it as a reference only, not a necessary tool.

Materials, Supplies, and Equipment:

1. Place value chart, only if necessary
2. Population maps of the world
3. *Worksheet 8*

Activities:

1. Read **Lesson 13 Explanation** together and complete the example problem. Have the students use the world population maps to find the countries with the largest populations. You might need to break the class into small groups if there are a limited supply of these maps. Have the groups/students find the five (5) countries with the largest populations. Once the students have found this information, have them write down each country's name and population (in standard form). Then have the student convert the numbers written in standard from into written form.
    Go over the answers together and make sure each student understands this concept.
2. The student should be able to complete **Lesson 13 Practice** independently.

*Woe to those who call evil good and good evil, who put
darkness for light and light for darkness...*
Isaiah 5:20a

Lesson 14

Concepts:

Place value, improper to mixed fractions, space figures, temperature, addition terms and facts, multiplication facts

Objectives:

1. The student will be able to read and write numbers in standard, written, and expanded forms.
2. The student will be able to read and write written numbers which contain place value through the thousands', millions' and billions' place.
3. The student will be able to convert improper fractions to mixed numbers.
4. The student will be able to correctly identify, label and draw specified space figures.
5. The student will be able to read temperatures using the Fahrenheit scale.
6. The student will be able to identify and give examples of addition terms and facts.
7. The student will be able to identify and complete specified multiplication facts.

Teaching Tips:

Remember to minimize the use of the place value chart. Students need to know this information without any visual aids or coaxing.

Materials, Supplies, and Equipment:

1. Place value chart, if necessary
2. Snap cubes
3. *Worksheet 9*

Activities:

1. Read **Lesson 14 Explanation** together. This lesson is fairly simple. Most students will have no difficulty with this material/concept because it is review. Remind the students that every number has a specific value on the place value chart. For this reason, when converting a number into written form, as done in previous lessons, the names of the column values are written out (Example: a *5* in the thousands' column is written "Five Thousand"). Expanded notation is similar, a *5* in the thousands' column is written "5,000."
2. Use the snap cubes to play a place value game. Place the students into pairs or groups of 3. Have the students "play" with the snap cubes and make a place value chart/snapping grid. Most snap cubes are colored differently. As a class, have the students chose different colors to represent different place value columns. All of the students need to use the same colors to represent each place value column. See the example diagram below:

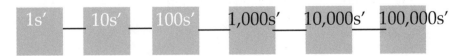

Give each group a large supply of snap cubes. The students will be expected to form the largest and smallest number possible with the supply of cubes they have been given. You may wish to make a game out of this activity by having the group with the largest number win points, groups with the smallest numbers win points, the largest number possible with a 4 in the thousands' column, etc. Be as creative as possible. The students may even come up with a new twist to the game. The goal is to have them recognize and understand place value.

3. The student should be able to complete **Lesson 14 Practice** independently.

To obey is better than sacrifice, and to heed is better than the fat of rams. For rebellion is like the sin of divination, and arrogance like the evil of idolatry.
1 Samuel 15:22b-23a

Lesson 15

Concepts:

Roman numerals, place value, addition of mixed numbers, perimeter, addition terms and facts, comparing decimals

Objectives:

1. The student will be able to read and write Roman numerals.
2. The student will be able to read and write numbers in standard, written, and expanded form.
3. The student will be able to read and write word numbers which contain place value through the billions' place.
4. The student will be able to add mixed numbers with like denominators.
5. The student will be able to find the perimeter of a given shape or object.
6. The student will be able to identify and give examples of addition terms and facts.
7. The student will be able to compare decimal numbers using the terms "greater than," "less than," and "equal to."

Teaching Tips:

Stressing the use of Roman numerals in every day life will help when teaching this concept. Have the students name the different areas and items which contain or use Roman numerals. This concept is much easier to understand once the student understands that Roman numerals follow place value just like regular standard (Arabic) numbers. Each Roman numeral has its place on the place value chart.

Materials, Supplies, and Equipment:

1. Place value chart
2. Index cards

Activities:

1. Have each student write down the basic Roman numerals (given in the text) on an index card. These may be used as a reference while instructing.
2. Demonstrate how each Roman numeral has a place value and coordinates with the place value chart.

   Example:

	Hundreds	Tens	Ones
XIX = 19		X	IX
		1	9
CXXV = 125	C	XX	V
	1	2	5

   Make up several numbers, have the students make up numbers also, and place them on the place value chart (like above) as both Roman numerals and Standard Arabic numbers.
3. Use the index cards to create a Roman numeral Concentration game for the students. The students can pair up and create their own Concentration games.
   Chose several Roman numerals and write them on cards (each numeral needs to be written on two cards to make a pair or "match"). Allow the students to play several games of Concentration.
4. The students should be able to complete **Lesson 15 Practice** independently.

Do nothing out of selfish ambition or vain conceit,
but in humility consider others better than yourselves.
Philippians 2:3

Lesson 16

Concepts:

Order numbers, Roman numerals, place value, addition of mixed numbers, perimeter, subtraction terms and facts

Objectives:

1. The student will be able to compare and order numbers from the largest number to the smallest number.
2. The student will be able to read and write Roman numerals.
3. The student will be able to read and write numbers in standard, written, and expanded form.
4. The student will be able to read and write word numbers which contain place value through the billions' place.
5. The student will be able to add mixed numbers with like denominators.
6. The student will be able to find the perimeter of a given shape or object.
7. The student will be able to complete given subtraction terms and facts.

Teaching Tips:

The students should not have difficulty with this concept. Explain that they already compare numbers each time they keep score to see who wins when they play a game, or when they argue over who has more of something.

Materials, Supplies, and Equipment:

1. Place value chart
2. The sports page from your local paper

Activities:

1. Write the numbers *2,068* and *2,078* on the board. Have the students write each of these numbers on the place value chart. Beginning with the thousands' column, and working over toward the ones' column, have the student compare each number to see which is larger. Since the Thousands' and Hundreds' columns are the same, the Tens' column is the first column where there is a difference in the numbers. 7 is larger than 6, therefore, 2,078 is larger than 2,068.
2. Have the students go through the sports pages from a local newspaper. Chose several scores from competing teams in local sports events (baseball, football, basketball, hockey, etc.) Have them write the scores on the place value chart and then compare to see which number is larger, which team won.
3. The students should be able to complete **Lesson 16 Practice** independently.

> *Do everything without complaining or arguing, so that you may*
> *become blameless and pure, children of God...*
> **Philippians 2:14-15a**

Lesson 17

Concepts:

> Rounding numbers, order, Roman numerals, place value, subtraction of mixed numbers, area, bar graphs, subtraction terms and facts

Objectives:

1. The student will be able to round numbers to the nearest 10.
2. The student will be able to compare and order numbers from the smallest to the largest.
3. The student will be able to identify and write Roman numerals.
4. The student will be able to read and write numbers in standard, written, and expanded forms.
5. The student will be able to subtract mixed numbers with like denominators.
6. The student will be able to find the area of a given shape or object.
7. The student will be able to read and interpret information contained in a bar graph.
8. The student will be able to complete given subtraction terms and facts.

Teaching Tips:

> Once again, it is important that the student understand that rounding is a skill that is used regularly. Give examples of everyday activities that use rounding such as estimating prices when shopping at a store.

Materials, Supplies, and Equipment:

1. A centimeter ruler or meter stick for each child (or 1 for every 2 children)

Activities:

1. Have each student look at the centimeter ruler. They should note that the centimeter markings for 10, 20, and 30 are written larger than the other numbers. Instruct them to notice numbers 10-20. When looking at the numbers 11-14, notice that they are closer to the 10 than to the 20. When looking at numbers 16-19, notice that they are closer to the 20. When rounding numbers instruct the student that they are estimating which number a given number is closer to. 13 is closer to 10 so it would round to 10. 17 is closer to 20, so it would round to 20. When looking at 15 instruct the students that because this is the   halfway point (middle) we round up.
2. Have the students draw number a line with numbers ranging from 30-50. Practice rounding numbers between 30 and 50 using this number line for assistance.
3. Explain that larger numbers can be rounded to specific places (Tens', Hundreds', Thousands'). Practice this process by making up, and rounding, several 4-digit numbers to the Tens' place.
4. Complete the example problems in the text **Lesson 17 Explanation**.
5. The student should complete **Lesson 17 Practice** independently.

> *"I tell you there is rejoicing in the presence of the angels*
> *of God over one sinner who repents."*
> **Luke 15:10**

Lesson 18

Concepts:

Rounding numbers, comparing numbers, Roman numerals, subtract mixed numbers, writing a check, area, circle graph, multiplication terms

Objectives:

1. The student will be able to round numbers to the nearest 100 and 1,000.
2. The student will be able to compare and order numbers from the largest to the smallest.
3. The student will be able to identify, read, and write Roman numerals.
4. The student will be able to subtract mixed numbers with like denominators.
5. The student will be able to correctly write a check for a specified amount.
6. The student will be able to find the area of a given shape or object.
7. The student will be able to read and interpret information contained in a circle graph.
8. The student will be able to complete given multiplication terms and facts.

Teaching Tips:

Allow the students to work through many problems while viewing a number line. When the student thoroughly grasps the concept, move on to the abstract.

Materials, Supplies, and Equipment:

1. Paper and pencil
2. Ruler (or straightedge for drawing number lines)
3. *Worksheet 10*

Activities:

1. Draw a number line on the board which ranges from 100 through 200 (numbered by 10s).

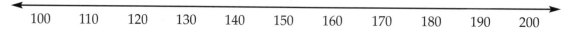

| 100 | 110 | 120 | 130 | 140 | 150 | 160 | 170 | 180 | 190 | 200 |

2. Tell the students that sometimes we don't want or need to use exact numbers. We want to use approximate numbers that are easy to add, subtract, multiply, and divide. Tell the students that they are going to approximate, or round, 124 to the nearest hundred.

3. Ask them to draw a red line showing where 124 would be placed on the number line.

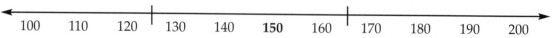

| 100 | 110 | 120 | 130 | 140 | **150** | 160 | 170 | 180 | 190 | 200 |

4. Ask the students if 124 is closer to 100 or 200 on the number line. It is closer to 100 so 124 rounds to 100 when rounded to the nearest 100.

5. Ask them where 165 would round to. Place a blue line on the number line which represents 165. 165 is past the "halfway point" of 150. Explain that a number on or past the "halfway point" of 5, 50, 500, 5,000, and so on, will round up.

6. Direct the students to read **Lesson 18 Explanation**.
    Read the directions and explanation together orally.
7. Work through one of each problem type on **Lesson 18 Practice**.
8. The students should be able to complete **Lesson 18 Practice** independently.
    Assist those who need help.

...there will be more rejoicing in heaven over one sinner who repents than over ninety-nine righteous persons who do not need to repent.
Luke 15:7

Lesson 19

Concepts:

Problem solving, rounding, comparing numbers, renaming fractions, line graphs, word problems, multiplication terms and facts

Objectives:

1. The student will be able to demonstrate the understanding of a mathematical question by completing a problem solving equation.
2. The student will be able to round numbers to the nearest 10, 100, and 1,000.
3. The student will be able to compare and order numbers.
4. The student will be able to rename fractions to their lowest terms.
5. The student will be able to read and interpret information contained in a line graph.
6. The student will be able to solve word problems.
7. The student will be able to complete multiplication terms and facts.

Teaching Tips:

If the student is having difficulty understanding the problem, have him read it several times (out loud if necessary) to himself and then restate it in his own words.

Materials, Supplies, and Equipment:

1. Pencil and paper

Activities:

1. Teacher instruction is of the utmost importance when discussing word problems. Read **Lesson 19 Explanation** with the students.
2. Work through the explanation together. Ask the student what data is needed in order to answer the questions. After working through the sample problem with the students, have them read through the first question on the page and decide if it can be answered with the data given in the problem. Additional questions which you might ask could be: How much will the movie tickets cost in all?; How much will Mrs. Smith have after purchasing 1 ticket and giving the cashier a $20.00 bill? How many tickets can Linda buy with $40.00? How many movie tickets can she buy?
3. The students should be instructed to complete **Lesson 19 Practice** independently.

The Lord Almighty will be exalted by his justice and the holy God
will show himself holy by his righteousness.
Isaiah 5:16

Lesson 20

Concepts:

Calculator, problem solving, rounding, comparing numbers, pictograph, missing minuends or subtrahends, division terms, and facts

Objectives:

1. The student will be able to complete given problem solving equations by using a calculator.
2. The student will be able to demonstrate the understanding of a mathematical question by completing a problem solving equation.
3. The student will be able to round numbers to the nearest 10, 100, and 1,000.
4. The student will be able to compare and order numbers.
5. The student will be able to read and interpret information contained in a pictograph.
6. The student will be able to solve for missing minuend or subtrahend.
7. The student will be able to complete division terms and facts.

Teaching Tips:

Allow the students time to "play" and become familiar with their calculators.
If the class each has the same calculators, consider having an instructional lesson on every function of the calculator.

Materials, Supplies, and Equipment:

1. Calculators
2. Newspaper or mail order catalogue

Activities:

1. Have each student find one item in the newspaper or mail order catalogue that they would like to purchase. On the chalkboard keep a record of the choices and costs. The same item may be selected more than once. Simply put a tally mark beside it to indicate how many students wish to purchase that item. Once each student has listed a desired item, have the students use a calculator to calculate the exact cost of all of the items on the list.
2. Ask the students why using a calculator for this problem is a good idea. **Because it can be worked more quickly and accurately with one.**
3. Ask the students what kind of problems are more easily worked with a calculator. **One can use a calculator for any problem. Long problems or problems containing larger numbers are easier to compute with a calculator.**
4. Read **Lesson 20 Explanation** together. Work through the example problem together.
5. Look at **Lesson 20** exercise **5**. Demonstrate simple problems with counters or beans to help the students know whether they should use addition or subtraction to solve for the missing number.
6. The students should be able to complete **Lesson 20 Practice** independently.

Test:
1. Test 2 covers Lessons 6-15.
2. Administer Test 2, allowing the students 30-40 minutes to complete the test.

Remember me...O my God, and show mercy to me according to your great love.
Nehemiah 13:22b

Lesson 21

Concepts:

Addition with two and three digits, fractions, value of money, problem solving, volume, place value, missing addends

Objectives:

1. The student will be able find the sum of two numbers which contain two- and three-digit addends, and may require use of the regrouping process.
2. The student will be able to add simple fractions.
3. The student will be able to identify and name the value of given sums of money.
4. The student will be able to complete given problem solving equations.
5. The student will be able to find the volume of a given shape or item.
6. The student will be able to identify place value through the billions place.
7. When given equations with missing addends, the student will be able to solve and give the missing addend.

Teaching Tips:

Allow the student to work through as many problem using manipulatives as you feel necessary. When the student thoroughly grasps the concept, move on to the abstract.

Materials, Supplies, and Equipment:

1. Base ten blocks or centimeter graph paper and place value squares from **Lesson 11**.

Activities:

1. Tell the students, **We are adding two-digit and three-digit numbers today. It is important that you can rename numbers (regroup) as hundreds, tens and ones. For instance, 13 has 1 set of ten and 3 ones.** (Demonstrate by showing one ten rod and three cubes. **Tell the students, "Rename the following as tens and ones and demonstrate with rods: 27, 38, 45, 221, 405, 353, and 91."**
2. Have the students demonstrate 28 + 14 using base ten blocks.
3. Direct the students' attention to **Lesson 21 Explanation**. Read orally.
4. Have the students demonstrate 241 + 174 using the base ten blocks. Check to see that the students are renaming correctly.
5. Allow the students to use base ten blocks as they complete **Lesson 21 Practice**, if necessary.

Thou shalt worship thy Lord the God, and him only shalt thou serve.
Deuteronomy 6:13

Lesson 22

Concepts:

Addition with four, five and six digits; addition with two and three digits, value of money, problem solving, volume, place value, missing addends

Objectives:

1. The student will be able to find the sum of two 4-, 5- or 6-digit numbers that may require use of the regrouping process.
2. The student will be able to find the sum of two numbers which contain two- and three-digit addends, and may require use of the regrouping process.
3. The student will be able to identify and name the value of given sums of money.
4. The student will be able to complete given problem solving equations.
5. The student will be able to find the volume of a given shape or item.
6. The student will be able to identify place value through the billions place.
7. When given equations with missing addends, the student will be able to solve and give the missing addend.

Teaching Tips:

Allow the student to work through as many problem using manipulatives as you feel necessary. When the student thoroughly grasps the concept, move on to the abstract.

Materials, Supplies, and Equipment:

1. Base ten blocks, or centimeter graph paper and place value squares from **Lesson 11**.
2. *Worksheet 11*

Activities:

1. Direct the students attention to **Lesson 22 Explanation**. Read orally.
2. This exercise should require no additional explanation if the student comprehends regrouping and the place value system.
3. Allow the students to work **Lesson 22 Practice** independently. If they find the manipulatives helpful, encourage the students to use them. With the larger numbers, the use of the manipulatives will be more difficult. The students might need to pair up and share manipulatives.
4. If the students have no difficulty grasping this concept, you might have the class play a game of solving larger problems on the board. Have the students divide into two teams. Each team sends a representative to the board to compete. The two representatives are given the same problem to work. The <u>first</u> student to complete the problem correctly gets 2 points; one point for finishing first and one point for finishing correctly, if it is correct. The problem must be correct for the student to get the points for finishing first. The student who completes the problem second also gets one point if the problem is completed correctly. No student should work the problem correctly and not receive points. The team with the most points at the end of the game wins.

> *He that is faithful in that which is least is faithful also in much:*
> *and he that is unjust in the least is unjust also in much.*
> **Luke 16:10**

Lesson 23

Concepts:

Column addition, addition with four, five, and six digits, addition with two and three digits, mixed numbers to improper fractions, problem solving, compare and order, geometric shapes

Objectives:

1. The student will be able to find the sum of three or four, two-digit numbers that require regrouping in the ones' and the tens' place.
2. The student will be able to find the sum of two four-, five- or six-digit numbers that may require use of the regrouping process.
3. The student will be able to find the sum of two numbers which contain two- and three-digit addends, and may require use of the regrouping process.
4. The student will be able to convert mixed numbers to improper fractions.
5. The student will be able to solve given word problems which require multi-step operations to find the answer.
6. The student will be able to compare and order whole numbers.
7. The student will be able to identify and label a trapezoid, rhombus, square, parallelogram, quadrilateral, and rectangle.

Teaching Tips:

Allow the student to work through as many problem using manipulatives as you feel necessary. When the student thoroughly grasps the concept, move on to the abstract.

Materials, Supplies, and Equipment:

1. Base ten blocks, or centimeter graph paper and place value squares from **Lesson 11**.
2. *Worksheet 12*

Activities:

1. Direct the students attention to **Lesson 23 Explanation**. Read orally.
2. This exercise should require no additional explanation if the student comprehends regrouping and the place value system.
3. Allow the students to work **Lesson 23 Practice** independently.
   If they find the manipulatives helpful, encourage the students to use them.
4. To make this activity more personal, you might have the students average their grades in one subject area. Have them do the column addition with out the aid of a calculator. Then allow them to use the calculator for the division part of the averaging process, if necessary.

> *...for this thy brother was dead, and is alive again; and was lost, and is found.*
> **Luke 15:32**

Lesson 24

Concepts:

Estimating sums, column addition with three-, four-, five-, and six-digit numbers, problem solving, compare and order, more than one operation, geometric shapes

Objectives:

1. The student will be able to estimate sums by rounding.
2. The student will be able to find the sum of three or four, two-digit numbers that require regrouping in the ones' and the tens' place.
3. The student will be able to find the sum of two four-, five- or six-digit numbers that may require use of the regrouping process.
4. The student will be able to find the sum of two numbers which contain two- and three-digit addends, and may require use of the regrouping process.
5. The student will be able to solve given word problems which require multi-step operations to find the answer.
6. The student will be able to compare and order whole numbers.
7. The student will be able to solve problems with more than one operation.
8. The student will be able to identify and label a trapezoid, rhombus, square, parallelogram, quadrilateral, and rectangle.

Teaching Tips:

This exercise combines the skills of rounding and regrouping. Allow the students to use number lines and manipulatives for reinforcement. Most of the students, however, should have little difficulty with this concept.

Materials, Supplies, and Equipment:

1. Base ten blocks
2. Number lines

Activities:

1. Draw a number line on the board.

| 50 | 51 | 52 | 53 | 54 | 55 | 56 | 57 | 58 | 59 | 60 |

2. Ask the student, **Does 58 round to 50 or 60? (60)**
3. Draw another number line on the board.

| 80 | 81 | 82 | 83 | 84 | 85 | 86 | 87 | 88 | 89 | 90 |

4. Ask the student, **Does 89 round to 80 or 90? (90)**
5. Direct the student to find the sum of the rounded numbers. (60 + 90 = 150)
6. Direct the students' attention to **Lesson 24 Explanation**. Read it together. The student should check their rounding process against the steps shown in the exercise.
7. Allow the student to work **Lesson 24 Practice** independently.

I am crucified with Christ; nevertheless I live, yet not I but Christ liveth in me: and the life which I now live in the flesh I live by the faith of the Son of God who loved me, and gave himself for me.
Galatians 2:20

Lesson 25

Concepts:
    Subtracting two- and three-digit numbers, estimating sums, column addition, addition
    with four-, five-, and six-digit numbers, rounding, addition terms and facts, addition
    equations

Objectives:
1. The student will be able to subtract two, two- or three-digit numbers using the
    regrouping process, if necessary.
2. The student will be able to estimate sums by rounding.
3. The student will be able to find the sum of three or four, two-digit numbers that
    require regrouping in the ones' and the tens' place.
4. The student will be able to find the sum of two four-, five- or six-digit numbers that
    may require use of the regrouping process.
5. The student will be able to round given numbers to the nearest 10, 100, or 1,000.
6. The student will be able to solve addition equations.

Teaching Tips:
    If the students are having difficulty keeping columns aligned, drawing in the place value
    columns onto the problem, turning a piece of notebook paper sideways to use the lines
    for an aid, or even using graph paper will help the students. Remind them that each row
    of numbers in the problem has a value on the place value chart.

Materials, Supplies, and Equipment:
1. Posterboard
2. Markers
3. Centimeter place value squares (from **Lesson 11**)

Activities:
1. Draw a place value chart (through the 100 thousands' column) on the posterboard.
    Make each column large enough to fit one 1,000 square centimeter block. Write the
    problem 39 – 27 down on the chalkboard for the students to see. Then illustrate the
    problem on the place value chart with the centimeter place value squares.

HUNDREDS	TENS	ONES
	3	9
	2	7
	1	2

This is a very helpful visual illustration of the subtraction process.
Try several more problems both together as a group and independently.
Here are a few suggestions: 120 + 34, 156 + 121, 45 + 61.

On the following page is another example using three-digit numbers.
Write the problem 930 – 912 on the board and illustrate it on the place value chart
with the centimeter square pieces. Show the regrouping process with the squares
and then solve.

Thousands	Hundreds	Ten	Ones
			2 (**regroup**) 10
	9	̶3̶	→ 0
	9	1	2
	0	1	8

The arrows point to the regrouping process which you will actually exchange place value squares and strips. Work several problems with regrouping to insure that the students understand the concept.

2. The students might chose to work the subtraction problems on the place value chart.

3. Work several problems with regrouping to insure that the student understand the concept.

4. The student should be able to complete **Lesson 25 Practice** independently.
   If the students feel a need to use the manipulatives, that is fine.
   The goal, however, is for them to work and understand the concept in the abstract.

The Lord is my rock, and my fortress, and the God of my rock; in him will I trust...
2 Samuel 22:2-3

Lesson 26

Concepts:

Subtracting two-, three-, four-, five-, and six-digit numbers, estimating sums, column addition, rounding, addition terms and facts, addition equations

Objectives:

1. The student will be able to subtract two, four-, five-, or six-digit numbers using the regrouping process as needed.
2. The student will be able to subtract two, two- or three-digit numbers using the regrouping process, if necessary.
3. The student will be able to estimate sums by rounding.
4. The student will be able to find the sum of three or four, two-digit numbers that require regrouping in the ones' and the tens' place.
5. The student will be able to round given numbers to the nearest 10, 100, or 1,000.
6. The student will be able to identify the parts of an addition problem and correctly solve for a sum.
7. The student will be able to solve addition equations.

Teaching Tips:

Review the concept that each row in a subtraction problem represents a column on the place value chart. When multiplying larger numbers keeping all columns straight becomes imperative and difficult for some students.

Materials, Supplies, and Equipment:

1. Centimeter squares, if necessary
2. Chalkboard and chalk or dry erase board and markers
3. *Worksheet 13*

Activities:

1. Read **Lesson 26 Explanation** with the students. Stick with using graph paper, turning a piece of notebook paper sideways, or drawing in place value columns so that the students keep all rows straight.

2. Continue to use the centimeter squares if necessary; however, the students should not need them at this point.
3. Have the students make up several problems and work them together.
   You may choose to play a game by dividing the students in half. The students take turns competing two at a time. Each student makes up a problem (no larger than 6 digits), they swap problems, work them, compare them. Then tell which answer is larger by writing it down as a mathematical sentence using >, <, and =.
   The students are given one point for answering the problem correctly and one point for writing the mathematical sentence correctly.

   See example:
   $$\begin{array}{r} 1,235 \\ -\ \ \ 567 \\ \hline 668 \end{array} \qquad \begin{array}{r} 3,078 \\ -\ 1,450 \\ \hline 1,628 \end{array}$$

   $$1,628 > 668 \quad \text{OR} \quad 668 < 1,628$$

4. The students should be able to work **Lesson 26 Practice** independently.

If we live in the Spirit, let us also walk in the Spirit.
Galatians 5:25

Lesson 27

Concepts:
> Estimating differences, subtracting two-, three-, four-, five-, and six-digit numbers, estimating sums. subtraction equations, subtraction terms and facts, space figures

Objectives:
1. The student will be able to estimate differences by rounding.
2. The student will be able to subtract two, four-, five-, or six-digit numbers using the regrouping process as needed.
3. The student will be able to subtract two, two- or three-digit numbers using the regrouping process, if necessary.
4. The student will be able to estimate sums by rounding.
5. The student will be able to complete subtraction equations.
6. The student will be able to identify the parts of a subtraction problem and correctly find the difference, using the regrouping process as needed.
7. The student will be able to identify and label triangular, rectangular, and hexagonal prisms and pyramids.

Teaching Tips:
> It is important that the student understand that rounding is a skill that is used regularly. Give examples of everyday activities that use rounding such as estimating prices when shopping at a store. Remind them of the estimating sums from **Lesson 24** and tell them that estimating differences is the same concept, with subtraction instead of addition.

Materials, Supplies, and Equipment:
1. Base ten blocks
2. Number lines
3. *Worksheet 14*

Activities:
1. Draw a number line on the board.

| 30 | 31 | 32 | 33 | 34 | 35 | 36 | 37 | 38 | 39 | 40 |

2. Ask the student, **Does 36 round to 30 or 40? (40)**

3. Draw another number line on the board.

| 80 | 81 | 82 | 83 | 84 | 85 | 86 | 87 | 88 | 89 | 90 |

4. Ask the student, **Does 86 round to 80 or 90? (90)**

5. Direct the student to find the sum of the rounded numbers. 40 + 90 = 130
6. Direct the students' attention to **Lesson 27 Explanation**. Read it together. The student should check their rounding process against the steps shown in the exercise.
   Remind them that they will be rounding to different places.
7. Allow the student to work **Lesson 27 Practice** independently.

For all flesh is as grass, and all the glory of man as the flower of grass. The grass withereth, and the flower thereof falleth away: But the word of the Lord endureth for ever.
1 Peter 1:24-25a

Lesson 28

Concepts:

Addition and subtraction of money, estimating differences, subtracting two-, three-, four-, five-, and six-digit numbers, subtraction equations, subtraction terms and facts, space figures

Objectives:

1. The student will be able to add and subtract given dollar amounts, using the regrouping process as needed.
2. The student will be able to estimate differences by rounding.
3. The student will be able to subtract two, four-, five-, or six-digit numbers using the regrouping process as needed.
4. The student will be able to subtract two, two- or three-digit numbers using the regrouping process, if necessary.
5. The student will be able to complete subtraction equations.
6. The student will be able to identify the parts of a subtraction problem and correctly find the difference, using the regrouping process as needed.
7. The student will be able to identify and label triangular, rectangular, and hexagonal prisms and pyramids.

Teaching Tips:

Students should have little difficulty adding or subtracting decimals.

Materials, Supplies, and Equipment:

1. *Worksheet 15*

Activities:

1. Direct the students' attention to **Lesson 28 Explanation**. Read together orally.
2. This exercise should require no additional explanation if the student comprehends regrouping. Emphasize that the decimal points need to be in a straight line.
3. Allow the students to work **Lesson 28 Practice** independently.
   Students who have alignment problems may want to use lined paper or graph paper to help with this problem.

Therefore thus saith the Lord God, Behold, I lay in Zion for a foundation a stone,
a tried stone, a precious corner stone, a sure foundation:
he that believeth shall not make haste.
Isaiah 28:16

Lesson 29

Concepts:

Word problems, money, estimating differences, subtracting four-, five-, and six-digit numbers, dividing ratios, geometric figures

Objectives:

1. The student will be able to use the 4-step problem solving process to correctly solve given word problems.
2. The student will be able to add and subtract given dollar amounts, using the regrouping process as needed.
3. The student will be able to estimate differences by rounding.
4. The student will be able to subtract two, four-, five-, or six-digit numbers using the regrouping process as needed.
5. The student will be able to divide given ratios.
6. The student will be able to identify a cone, cylinder, specified pyramids and prisms, and a sphere.

Teaching Tips:

Students are successful at solving word problems if they understand and apply the Four Steps to a Solution when solving word problems.

Materials, Supplies, and Equipment:

1. Index cards
2. *Worksheet 23*

Activities:

1. Read **Lesson 29 Explanation** together orally.
2. Have the students write the Four Steps to a Solution on an index card that they can keep.
3. Read the first problem in **Lesson 29 Practice** orally.
   Work the problem through step 2 together.
   Instruct the students to complete steps 3 and 4 independently, following each step carefully. Check together.
4. The students should be able to complete **Lesson 29 Practice** independently.

My help cometh from the Lord which made heaven and earth.
He will not suffer thy foot to be moved: he that keepeth thee will not slumber.
Psalm 121:3-4

Lesson 30

Concepts:

Problem solving, money, estimating differences, even and odd, number recognition, multiplication terms and facts, geometric figures

Objectives:

1. The student will be able to read a story problem and use key words to determine what operation to use in order to solve the problem.
2. The student will be able to add and subtract given dollar amounts, using the regrouping process as needed.
3. The student will be able to estimate differences by rounding.
4. The student will be able to use given clues to solve for a mystery number.
5. The student will be able to identify even and odd numbers.
6. The student will be able to identify the parts of a multiplication problem and correctly solve for products.
7. The student will be able to identify a cone, cylinder, specified pyramids and prisms, and a sphere.

Teaching Tips:

Review the Four Steps to a Solution from **Lesson 29**.

Materials, Supplies, and Equipment:

Activities:

1. Direct the students' attention to **Lesson 30 Explanation**. Read together orally.
2. Have the students write their own simple story problems that require one operation. Use the problems to play **STUMPER**.
3. **STUMPER:** Choose a student to be the head of the class.
   The class is going to try and stump that person. The head of the class may choose any student to read their problem. If he is correct, he stays in the game, If he loses, the student who stumped him comes to the head of the class.
   If a student stays at the head of the class for five question in a row, they get their name in the HALL OF FAME.
   The HALL OF FAME is a poster prominently placed in the room listing the names of all students who have accomplished exceptional feats in the classroom, not limited to math.
4. Students should be able to complete **Lesson 30 Practice** independently.

Test:

1. Test 3 covers Lessons 16-25.
2. Administer Test 3, allowing the students 30-40 minutes to complete the test.

The Lord liveth; and blessed by my rock; and
exalted be the God of the rock of my salvation.
2 Samuel 22:47

Lesson 31

Concepts:

Multiplication, fractions and decimals, column addition, division, word problems, five-digit addition

Objectives

1. The student will be able to complete a multiplication table.
2. The student will be able to use a multiplication table to locate multiples, products, and factors.
3. The student will be able to convert fractions to decimals.
4. The student will be able to add numbers in a column.
5. The student will be able to divide with one-digit divisors.
6. The student will be able to solve word problems with different operations.
7. The student will be able to add two, five-digit numbers.

Teaching Tips:

Allow a little extra time for this activity. Students enjoy completing the table, but it is time consuming.

Materials, Supplies, and Equipment:

1. Multiplication Chart
2. Markers
3. Rulers

Activities:

1. Read through **Lesson 31 Explanation** with the students.
2. Give each student a multiplication chart, a ruler, and marker. Demonstrate use of the chart with the problem 3 x 5 = 15. Have the students find the 3 across the top line and put a marker line on that number. Then have them find the 5 on the vertical column and place a marker line on that number. As they follow the lines, they will see the lines intersect at the 15. 3 x 5 = 15. Let them draw over these lines with markers.
3. Repeat the procedure with the following problems:
   2 x 3 = 6, 1 x 1 = 1, 3 x 4 = 12.
   5 x 4 = 20, and 0 x 1 = 0.
4. Have the students find the multiples of 3 (3, 6, 9, 12, 15).
5. Have the students find the multiples of 4 (4, 8, 12, 16, 20).
6. Assist the students as they complete the multiplication table on **Lesson 31-1** and **Lesson 31-2**.

For unto us a child is born...and his name shall be called Wonderful Counselor,
The Mighty God, The Everlasting Father, The Prince of Peace.
Isaiah 9:6

Lesson 32

Concepts:

Factoring, multiplication tables, addition, mystery numbers, division, five-digit addition

Objectives:

1. Given a product and a factor, the student will be able to find the missing factor.
2. The student will be able to complete a multiplication table.
3. The student will be able to add two, three-digit numbers.
4. The student will be able to use logical reasoning to find mystery numbers.
5. The student will be able to divide with one-digit divisors.
6. The student will be able to add two, five-digit numbers.

Teaching Tips:

Students will enjoy finding missing factors when they play the factor game described below.

Materials, Supplies, and Equipment:

1. *Worksheet 16*

Activities:

1. Read **Lesson 32 Explanation** with the students.
2. Play the factor game below until students understand the concepts.

    Factor Game

    Getting Ready: Get a small jewelry box and decorate to look like a treasure box.
      Supplies: a small jewelry box, plastic money
    Directions:
    a. Divide the class into two equal teams.
    b. Decide which team will go first.
       Team One player comes to the board and writes a multiplication sentence with a one-digit factor, a symbol for a missing one-digit factor, and a product on the board. (For example: 2 x ? = 18.)
       They put the answer to the missing factor in the treasure box.
       (The number is 9 in our example.)
    c. Team Two player will come to the board and write the missing factor.
       He checked the treasure box for the correct answer.
       If he is correct, he gets ten cents worth of coins.
    d. The player from Team Two makes up a problem using the same instructions.
    e. Continue with the game until one team gets $1.00 worth of coins.

3. The students should be able to complete **Lesson 32 Practice** independently.

Good and upright is the Lord; therefore will he teach sinners in the way.
Psalms 25:8

Lesson 33

Concepts:

Prime/composite, multiplication tables, liters, meters and grams, addition, missing addends, place value

Objectives:

1. The student will be able to define and find prime and composite numbers.
2. The student will be able to complete a multiplication table.
3. The student will be able to complete a sentence with the following terms: liter, meter or gram.
4. The student will be able to add two four-digit numbers.
5. The student will be able to find missing addends.
6. The student will be able to match numbers in numerical form with those in written form.

Teaching Tips:

Allow the students to use the multiplication chart for additional assistance.

Materials, Supplies, and Equipment:

1. Multiplication Chart
2. Markers
3. Chart paper
4. *Worksheet 17*

Activities:

1. Read **Lesson 33 Explanation** with the students. Have the students define prime numbers and composite numbers in their own words and write them on the chart paper. Give at least 5 examples of each type of number.
2. Give the students the opportunity to make factor trees using the factors 4 x 3 (The prime numbers are 2, 2, and 3).
3. Allow them to continue making factor trees until they are confident and ready to work independently.
   Possible examples follow:
   > 4 x 7 (the prime factors are 2, 2, 7),
   > 3 x 8 (the prime factors are 3, 2, 2, 2),
   > 4 x 9 (the prime factors are 2, 2, 3, 3),
   > 4 x 6 (the prime factors are 2, 2, 2, 3).
4. The students should be able to complete **Lesson 33 Practice** independently.

And the Lord shall guide thee continually, and satisfy thy soul in drought, and
make fat thy bones: and thou shall be like a watered garden,
and like a spring of water, whose waters fail not.
Isaiah 58:11

Lesson 34

Concepts:

Multiplication, ratio, subtraction, divisibility, place value, prime numbers

Objectives:

1. The student will be able to multiply a three-digit number by a one-digit number.
2. The student will be able to write a ratio as a fraction.
3. The student will be able to subtract two four-digit numbers.
4. The student will be able to determine if a number is divisible by 2, 3, 5, or 10.
5. Given a set of numbers, the student will be able to order numbers from largest to smallest.
6. The student will be able to find prime numbers using a factor tree.
7. The student will be able to find the prime numbers, given a number chart with the numbers 1-50.

Teaching Tips:

Allow the students to use the multiplication chart for additional assistance.

Materials, Supplies, and Equipment:

1. Multiplication Chart

Activities:

1. Read **Lesson 34 Explanation** with the students.
2. Have the students work the following problems while you work them at the board:

369	802	491	299
x 5	x 7	x 9	x 8
1,845	5,614	4,419	2,392

3. The students should be able to complete **Lesson 34 Practice** independently.

The eye is the lamp of the body. So if your eye is sound,
your whole body will be full of light.
Matthew 6:22

Lesson 35

Concepts:
Multiply by 10, 100, and 1,000; multiplication, ratio, place value, prime numbers, factor trees

Objectives:

1. The student will be able to multiply by 10, 100, and 1,000.
2. The student will be able to multiply a three-digit number by a one-digit number.
3. The student will be able to complete a ratio table.
4. The student will be able to order numbers in written form from least to greatest.
5. Given a set of numbers, the student will be able to find prime numbers.
6. The student will be able to find prime numbers using a factor tree.

Teaching Tips:

Allow the students to use the multiplication chart for additional assistance.

Materials, Supplies, and Equipment:

1. Multiplication Chart
2. *Worksheet 18*

Activities:
1. Write the following information on the board:

   2 x 4 = 8

   2 x 40 = 80

   2 x 400 = 800

   2 x 4,000 = 8,000

2. Ask the students:

   "How does the number of zeros in one factor relate to the number of zeros in the product?"   "They are the same."

3. Direct the students to solve the following problems at the board.

   3 x 2 = _____ **6**

   3 x 20 = _____ **60**

   3 x 200 = _____ **600**

   3 x 2,000 = _____ **6,000**

4. Ask the students:

   "How can the number of zeros in the factors help you solve this problem?"

   20 x 300 = _____ 6,000

   "Multiply the 2 x 3 and add the zeros in the factors."

5. Read **Lesson 35 Explanation** with the students.

6. The students should be able to complete **Lesson 35 Practice** independently.

You shall love the Lord thy God with all your heart, and
with all thy soul, and with all thy mind.
Matthew 22:37

Lesson 36

Concepts:

Multiplication by two-digit factors, subtraction, two operations, multiplication by multiples of ten, factor trees, prime numbers, multiplication by one-digit factors

Objectives:

1. The student will be able to multiply by a two-digit factor.
2. The student will be able to find missing numbers.
3. The student will be able to solve problems with more than one operation.
4. The student will be able to find the product of multiples of 10.
5. The student will be able find prime numbers using a factor tree.
6. The student will be able to find prime and composite numbers.
7. Given a composite number, the student will be able to find the prime numbers.
8. The student will be able to multiply by a one-digit factor.

Teaching Tips:

Students often have alignment problems when multiplying by two digits.
They forget to place a zero in the ones' place when multiplying by the factor in the tens' place.

Materials, Supplies, and Equipment:

1. *Worksheet 19*

Activities:

1. Read **Lesson 36 Explanation** with the students.
2. Have the students complete the following problems at their desks, as you do them at the board:

34	56	78	91
x 16	x 37	x 47	x 34
204	392	546	364
340 ←	1,680 ←	3,120 ←	2,730 ←
544	2,072	3,666	3,094

Notice the zeros indicated by arrows.
The students have difficulty remembering to put the zero here.

3. The students should be able to complete **Lesson 36 Practice** independently.

Peace I leave with you, my peace I give unto you; not as this world giveth,
give I unto you. Let not your heart be troubled, neither let it be afraid.
John 14:27

Lesson 37

Concepts:

Multiplication by three-digit factors, multiplication by multiples of 10, five- and six-digit addition, prime factors, multiplication by one-digit factors

Objectives:

1. The student will be able to multiply by a three-digit factor.
2. The student will be able to multiply by a two-digit factor.
3. The student will be able to multiply by multiples of ten.
4. The student will be able to find the sum of two, six-digit numbers.
5. The student will be able to find prime factors of a composite number.
6. The student will be able to multiply by a one-digit factor.

Teaching Tips:

Students often have alignment problems when multiplying by more than one digit. It is helpful to turn the paper sideways and use the lines to align digits.

Materials, Supplies, and Equipment:

1. *Worksheet 20*

Activities:

1. Read **Lesson 37 Explanation** with the students.
2. Have the students complete the following problems at their desks, as you do them at the board:

117	164	208	291
x 168	x 314	x 437	x 144
936	656	1,456	1164
7,020 ←	1,640 ←	6,240 ←	11,640 ←
11,700 ←	49,200 ←	83,200 ←	29,100 ←
19,656	51,496	90,896	41,904

Notice the zeros indicated by arrows.
The students have difficulty remembering to put the zero(s) here.

3. The students should be able to complete **Lesson 37 Practice** independently.

Rejoice in the Lord always, and again I say rejoice.
Philippians 4:4

Lesson 38

Concepts:

Estimating products, multiplication, multiplication by factors of ten, subtraction, addition equations

Objectives:

1. The student will be able to estimate products.
2. The student will be able to multiply by a two-digit factor.
3. The student will be able to multiply by factors of ten.
4. The student will be able to label a subtraction problem and find the difference of basic subtraction problems.
5. The student will be able to find the difference of two five-digit numbers.
6. The student will be able to solve addition equations.

Teaching Tips:

Materials, Supplies, and Equipment:

Activities:

1. Read **Lesson 38 Explanation** with the students.
2. Complete several example problems with the students, as follows:

   4 x 521 =   6 x 389 =   22 x 609 =

   4 x 500 = 2,000   6 x 400 = 2,400   20 x 600 = 12,000

3. The students should be able to complete **Lesson 38 Practice** independently.

Be not forgetful to entertain strangers; for thereby some
have entertained angels in unawares.
Hebrews 13:2

Lesson 39

Concepts:

Multiplication equations, estimating products, polygons, multiplication, subtraction equations

Objectives:

1.   The student will be able to solve multiplication equations.
2.   The student will be able to estimate products.
3.   Given a picture, the student will be able to recognize the following polygons: octagon, square, hexagon, pentagon, decagon.
4.   The student will be able multiply two, one-digit numbers, and follow the products through a maze from the smallest to largest number.
5.   The student will be able to solve subtraction equations.
6.   The student will be able to multiply by a two-digit factor.

Teaching Tips:

Materials, Supplies, and Equipment:

1.   *Worksheet 21*

Activities:

1.   Read **Lesson 39 Explanation** with the students.
2.   The students should be able to complete **Lesson 39 Practice** independently.

And ye shall know the truth and the truth shall make you free!
John 8:32

O give thanks unto the Lord, for He is good; for his mercy endureth for ever.
Psalm 107:1

Lesson 40

Concepts:

Exponents, multiplication equations, estimating products, geometric shapes, multiplication, prime numbers

Objectives:

1. The student will be able to define an exponent.
2. Given a base and exponent, the student will be able to write the factors and product.
3. The student will be able to solve a multiplication equation.
4. The student will be able to estimate products.
5. The student will be able to match the following: geometric terms, definitions, geometric shapes.
6. The student will be able to multiply by a two-digit factor.
7. The student will be able to complete multiplication tables.
8. The student will be able to find and shade prime numbers in a table.

Teaching Tips:

Begin instruction at the concrete level.

Materials, Supplies, and Equipment:

1. *Worksheet 22*

Activities:

1. Display a 3-unit by 3-unit square.

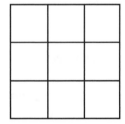

3 x 3 = 9

If you multiply the number of squares on one side by the number of squares on the other side (3 x 3), the product is 9. 3 x 3 can be written as 3^2, three squared, or three to the second power.

2. Read **Lesson 40 Explanation** with the students.
3. The students should be able to complete **Lesson 40 Practice** independently

Tests:

1. Test 4 covers Lessons 26-35.
2. Administer Test 4, allowing the students 30-40 minutes to complete the test.
3. Quarter Test 1 covers Lessons 1-40.
4. Administer Quarter Test 1, allowing the students 40-60 minutes to complete the test.

Lesson 41

Concepts:

Division, two- and three-digit addition, factor trees, customary units of measure, temperature (Fahrenheit), century, multiplication terms

Objectives:

1. The student will be able to complete division problems which contain a one-digit quotient and a remainder.
2. The student will be able to complete two- and three-digit addition problems.
3. The student will be able to complete factor trees.
4. The student will be able to identify and use Customary (standard) measurements of ounces, pounds, and tons.
5. The student will be able to identify and read Fahrenheit temperatures.
6. The student will be able to identify centuries.
7. The student will be able to label multiplication terms and answer multiplication facts.

Teaching Tips:

If students have difficulty with division, these two strategies will be helpful.

Take the student back to the manipulative stage to reinforce basic concepts.

Help students see the relationship between multiplication and division as outlined in activity 5 & 6.

Materials, Supplies, and Equipment:

1. Multiplication Test and counters

Activities:

1. Have the students take the multiplication test.
2. Read the explanation in **Lesson 41** with the students.
   Have a volunteer gather 39 counters.
   Have a student group the counters in even stacks of 9.
   How many stacks? **(4 with 3 left over)**.
3. Ask the students how one can check for accuracy.
   (Multiply the quotient by the divisor and add any remainder to the answer.)
4. Have the students orally solve the following problems:
   $16 \div 8 =$ ____ $24 \div 6 =$ ____ ; $40 \div 5 =$ ____ $15 \div 3 =$ ____ **(Answers: 2, 4, 8, 5.)**
5. Tell the students that one can use multiplication to solve division problems.
   For instance, in the problem $16 \div 8 =$ ____ , one might ask, ____ x 8 = 16.
   In the problem $24 \div 6 =$ ____ , one might ask, ____ x 6 = 24. **(Answers: 2, 4)**
6. What might one ask for $40 \div 5 =$ ____ , and $15 \div 3 =$ ____ ? **(Answer ___ x 5 = 40, ____ x 3 = 15)**
7. The students should be able to complete **Lesson 41 Practice** independently.

This is my body which is given for you; this do in remembrance of me.
Luke 22:19b

Lesson 42

Concepts:

One- and two-digit quotient division, two- and three-digit addition, factor trees, Customary units of measure, time measurement definitions, division terms

Objectives:

1. The student will be able to complete division problems which contain two-digit quotients with remainders.
2. The student will be able to complete division problems which contain a one-digit quotient and a remainder.
3. The student will be able to complete two- and three-digit addition problems.
4. The student will be able to complete factor trees.
5. The student will be able to identify and use Customary (standard) measurements using inches, feet, yards, and miles.
6. The student will be able to identify and label time equivalents such as a century, decade, millennium, B.C., and A.D.
7. The student will be able to label division terms and complete division facts.

Teaching Tips:

Using graph paper or lined paper, will be a helpful if the students are having difficulty keeping the numbers and lines straight.

Materials, Supplies, and Equipment:

1. Graph paper or lined paper
2. Calculator (for multiplication steps and checking ONLY)

Activities:

1. Read **Lesson 42 Explanation** together. Have the students copy the sample problem onto their graph paper. Follow the sample directions and use the class acronym developed to remember the steps in the division process (see **Lesson 42 Explanation**).
2. Allow the students to work in pairs and complete the first problem (after the example) on **Lesson 42 Practice**. The paired students should take turns working different steps of the problem. For example student 1 might complete steps 1 & 2 of the division process, while student 2 completes steps 3 & 4. Once the problem is completed, one set of paired students should swap problems with another set of paired students and check each others' work. If one group has worked the problem incorrectly, then their original problem is returned to them and they must find the error and correct it.
3. The student should be able to complete **Lesson 42 Practice** independently.

Do everything without complaining or arguing, so that you may become blameless and pure, children of God without fault in a crooked and depraved generation...
Philippians 2:14-15a

Lesson 43

Concepts:

1- and 2-digit quotient division, division of money, four-, five-, and six-digit addition, prime/composite, customary units of measure, missing addends

Objectives:

1. The student will be able to divide money.
2. The student will be able to complete division problems which contain two-digit quotients with remainders.
3. The student will be able to complete division problems which contain a one-digit quotient and a remainder.
4. The student will be able to complete four-, five-, and six-digit addition problems.
5. The student will be able to identify prime and composite numbers.
6. The student will be able to identify and use Customary (standard) measurements using cups, pints, quarts, and gallons.
7. The student will be able to solve for missing addends.

Teaching Tips:

The graph or lined paper will be an aid in keeping columns and lines straight. This will also be an added help when trying to line up the decimal point in the answer (quotient.)

Materials, Supplies, and Equipment:

1. Graph paper, or lined paper
2. Calculator (for multiplication steps and checking ONLY)
3. One individual candy bar
4. One package of several (5 or 6) individual candy bars
5. *Worksheet 23*

Activities:

1. Show the students the packaged candy bars and tell them that the package price is $2.95. Tell the students that an individual candy bar can be purchased for $0.65.

    Ask the students which is a better value, purchasing 5 (or 6, however, many are packaged together) at the individual price or purchasing the packaged candy bars for $2.95.

2. Read the beginning of **Lesson 43 Explanation**. Then have the students divide $2.95 by the number of candy bars in the package (5 or 6). Make sure they follow the division steps only after placing the decimal point in the quotient. **($2.95 ÷ 5 = $0.59 each. It is cheaper to purchase the bag than purchase the individual candy bars.)**

3. Complete the example problems on **Lesson 43 Explanation** together.
    Have the students use the graph paper or lined paper, to avoid errors.

4. The students should be able to complete **Lesson 43 Practice** independently.

Have nothing to do with godless myths and old wives' tales; rather, train yourself to be godly. For physical training is of some value, but godliness has value for all things, holding promise for both the present life and the life to come.
1 Timothy 4:7-8

Lesson 44

Concepts:

Division equations, one- and two-digit quotient division, division of money, four-, five-, and six-digit addition, place value, missing addends

Objectives:

1. The student will be able to solve division equations.
2. The student will be able to divide money.
3. The student will be able to complete division problems which contain two-digit quotients with remainders.
4. The student will be able to complete multiplication problems which contain a three-digit multiplicand and a one-digit multiplier.
5. The student twill be able to complete four-, five-, and six-digit addition problems.
6. The student will be able to identify place value through the billions' place.
7. The student will be able to solve for missing addends.

Teaching Tips:

Help the students who have difficulty by demonstrating the problem using counters. For instance, $n \div 2 = 7$. Have the student make 7 groups of counters with 2 counters in each group. Add the counters to find that $n = 14$.

Materials, Supplies, and Equipment:

1. *Worksheet 24*

Activities:

1. Review the terms *equation* and *variable*.
2. Read the example problems in **Lesson 44 Explanation**.
3. Solve the problem explaining each step verbally to the students.
4. Observe the students as they work the following problems:
   $n \div 9 = 4$ and $n \div 7 = 4$ **(answers 36, 28)**.
   Use the counters and assist any students who need additional help.
5. The students should be able to complete **Lesson 44 Practice** independently.

Behold, I am coming soon!…I am the Alpha and the Omega,
the First and the Last, the Beginning and the End.
Revelation 22: 12a & 13

Lesson 45

Concepts:

Two- and three-digit quotient division, division of money, three-digit multiplication, two- and three-digit subtraction, place value, multiple operations

Objectives:

1. The student will be able to complete division problems which contain three-digit quotients with remainders.
2. The student will be able to complete multiplication problems which contain a three-digit multiplier and a one-digit multiplicand.
3. The student will be able to divide money.
4. The student will be able to complete division problems which contain a two-digit quotient with remainders.
5. The student will be able to complete two- and three-digit subtraction problems.
6. The student will be able to identify place value through the billions.
7. The student will be able to complete problems which require the use of more than one operation to solve.

Teaching Tips:

By this time, students should have a basic understanding of the division process and all the steps involved in solving a division problem. Stress that solving a larger division problem simply means that the same division steps (Divide, Multiply, Subtract, Check, Bring Down) used in smaller problems, will be repeated in the larger problem.

Materials, Supplies, and Equipment:

1. Graph paper or lined paper
2. Calculator (for multiplication steps and checking ONLY)

Activities:

1. Remind the students of the steps involved in a division problem (Divide, Multiply, Subtract, Check, Bring Down). Have them repeat the class acronym if needed.
2. Complete the following problems together for review:
   $212 \div 3 =$, $302 \div 5 =$, and $363 \div 4 =$ **(Answers: 70 r 2, 60 r 3, and 90 r 3).**
   You may wish to have the students play "teacher."
   Pick a different student to complete each problem. The student must come to the board, work the problem, and explain each step as he completes the problem, just like the teacher would. If the student has difficulty with any portion of the division problem, he may stop at any point and have another student complete the task.
3. Read **Lesson 45 Explanation** together. Work through the sample problem and discuss each step.
4. Use the following problems as additional practice problems, if needed:
   $2,825 \div 3 =$, $2,457 \div 6 =$, and $2,560 \div 4 =$ **(Answers: 941 r 2, 409 r 3, and 640).**
5. The student should be able to complete **Lesson 45 Practice** independently.
   Allow them to use graph paper or lined paper, if necessary, to keep all columns straight. Also allow the students to use calculators for checking and difficult multiplication problems, but not for calculating answers without showing work.

God opposes the proud but gives grace to the humble.
Proverbs 3:34

Lesson 46

Concepts:

Division with zeros in the quotient, three-digit quotient division, division of money, two-digit multiplication, compare/order whole numbers, addition, multiple operations

Objectives:

1. The student will be able to complete division problems which have a zero in the quotient.
2. The student will be able to complete multiplication problems which have a two-digit multiplicand and a two-digit multiplier.
3. The student will be able to divide money.
4. The student will be able to compare and order whole numbers.
5. The student will be able to solve addition problems.
6. The student will be able to complete problems which require more than one operation.

Teaching Tips:

Students often leave out zeros in the quotient when dividing, especially if the zero is at the end of the answer. Encourage them to work carefully and check their work using multiplication. Remind them that every number in the dividend must be used when dividing.

Materials, Supplies, and Equipment:

1. Graph paper or lined paper
2. Calculator (for multiplication steps and checking ONLY)
3. Posterboard and marker

Activities:

1. Review the division steps.
2. Prior to the lesson, write the following examples onto the posterboard.

$$
\begin{array}{r}
12\ \text{r}\ 2 \\
5{\overline{\smash{)}\,512}} \\
-5 \\
\hline
012 \\
-\ 10 \\
\hline
2
\end{array}
\qquad
\begin{array}{r}
102\ \text{r}\ 2 \\
5{\overline{\smash{)}\,512}} \\
-5 \\
\hline
01 \\
-\ 0 \\
\hline
12 \\
-\ 10 \\
\hline
2
\end{array}
$$

Have the students examine each problem, check each answer by multiplication, and explain which one is correct. **The second example problem is correct because there is supposed to be a zero in the quotient.** Emphasize that every time we bring down a digit, we must divide and write a digit in the quotient. Also emphasize that we bring down only one number at a time.

© MCMXCVIII Alpha Omega Publications, Inc.

3. On the same posterboard, have the following additional examples:

$$
\begin{array}{r}
90\ \text{r}\ 2 \\
6\overline{)542} \\
-54 \\
\hline
02 \\
-\ \ \ 0 \\
\hline
2
\end{array}
\qquad\qquad
\begin{array}{r}
9\ \ \ \text{r}\ 2 \\
6\overline{)542} \\
-54 \\
\hline
02
\end{array}
$$

Ask the students to check each answer by multiplying and determine which one of these two examples is correct and explain why. **The first problem is correct because each digit in the dividend is brought down and divided into. The second problem is incorrect because it is incomplete.**

4. Read **Lesson 46 Explanation**. Discuss and work the sample problem.
5. The students should be able to complete **Lesson 46 Practice** independently.

Submit yourselves to God. Resist the devil, and he will flee from you.
James 4:7

Lesson 47

Concepts:

Estimating quotients, division, three-digit quotients, zeros in quotients, two-digit multiplication, two- and three-digit subtraction, compare/order whole numbers, addition terms, addition, addition equations

Objectives:

1. The student will be able to estimate quotients.
2. The student will be able to complete division problems which have a zero in the quotient.
3. The student will be able to complete division problems which contain three-digit quotients with remainders.
4. The student will be able to complete multiplication problems which have a two-digit multiplicand and a two-digit multiplier.
5. The student will be able to complete two- and three-digit subtraction problems.
6. The student will be able to compare and order whole numbers.
7. The student will be able to label addition terms and to solve addition equations.

Teaching Tips:

A rounding review will be helpful before beginning the lesson.

Materials, Supplies, and Equipment:

1. Calculator, if necessary for multiplication and checking ONLY

Activities:

1. Read **Lesson 47 Explanation** together. Discuss and work the sample problem.
2. Use these additional problems if extra practice is needed:

    $4,854 \div 7 =$ ___ , $4,189 \div 7 =$ ___ , $7,241 \div 9 =$ ___ , **(Answers: 700, 600, 800).**
    You may have the students round each problem to the thousand, hundred, or ten to create several additional practice problems.
3. The students should be able to complete **Lesson 47 Practice** independently.

Keep your lives free from the love of money and be content with what you have, because God has said, Never will I leave you; never will I forsake you.
Hebrews 13:5

© MCMXCVIII Alpha Omega Publications, Inc.

Lesson 48

Concepts:

Averaging, estimating quotients, division, three-digit quotients, four-, five-, and six-digit subtraction, three-digit multiplication, subtraction terms, subtraction, addition equations

Objectives:

1. The student will be able to average a set of numbers.
2. The student will be able to estimate quotients.
3. The student will be able to complete division problems which have a zero in the quotient.
4. The student will be able to complete division problems which contain three-digit quotients with remainders.
5. The student will be able to complete four-, five-, and six-digit subtraction problems.
6. The student will be able to complete multiplication problems which contain a three-digit multiplicand and a three-digit multiplier.
7. The student will be able to identify subtraction terms and complete subtraction facts.
8. The student will be able to solve addition equations.

Teaching Tips:

Try to find as several real life examples where averaging is used.

Make the lesson relevant. It also may be useful to review the Addition Properties; specifically the Order Property.

Materials, Supplies, and Equipment:

1. Calculators for checking

Activities:

1. Ask the students to give examples of when averages are used.
   (Baseball averages, grades, averages heights, weights, and average temperatures.)
2. Read **Lesson 48 Explanation** with the students.
3. Ask the students **Can I change the order of the addends and make them easier to add, or do I need to leave them as they are written?**
   (The Order Property of Addition states that any order is acceptable.)
4. Ask the student **Why is 455 divided by the number 5?**
   (You divide by the number of addends.)
5. Work the first number in **Lesson 48-1** together and work with any students that need additional assistance.

   Allow the students to complete the lesson independently.

For He has rescued us from the dominion of darkness and brought us into the kingdom of the Son He loves in whom we have redemption, the forgiveness of sins.
Colossians 1:13-14

Lesson 49

Concepts:

Averaging, estimating quotients, division, zeros in quotients, four-, five-, and six-digit subtraction, rounding to 10, 100 and 1,000, subtraction terms, subtraction equations

Objectives:

1. The student will be able to average a set of numbers which yield a remainder.
2. The student will be able to average a set of numbers.
3. The student will be able to estimate quotients.
4. The student will be able to complete division problems which have a zero in the quotient.
5. The student will be able to complete four-, five-, and six- digit subtraction problems.
6. The student will be able to round numbers to the nearest 10, 100, & 1,000.
7. The student will be able to identify subtraction terms and complete subtraction facts.
8. The student will be able to solve subtraction equations.

Teaching Tips:

Review the averaging process discussed in **Lesson 48**. Students grasp a visual representation. It may be necessary to show all fractional remainders through a visual representation using manipulatives (pattern blocks) for some students.

Materials, Supplies, and Equipment:

1. Calculators for multiplication and checking
2. *Worksheet 25*

Activities:

1. Read **Lesson 49 Explanation** together. Explain to the students that many times when averaging numbers, the division problem will yield a remainder. These remainders may be in decimal form if using a calculator, or in fractional form, if manual computation is used. In either event, the remainder will need to be rounded to the nearest whole number to determine the average.
2. Complete the first example problem together, explaining each step.
3. The second example problem shows the answer that would be displayed if worked on a calculator. You may need to explain to the students that calculators do not automatically show remainders as fractions, they convert any remainders to decimals. ¼ is equal to .25.
4. Have the students manually complete the first problem on **Lesson 49-1** and check this answer together. After manually calculating the answer and remainder, have the students complete the same problem using a calculator.
   Once rounded, the answers should be the same:
   36 R 3 (¾) manually, 36.75 on calculator both round to 37.
5. The students should be able to complete **Lesson 49 Practice** independently. Allow them to check their answers with a calculator, but insist that they show all their work manually.

Whatever happens, conduct yourselves in a manner worthy of the gospel of Christ.
Philippians 1:27

Lesson 50

Concepts:

Interpreting answers, averaging, estimating quotients, division, exponents, multiplication equations, subtraction equations

Objectives:

1. Given division problems, the student will be able to interpret remainders.
2. The student will be able to average a set of numbers which yield a remainder.
3. The student will be able to average a set of numbers.
4. The student will be able to estimate quotients.
5. The student will be able to read and write exponents.
6. The student will be able to complete multiplication equations.
7. The student will be able to solve subtraction equations.

Teaching Tips:

Review **Lesson 49** rounding of remainders. Have manipulatives (pattern blocks) necessary to represent fractional remainders on division problems.

Materials, Supplies, and Equipment:

1. Calculators for checking
2. 29 counters, 5 sandwich bags

Activities:

1. Tell the student to place the 29 counters <u>EVENLY</u> into 4 bags **(7 counters will go in each bag with one remaining).**
2. Point out that what is done with the leftover counter depends on the question being asked.
3. Ask the students **How many bags would be needed to hold 29 counters if only 7 counters could go in each bag?**
   (The answer is 5. One bag would only have 1 counter.)
4. Ask the students **How many bags can be filled with 7 counters each?**
   (The answer is 4. The remaining counter can be discounted.)
5. Work the problems in **Lesson 50 Explanation** orally, verbalizing each step in the process.
6. Guide the students as they solve the story problems in **Lesson 50-1.**
   If there are students that do not need additional assistance, allow them to complete the problems independently.

Test:

1. Test 5 covers Lessons 36-45.
2. Administer Test 5, allowing the students 30-40 minutes to complete the test.

You, my brother, were called to be free. But do not use your freedom to indulge in the sinful nature, rather, serve one another in love.
Galatians 5:13

Lesson 51

Concepts:

Division, factor trees, solid figures, metric definitions, geometric figures, multiplication, division by two-digit divisors

Objectives:

1. The student will be able to divide by multiples of ten.
2. The student will be able to use a factor tree to find prime numbers.
3. Given a solid figure, the student will be able to find the number of faces, edges, and vertices.
4. The student will use the terms liter, meter, and gram to complete sentences.
5. The student will match geometric names to geometric figures.
6. The student will be able to find products.
7. The student will be able to solve word problems involving two-digit divisors.

Teaching Tips:

Students get confused when dividing by multiples of ten and often add an extra zero in the quotient. Checking the answer helps them understand the concept and correct the error.

Materials, Supplies, and Equipment:

1. Base ten blocks
2. *Worksheet 26*

Activities:

1. Getting Ready to Divide—Write these problems on the board.
   10 x 5 = 50, 10 x 30 = 300, 10 x 40 = 400   (Have a student circle the multiples of 10)
   (Answers: 50, 30, 300, 10, 40, 400)
2. Explain that today we are dividing by multiples of 10. Write 70 ÷ 10 on the board.
   Demonstrate the meaning of dividing by a 2-digit multiple of 10 using blocks.

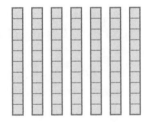

3. If 70 represents the number of small tiles and there are ten rows of tiles, how many columns are there? **(7)**
4. Read **Lesson 51 Explanation** with the students. Emphasize the importance of checking each problem.
5. Work the following problems on the board:

$$
\begin{array}{cccc}
\overset{5}{50\overline{)250}} & \overset{7}{30\overline{)210}} & \overset{7\,\text{r}\,2}{40\overline{)282}} & \overset{4\,\text{r}\,5}{70\overline{)285}}
\end{array}
$$

6. The students should be able to complete **Lesson 51 Practice** independently.

Heaven and earth shall pass away, but my words shall not pass away.
Luke 21:33

Lesson 52

Concepts:

Division with two-digit divisors, factor trees, solid figures, divisibility, measurement, division

Objectives:

1. The student will be able to divide by two-digit divisors to find a one-digit quotient.
2. The student will be able to use a factor tree to find prime numbers.
3. Given a solid figure, the student will be able to find the number of faces, edges, and vertices.
4. The student will be able to test numbers for divisibility by 2, 3, 5, and 10.
5. The student will be able to measure to the ¼ inch.
6. The student will be able to solve simple division problems.

Teaching Tips:

The most common error is forgetting to check and see if the remainder is less than the divisor.

Materials, Supplies, and Equipment:

Activities:

1. Read **Lesson 52 Explanation** with the students.
2. Write this problem on the board and ask the students to find the error.

$$
\begin{array}{r}
6 \text{ r } 44 \\
42\overline{)296} \\
-252 \\
\hline
44
\end{array}
$$

The answer should be 7 r 2. The remainder is larger than the divisor.

3. The students should be able to complete **Lesson 52 Practice** independently.

Consider the ravens, for they neither sow nor reap, and they have no storeroom or barn, and yet God feeds them. How much more valuable you are than the birds!
Luke 12:24

Lesson 53

Concepts:

Division with two-digit quotients, prime numbers, divisibility, measurement, simple division

Objectives:

1. The student will be able to divide by two-digit divisors to find two-digit quotients.
2. The student will be able to find prime numbers and follow them through a maze.
3. The student will be able to test numbers for divisibility by 2, 3, 5, and 10.
4. The student will be able to measure to the ¼ inch.
5. The student will be able to solve simple division problems.

Teaching Tips:

The most common error when dividing a three-digit number by a two-digit number is placing the first digit of the quotient in the hundreds' place instead of the tens' place. Encourage the students to place a star or happy face above the hundreds' place as a place holder.

Materials, Supplies, and Equipment:

1. *Worksheet 27*

Activities:

1. Read **Lesson 53 Explanation** with the students.
2. Write these problems on the board for more practice.
   Remind the students to put a place holder in the hundreds' place.

$$15\overline{)295} \quad \text{H19 r 10}$$

$$23\overline{)628} \quad \text{H27 r 7}$$

$$36\overline{)798} \quad \text{H22 r 6}$$

3. **Calculator Tips–Changing a decimal remainder.**
   a. Divide 568 by 32 on the calculator.

$$32\overline{)568} \quad \textbf{17.75}$$

   b. Find the whole number to the left of the decimal point. **17**
   c. Multiply the quotient by the divisor. **17 x 32 = 544**
   d. Subtract the product from the dividend. **568 − 544 = 24**
   e. **The quotient is 17. The remainder is 24.**
4. Students should be able to complete **Lesson 53 Practice** independently.

And Jesus, when He was baptized, went straightway out of the water; and lo, the heavens were opened unto Him, and He saw the Spirit of God descending like a dove, and lighting upon Him. And lo, a voice from heaven, saying, "This is my beloved Son, in whom I am well pleased."
Matthew 3:16-17

Lesson 54

Concepts:

Division and estimation, divide by multiples of ten, prime and composite, missing addends, bar graphs, magic squares

Objectives:

1. The student will be able to divide by a two-digit divisor to find a one-digit quotient where the estimates must be changed.
2. The student will be able to divide by multiples of ten.
3. The student will be able to determine if a number is prime or composite. If the number is composite, the student will be able to write the prime factors.
4. The student will be able to find the missing addends.
5. The student will be able to read a bar graph and answer questions.
6. The student will be able to solve a magic square requiring the addition of fractions.

Teaching Tips:

Students may need vertical lines to help keep columns straight as the problems become more complex. Turning lined paper sideways is one solution.

Materials, Supplies, and Equipment:

Activities:

1. Read **Lesson 54 Explanation** with the students.
2. Write these problems on the board for more practice.

$$70\overline{)1597} \quad 63 \text{ r } 22$$

$$64\overline{)4382} \quad 68 \text{ r } 30$$

3. The students should be able to complete **Lesson 54 Practice** independently.

And ye shall know the truth, and the truth shall make you free.
John 8:32

Lesson 55

Concepts:

Division with three-digit quotient, division with two-digit quotient, multiplication, missing addends, place value, subtraction

Objectives:

1. The student will be able to divide to find a three-digit quotient.
2. The student will be able to divide to find a two-digit quotient.
3. The student will be able to find products and use logical reasoning to solve a puzzle.
4. The student will be able to find missing addends.
5. The student will be able to use knowledge of place value to solve a puzzle.
6. The student will be able to find the difference.

Teaching Tips:

Students may need vertical lines to help keep columns straight as the problems become more complex. Turning lined paper sideways is one solution.

Materials, Supplies, and Equipment:

Activities:

1. Read **Lesson 55 Explanation** with the students.
2   Encourage the students to work the problems carefully to avoid errors.
3. The students should be able to complete **Lesson 55 Practice** independently.

Prove all things; hold fast that which is good.
2 Thessalonians 5:21

Lesson 56

Concepts:

Division with zeros in the quotient, multiplication, division with two-digit quotients, column addition, place value, problems with two operations, multiplication

Objectives:

1. The student will be able to divide with zeros in the quotient.
2. The student will be able to find products to solve a riddle.
3. The student will be able to divide to find one- and two-digit quotients.
4. The student will be able to find sums when given columns of numbers.
5. The student will be able to match written numbers with numeric numbers.
6. The student will be able to solve problems with two operations.
7. The student will be able to find products and solve a puzzle.

Teaching Tips:

Students often forget to place the zero in the quotient when they divide. Using multiplication to check answers will help them discover their error.

Materials, Supplies, and Equipment:

1. *Worksheet 28*

Activities:

1. Read **Lesson 56 Explanation** with the students.
2. Write these problems on the board for more practice.

$$\frac{104}{42)4368} \qquad \frac{105}{52)5460}$$

3. The students should be able to complete **Lesson 56 Practice** independently.

I love the Lord because he hears my prayers and answers them.
Because he bends down and listens, I will pray as long as I breathe.
Psalms 116: 1-2

Lesson 57

Concepts:

Division to estimate quotients, addition, division with two-digit divisors, ordering numbers, division with two- and three-digit quotients, problems with two operations, multiplication equations

Objectives:

1. The student will be able to solve division problems by estimating quotients.
2. The student will be able to find simple sums.
3. The student will be able to solve division problems with two-digit divisors.
4. The student will be able to order numbers from least to greatest.
5. The student will be able to solve division problems with two-digit divisors and three-digit quotients.
6. The student will be able to place the parentheses in a problem with two operations to make a statement true.
7. The student will be able to solve multiplication equations.

Teaching Tips:

Materials, Supplies, and Equipment:

Activities:

1. Read **Lesson 57 Explanation** with the students.
2. Write these problems on the board for more practice.
   Have the students estimate by rounding the divisor and the dividend to the first digit.

$$80\overline{)427}\qquad\qquad 52\overline{)3172}\qquad\qquad 27\overline{)61,420}$$

$$\overset{5}{80\overline{)400}}\qquad\qquad \overset{60}{50\overline{)3000}}\qquad\qquad \overset{2,000}{30\overline{)60,000}}$$

3. The students should be able to complete **Lesson 57 Practice** independently.

But it is good for me to draw near to God: I have put my trust
in the Lord God, that I may declare all thy works.
Psalms 73: 28

Lesson 58

Concepts:

Divide money, exponents, addition equations, addition, place value, magic squares

Objectives:

1. The student will be able to divide money.
2. The student will be able to find products given exponents.
3. The student will be able to solve addition equations.
4. The student will be able to find sums and color a puzzle.
5. The student will be able to match written numbers with numeric numbers.
6. The student will be able to solve a magic square by finding sums.

Teaching Tips:

Encourage students to place the decimal point and dollar sign in the problem BEFORE they divide. This will alleviate the most common mistake in dividing money.

Materials, Supplies, and Equipment:

Activities:

1. Read **Lesson 58 Explanation** with the students.
2. This lesson is a review of skills previously taught. Students should be able to complete **Lesson 58 Practice** independently.

Great is the Lord, and greatly to be praised; and his greatness is unsearchable.
Psalms 145:3

Lesson 59

Concepts:
Divisibility, dividing money, addition, addition equations, averaging, three-digit addition

Objectives:

1. The student will be able to determine if a number is divisible by 2, 3, 5, or 10.
2. The student will be able to divide money.
3. The student will be able to find the sum of two five-digit numbers.
4. The student will be able to solve addition equations.
5. The student will be able to find the average of three or four numbers.
6. The student will be able to find the sum of two- and three-digit numbers.

Teaching Tips:

Students enjoy playing games that involve divisibility. Try playing "Three in a Row."

Materials, Supplies, and Equipment:

1. *Worksheet 29*

Activities:
1. Read **Lesson 59 Explanation** with the students.
2. Play "Three in a Row"

"Three in a Row"
Materials: markers, large index cards
Getting Ready: Make 10 game cards on large index cards as follows:

9	22	25
5	11	40
63	12	17

11	12	70
14	13	5
25	75	9

5	7	80
3	29	15
9	12	63

50	15	3
13	9	25
22	11	14

9	20	22
25	13	11
30	3	85

62	22	29
15	65	9
20	6	7

43	5	13
81	25	50
14	9	3

63	25	2
22	7	60
11	9	35

3	11	40
35	2	16
23	9	25

15	45	60
9	17	44
19	22	3

Make 4 instruction cards for each category as follows: Divisible by 2, Divisible by 10, Divisible by 3, Divisible by 5, Prime
Directions: Give each student a game card. Every number on the cards is divisible by 2, 10, 3, 5, or is prime. Some numbers only fit one category. For instance 11 is prime. Some numbers fit several categories. 40 is divisible by 2, 5, and 10. The goal of the game is to get three spaces covered in a row vertically, horizontally, or diagonally.
  a. The leader will read the instruction card, and the student may cover one space that fits that category. Once a space is covered, it may not be changed for another category later.
  b. The leader will pick another instruction card and the student will cover another space. This continues until someone calls "Three in a Row."
  c. The leader will compare the instruction cards with the numbers covered to test the validity of the student's answers. If all the answers are correct. That student is the winner and becomes the new leader.
3. Students should be able to complete **Lesson 59 Practice** independently.

Set a watch, O Lord, before my mouth; keep the door of my lips.
Psalms 141:3

Lesson 60

Concepts:

Problem solving, divide money, subtraction, divisibility, subtraction equations, averaging with decimal remainders, averaging with fractional remainders

Objectives:

1. The student will be able to solve word problems that contain too much information. The student will be able to find the information that is not needed.
2. The student will be able to divide money.
3. The student will be able to find the difference in simple subtraction problems.
4. The student will be able to find numbers that are prime or divisible by 3 or 2.
5. The student will be able to solve subtraction equations.
6. Given an averaging problem, the student will be able to look at the decimal portion and determine whether the problem should be rounded up or down.
7. Given an averaging problem, the student will be able to look at a fractional remainder and determine whether the problem should be rounded up or down.

Teaching Tips:

Students enjoy making problems similar to these for their classmates to solve.

Materials, Supplies, and Equipment:

Activities:

1. Read **Lesson 60 Explanation** with the students.
2. Students should be able to complete **Lesson 60 Practice** independently

Test:

1. Test 6 covers Lessons 46-55.
2. Administer Test 6, allowing the students 30-40 minutes to complete the test.

Teach me Thy way, O Lord; I will walk in Thy truths.
Psalms 86:11a

Lesson 61

Concepts:

Time definitions, polygons, number identification, division with one-digit quotients, factor trees, multiplication facts and terms, addition equations

Objectives:

1. The student will be able to identify time definitions.
2. The student will be able to find a mystery numbers when given a set of clues.
3. The student will be able to draw and identify 5, 6, 7, 8, and 10-sided polygons.
4. The student will be able to solve division problems which yield a one-digit quotient with a remainder.
5. The student will be able to complete factor trees.
6. The student will be able to label multiplication terms and complete multiplication facts.
7. The student will be able to solve addition equations.

Teaching Tips:

Most of the students will not have any difficulty grasping this concept.
For most of them it will be review. Try to make it as interesting as possible.

Materials, Supplies, and Equipment:

Activities:

1. Read **Lesson 61 Explanation** together and discuss it with the students.
2. The student should be able to complete **Lesson 61 Practice** independently.

If we confess our sins, he is faithful and just to forgive us our sins
and purify us from all unrighteousness.
1 John 1:9

Lesson 62

Concepts:

A.M. & P.M., 3-D figures: faces, edges, vertices; line graphs, division with two-digit quotients, factor trees, problem solving, multiplication terms and facts

Objectives:

1. The student will be able to correctly write times using the designations A.M. and P.M.
2. The student will be able to identify and draw 3-D figures identifying each figure's faces, edges, and vertices.
3. The student will be able to read and interpret information from a line graph.
4. The student will be able to solve division problems which yield a two-digit quotient with a remainder.
5. The student will be able to complete factor trees.
6. The student will be able to solve given problem solving activities.
7. The student will be able to label multiplication terms and complete multiplication facts.

Teaching Tips:

The abbreviation A.M. stands for "ante meridian" the time between midnight and noon. The abbreviation P.M. means "post meridian" is the time between noon and midnight.

Materials, Supplies, and Equipment:

1. Demonstration clock
2. *Worksheet 30*

Activities:

1. Read **Lesson 62 Explanation** together. Write the following times on the board: 2:00 P.M., 11:00 A.M., 9:45 P.M., and 6:25 A.M.
   Have the students take turns reading the time and telling whether each is morning, afternoon or night. Have them show each time on the demonstration clock.
2. The student should be able to complete **Lesson 62 Practice** independently.

*Do not love the world or anything in the world. If anyone loves
the world, the love of the Father is not in him.*
1 John 2:15

Lesson 63

Concepts:

Centuries, types of angles, pie graphs, division with three-digit quotients, prime and composite numbers, division terms and facts

Objectives:

1. The student will be able to properly identify various centuries.
2. The student will be able to identify and label acute, obtuse, and right angles.
3. The student will be able to read and interpret information presented in a pie graph.
4. The student will be able to solve division problems which yield a three-digit quotient with a remainder.
5. The student will be able to identify prime and composite numbers.
6. The student will be able to label division terms and complete division facts.

Teaching Tips:

Most students will want to know why the century numbers do not match the beginning numbers of each year; for example, why 1809 is not the 18th century.

Remind them that a time period of 100 years has to pass before it can be considered a century, the years A.D. 0-99 are considered the 1st century.

Materials, Supplies, and Equipment:

1. A timeline of historical events (can be obtained from any history book or encyclopedia)

Activities:

1. Read **Lesson 63 Explanation** together and look over the listing of century dates. Take the historical timelines and have the students pick any 4 historical events (for example, the American Revolution, World War II, The Civil War, and The Louisiana Purchase).

   Have the students name the date and century in which each major event occurred.
2. The student should be able to complete **Lesson 63 Practice** independently.

   Praise be to the name of God for ever and ever; wisdom and power are his.
   Daniel 2:20

Lesson 64

Concepts:

Time equivalents, perimeter, division terms and facts, division with zeros in the quotient, prime and composite numbers, geometric figures

Objectives:

1. The student will be able to identify time equivalents.
2. The student will be able to read and interpret information presented in a bar graph.
3. The student will be able to calculate the perimeter of a shape.
4. The student will be able to label division terms and complete division facts.
5. The student will be able to solve division problems which contain zeros in the quotient.
6. The student will be able to identify prime and composite numbers.
7. The student will be able to identify and label a parallelogram; square, rectangle, rhombus and trapezoid.

Teaching Tips:

Link time conversions and equivalents to everyday life.

Always remember that relevancy to real world activities is necessary for the students to grasp the importance of all math concepts.

Materials, Supplies, and Equipment:

1. Several popular videos (age and content appropriate)
2. Demonstration clock
3. *Worksheet 31*

Activities:

1. Show the display clock and ask the students how many minutes are in an hour, how many minutes are in two hours, how many hours are in one day, and how many seconds are in two minutes. Call on students to answer individually and then have them come up and give the correct answer on the demonstration clock. This should enable the students thinking in the correct direction.
2. Tell the students that you have planned to show a movie in class today.
   You only have 1 hour to show the movie, and the movie is 120 minutes long.
   Ask the students if they will have enough time to see the entire movie in the 1 hour time slot. The answer, of course, is no.
   Have the students who answered correctly how they arrived at their answer.
   The response should be that 120 minutes is 2 hours, and therefore the movie is longer than the allotted viewing time.
3. Read **Lesson 64 Explanation** together.
   Answer any questions that the students might have about the lesson.
4. The student should be able to complete **Lesson 64 Practice** independently.

Do not repay anyone evil for evil. Be careful to do what
is right in the eyes of everybody.
Romans 12:17

Lesson 65

Concepts:

Elapsed time, time equivalents, area, averaging, three-digit multiplication, two- and three-digit subtraction, problem solving- more than one operation

Objectives:

1. The student will be able to calculate elapsed times.
2. The student will be able to identify time equivalents.
3. The student will be able to calculate the area of a shape or object.
4. The student will be able to average a set of numbers.
5. The student will be able to solve multiplication problems which contain a three-digit multiplicand and a one-digit multiplier.
6. The student will be able to solve two- and three-digit addition problems.
7. The student will be able to solve for missing addends.

Teaching Tips:

Explain that estimating elapsed time and calculating elapsed time are extremely important in the workplace. In order to schedule appointments, a salesperson needs to properly calculate elapsed travel time when arranging appointments and meeting customers. If a salesman did not have this skill he might have customers waiting for him, missing him, and consequently losing business.

Materials, Supplies, and Equipment:

1. Demonstration clock
2. Daily planner sheets (taken from a business planner which a business person would use)
3. *Worksheet 30*

Activities:

1. Put the following appointments on the board:
    > 9:15 – meeting with Pastor Kendall
    > 12:00 – Lunch with Mr. Wallace
    > 1:30 – meeting with Mr. Carmichael of APNC Industries
    > 3:00 – pick up Caroline from school

    Instruct the students to write each event on their daily planner sheets by the appropriate time slot. Then instruct them to pretend that they are a businessman/woman and need to attend all of these appointments for the day. Travel time between each appointment is at least 30 minutes. Have the students calculate the maximum amount of time which can be spent at each appointment without being late for the next appointment. After the students have had time to work, explain that this is an example of calculating elapsed time.
2. Read **Lesson 65 Explanation** together. Complete the sample problems. Answer any questions the students might have.
3. The student should be able to complete **Lesson 65 Practice** independently. Monitor the students in case further assistance is needed.

If you enemy is hungry, feed him; if he is thirsty, give him something to drink.
In doing this you will heap burning coals on his head.
Romans 12:20

Lesson 66

Concepts:

Calendar, elapsed time, time equivalents, averaging with remainder, three-digit multiplication, four-, five-, and six-digit multiplication, missing addends

Objectives:

1. The student will be able to calculate time and elapsed time using a calendar.
2. The student will be able to calculate elapsed times.
3. The student will be able to identify time equivalents.
4. The student will be able to average a set of numbers and properly round any remainders to the nearest whole number.
5. The student will be able to solve multiplication problems which contain a three-digit multiplicand and a two-digit multiplier.
6. The student will be able to solve four-, five-, and six-digit addition problems.
7. The student will be able to solve for missing addends.

Teaching Tips:

There is a poem which reads "Thirty days have September, April, June, and November. And just for fun, all the rest have 31, except February. February alone doesn't hold the line. For three years it has 28, and in the fourth it has 29." The students probably know and can recite this poem. It is a fun exercise.

Materials, Supplies, and Equipment:

1. A calendar for the entire year.

Activities:

1. Take the calendar apart and place all the months on the board (in order) so that the students can see the entire year at once (see below).

January	February	March	April	May	June

July	August	September	October	November	December

Check the number of days in each month to ensure that the poem (discussed in the teaching tip) is correct. Then have the students answer several questions using these monthly calendars.

Ask questions like: How many days are between Thanksgiving and Christmas? How many weeks is that? or

How many weeks are there between Easter and Labor Day.

2. Have the students read **Lesson 66 Explanation**. Complete the sample questions together and discuss any questions together.
3. The student should be able to complete **Lesson 66 Practice** independently.

Whatever happens, conduct yourselves in a manner worthy of the gospel of Christ.
Then, whether I come and see you or only hear about you in my absence, I will know that
you stand firm in one spirit, contending as one man for the faith of the gospel without
being frightened in any way by those who oppose you.
Philippians 1:27-28

Lesson 67

Concepts:

Time zones, calendar, elapsed time, time equivalents, two-digit divisors and one-digit quotients, three-digit multiplication, two- and three-digit subtraction, problem solving, using more than one operation

Objectives:

1. The student will be able to identify and use time zones to calculate time.
2. The student will be able to calculate time and elapsed time using a calendar.
3. The student will be able to calculate elapsed times.
4. The student will be able to identify time equivalents.
5. The student will be able to solve division problems which contain a two-digit divisor and yield a one-digit quotient.
6. The student will be able to complete multiplication problems which contain a three-digit multiplicand and three-digit multiplier.
7. The student will be able to solve two- and three-digit subtraction problems.
8. The student will be able to complete problems which require the use of more than one operation to solve.

Teaching Tips:

With satellite dishes easily available and affordable these days, some students have experienced time zone differences by watching news or sporting events on channels which are broadcast from cities in different time zones than their own.

Materials, Supplies, and Equipment:

1. Local television viewing guide (schedule)
2. Flashlight
3. Tennis ball (or some other small round ball)
4. 2 Push pins
5. *Worksheet 32*

Activities:

1. Have the students browse through the television viewing guides and pick out stations which broadcast the news (or favorite TV shows) at a different hour than the local channels (for example, if living in Atlanta where the news is broadcast at 12:00 P.M., 6:00 P.M., and 11:00 P.M., watching a channel in Chicago would show the news at 11:00 A.M., 5:00 P.M., and 10:00 P.M. Georgia time because of the time zone difference). Discuss why the news in Chicago would be shown in Atlanta at 10:00 P.M. rather than 11:00 P.M..
2. Read **Lesson 67 Explanation** together. Work the sample problems together and answer any questions.
3. Illustrate how the rotation of the Earth results in the necessity for different time zones. Tell the students to imagine that the tennis ball is Earth and the flashlight is the Sun. Push one pushpin into the tennis ball and have it represent Atlanta. Push the second pushpin into the ball at least 2 inches to the left of the first pin.

This second pin will represent Los Angeles. While shining the light on the ball, rotate the ball to show that the Earth is constantly rotating.

Discuss that the rotation of the Earth as the Sun shines on cities in the East before shining on cities in the West.

Point out that the sun shines on the push pin representing Atlanta before it shines on the pin representing Los Angeles. By the time the sun is shining on Los Angeles, the Atlanta pushpin is in darkness. This illustrates why it is 10:00 in Atlanta, 9:00 in Chicago, 8:00 in Denver, 7:00 in Los Angeles and 5:00 in Hawaii. Remember to make sure the student understands that there are 24 time zones in all (24 hours in the day). This might be a good time to correlate geography and math by discussing the Prime Meridian and the International Date Line.

4. The student should be able to complete **Lesson 67 Practice** independently.

Have nothing to do with godless myths and old wives'
tales; rather, train yourself to be godly.
1 Timothy 4:7

Lesson 68

Concepts:

Counting money, time zones, calendar, elapsed time, two-digit divisor and two-digit quotient, multiplication equations, problem solving, using more than one operation, four-, five- and six-digit multiplication

Objectives:

1. The student will be able to identify and count money.
2. The student will be able to identify and use time zones to calculate time.
3 The student will be able to calculate time and elapsed time using a calendar.
4. The student will be able to calculate elapsed times.
5. The student will be able to solve division problems that have a two-digit divisor and yield a two-digit quotient.
6. The student will be able to solve multiplication equations.
7. The student will be able to add and subtract money.

Teaching Tips:

Most of the students will not have difficulty identifying the various denominations of money, both bills and coins. Try to make the lesson more interesting by contacting your local bank, or the local Federal Reserve Bank, and gathering some information on the various items printed on a dollar bill. You may also be able to gather information on what to look for when looking for counterfeit money. The Federal Reserve has a packet of materials which explains the history of money and shows the way money has changed over the years.

Materials, Supplies, and Equipment:

1. Play money (both bills and coins)
2. Information on counterfeit money and the printing of money.
3. Place value chart (if necessary)
4. *Worksheet 33*

Activities:

1. Pick three students to come to the front of the room. Give one student a $20.00 bill, one student $15.00 and one student a $1.00 bill. Ask them which student has the least amount of money and which student has the most money.
2. Do this same activity again with various coins. Remind the students that coins are fractional (decimal) parts of a dollar. Use the place value chart, if necessary, to illustrate.
3. Read **Lesson 68 Explanation** together. Ask one student to use the play money and demonstrate the answer to the example problem.
4. Have the students make up several subtraction problems and demonstrate them with the play money.
5. If you have been able to obtain information on the history of money and the counterfeiting of money, from the Federal Reserve Bank, discuss this information with the students. It really is fascinating!
6. The students should be able to complete **Lesson 68 Practice** independently.

We brought nothing into the world, and we can take nothing out of it.
1 Timothy 6:7

Lesson 69

Concepts:

Giving change, counting money, time zones, calendar, two-digit divisor and three-digit quotient, exponents, addition and subtraction of money, addition equations

Objectives:

1. The student will be able to calculate the amount of change due from a specific transaction or purchase.
2. The student will be able to identify and count money.
3. The student will be able to identify and use time zones to calculate time.
4. The student will be able to calculate time and elapsed time using a calendar.
5. The student will be able to solve division problems which contain a one-digit divisor and yield a three-digit quotient.
6. The student will be able to calculate the value of exponential numbers.
7. The student will be able to add and subtract money.
8. The student will be able to solve addition equations.

Teaching Tips:

Most students know their coins and bills but cannot not count back change because computer technology now makes that an underutilized skill. Try to give examples of times when a student would need to count back change without the assistance of a calculator or computer (concessions stands at a ballpark, cashiering during a power outage, verifying a cashier gave you the correct change).

Materials, Supplies, and Equipment:

1. Play money and coins
2. *Worksheet 34*

Activities:

1. Review the value of coins–pennies, nickels, dimes, quarters and half dollars. Then ask the following types of questions:

   1 quarter, 5 dimes, 17 pennies.   How much altogether?
   3 dimes, 5 pennies.   How much altogether?
   3 quarters, 1 dime, 3 pennies.   How much altogether?

2. Read **Lesson 69 Explanation** together. Go through each step and actually do the problem with the aid of play money and coins. Have several students experience counting the change. Create several new problems and allow several more students to count change.

3. Break the students into pairs. Have them work the first two problems on **Lesson 69-1** together with the play money and coins. Then check their answers.
   The first problem is an example and has been answered for them.
   They can demonstrate this one and the next problem as the two practice problems.

4. The students should be able to complete the rest of **Lesson 69 Practice** independently.

God opposes the proud but gives grace to the humble.
Proverbs 3:34

Lesson 70

Concepts:

Problem solving, reasonable answers, giving change, counting money, time zones, divisibility, exponents, subtraction equations

Objectives:

1. The student will be able to evaluate a problem solving solution and tell whether an answer is reasonable or not reasonable.
2. The student will be able to calculate the amount of change due from a specific transaction or purchase.
3. The student will be able to identify and count money.
4. The student will be able to identify and use time zones to calculate time.
5. The student will be able to calculate the value of exponential numbers.
6. The student will be able to solve subtraction equations.
7. The student will be able to evaluate a number and identify which numbers it is divisible by.

Teaching Tips:

If the student is having difficulty, have them read the problem several times and restate it in their own words. Then have them state what options they have for solving the problem.

Materials, Supplies, and Equipment:

Activities:

1. Read **Lesson 70 Explanation** with the students. Explain why the example answer is not reasonable. Ask the students if there is another way to explain why the answer is incorrect, other than the example explanation.
2. Have the student complete the first problem on **70-1** independently. Then check the answer together and discuss the different ways several students arrived at the answer.
3. The students should be able to complete **Lesson 70 Practice** with little or no assistance. Monitor the students and help those who seem to be having difficulty with the exercise.

Test:

1. Test 7 covers Lessons 56-65.
2. Administer Test 7, allowing the students 30-40 minutes to complete the test.

For the Lamb at the center of the throne will be their shepherd; He will lead them to springs of living water. And God will wipe away every tear from their eyes.
Revelation 7:17

Lesson 71

Concepts:

Points, lines, segments, mystery numbers, subtraction of fractions, liquid measure, time definitions, division by multiples of 10

Objectives:

1. The student will be able to define in pictures, symbols and words the following: point, line, line segment, ray, and plane.
2. Given clues, the student will be able to find a mystery number.
3. The student will be able to subtract fractions with common denominators.
4. The student will be able to find equivalent liquid measures.
5. The student will be able to define the following time definitions:
    B.C., A.D., decade, century, and millennium.
6. The student will be able to divide by multiples of 10.

Teaching Tips:

Materials, Supplies, and Equipment:

1. *Worksheet 35*

Activities:

1. Read **Lesson 71 Explanation** with the students.
2. Practice writing and reading the geometry terms.
3. Students should be able to complete **Lesson 71 Practice** independently.

We do however, speak a message of wisdom among the mature,
but not the wisdom of this age or the rulers of this age, who are coming to nothing.
No, we speak of God's secret wisdom, a wisdom that has been hidden and that God has
destined for our glory before time began.
1 Corinthians 2:6-7

Lesson 72

Concepts:

Intersecting, parallel, and perpendicular lines, points, lines, segments, adding fractions, A.M. and P.M., linear measure, division

Objectives:

1. The student will be able to define intersecting, parallel, and perpendicular lines.
2. The student will be able to define in pictures, symbols and words the following: point, line, line segment, ray, and plane.
3. The student will be able to add fractions with common denominators.
4. The student will be able to determine if a given time is A.M. or P.M..
5. The student will be able to find equivalent linear measures.
6. The student will be able to divide by a two-digit divisor.

Teaching Tips:

These concepts are not difficult to understand, but takes repeated practice to memorize.

Materials, Supplies, and Equipment:

1. Manila paper
2. 9 index cards
3. *Worksheet 36*

Activities:

1. Write each of the following terms on manila paper and ask the students to think of examples of each: point, line, line segment, ray, intersecting lines, parallel lines, perpendicular lines and plane. For instance, a thumbtack might be an example of a point; the top and bottom of the chalkboard might be an example of parallel lines.
2. Students have little difficulty memorizing the definitions, but they need practice writing the geometric pictures, symbols, and words. To help with this skill, play Geometry Wizard.
3. Have the student complete **Lesson 72 Practice** with the help of the chart in **Lessons 71** and **72**.

Geometry Wizard

Materials:

9 index cards and a chalkboard.

Getting Ready:

Write the following phrases on three index cards: Geometry in Pictures, Geometry in Symbols, Geometry in Words. Draw a game board on the chalkboard like the one on the following page:

© MCMXCVIII Alpha Omega Publications, Inc.

Geometry Terms	Geometry in Pictures	Geometry in Symbols	Geometry in Words
Point			
Line			
Line Segment			
Plane			
Ray			
Intersecting Lines			
Parallel Lines			
Perpendicular Lines			

Procedure:

1. Divide the class into two groups and decide who will go first.
   This may also be played with two players.
2. Place the index cards on a table word-side down.
3. Player One draws a card, reads it, and places it on the bottom of the deck.
   If he turns over **Geometry in Pictures**, the player will choose any of the lines under the column **Geometry in Pictures** and draw and label a picture. If the card is impossible to use because all the spaces are taken, draw again.
   Check the table in **Lessons 71** and **72** for accuracy. The student may label the picture with letters of his choice. If the player's example is incorrect, he loses his turn and the example is erased. If it is correct, the drawing remains on the board.
4. Player Two follows the same procedure. If he draws a card for **Geometry in Symbols**, the player will choose any of the lines not completed under the column **Geometry in Symbols**. If the student chooses a row that already has a label, the same label must be used. For instance, if Player Two wants to place a letter under **Geometry in Symbols** in the row **Point** and a •K has already been placed under **Geometry in Pictures,** player two would need to use the label *K*.
5. **Strategy:** Points may be obtained by completing a row. For instance, if two of the columns have been completed under **Point**, the team to fill in the last column will score one point. They will also get to take another turn.
6. The team that gets the most points after the chart is completed wins the game.

A rich man may be wise in his own eyes, but a poor man
who has discernment sees through him.
Proverbs 28:11

Lesson 73

Concepts:

Angles, types of lines, intersecting, parallel, and perpendicular lines, equivalent fractions, century, time equivalents

Objectives:

1. The student will be able to define types of angles.
2. The student will be able to define intersecting, parallel, and perpendicular lines.
3. The student will be able to define in pictures, symbols and words the following: point, line, line segment, ray, and plane.
4. The student will be able to find equivalent fractions.
5. Given dates, the student will be able to determine the century.
6. The student will be able to find equivalent time measures.

Teaching Tips:

Students enjoy making tagboard strip angles and readily understand the concept.

Materials, Supplies, and Equipment:

1. Tagboard strips one inch wide and six inches long (2 per child).
    Punch a hole in one end of each strip.
2. Metal brads (1 per child)
3. *Worksheet 35*

Activities:

1. Read **Lesson 73 Explanation** with the students. Emphasize that an angle is two rays that meet at a vertex. Explain that there are three names for any one angle.
2. Give each child two tag board strips and a metal brad. Have them join the two pieces of tag board together so the holes match. Place the brad through the hole and spread the ends of the brad.

3. Have the students label their angle $\angle$**ABC**
4. Ask the students to name each ray $(\overrightarrow{BA}$ and $\overrightarrow{BC})$.
5. Ask the students to name the vertex **(vertex B)**.
6. Ask the students to name the three different ways to label this angle **($\angle$ABC, $\angle$CBA, $\angle$B)**.
7. Ask the students to move the tagboard so that their angle is acute, obtuse, and right. Check each student's angle for accuracy.
8. Students should be able to complete **Lesson 73 Practice** independently.

Wisdom, like an inheritance, is a good thing and benefits those who see the sun.
Ecclesiastes 7:11

Lesson 74

Concepts:

Protractor, intersecting, parallel, and perpendicular lines; types of lines, time equivalents, factor trees, division, missing addends

Objectives:

1. The student will be able to use a protractor to measure angles.
2. The student will be able to define intersecting, parallel, and perpendicular lines.
3. The student will be able to define in pictures, symbols and words the following: point, line, line segment, ray, and plane.
4. The student will be able to complete a factor tree.
5. The student will be able to divide with a one-digit divisor.
6. The student will be able to find the missing addends.
7. The student will be able to find equivalent time measures.

Teaching Tips:

Allow the students plenty of opportunity to measure angles.

Materials, Supplies, and Equipment:

1. One protractor per student
2. *Worksheet 37*

Activities:

1. Draw a large acute, obtuse, and right angle on paper.
2. Demonstrate the procedure for measuring with a protractor:
   a. Place the arrow of the protractor on the vertex of the angle.
   b. Place the zero edge on one side of the angle.
   c. Read the measure.
3. Have the students measure the angles on the paper as you help them.
4. Students will be able to complete **Lesson 74 Practice** independently.

Man looks at the outward appearance, but the Lord looks at the heart.
1 Samuel 16:7b

Lesson 75

Concepts:

Types of triangles, protractor, types of angles, word problems, division

Objectives:

1. The students will be able to define the following types of triangles: scalene, equilateral, and isosceles.
2. The student will be able to define right triangles.
3. The student will be able to use a protractor to measure angles.
4. The student will be able to define types of angles.
5. The student will be able to solve word problems.
6. The student will be able to divide with a two-digit divisor.

Teaching Tips:

Materials, Supplies, and Equipment:

1. Geoboards
2. *Worksheet 38*

Activities:

1. Have the students make a triangle on their Geoboard.
2. Place the Geoboards with similar triangles together.
   Discuss how the triangles are alike and different.
3. Read **Lesson 75 Explanation** together.
   Now you can give the groups of triangles names.
4. Ask the student to make the following triangles on their Geoboards: scalene, equilateral, and isosceles.
5. Ask the students if any of the triangles are right triangles.
6. Students will be able to complete **Lesson 75 Practice** independently.

Dear friend, do not imitate what is evil but what is good.
Anyone who does what is evil has not seen God.
3 John 11

Lesson 76

Concepts:

Quadrilaterals, triangles, multiplication, place value

Objectives:

1. The student will be able to define quadrilaterals.
2. The student will be able to define types of angles.
3. The student will be able to define the following types of triangles: scalene, equilateral, and isosceles.
4. The student will be able to find the product given a three-digit factor and a one-digit factor.
5. The student will be able to determine place value to the hundred billions' place.

Teaching Tips:

Materials, Supplies, and Equipment:

1. Geoboards
2. *Worksheet 39*

Activities:

1. Read **Lesson 76 Explanation** together.
2. Have the students make the following figures on their Geoboards: square, rectangle, parallelogram, trapezoid, and rhombus.
3. Point out that there are many figures that fall under each category.
    For instance, a square, rhombus, and rectangle are all parallelograms.
    A square is also a rectangle.
4. The students will be able to complete **Lesson 76-2** independently.
    Help them with **Lesson 76-1** and **Lesson 76-3**.
    Many students are confused, giving several names to one figure.

And He said to man, "The fear of the Lord—
that is wisdom, and to shun evil is understanding."
Job 28:28

Lesson 77

Concepts:

Polygons, quadrilaterals, triangles, protractor, angles, A.M., P.M., multiplication

Objectives:

1. The student will be able to define the following polygons: triangle, quadrilateral, pentagon, hexagon, octagon and decagon.
2. The student will be able to find the diagonals of polygons.
3. The student will be able to define the following types of triangles: scalene, equilateral, and isosceles.
4. The student will be able to define types of angles.
5. The student will be able to determine if a given time is A.M. or P.M..
6. The student will be able to find the product of two, two-digit factors.

Teaching Tips:

Students enjoy making tagboard strip polygons and readily learn the information.

Materials, Supplies, and Equipment:

1. 10 tagboard strips 1 inch wide and 5 inches long. (per child).
   Punch a hole in each end.
2. 2 tagboard strips 1 inch wide and 2½ inches long (per child).
   Punch a hole in each end.
3. 10 brads (per child)
4. *Worksheet 40*

Activities:

1. Read **Lesson 77 Explanation** orally with the students.
   Emphasize the definition of a polygon and the difference between a polygon and a regular polygon.
2. Pass out the tagboard and brads.
3. Tell the students to make one of the figures found in the lesson out of their tagboard and brads. They should be ready to tell the name of the polygon, number of sides, and number of vertices.
4. Allow the students to come to the front of the room and show their polygon. They should be able to tell the name of the polygon, number of sides, and number of vertices.
5. Students will be able to complete **Lesson 77 Practice** independently.

I press on toward the goal to win the prize for which God has called me heavenward in Christ Jesus.
Philippians 3:14

Lesson 78

Concepts:

Circles, polygons, quadrilaterals, triangles, averaging, multiplication, place value, mystery number

Objectives:

1. The student will be able to define the following terms: diameter, chord, radius, center.
2. The student will be able to match names and pictures of polygons.
3. The student will be able to define types of quadrilaterals.
4. The student will be able to average grades.
5. The student will be able to find the product given two, three-digit factors.
6. The student will be able to order numbers from largest to smallest.
7. The student will be able to find a mystery number.

Teaching Tips:

Allow plenty of time to learn to use a compass.

Materials, Supplies, and Equipment:

1. 1 compass (per child)
2. 1 ruler (per child)
3. *Worksheet 41*

Activities:

1. Read **Lesson 78 Explanation** orally with the students.
2. Ask the students to name things in the room that are circular.
3. Distribute a compass and a ruler to each student.
4. Demonstrate how to draw a circle using a compass.
   Draw the students attention to the center point and how each point on the circle is equidistant from that point.
5. Have the students draw circles using their compasses.
   Let them practice until they feel comfortable with the equipment.
6. Allow each child to draw a circle and label it.
   Tell them that you want circles of different sizes.
7. Ask each child to measure the diameter and radius of their circle in centimeters.
8. Place a chart on the board and have the students come to the board and place the measurements from their circle.

Radius	Diameter

9. What did the students notice about the radius and diameter?
   (The radius x 2 equals the diameter.)

10. Ask the students the following questions about their circle:
   Name the circle **(Circle B)**.
   Name the diameter **(AC)**.
   Name the three radii **(AB, BC, BD)**.

11. The students should be able to complete **Lesson 78 Practice** independently.

Cast your bread upon the waters for after many days you will find it again. Give portions to seven, yes to eight, for you do not know what disaster may come upon the land.
Ecclesiastes 11:1-2

Lesson 79

Concepts:

Graphing, circles, polygons, multiplication of equations, place value, addition

Objectives:

1. The student will be able to find points on a graph given ordered pairs of numbers.
2. The student will be able to define the following terms: diameter, chord, radius, center.
3. The student will be able to use a compass to draw circles.
4. The student will be able to define the following polygons:
   square, rectangle, and equilateral triangle.
5. The student will be able to solve multiplication equations.
6. The student will be able to order numbers from largest to smallest.
7. The student will be able to find the sum.

Teaching Tips:

Have the students draw a simple design on grid paper with plotted points.
Tell them to give the ordered pairs to another student.
See if the student can plot the points and draw the same design.

Materials, Supplies, and Equipment:

1. *Worksheet 42*

Activities:

1. Read **Lesson 79 Explanation** with the students.
2. Use the grid on **Lesson 79 Explanation** and have the students plot these points:
   (4, 2), (4, 4), (1, 4), (1, 2).
3. Have the students draw a line to connect the points in order.
   Finally, connect point (1, 2) and (4, 2).
4. Have the students name the figure drawn **(rectangle)**.
5. Ask the students if there are other names to define that figure **(quadrilateral, parallelogram)**.
6. The students will be able to complete **Lesson 79 Practice** independently.

Peacemakers who sow in peace raise a harvest of righteousness.
James 3:18

Lesson 80

Concepts:

Guess and check, circles, polygons, more polygons, exponents, subtraction, rounding

Objectives:

1. The student will be able to solve word problems using the "guess and check method."
2. The student will be able to use a compass to draw circles with a given radius and diameter.
3. The student will be able to define the following polygons: triangle, parallelogram, pentagon, hexagon, octagon, rhombus, trapezoid and decagon.
4. The student will be able to decide if a given polygon is a square, parallelogram, quadrilateral or polygon.
5. The student will be able to write the value of an exponent.
6. The student will be able to find the difference between two, two-digit numbers.
7. The student will be able to round numbers to the nearest 10.

Teaching Tips:

These problems involve trial and error. Tell the students that they should not expect to get the answer quickly. Every incorrect answer will help determine the one correct answer.

Materials, Supplies, and Equipment:

Activities:

1. Read **Lesson 80 Explanation** with the students.
2. Ask the students to solve the following problem:
   a. Sam had 24 boxes of cookies to sell. She had 10 more boxes of chocolate chip than peanut butter cookies.
      How many boxes of peanut butter did she have?
   b. Remind them to use the strategy called guess and check.
      The clues to the first guess will help to make the next guess, until they narrow down possible answers.
   c. The answer is 7.

$$
\begin{array}{rl}
  7 & \text{boxes of peanut butter} \\
+ 17 & \text{boxes of chocolate chip} \\
\hline
 24 & \text{boxes total}
\end{array}
$$

3. The students may need assistance as they complete **Lesson 80 Practice**.

Tests:

1. Test 8 covers Lessons 66-75.
2. Administer Test 8, allowing the students 30-40 minutes to complete the test.
3. Quarter Test 2 covers Lessons 41-80.
4. Administer Quarter Test 2, allowing the students 40-60 minutes to complete the test.

Gold there is, and rubies in abundance, but lips that speak knowledge are a rare jewel.
Proverbs 20:15

© MCMXCVIII Alpha Omega Publications, Inc.

Lesson 81

Concepts:

Symmetry, geometric terms, time definitions, division, rounding numbers, subtraction

Objectives:

1. Given a symmetrical geometric figure, the student will be able to draw the line or lines of symmetry.
2. The student will be able to find examples of parallel, perpendicular and intersecting lines.
3. The student will be able to define geometric terms in pictures, symbols and words.
4. The student will be able to define time definitions.
5. The student will be able to divide a two-digit dividend by a one-digit divisor.
6. The student will be able to round numbers to the nearest 100.
7. Given the difference, the student will be able to find possible subtrahends and minuends.

Teaching Tips:

Materials, Supplies, and Equipment:

1. 2 pieces of paper (per child)
2. 1 pair of scissors (per child)

Activities:

1. Read **Lesson 81 Explanation** orally with the students. Complete the activity as directed in the example.
2. Have the children fold one piece of paper in half lengthwise. Then have the children fold it again across the width. (When opened, the paper will form a cross.)
    Cut out a design, being careful not to cut along the fold line. Open the paper and ask them what they notice. **(It is symmetrical with two lines of symmetry along each fold.)**
3. The children should be able to complete **Lesson 81 Practice** independently.
4. JUST FOR FUN — Have the students design a symmetrical shape that they might want to use as a wallpaper design for their walls, or tile for their floor.
5. JUST FOR FUN — Give the students grid paper and have them fold it into fourths. The students can cut along the lines in the grid paper and create some intricate angular designs.
6. JUST FOR FUN — Divide the students into even-numbered groups, and give them five minutes to go on a discovery trip. They will be hunting for objects that are exactly symmetrical, and recording their discoveries on paper. The team with the most objects found wins the game. **Take it Further** — Look for objects with *two* lines of symmetry.

We ponder God's withholding or bestowing and while we pine for what was never given and what was taken, today slips through our fingers.
Teresa Burleson

Lesson 82

Concepts:

Congruent, geometric terms, symmetry, angles, time definitions, word problems, logical reasoning

Objectives:

1. The student will be able to find pairs of congruent lines, angles and polygons.
2. The student will be able to find lines of symmetry.
3. The students will be able to determine if an angle is acute, right or obtuse.
4. The student will be able to match time definitions with terms.
5. The student will be able to solve word problems involving money.
6. The student will be able to solve logic problems.

Teaching Tips:

Materials, Supplies, and Equipment:

1. 1 piece of paper (per child)
2. 1 protractor (per child)
3. 1 ruler (per child)
4. *Worksheet 43*

Activities:

1. Read **Lesson 82 Explanation** orally with the students.
2. Pair the students. Have the students draw a line on their paper of any length and label it line segment $\overline{AB}$. The students should trade papers with their partner and draw a congruent line. Trade the papers back.
3. Instruct the students to draw an angle on their paper and label it angle $\angle ABC$. The students should trade papers with their partner and using a protractor and ruler, draw a congruent angle. Trade the papers back.
4. Have the students draw a triangle and label it triangle $\triangle XYZ$. The students should trade papers with their partner and draw a congruent triangle using a ruler and protractor. Trade the papers back.
5. The students should be able to complete **Lesson 82 Practice** independently.

Enjoy the little things for one day you may look back and
realize that they are the big things.
Robert Brault

Lesson 83

Concepts:

Similar figures, symmetry, types of triangles, division, word problems, multiplication

Objectives:

1. The student will be able to draw similar figures.
2. The student will be able to draw congruent figures.
3. The student will be able to design a symmetrical design.
4. The student will be able to define the following triangles: scalene, equilateral, isosceles and right.
5. The student will be able to divide a four-digit dividend by a two-digit divisor.
6. The student will be able to solve word problems involving money.
7. The student will be able to find the products of two one-digit factors.

Teaching Tips:

Materials, Supplies, and Equipment:

1. 1 piece of grid paper (per child)
2. *Worksheet 44*

Activities:

1. Read **Lesson 82 Explanation** orally with the students.
2. Explain to the students how architects use scale drawing to provide a smaller version of a house or building.
3. Draw a rectangle on grid paper. Count the number of squares used in the length and width of the rectangle. Have the students draw a similar rectangle on their grid paper. Tell them that it can be 2, 3, 4, etc. times bigger. If the length is three times bigger, the width must also be three times bigger.
4. Have the students draw a polygon on their grid paper, and trade it with a neighbor. Draw a similar polygon to the one drawn.
5. The students should be able to complete **Lesson 83 Practice** independently.

My son, keep your father's commandments and do not forsake your mother's teaching.
Bind them upon your heart forever; fasten them around your neck.
Proverbs 6:20-21

Lesson 84

Concepts:

Space figures, faces, edges, vertices, congruent, types of triangles, symmetry, century, rounding, division

Objectives:

1. The student will be able to define cones, cylinders, pyramids, spheres and prisms.
2. Given a geometric shape, the student will be able to find the number of faces, edges and vertices.
3. The student will be able to determine if two lines, triangles, or polygons are congruent.
4. The student will be able to determine if two triangles are similar.
5. The student will be able to draw a symmetrical shape given one half of the design.
6. The student will be able to write a year that falls in a specific century.
7. The student will be able to round three-digit numbers to the nearest ten and four-digit numbers to the nearest hundred.
8. The student will be able to divide one- and two-digit dividends by one-digit divisors.

Teaching Tips:

Leave the solid space figures in the room with the names on them.

Review the names on a daily basis.

Materials, Supplies, and Equipment:

1. Solid space figures
2. *Worksheet 45*

Activities:

1. Read **Lesson 84 Explanation** orally with the students.
   Review the types of space figures.
2. Show the students the various solid space figures identifying them by name.
   Ask the students to find the number of faces, edges and vertices on each figure.
3. The students should be able to complete **Lesson 84 Practice** independently.

I set My rainbow in the cloud, and it shall be for the sign of the covenant between Me and the earth.
Genesis 9:13

Lesson 85

Concepts:

Perimeter, space figures, quadrilaterals, elapsed time, division, similar figures

Objectives:

1. The student will be able to find the perimeter of a given polygon.
2. The student will be able to construct and identify space figures.
3. The student will be able to draw the following figures: square, rectangle, parallelogram, trapezoid and rhombus.
4. The student will be able to compute elapsed time.
5. The student will be able to divide three-digit dividends by two-digit divisors.
6. The student will be able to divide one- and two-digit dividends by one-digit divisors.
7. The student will be able to draw two similar figures.

Materials, Supplies, and Equipment:

1. 1 tape measure (per child)
2. *Worksheet 46*

Activities:

1. Read **Lesson 85 Explanation** orally with the students.
2. Review measuring with a tape measure.
3. Allow the students to work with partners and measure the perimeter of four objects in the room. They must include a drawing of the object, the measurement of each side, and the perimeter of the object.
4. Have the children share one of their drawings with the class.
5. The students should be able to complete **Lesson 85 Practice** independently.
6. JUST FOR FUN — Have the students guess which room in the learning center has the largest perimeter. What do they think the perimeter will be?
Measure to determine who had the closest estimate.

If you can not lift the load off another's back, do not walk away. Try and lighten it.
Tyger

Lesson 86

Concepts:

Area, perimeter, space figures, faces, edges, vertices, similar figures, addition, division

Objectives:

1. The student will be able to find the area and perimeter of a given polygon.
2. The student will be able to construct and identify space figures.
3. Given a geometric shape, the student will be able to find the number of faces, edges and vertices.
4. The student will be able to find similar figures from a given set of figures.
5. The student will be able to find the sum of two three-digit numbers.
6. The student will be able to divide four-digit divisors by two-digit dividends.

Teaching Tips:

Emphasize that when we label area, we use square units (m^2, cm^2, mm^2).

Materials, Supplies, and Equipment:

1. Two pieces of grid paper (per student)
2. *Worksheet 47*

Activities:

1. Read **Lesson 86 Explanation** orally with the students.
2. Distribute the grid paper. Have each child color a shape with the following dimensions: 15 square units long and 4 square units wide. Count the squares to compute the area **(60 square units)**.
3. Have the students use the formula to compute the area for the same figure **(A = L x W, 60 = 15 x 4)**.
4. Using the remaining grid paper, have the student draw and color a closed figure. Encourage them to use some squares in their drawing. Have the students compute the perimeter and area and place the answers on the back.
5. Choose several pictures the students have created and have the class find the perimeter and area.
6. The students should be able to complete **Lesson 86 Practice** independently.

Those who are lifting the world upward and onward are those who encourage more than criticize.
Elizabeth Harrison

Lesson 87

Concepts:

Volume, perimeter, area, addition, divisibility, missing addends

Objectives:

1. The student will be able to determine the volume of a given figure.
2. The student will be able to use the correct symbol for cubic units.
3. The student will be able to find the length, width, perimeter and area of polygons.
4. Given a geometric shape, the student will be able to find the number of faces, edges and vertices.
5. The student will be able to find the sum of two four-digit numbers.
6. The student will be able to find numbers that are divisible by five.
7. The student will be able to find missing addends.

Teaching Tips:

Emphasize that when we label volume, we use cubic units (m^3, cm^3, mm^3).

Materials, Supplies, and Equipment:

1. Centimeter cubes
2. *Worksheet 48*

Activities:

1. Read **Lesson 87 Explanation** orally with the students.
   Demonstrate using centimeter cubes.
2. Have each student make a cube with 4 centimeter cubes on the bottom and 4 on the top.
   Have the students determine the volume by counting the blocks **(8 cubic units)**.
   Have the students compute the volume using the formula V = L x W x H **(8 = 2 x 2 x 2)**.
3. The students should be able to complete **Lesson 87 Practice** independently.

Those who are wise will shine like the brightness of the heavens, and those who lead many to righteousness, like the stars for ever and ever.
Daniel 12:3

Lesson 88

Concepts:

Surface area, volume, area, circles, column addition, dividing money, mystery number

Objectives:

1. Given a three-dimensional figure, the student will be able to find the surface area.
2. The student will be able to determine the volume of a given figure.
3. The student will be able to draw a figure given the width and area of that figure.
4. The student will be able to draw defined circles.
5. The student will be able to find the sum of a column of numbers.
6. The student will be able to divide four-digit dividends by two-digit divisors with decimals.
7. Given clues, the students will be able to find a mystery number.

Teaching Tips:

Materials, Supplies, and Equipment:

1. Grid paper
2. *Worksheet 49*

Activities:

1. Read **Lesson 88 Explanation** orally with the students.
2. Using the grid paper, draw the front, top, and side of the figure in the explanation.
    Have the students compute the area of each part.
    Multiply by 2 and compute the total surface area.
3. The students should be able to complete **Lesson 88 Practice** independently.
4. JUST FOR FUN — Have boxes of several sizes in your learning center.
    Challenge the students to compute the surface area of each box.
5. JUST FOR FUN — Have the students compute the surface area of their favorite cereal box.

Be kind and compassionate to one another, forgiving each other
as in Christ, God forgave you.
Ephesians 4:32

Lesson 89

Concepts:

Word problems, surface area, perimeter, area, money, subtraction, more than one operation

Objectives:

1. The student will be able to find the width of a figure given the perimeter and length.
2. Given a three-dimensional figure, the student will be able to find the surface area.
3. The student will be able to draw three rectangles with a given perimeter.
4. The student will be able to determine the least number of coins and bills needed for change.
5. Given two four-digit numbers, the student will be able to find the difference.
6. The student will be able to put parentheses in the proper place to make number sentences true.

Teaching Tips:

Materials, Supplies, and Equipment:

Activities:

1. Read **Lesson 89 Explanation** orally with the students.
2. The students should be able to complete **Lesson 89 Practice** independently.
3. JUST FOR FUN — Have the students write their own geometry problem for their classmates to solve. Have them include the width of a rectangle and the perimeter. Their classmates should be able to find the length of the rectangle.

Is it possible that I am so busy doing that I no longer have time to enjoy being?
Wilson

Lesson 90

Concepts:
Problem solving, word problems, surface area, volume, area, perimeter, subtraction, ordering numbers

Objectives:
1. The student will be able to solve word problems using the strategy known as "making an organized list."
2. The student will be able to solve geometric word problems.
3. Given a three-dimensional figure, the student will be able to find the surface area.
4. Given a three-dimensional figure, the student will be able to find the volume.
5. Given the length and width of a figure, the student will be able to draw the figure and determine the area and perimeter.
6. Given two four-digit numbers, the student will be able to find the difference.
7. The student will be able to order whole numbers from greatest to least.

Teaching Tips:

Materials, Supplies, and Equipment:

Activities:
1. Read **Lesson 90 Explanation** orally with the students.
2. The students should be able to complete **Lesson 90 Practice** independently.

Test:
1. Test 9 covers Lessons 76-85.
2. Administer Test 9, allowing the students 30-40 minutes to complete the test.

Love doesn't make the world go round. Love is what makes the ride worthwhile.
Franklin P. Jones

Lesson 91

Concepts:

Fractions, symmetry, division, rounding numbers, geometric terms

Objectives:

1. The students will be able to define the numerator and denominator of a fraction.
2. The students will be able to give the fraction of a colored region.
3. The students will be able to give the fraction of specific objects in a given set.
4. The students will be able to draw two objects with one and two lines of symmetry.
5. The students will be able to solve subtraction equations.
6. The students will be able to find two-digit quotients given a three-digit dividend and a two-digit divisor that is a multiple of 10.
7. The students will be able to round numbers to the nearest 10, 100, and 1,000.
8. The students will be able to match geometric terms to their pictorial representation.

Teaching Tips:

Students can readily determine what fraction represents part of a whole. They often find fractions like ⅔ and ⅓ confusing. Give the students concrete examples of these fractions.

Materials, Supplies, and Equipment:

1. 2 paper plates
   Getting Ready: Draw lines on each paper plate dividing them as follows:
   thirds and fourths
2. *Worksheet 50*

Activities:

1. Place the paper plates in front of the students, and ask them which paper plate is divided into fourths.
2. After the correct plate has been chosen, ask a volunteer to color the plate so that ¼ of the plate is colored.
3. Tell the students, **"In the fraction ¼, the number over the line is the *numerator* and the number under the line is the *denominator*."** Write the terms on the board.
4. Ask the students which paper plate is divided into thirds.
5. After the correct plate has been chosen, ask a volunteer to color the plate so that ⅔ of the plate is colored.
6. Write the fraction ⅔ on the board.
   Ask a student to identify the numerator and denominator.
7. Read **Lesson 91 Explanation** with the students.
8. The students should be able to complete **Lesson 91 Practice** independently.

Be strong and courageous. Do not be terrified; do not be discouraged,
for the Lord your God will be with you wherever you go.
Joshua 1:9

Lesson 92

Concepts:
Equivalent fractions, congruent figures, angles, A.M. and P.M., rounding numbers, division

Objectives:
1. The students will be able to find equivalent fractions.
2. The students will be able to give the fraction of a colored region.
3. The students will be able to find a congruent figure.
4. The students will be able to define a right angle, acute angle and obtuse angle.
5. The students will be able to determine if an event is taking place in the A.M. or P.M..
6. The students will be able to shade numbers that round to 100.
7. The students will be able to find two-digit quotients given a three-digit dividend and a two-digit divisor.

Teaching Tips:

Materials, Supplies, and Equipment:
1. Three paper plates
2. magic markers
   Getting Ready: Draw lines on each paper plate dividing them as follows: halves, fourths, and sixths
3. *Worksheet 51*

Activities:
1. Show the students the paper plate divided into halves.
   Ask them to identify the fractional representation for one part of the paper plate (½).
2. Show the students the paper plate divided into fourths.
   Ask them to identify the fractional representation for one part of the paper plate (¼).
3. Show the students the paper plate divided into sixths.
   Ask them to identify the fractional representation for one part of the paper plate (⅙).
4. Take the paper plate divided into halves and cut out the fractional representation of ½. Write ½ on the paper plate with magic marker.
5. Place the fractional representation for ½ on the paper plate divided into fourths. What fraction of the plate is covered (²⁄₄)?
6. Place the fractional representation for ½ on the paper plate divided into sixths. What fraction of the plate is covered (³⁄₆)?
7. What statement can be made about the fractions ½, ²⁄₄, and ³⁄₆?
   They are all equal or equivalent.
8. Read **Lesson 92 Explanation** with the students.
   Work the following problems solving for a missing numerator:

$$\frac{1}{3} = \frac{n}{12} \qquad \frac{3}{7} = \frac{n}{21} \qquad \frac{4}{5} = \frac{n}{25}$$
$$n = 4 \quad n = 9 \quad n = 20$$

9. The students should be able to complete **Lesson 92 Practice** with assistance.

And I pray that you, being rooted and established in love, may have power, together with all the saints, to grasp how wide and long and high and deep is the love of Christ.
Ephesians 3:17b-18

Lesson 93

Concepts:

Greatest common factors, equivalent fractions, measuring with a protractor, perimeter, division, time equivalents, similar figures

Objectives:

1. The students will be able to find the greatest common factor of two numbers.
2. The students will be able to find equivalent fractions.
3. The students will be able to use a protractor to measure angles.
4. Given a regular polygon and the length of one side, the student will be able to find the perimeter.
5. The students will be able to find three-digit quotients given a four-digit dividend and a two-digit divisor.
6. Given dates, the student will be able to determine the century in which the event occurred.
7. The students will be able to draw a similar figure to a given figure.

Teaching Tips:

These concepts are difficult at first. It is important to work many examples and supply the students with a lot of opportunities to practice finding the GCF.

Materials, Supplies, and Equipment:

Activities:

1. Read **Lesson 93 Explanation** with the students.
2. Work the following problems with the students:

   10: *1, 2, 5, 10*   12: *1, 2, 3, 4, 6, 12*   16: *1, 2, 4, 8, 16*

   16: *1, 2, 4, 8, 16*   18: *1, 2, 3, 6, 9, 18*   20: *1, 2, 4, 5, 10*

   common factors: *1, 2*   common factors: *1, 2, 3, 6*   common factors: *1, 2, 4*

   greatest common factor: *2*   greatest common factor: *6*   greatest common factor: *4*

3. The students should be able to complete **Lesson 93 Practice** with assistance.

Now suppose one of you fathers is asked by his son for a fish; he will not give him a snake instead of a fish, will he? Or if he is asked for an egg, he will not give him a scorpion, will he? If you then, being evil, know how to give good gifts to your children, how much more shall your Heavenly Father give the Holy Spirit to those who ask Him.
Luke 11:11-13

Lesson 94

Concepts:

Lowest term fractions, greatest common factors, equivalent fractions, volume, space figures, division, time equivalents, logical reasoning

Objectives:

1. The students will be able to find lowest term fractions.
2. The students will be able to find the greatest common factor of two numbers.
3. Given two equivalent fractions, the student will be able to find the missing numerator or denominator.
4. The students will be able to find the volume of a three-dimensional figure.
5. The student will be able to define the following space figures: rectangular pyramid, rectangular prism, hexagonal prism, cylinder, octagonal pyramid, octagonal prism.
6. Given a division problem, the student will be able to find missing numbers.
7. The students will be able to find equivalent time definitions.
8. The students will be able to find numbers in a number puzzle using logical reasoning.

Teaching Tips:

Students often write an equivalent fraction that is not in the lowest terms. If they find the GCF first, this error can be avoided.

Materials, Supplies, and Equipment:

1. 3 paper plates, black magic marker
   Getting Ready: Draw lines with magic marker on each paper plate dividing them as follows: halves, sixths, and twelfths
2. *Worksheet 52*

Activities:

1. Display the paper plate divided into twelfths.
   Ask a volunteer to shade the paper plate to represent ⁶⁄₁₂.
2. Cut out the shaded portion. Display the other paper plates. Place the cut out portion on top of the other two paper plates. It is obvious that ⁶⁄₁₂ is equivalent to ³⁄₆ and ½. The lowest terms representation of that fraction would be ½.
3. Read **Lesson 94 Explanation** with the students.
   Tell the students that both methods will help you find the lowest terms fraction, but the GCF method is the most accurate method.
4. The students should be able to complete **Lesson 94 Practice** independently.

For the grace of God that brings salvation has appeared to all men. It teaches us to say "No" to all ungodliness and worldly passions, and to live self-controlled upright and godly lives in this present age.
Titus 2:11-12

Lesson 95

Concepts:

Compare and order fractions, lowest term fractions, greatest common factor, equivalent fractions, quadrilaterals, perimeter and area, division of decimals

Objectives:

1. The students will be able to compare and order fractions.
2. The students will be able to find lowest term fractions.
3. The students will be able to find the greatest common factor of two numbers.
4. The students will be able to find equivalent fractions.
5. The students will be able to draw pictures that represent the following quadrilaterals: square, rectangle, parallelogram, trapezoid and rhombus.
6. Given the length and width of a quadrilateral, the student will be able to find the perimeter and area.
7. The student will be able to divide a four-digit dividend by a two-digit divisor that involves decimal points.

Teaching Tips:

When comparing fractions students often think that a fraction with a larger denominator represents a larger fraction. Give students several examples to show that this is incorrect.

Materials, Supplies, and Equipment:

Activities:

1. Read **Lesson 95 Explanation** with the students.
   Work several of the examples below to reinforce the concepts of the lesson.

   Compare ⅔ and ½ by renaming them as like fractions:

   $$\frac{2 \times 2}{3 \times 2} = \frac{4}{6}$$

   $$\frac{1 \times 2}{2 \times 3} = \frac{3}{6}$$

   ⅔ > ½

   Compare 2/7 and ²¹/₂₈ by renaming them as like fractions:

   $$\frac{2 \times 4}{7 \times 4} = \frac{8}{28}$$

   $$\frac{3 \times 7}{4 \times 7} = \frac{21}{28}$$

   2/7 < ²¹/₂₈

2. Play Fractions Buster 1 or Fraction Buster 2 with the students (Below).
3. The students should be able to complete **Lesson 95 Practice** independently.

Fraction Buster 1

        Materials: 32 large index cards

Getting Ready: Write two copies of the following fractions on each of the 16 index cards: $\frac{1}{16}$, $\frac{2}{16}$, $\frac{3}{16}$, $\frac{4}{16}$, $\frac{5}{16}$, $\frac{6}{16}$, $\frac{7}{16}$, $\frac{8}{16}$, $\frac{9}{16}$, $\frac{10}{16}$, $\frac{11}{16}$, $\frac{12}{16}$, $\frac{13}{16}$, $\frac{14}{16}$, $\frac{15}{16}$, and $\frac{16}{16}$

1. Each student gets 16 cards that will be placed face down in front of him.
2. Both players turn over their first card and compare the fractions. The student with the highest card takes both cards. The cards that are "won" should be placed on the bottom of the player's pile.
3. If two cards are the same, each player turns over two more cards and finds the sum of the two fractions. The person with the largest sum wins all of the cards.
4. Play continues until one player has all of the cards.

Fraction Buster 2

        Materials: 40 large index cards

Getting Ready: Write two copies of the following fractions on each of the 20 index cards: $\frac{1}{16}$, $\frac{2}{16}$, $\frac{4}{16}$, $\frac{6}{16}$, $\frac{8}{16}$, $\frac{10}{16}$, $\frac{12}{16}$, $\frac{14}{16}$, $\frac{16}{16}$, $\frac{1}{8}$, $\frac{2}{8}$, $\frac{4}{8}$, $\frac{6}{8}$, $\frac{8}{8}$, $\frac{1}{2}$, $\frac{2}{2}$, $\frac{1}{4}$, $\frac{2}{4}$, $\frac{3}{4}$, and $\frac{4}{4}$

1. Each student gets 20 cards that will be placed face down in front of them.
2. Both players turn over their first card and compare the fractions. The student with the highest card takes both cards. The cards that are "won" should be placed on the bottom of the player's pile.
3. If two cards are the same, each player turns over two more cards and finds the sum of the two fractions. The person with the largest sum wins all of the cards.
4. Play continues until one player has all of the cards.

And I will dwell in the house of the Lord forever.
Psalms 23:6b

Lesson 96

Concepts:

Add and subtract fractions, compare and order fractions, lowest term fractions, define polygons, mystery numbers, addition, rounding numbers

Objectives:

1. The students will be able to add and subtract fractions with like denominators.
2. The students will be able to compare and order fractions.
3. The students will be able to find lowest term fractions.
4. The students will be able to define the following figures: pentagon, hexagon, and octagon.
5. Given number clues, the students will be able to find the mystery number.
6. The students will be able to add two, three-digit numbers.
7. The students will be able to round three-digit numbers to the nearest ten and four-digit numbers to the nearest hundred. The student will be able to divide rounded numbers.

Teaching Tips:

When students add and subtract fractions they often add the numerator and denominator. Use concrete examples to show them the error in this thinking.

Materials, Supplies, and Equipment:

1. Three paper plates
    Getting Ready: Draw lines on 3 paper plates dividing them into four equal parts.
2. *Worksheet 53*

Activities:

1. Display one of the paper plates.
    Have a student shade ¼ of the paper plate and cut it out.
2. Display another paper plate.
    Have a student shade ²⁄₄ of the paper plate and cut it out.
3. Ask the students: **"What is the sum of ²⁄₄ and ¼ (¾)?"**
4. Place the shaded ¼ and ²⁄₄ over the whole paper plate.
    It will be easy to see that ¾ of the paper plate is covered.
5. Display the whole paper plate and the shaded ²⁄₄.
    Place the ²⁄₄ over the ⁴⁄₄ and ask the students: **"What is the difference of ⁴⁄₄ and ²⁄₄ ? ²⁄₄ or ½ ?"**
6. Read **Lesson 96 Explanation** with the students.
7. The students should be able to complete **Lesson 96 Practice** independently.

So whether you eat or drink or whatever you do, do it all for the glory of God.
1 Corinthians 10:31

Lesson 97

Concepts:

Mixed numbers to improper fractions, add and subtract fractions, order fractions, renaming fractions, prime numbers, divisibility, time zones

Objectives:

1. The student will be able to change a mixed number to an improper fraction.
2. The students will be able to add and subtract fractions with like denominators.
3. The students will be able to order fractions with different denominators from least to greatest.
4. The students will be able to match fractions to equivalent lowest term fractions.
5. The students will be able to use a factor tree to find prime numbers.
6. The students will be able to determine if a given number is divisible by 2, 5, 10, or 3.
7. Given the time in New York City, the students will be able to use a time zone map and determine times in each time zone.

Teaching Tips:

Explanation of these concepts will be enhanced by the use of manipulatives.

Materials, Supplies, and Equipment:

1. Paper

Activities:

1. Take two pieces of paper divided into sixths.
   Ask the students, **"Who can color these pieces of paper to represent $1\frac{1}{6}$?"**
   (One whole sheet and $\frac{1}{6}$ of the other sheet.)
2. Take two pieces of paper divided into sixths.
   Ask the students, **"Who can color these pieces of paper to represent $\frac{7}{6}$?"**
   (One whole sheet and $\frac{1}{6}$ of the other sheet.)
3. The students can easily see that these two fractional representations are equal.
4. Read **Lesson 97 Explanation** with the students.
5. Allow the students to work the following problems on the board with guidance:
   Change each mixed fraction to an improper fraction:
   $1\frac{1}{2}$, $3\frac{6}{8}$, $4\frac{2}{7}$, $1\frac{5}{10}$, $1\frac{6}{6}$ ($\frac{3}{2}$, $\frac{30}{8}$, $\frac{30}{7}$, $\frac{15}{10}$, **2**).
6. The students should be able to complete **Lesson 97 Practice** independently.

But he said to me, "My grace is sufficient for you, for my power
is made perfect in weakness.
2 Corinthians 12:9

© MCMXCVIII Alpha Omega Publications, Inc.

Lesson 98

Concepts:

Improper fractions to mixed numbers, add fractions, subtract fractions, comparing fractions, prime and composite numbers, subtraction

Objectives:

1. The student will be able to change an improper fraction to a mixed number.
2. The student will be able to draw a pictorial representation of mixed numbers.
3. The students will be able to add fractions with like denominators.
4. The students will be able to subtract fractions with like denominators.
5. The students will be able to determine if fractions are larger than ½ or smaller than ½.
6. The students will be able to find the prime factors of composite numbers.
7. The students will be able to find the difference of two three-digit numbers.

Teaching Tips:

Explanation of these concepts will be enhanced by the use of manipulatives.

Materials, Supplies, and Equipment:

1. Paper
2. *Worksheet 54*

Activities:

1. Ask the students, **"Who remembers what mathematical concept we covered yesterday?" (We changed mixed numbers to improper fractions.)**
2. Say, **"Today we are going to do the opposite, we are going to change improper fractions to mixed numbers."**
3. Say, **"Remember, we found that 1⅙ equals ⁷⁄₆."** Demonstrate using paper. **"Can anyone tell us what mathematical operation we might use to change ⁷⁄₆ to 1⅙ ?" (Division)**
4. Direct the students' attention to **Lesson 98 Explanation.**
   Read the lesson with the students answering questions.
5. Allow the students to work the following problems on the board with guidance.
   Change each improper fraction to a mixed number:
   ¹⁰⁄₃, ⁷⁄₂, ³⁄₁, ⁸⁄₅, ⁸⁄₂, ³⁄₃ (**3⅓ r 1, 3½ r 1, 3, 1⅜ r 3, 4, 1**)
6. The students should be able to complete **Lesson 98 Practice** independently.

When I am afraid, I will trust in you.
Psalm 56:3

Lesson 99

Concepts:

Least common multiple and least common denominator, add fractions, subtract fractions, improper fractions to mixed numbers, mixed numbers to improper fractions, multiplication, subtraction, place value

Objectives:

1. The students will be able to find the least common multiple of two denominators and the least common denominator of two fractions.
2. The students will be able to add fractions with like denominators.
3. The students will be able to subtract fractions with like denominators.
4. The student will be able to change an improper fraction to a mixed number.
5. The student will be able to change a mixed number to an improper fraction.
6. The student will be able to find the product of a three-digit factor by a one-digit factor.
7. The student will be able to find the difference between two five-digit numbers.
8. The student will be able to define place value to the millions' place.

Teaching Tips:

Materials, Supplies, and Equipment:

Activities:

1. Read **Lesson 99 Explanation** with the students.
   Use the examples below for additional practice.
2. Find the LCM of 3 and 4.
   What are the first 10 multiples of 3? 3, 6, 9, 12, 15, 18, 21, 24, 27, 30
   What are the first 10 multiples of 4? 4, 8, 12, 16, 20, 24, 28, 32, 36, 40
   The common multiples of 3 and 4 are 12 and 24.
   The least common multiple is 12.
3. Find the LCM of 5 and 7.
   What are the first 10 multiples of 5? 5, 10, 15, 20, 25, 30, 35, 40, 45, 50
   What are the first 10 multiples of 7? 7, 14, 21, 28, 35, 42, 49, 56, 63, 70
   The common multiple of 5 and 7 is 35.
   The least common multiple is 35.
4. The students should be able to complete **Lesson 99 Practice** independently.

I sought the Lord, and he answered me; he delivered me from all my fears…
The angel of the Lord encamps around those who fear him, and he delivers them.
Psalm 34:4, 7

Lesson 100

Concepts:

Problem solving, least common multiple and least common denominator, improper fractions and mixed numbers, add and subtract fractions, multiplication equations, coordinate graphs

Objectives:

1. The student will be able to solve word problems using the strategy, "Make it Simpler."
2. The students will be able to find the least common multiple of two denominators and the least common denominator of two fractions.
3. The student will be able to match an improper fraction to an equivalent mixed number.
4. The students will be able to add and subtract fractions with like denominators.
5. The students will be able to solve multiplication equations.
6. The students will be able to graph points on a coordinate graph.

Teaching Tips:

Materials, Supplies, and Equipment:

Activities:

1. Read **Lesson 100 Explanation** with the students.
2. The students should be able to complete **Lesson 100 Practice** independently.

Test:

1. Test 10 covers Lessons 86-95.
2. Administer Test 10, allowing the students 30-40 minutes to complete the test.

...Be strong in the grace that is in Christ Jesus.
2 Timothy 2:1b

© MCMXCVIII Alpha Omega Publications, Inc.

Lesson 101

Concepts:

Adding fractions with unlike denominators, addition terms and facts, symmetry, perimeter, area, volume, multiplication by 10, 100, and 1,000; compare and order of whole numbers, points, lines, segments, parallel lines, intersecting lines, perpendicular lines

Objectives:

1. The student will be able to add fractions with unlike denominators.
2. The student will be able to identify addition terms and complete addition facts.
3. The student will be able to identify line symmetry and symmetric figures.
4. The student will be able to calculate the perimeter, area, and volume of a shape or item.
5. The student will be able to multiply by 10, 100, and 1,000.
6. The student will be able to compare and order whole numbers.
7. The student will be able to identify points, lines, and segments, as well as parallel, intersecting and perpendicular lines.

Teaching Tips:

Marked fraction strips are very useful tools when explaining how to add and subtract fractions with unlike denominators. They allow the students to visually see the equivalent relationships between the equivalent fractions.

Materials, Supplies, and Equipment:

1. Marked fraction strips

Activities:

1. Have the students look at the marked fraction strips.
    Practice showing several equivalent relationships such as ½ = ²⁄₄, ⅓ = ²⁄₆, and ¼ = ²⁄₈. Remind the students that these fractions show the same shaded amount, are equal, and are therefore called *equivalent fractions*.
2. Read **Lesson 101 Explanation** together. Look at the example problem and the graphic illustrations of the problem. Have the students work this problem using the fraction strips. They may need to work with a partner.
3. If additional problems and instructions are needed, work these problems with the fraction strips.

> *Thou shalt love the Lord the God, and keep His charge, and His statutes*
> *...and His commandments, always.*
> **Deuteronomy 11:1**

Lesson 102

Concepts:

Subtracting fractions with unlike denominators, adding fractions with unlike denominators, least common multiple, rays , angles, using a protractor, two-digit multiplication, rounding to the nearest 10, 100, or 1,000; subtraction terms and facts

Objectives:

1. The student will be able to subtract fractions with unlike denominators.
2. The student will be able to add fractions with unlike denominators.
3. The student will be able to find the least common multiple of two numbers.
4. The student will be able to identify rays, angles and correctly measure them using a protractor.
5. The student will be able to multiply two-digit numbers.
6. The student will be able to round numbers to the nearest 10, 100, or 1,000.
7. The student will be able to identify subtraction terms and solve subtraction facts.

Teaching Tips:

Again, use the marked fraction strips to show the equivalent relationships between fractions.

Materials, Supplies, and Equipment:

1. Marked fraction strips
2. Pattern Block Fraction Pieces (out of either wood or construction paper)
3. *Worksheet 55*

Activities:

1. Reinforce the concept of equivalent fractions by asking the student to look at their marked fraction strips and find all the fractions that equal the following:

   $\frac{1}{2}$ ($\frac{2}{4}$, $\frac{3}{6}$, $\frac{4}{8}$, $\frac{5}{10}$, $\frac{6}{12}$); $\frac{1}{5}$ ($\frac{2}{10}$); $\frac{2}{3}$ ($\frac{4}{6}$, $\frac{8}{12}$); $\frac{3}{4}$ ($\frac{6}{8}$, $\frac{9}{12}$).

2. Read **Lesson 102 Explanation** together.

   Go over each step shown in the explanation and work it with the Pattern Block Fraction Pieces to illustrate each step of the problem.

3. Have the students work the first problem on **Lesson 102-1** independently, or with a partner, using the Pattern Blocks. Check the answer together.

   Allow the students that grasp the concept to complete **Lesson 102-1** independently. Assist any students that need further explanation with another problem.

   Most should be able to complete the exercise with little assistance.

Love your enemies and pray for those who persecute you,
that you may be sons of your Father in heaven.
Matthew 5: 44-45

Lesson 103

Concepts:

Addition and subtraction of mixed numbers with like denominators, addition and subtraction of fractions with unlike denominators, triangles, three-digit multiplication, rounding to the nearest 10, 100, or 1,000; subtraction terms and facts

Objectives:

1. The student will be able to add and subtract mixed numbers with like denominators.
2. The student will be able to subtract fractions with unlike denominators.
3. The student will be able to add fractions with unlike denominators.
4. The student will be able to identify and draw specific triangles.
5. The student will be able to multiply three-digit numbers.
6. The student will be able to identify subtraction terms and solve subtraction facts.
7. The student will be able to round numbers to the nearest 10, 100, and 1,000.

Teaching Tips:

Use as many manipulatives as possible when teaching fractions.
Students usually need concrete examples before they can move to abstract thinking.

Materials, Supplies, and Equipment:

1. Split-color demonstration posterboard
2. Demonstration Pattern Block pieces
3. Pattern Block pieces
4. Colored construction paper

Activities:

1. Remind the students that mixed numbers are whole numbers and fractional pieces together. Prior to the lesson take a piece of green posterboard and a piece of white posterboard. Cut the green piece in half and glue onto the white posterboard so that ½ of the board is green and ½ of the board is white.

   See the example:

   The green side will represent the whole number side of the mixed number. The white side will represent the fractional side of the mixed number. Use this board with larger demonstration pattern block pieces (also made prior to the lesson) to work problems as a class. You may use construction paper to have the students make their own individual green/white charts if needed, or desired. These charts could be used in conjunction with the Pattern Blocks.

2. Read **Lesson 103 Explanation** together and work the example problem on the demonstration board using the Demonstration Pattern Block Pieces. At the same time you are working the problem with the manipulatives, show each written step of the problem.

$$4 \frac{1}{2}$$

$$+ \ 3 \frac{1}{2}$$

$$7 \frac{2}{2} = 8$$ Remember to always start with the fractional side of the problem first.

3. Have the students work the second example problem independently with the Pattern Blocks. Chose one student to come to the large demonstration board and work the problem while another student writes the problem on the board.

4. The students should be able to complete **Lesson 103-1** independently. Allow them to use the Pattern Blocks if necessary, but encourage them to move to the written stage without the use of manipulatives.

Do not seek revenge or bear a grudge against one of your people, but love you neighbor as yourself...
Leviticus 19:18

Lesson 104

Concepts:

Addition and subtraction of mixed numbers with unlike denominators, addition and subtraction of mixed numbers with like denominators, addition and subtraction of fractions with unlike denominators, estimating products, problem solving, multiplication terms and facts, quadrilaterals, construction of bar graphs

Objectives:

1. The student will be able to add and subtract mixed numbers with unlike denominators.
2. The student will be able to add and subtract mixed numbers with like denominators.
3. The student will be able to subtract fractions with unlike denominators.
4. The student will be able to add fractions with unlike denominators.
5. The student will be able to estimate products.
6. The student will be able to complete problem solving problems.
7. The student will be able to identify multiplication terms and solve multiplication facts.
8. The student will be able to identify, draw and label a quadrilateral.
9. The student will be able to identify, draw and label a bar graph.

Teaching Tips:

Practice subtracting and adding fractions with unlike denominators, as a review, before beginning the lesson.

Materials, Supplies, and Equipment:

1. Split-color demonstration posterboard
2. Demonstration Pattern Block pieces
3. Pattern Block pieces
4. *Worksheet 56*

Activities:

1. Read **Lesson 104 Explanation** together.
   Follow the steps in the explanation and work the example problem on the demonstration board with the Demonstration Pattern Blocks. Begin with the fractional side of the problem. Then move to the whole number side of the problem.
2. Through the use of the pattern block pieces, you should be able to easily show how the answer ⁴⁄₆ can be renamed to lowest terms (²⁄₃).
3. The students should be able to complete **Lesson 104-1** independently.
   Work with those students that need additional help.

Do not store up for yourselves treasures on earth, where moth and rust destroy, and where thieves break in and steal. But store up for yourselves treasures in heaven, where moth and rust do not destroy, and where thieves do not break in and steal. For where your treasure is, there your heart will be also.
Matthew 6:19-21

Lesson 105

Concepts:

Renaming improper fractions to mixed numbers, addition and subtraction of mixed numbers with unlike (and like) denominators, addition and subtraction of fractions with unlike denominators, multiplication equations, problem solving, multiplication terms and facts, circles and using a compass

Objectives:

1. The student will be able to rename improper fractions to mixed numbers.
2. The student will be able to add and subtract mixed numbers with unlike denominators.
3. The student will be able to add and subtract mixed numbers with like denominators.
4. The student will be able to subtract fractions with unlike denominators.
5. The student will be able to complete multiplication equations.
6. The student will be able to complete problem solving equations.
7. The student will be able to identify multiplication terms and solve multiplication facts.
8. The student will be able to draw a circle using a compass and label the parts of a circle.

Teaching Tips:

Materials, Supplies, and Equipment:

1. Pattern Blocks, if necessary
2. apples
3. *Worksheet 57*

Activities:

1. Begin the lesson by cutting the apples into halves. Give one child 3 halves. Give another child 5 halves. Ask the students, **"How many halves do you have?"** (Child 1: 3 halves, Child 2: 5 halves) **"How many whole apples do you have?"** (Child 1: 1½, Child 2: 2½).
   Write each answer on the board, in chart form, as the student responds.
   Use the chart below:

Apple Halves	=	Whole Apples
³⁄₂	=	1½
⁵⁄₂	=	2½

   This should illustrate the relationship between improper fractions and mixed numbers.

2. Read **Lesson 105 Explanation** together.
   Have the students look at the illustrations which show how 1½ and 2½ are the same. Use the cut up apple halves to re-illustrate it, if necessary.
3. Go over the practice examples given in **Lesson 105 Explanation**.
4. The student should be able to complete **Lesson 105-1** independently.
   Allow them to use the Pattern Blocks, if necessary.

Blessed are you when men hate you, when they exclude you and insult you and reject your name as evil, because of the Son of Man.
Luke 6:22

Lesson 106

Concepts:

Addition of mixed numbers and renaming improper fractions in sums, converting improper fractions to mixed numbers, addition and subtraction of mixed numbers with unlike denominators, dividing with one-digit divisor and one-digit quotient, exponents, division terms and facts, capacity

Objectives:

1. The student will be able to add mixed numbers and rename improper fractions in their sums.
2. The student will be able to rename improper fractions to mixed numbers.
3. The student will be able to add and subtract mixed numbers with unlike denominators.
4. The student will be able to add and subtract mixed numbers with like denominators.
5. The student will be able to complete division problems which contain a one-digit divisor and a one-digit quotient.
6. The student will be able to correctly use and calculate exponents.
7. The student will be able to identify division terms and solve division facts.
8. The student will be able to calculate capacity of a given figure or item.

Teaching Tips:

Review **Lesson 105** on renaming improper fractions to mixed numbers before beginning **Lesson 106**. You may also want to review **Lessons 103** and **104** on adding and subtracting mixed numbers. By this time, the students should be very comfortable with the addition and subtraction of fractions with unlike denominators and mixed numbers.

They should be past the manipulative stage and into the abstract, written stage.

Materials, Supplies, and Equipment:

1. Pattern Blocks, if necessary
2. *Worksheet 58*

Activities:

1. Read **Lesson 106 Explanation** together. Write the sample problem on the board and work it according to the steps in the explanation. It might help the students, visually, if you draw a line down the middle of the problem and separate the fractional part of the problem from the whole number part of the problem.

   Look below:

   $$2\frac{1}{2}$$

   $$+\quad 3\frac{3}{4}$$

   When the answer is calculated it will be an improper fraction: 5¾. Have the students rename the fraction to a mixed number. Use the pattern blocks, if necessary.
2. The students should be able to complete **Lesson 106-1** independently.
   Use pattern blocks to aid any students that need further assistance.

No good tree bears bad fruit, nor does a bad tree bear good fruit.
Each tree is recognized by its own fruit.
Luke 6:43-44

Lesson 107

Concepts:

Addition of mixed numbers and renaming improper fractions in sums, converting improper fractions to mixed numbers, adding and subtracting mixed numbers with unlike denominators, least common multiple, division with one-digit divisor and two- digit quotient

Objectives:

1. The student will be able to add and subtract mixed numbers and rename improper fractions in the sum or difference.
2. The student will be able to add mixed numbers and rename improper fractions in their sums.
3. The student will be able to rename improper fractions to mixed numbers.
4. The student will be able to add and subtract mixed numbers with unlike denominators.
5. The student will be able to add and subtract mixed numbers with like denominators.
6. The student will be able to find the least common multiple of two numbers.
7. The student will be able to complete a division problem which contains a one-digit divisor and a two-digit quotient.

Teaching Tips:

Review **Lesson 106**. Review **Lessons 103-105** for students that are not up to speed yet on the addition and subtraction of mixed numbers and fractions with unlike denominators.

Materials, Supplies, and Equipment:

1. *Worksheet 59*

Activities:

1. Read **Lesson 107 Explanation** as a class. Have a student volunteer come to the board and explain how to work the problem step by step. At any point in the explanation, if the student gets stumped, he has the prerogative to call on another student for assistance. Students love to be "in charge" and be the "teacher." This gives them the chance to show what they know, but also gives them an escape if they get in over their head.
2. Divide the class into two teams and play a game. Take turns having students come to the board, one team at the time, and work mixed number addition and subtraction problems. If the student correctly works the problem, his team receives one point. If the student misses the problem, the opposing team may "steal" the point by having the next contestant come correct the problem and explain the error. After everyone has had a turn, the team with the most points wins a "prize."
3. The students should be able to complete **Lesson 107-1** independently.

Love must be sincere. Hate what is evil; cling to what is good.
Romans 12:9

Lesson 108

Concepts:

Subtraction of mixed numbers (with like denominators) using borrowing (renaming) from whole numbers, renaming improper fractions to mixed numbers, addition and subtraction of mixed numbers with unlike denominators, dividing money, factor trees, two- and three-digit addition, missing addends

Objectives:

1. The student will be able to subtract mixed numbers with like denominators, borrowing from the whole number and renaming when necessary.
2. The student will be able to add and subtract mixed numbers and rename improper fractions in the sum or difference.
3. The student will be able to add and subtract mixed numbers and rename answers with improper fractions.
4. The student will be able to rename mixed numbers.
5. The student will be able to divide money.
6. The student will be able to complete factor trees.
7. The student will be able to add two- and three-digit numbers.
8. The student will be able to solve for missing addends.

Teaching Tips:

Materials, Supplies, and Equipment:

1. Pattern Blocks
2. four candy bars
3. blunt knife

Activities:

1. Have three students come to the front of the room. Give one student all of the four candy bars. Instruct him to give one of the other students 1 and ⅓ candy bars. Instruct him also to give the third student 1 and ⅓ candy bars. Ask him how he will do this with five whole candy bars. He should understand to split one of the candy bars into 3 equal pieces, or "thirds." Use this demonstration to illustrate one whole candy bar had to be separated in order to create fractional pieces between the other students.
2. Read **Lesson 108 Explanation**. Follow the steps in the explanation and show how the problem in the example is worked the same way that Student #1 divided the candy bars between his friends.
3. Have the students work problem number 2 in **Lesson 108-1** independently. Check the answer together once everyone has completed it. You may use pattern blocks to illustrate it, if necessary.
4. Have the students complete **Lesson 108-1** independently, or with a partner, if you feel that is necessary.

Do not repay evil for evil. Be careful to do what is right in the eyes of everybody.
Romans 12:17

Lesson 109

Concepts:

Subtraction of mixed numbers (with unlike denominators) using borrowing (renaming) from the whole number, subtraction of mixed numbers (with like denominators) using borrowing (renaming) from whole numbers, renaming improper fractions to mixed numbers, prime and composite numbers, four-, five-, and six-digit addition, place value through billions, missing addends

Objectives:

1. The student will be able to subtract mixed numbers with unlike denominators, borrowing from the whole number and renaming when necessary.
2. The student will be able to subtract mixed numbers with like denominators, borrowing from the whole number and renaming when necessary.
3. The student will be able to rename mixed numbers.
4. The student will be able to add mixed numbers and rename improper fractions in their sums.
5. The student will be able to identify prime and composite numbers.
6. The student will be able to add four-, five-, and six-digit numbers.
7. The student will be able to identify place value through the billions.
8. The student will be able to solve for missing addends.

Teaching Tips:

Review **Lesson 108** before beginning **Lesson 109**.

Materials, Supplies, and Equipment:

1. 5¼ apples
2. knife
3. Pattern Blocks

Activities:

1. Begin the lesson by having two students volunteer. Give one student the 5¼ apples. Instruct him to give 3½ apples to the other volunteer. Ask the student to explain how he will accomplish this with what he has been given. The student will need to divide one of the whole apples in half. He can then give 3½ to the other student. Once this happens, ask the first student how many apples he has left (1¾ because 1½ plus the ¼ he originally had = 1¾). This process will illustrate the example problem in **Lesson 109**.
2. Read **Lesson 109 Explanation** together. Explain to the students that the apple demonstration was the example problem. Go over each explanation step and relate it to the apple experiment.
3. Have the students work problem number 1 on **Lesson 109-1**. They may use Pattern Blocks, if needed. Check the answer as a class once each student has worked the problem independently.
4. The student should be able to complete the rest of **Lesson 109-1** independently. Help those that need additional assistance. Allow the students to use Pattern Blocks, if necessary. Encourage them not to use them if they understand the process and can work the problem without the manipulatives.

Don't you know that friendship with the world is hatred toward God?
Anyone who chooses to be a friend of the world becomes an enemy of God.
Hebrews 4:4

Lesson 110

Concepts:

Adding and subtracting of whole numbers, mixed numbers, and fractions, subtraction of mixed numbers (with like and unlike denominators) using borrowing (renaming) from the whole number, rename mixed numbers, add using column addition, place value, more than one operation

Objectives:

1. The student will be able to add and subtract whole numbers, mixed numbers, and fractions.
2. The student will be able to subtract mixed numbers with like and unlike denominators, borrowing from the whole number and renaming when necessary.
3. The student will be able to rename mixed numbers.
4. The student will be able to add using column addition.
5. The student will be able to identify place value through the billions.
6. The student will be able to solve problems which require the use of more than one operation.

Teaching Tips:

If the students understood **Lesson 109**, they will have no difficulty with **Lesson 110**. It is an extension of **Lesson 109**. Review **Lesson 109** before beginning the new lesson.

Materials, Supplies, and Equipment:

1. Pattern Blocks, if necessary
2. *Worksheet 60*

Activities:

1. Read **Lesson 110 Explanation** together. Go through each example and work it on the board as a class. You may want to have the students explain the steps as you write them.
2. Have the students work with a partner and complete problems one and two on **Lesson 110-1**. After working these two problems, work them as a class and have the students correct their work. Any students that need additional assistance should be grouped together and work with the teacher. Students that grasp the concept, should be assigned to work the rest of **Lesson 110-1** independently.

Test:

1. Test 11 covers Lessons 96-105.
2. Administer Test 11, allowing the students 30-40 minutes to complete the test.

Do not imitate what is evil but what is good. Anyone who does what is good is from God. Anyone who does what is evil has not seen God.
3 John 11

Lesson 111

Concepts:

Fraction of a number, subtraction of fractions, least common denominator, addition of fractions, two operations, calculator division

Objectives:

1. Given pictorial representations, the students will be able to find the fraction of a number.
2. The students will be able to find the difference of two mixed fractions.
3. Given two fractions, the students will be able to find the least common denominator.
4. The students will be able to find the sum of two mixed fractions.
5. The students will be able to solve problems with two operations.
6. The students will be able to find the quotient and remainder of a division problem using a calculator.

Teaching Tips:

Allow the students many opportunities to work with concrete examples before they solve written problems.

Materials, Supplies, and Equipment:

Activities:

1. Read **Lesson 111 Explanation** with the students.
2. Share concrete examples of this type of problem with the students.

   A few examples follow:

   a. Place 10 pencils on the table.
   b. Ask the students to find ⅖ of the 10 pencils.
   c. Help them to first divide the pencils into 5 even groups, then determine how many pencils are in two groups.

⅖ of 10 equals 4.

   a. Place 16 counters on the table.
   b. Ask the students to find of the counters.
   c. They should be able to divide the counters into four even groups, and determine how many counters are in 3 groups.

¾ of 16 equals 12.

3. Challenge the students to develop problems for others to solve.
4. The students will be able to complete **Lesson 111 Practice** independently.

*Many individuals have, like uncut diamonds, shining qualities
beneath a rough exterior.*
Juvenal

Lesson 112

Concepts:

Multiplying fractions, fraction of a number, addition and subtraction of fractions, division, triangles, five-digit subtraction, place value

Objectives:

1. The students will be able to multiply fractions.
2. The students will be able to find the fraction of a number.
3. The students will be able to find the difference of two mixed fractions.
4. The students will be able to find a two-digit quotient given a three-digit dividend and a two-digit divisor.
5. The students will be able to define triangles as equilateral, scalene and isosceles. The students will be able to determine whether a triangle is a right triangle.
6. The students will be able to find the difference of two five-digit numbers.
7. The students will be able to order numbers from greatest to least.

Teaching Tips:

Allow the students many opportunities to work with concrete examples before they solve written problems.

Materials, Supplies, and Equipment:

1. *Worksheet 61*

Activities:

1. Students learn to multiply fractions quite easily, but it takes working many concrete examples before they understand the application of the concept. Use the concrete examples that follow or develop your own.
2. Display the picture below and ask the students to shade $\frac{1}{3}$ times $\frac{1}{2}$.

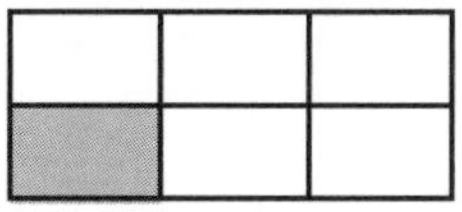

$\frac{1}{3} \times \frac{1}{2} = \frac{1}{6}$

3. Display the picture below and ask the students to shade $\frac{2}{4}$ times $\frac{2}{3}$.

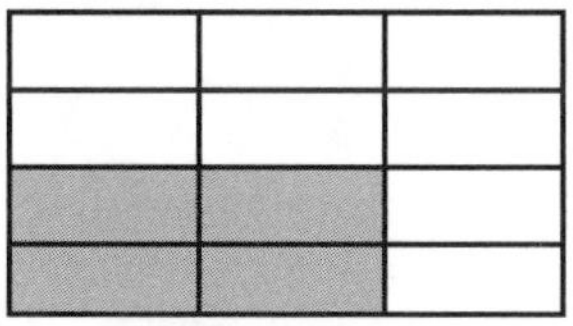

$\frac{2}{4} \times \frac{2}{3} = \frac{4}{12} = \frac{1}{3}$

4. Display the picture below and ask the students to shade $\frac{1}{4}$ times $\frac{3}{5}$.

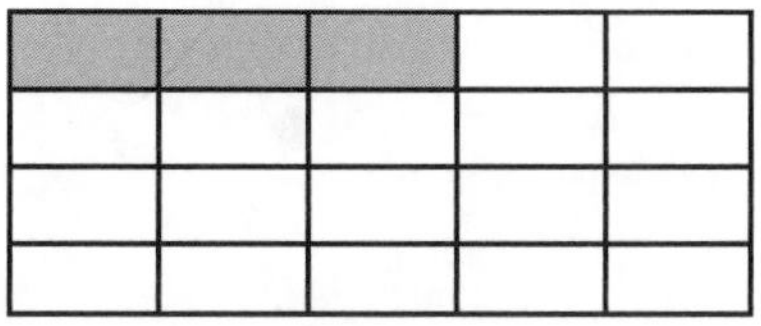

$\frac{1}{4} \times \frac{3}{5} = \frac{3}{20}$

5. Read **Lesson 112 Explanation** with the students.
6. The students will be able to complete **Lesson 112 Practice** independently.

You will find men who want to be carried on the shoulders of others, who think that the world owes them a living. They don't seem to see that we must all lift together and pull together.
Henry Ford II

Lesson 113

Concepts:

Multiplying mixed numbers, multiplying fractions, making change, fraction of a number, subtraction of equations, rounding to 100, protractors

Objectives:

1. The students will be able to multiply mixed numbers.
2. The students will be able to multiply fractions.
3. The students will be able to make the correct change using the fewest bills and coins.
4. The students will be able to find the fraction of a number.
5. The students will be able to solve subtraction equations.
6. The students will be able to round numbers to the nearest 100.
7. The students will be able to use a protractor and find the measure of given angles.

Teaching Tips:

These problems are difficult because they combine many skills the students have been learning into one problem. Help the students break the problems into simple steps and encourage them to work slowly.

Materials, Supplies, and Equipment:

1. *Worksheet 62*

Activities:

1. Read **Lesson 113 Explanation** with the students.
    Work the following example problem with the students.
    a. $1\frac{1}{3} \times 2\frac{1}{4} =$

        Step 1: Change the mixed numbers to improper fractions.
        $\frac{4}{3} \times \frac{9}{4} =$

        Step 2: Multiply the numerators.
        $\frac{4}{3} \times \frac{9}{4} = \frac{36}{}$

        Step 3: Multiply the denominators.
        $\frac{4}{3} \times \frac{9}{4} = \frac{36}{12}$

        Step 4: Change the improper fraction to a mixed number.
        $\frac{36}{12} = 3$

2. The students will be able to complete **Lesson 113 Practice** independently.

    My son, keep my words, and treasure my commandments within you.
    Proverbs 7:1

Lesson 114

Concepts:

Dividing fractions, multiplying mixed numbers, multiplying fractions, averaging, multiplication, rounding to 1,000, fraction of a number

Objectives:

1. The students will be able to divide a whole number by a fraction.
2. The students will be able to multiply two mixed numbers.
3. The students will be able to multiply two fractions.
4. The students will be able to find the average of three numbers.
5. The students will be able to find the product of a three-digit number by a one-digit number.
6. The students will be able to round numbers to the nearest 1,000.
7. The students will be able to find the fraction of a whole number.

Teaching Tips:

It is important that students see that dividing by a fraction is the same as multiplying by the reciprocal. Provide them with many examples of this principle before they begin dividing fractions.

Materials, Supplies, and Equipment:

Activities:

1. Read **Lesson 114 Explanation** with the students.
   Work the following example problems with the students.
2. Ask the students. **"How many fourths are in 5?"** **(20)**
   a. Provide the students with a pictorial model to verify their answer or to disprove their incorrect answer.

$$5 \div \frac{1}{4} = 20 \quad \text{and} \quad 5 \times \frac{4}{1} = 20$$

3. Ask the students. **"How many halves are in 4?"** **(8)**
   a. Provide the students with a pictorial model to verify their answer or to disprove their incorrect answer.

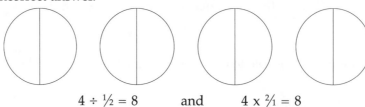

$$4 \div \frac{1}{2} = 8 \quad \text{and} \quad 4 \times \frac{2}{1} = 8$$

4. The students will be able to complete **Lesson 114 Practice** independently.

The Lord is my shepherd, I shall not want. He makes me lie down in green pastures;
He leads me beside quiet waters. He restores my soul; He guides me in paths of
righteousness for His name's sake. Even though I walk through the valley of the shadow
of death, I fear no evil; for Thou art with me; Thy rod and Thy staff, they comfort me.
Psalm 23:1-4

Lesson 115

Concepts:

Dividing a fraction by a whole number, dividing a whole number by a fraction, multiplying fractions, averaging, two-digit multiplication, word problems

Objectives:

1. The students will be able to divide a fraction by a whole number.
2. The students will be able to divide a whole number by a fraction.
3. The students will be able to multiply mixed numbers.
4. The students will be able to multiply fractions.
5. The students will be able to find the average of three numbers.
6. The students will be able to find the product of a three-digit number by 10, 100 or 1,000.
7. The students will be able to solve fraction word problems.

Teaching Tips:

Remind the students that a whole number can be written in an equivalent fraction by placing the number over 1. $3 = \frac{3}{1}$, $5 = \frac{5}{1}$.

Materials, Supplies, and Equipment:

1. *Worksheet 63*

Activities:

1. Read **Lesson 115 Explanation** with the students.
   Work the example problems written in the explanation with the students.
2. The students will be able to complete **Lesson 115 Practice** independently.

Teach me Thy way, O Lord ; I will walk in Thy truth.
Psalm 86:11

Lesson 116

Concepts:

Dividing two fractions, divide a fraction by a whole number, word problems, adding fractions, division, two-digit multiplication, missing digits

Objectives:

1. The students will be able to divide a fraction by a fraction.
2. The students will be able to divide a fraction by a whole number.
3. The students will be able to solve fraction word problems.
4. The students will be able to add mixed numbers.
5. The students will be able to divide a two-digit dividend by a three-digit divisor.
6. The students will be able to multiply two, two-digit numbers.
7. The students will be able to use logical reasoning to define missing digits.

Teaching Tips:

Remind the students that a whole number can be written as a fraction by placing the number over 1 (3 = ³⁄₁, 5 = ⁵⁄₁). Stress that every whole number has a reciprocal.

Materials, Supplies, and Equipment:

Activities:

1. Begin this lesson with a game. Tell the students that you will give them clues, and you want them to figure out the fraction that you are thinking of. They may only ask you "yes" and "no" questions to narrow down the correct fraction. When they think they have figured out the answer, they need to say the fraction and the reciprocal. If they are correct, they will get to be the leader and give the clues.
2. Example:
   a. "I am thinking of a fraction with an even numerator, and a denominator that is 1." Let the students begin asking "yes" or "no" questions.
   b. The numerator is divisible by 5. Let the students begin asking "yes" and "no" questions.
   c. The numerator is less than 50 and greater than 20. Let the students guess the fraction which is ³⁵⁄₁. The reciprocal is ¹⁄₃₅.
   d. The person with the correct guess becomes the leader.
3. Read **Lesson 116 Explanation** with the students. Explain to the students that they will be multiplying by the reciprocal of the fraction to find the products.
4. The students will be able to complete **Lesson 116 Practice** independently.

How great is Thy goodness.
Psalm 31:19

Lesson 117

Concepts:

Reading and writing ratios, dividing a whole number by a fraction, dividing a fraction by a whole number, dividing two fractions, three-digit multiplication, division

Objectives:

1. The students will be able to read and write ratios.
2. The students will be able to divide a whole number by a fraction.
3. The students will be able to divide a fraction by a whole number.
4. The students will be able to divide a fraction by a fraction.
5. The students will be able to multiply three, three-digit numbers.
6. The students will be able to divide a two-digit dividend by one-digit divisor.

Teaching Tips:

Help the students to see the relationship between a ratio and a fraction.

Materials, Supplies, and Equipment:

1. *Worksheet 64*

Activities:

1. Write ⅔ on the board. Explain to the students that we usually think of this as a fraction, but it can also be called a ratio. A ratio is used to compare two numbers.
2. Draw this example on the board.

   a. Ask the students, **"How many blue stars are on the board?"** **(3)**
   b. Ask the students, **"How many red stars are on the board?"** **(1)**
   c. Ask the students, **"How many black stars are on the board?"** **(2)**
3. Tell the students that there are 2 black stars to every 3 blue stars, so the ratio is 2 to 3. We can also express this relationship as 2:3 or ⅔.
4. Ask the students, **"What is the ratio of red stars to black stars?"** **(1 to 2, 1:2, ½)**
   a. Ask the students, **"What is the ratio of red stars to blue stars?"** **(1 to 3, 1:3, ⅓)**
   b. Ask the students, **"What is the ratio of blue stars to black stars?"** **(3 to 2, 3:2, 3⁄2)**
5. Read **Lesson 117 Explanation** with the students.
6. The students will be able to complete **Lesson 117 Practice** independently.

How blessed is he whose transgression is forgiven, whose sin is covered!
Psalm 32:1

Lesson 118

Concepts:

Multiplying to find equal ratios, reading and writing ratios, dividing two fractions, dividing a whole number by a fraction, multiplication equations

Objectives:

1. The students will be able to multiply to find equal ratios.
2. The students will be able to read and write ratios.
3. The students will be able to divide a mixed number by a fraction.
4. The students will be able to divide a fraction by a whole number.
5. The students will be able to divide a whole number by a fraction.
6. The students will be able to solve equations.

Teaching Tips:

Help the students to see the relationship between a ratio and a fraction.
Students quickly understand this concept because they have recently studied equivalent fractions.

Materials, Supplies, and Equipment:

Activities:

1. Read **Lesson 118 Explanation** with the students.
2 The students will be able to complete **Lesson 118 Practice** independently.

What you dislike in another take care to correct in yourself.
Thomas Sprat

Lesson 119

Concepts:

Dividing to find equal ratios, multiplying to find equal ratios, word problems with ratios, ordering fractions, two-digit multiplication, division, mystery number

Objectives:

1. The students will be able to divide to find equal ratios.
2. The students will be able to multiply to find equal ratios.
3. The students will be able to solve word problems using equal ratios.
4. The students will be able to order fractions from least to greatest.
5. The students will be able to multiply a two-digit number by a two-digit number.
6. The students will be able to divide a three-digit dividend by a two-digit divisor
7. Given word clues, the students will be able to find a mystery number.

Teaching Tips:

Students need very little guidance with this concept.

Materials, Supplies, and Equipment:

1. *Worksheet 65*

Activities:

1. Read **Lesson 119 Explanation** with the students.
2. Encourage the students to make their own equal ratio charts for their classmates to solve.
3. The students will be able to complete **Lesson 119 Practice** independently.

People in the long run are going to do more to promote peace than governments.
Dwight D. Eisenhower

Lesson 120

Concepts:

Ratios and the calculator, finding equal ratios, exponents, four-digit addition, comparing fractions, equations

Objectives:

1. The students will be able to use a calculator to determine if ratios are equal or not equal.
2. The students will be able to multiply to complete an equal ratio chart.
3. The students will be able to find the value of numbers and exponents.
4. The students will be able to find the sum of two, four-digit numbers and complete a crossword puzzle.
5. The students will be able to use >, <, and = to compare fractions.
6. The students will be able to solve equations.

Teaching Tips:

Materials, Supplies, and Equipment:

Each student will need a calculator.

Activities:

1. Read **Lesson 120 Explanation** with the students.
2. Have the students try the following examples on their calculators.
   a. Is $\frac{1}{7}$ equivalent to $\frac{2}{13}$? (**No**)
   b. Is 1 to 3 equivalent to 7 to 21? (**Yes**)
   c. Is 2:5 equivalent to 20:50? (**Yes**)
   d. Is $\frac{2}{9}$ equivalent to $\frac{4}{16}$? (**No**)
3. The students will be able to complete **Lesson 120 Practice** independently.

Tests:

1. Test 12 covers Lessons 106-115.
2. Administer Test 12, allowing the students 30-40 minutes to complete the test.
3. Quarter Test 3 covers Lessons 81-120.
4. Administer Quarter Test 3, allowing the students 40-60 minutes to complete the test.

And you shall love the Lord your God with all your heart, and with all your soul,
and with all your mind, and with all your strength.
Mark 12:30

Lesson 121

Concepts:

Decimals — tenths, mystery number, time equivalents, two-digit divisors and three-digit quotients, addition of mixed numbers with renamed sums

Objectives:

1. The student will be able to identify and write decimals through the tenths' place.
2. The student will be able to convert percents to decimals and decimals to percents.
3. The student will be able to identify and use time definitions.
4. The student will be able to complete a division problem that contains a two-digit divisor and a three-digit quotient.
5. The student will be able to add mixed numbers and rename improper sums, when necessary.

Teaching Tips:

A review of place value through the hundred billions' place would be beneficial before beginning the lesson. It is important to tell the students that fractions, percents, and decimals are all parts of whole numbers. They are different representations for the same concept.

Materials, Supplies, and Equipment:

1. Two pieces of posterboard, one green, the other white
2. Black magic marker
3. Flashcards with decimal numbers, as well as whole numbers through millions, written in standard form
4. King-sized KitKat® candy bar(s)
5. Student place value charts

Activities:

1. Prior to the lesson make a place value chart using the two pieces of posterboard listed under Materials, Supplies, and Equipment #1. The green posterboard should be used to make a section for the whole number side of the place value chart. The white posterboard should be used to make a section for the decimal part of the place value chart (See diagram below).

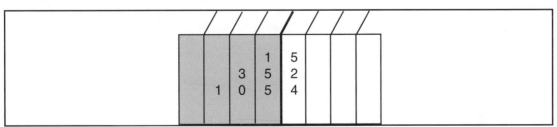

The bold line between the ones' and tenths' columns represents where the poster-boards will be taped together AND the exact point where the decimal should be. A great way to illustrate this concept is with money. The whole number side would represent dollars ("green money"), the fractional side represents the change side ("white money").

The word "AND" in math should be used ONLY WHEN A DECIMAL IS PRESENT! The problems shown in the chart above should be read "one **and** five tenths," "thirty-five **and** two tenths," and "one hundred five **and** four tenths." To mispronounce a number (for example, *One Hundred and One Dalmatians*), is to change the entire value of the number. This example, when written as pronounced, would actually be 100.1 **NOT** 101. Have the students add this portion of the decimal place value chart onto their existing place value charts (from Lessons 10 through higher lessons).

2. Read **Lesson 121 Explanation** together and discuss the example problem. Today's lesson will be dealing with the tenths' place.

3. Practice having the students read decimal numbers aloud by having a class competition between teams. Take turns reading decimal numbers off of pre-made flashcards. The key is to read the decimal as "AND," and not to read regular numbers with the word "AND."

4. Another good tactile example would be to use a KitKat® candy bar. It is divided into strips which are easily broken apart. A king sized KitKat® bar has 10 strips. Having the students break into groups and eat portions of each candy bar would be a good way to show what fractional portions of each candy bar had been eaten. Make sure there are enough for each student.

5. The student should be able to complete **Lesson 121-1** with little or no assistance.

Learn to do right! Seek justice, encourage the oppressed. Defend the cause of the fatherless, plead the case of the widow.
Isaiah 1:17

Lesson 122

Concepts:

Decimals — hundredths, decimals — tenths, A.M./P.M./century, division — two-digit divisor with zero in quotient, prime and composite, four-, five-, and six-digit subtraction, subtraction of mixed numbers with common denominators

Objectives:

1. The student will be able to identify and write decimals through the hundredths' place.
2. The student will be able to identify and write decimals through the tenths' place.
3. The student will be able to identify and use the terms A.M., P.M., and *century*.
4. The student will be able to complete division problems that contain a two-digit divisor and a zero in the quotient.
5. The student will be able to identify prime and composite numbers.
6. The student will be able to subtract four-, five-, and six-digit numbers.
7. The student will be able to subtract mixed numbers with a common denominator.

Teaching Tips:

Review the place value chart again. Use the same posterboard chart created for **Lesson 121**. It would be a good idea to laminate these posters for use with dry erase or overhead projector pens.

Materials, Supplies, and Equipment:

1. Posterboard place value chart
2. Place value centimeter blocks or wooden place value blocks.
3. Play money (bills and coins)

Activities:

1. Read **Lesson 122 Explanation** together and discuss.
   Use the posterboard place value chart and place value blocks to illustrate the hundredths' place. Review the information from **Lesson 121** concerning the tenths' place. Also review the information concerning the proper pronunciation of each written number.
2. Have the students create several numbers and write them on the place value chart. Remind them that the tenths' place value column is like having dimes, and the hundredths' column is like having pennies ("change side of chart"— it takes 10 dimes to make $1.00 and 100 pennies to make $1.00).
3. Have the students write the following numbers on their place value charts: 5.42, 5.12, and 2.89. Then have the students illustrate each number using the play money. This will reinforce the information given in Activities #2 stating that the decimal (or "change") side of the place value chart is part of a whole, like dimes and pennies are to whole dollars or currency.
4. The student should be able to complete **Lesson 122-1** independently.

He has shown you, o man, what is good. And what does the Lord require of you?
To act justly and to love mercy, and to walk humbly with your God.
Micah 6:8

Lesson 123

Concepts:
> Decimals — thousandths, decimals — hundredths and tenths, mystery number, least common multiple, subtraction of mixed numbers with unlike denominators, addition and subtraction of money, subtraction, factor trees

Objectives:
1. The student will be able to identify and write decimals though the thousandths' place.
2. The student will be able to identify and write decimals through the hundredths' place.
3. The student will be able to identify and write decimals through the tenths' place.
4. The student will be able to calculate a given percent of a given number.
5. The student will be able to calculate the least common multiple of two numbers.
6. The student will be able to subtract mixed numbers with unlike denominators.
7. The student will be able to add and subtract money.
8. The student will be able to complete subtraction problems.
9. The student will be able to complete factor trees.

Teaching Tips:
> By this point, the place value chart should be memorized and place value should be memorized. The students should easily understand the concept of thousandths, ten thousandths, and so on.

Materials, Supplies, and Equipment:
1. Place value charts (only to add on additional columns)
2. Decimal flashcards
3. *Worksheet 66*

Activities:
1. Read **Lesson 123 Explanation** together. Look at the additional columns which have been added to the place value chart. Stress to the students that just like the whole number side of the place value chart is infinite, so is the decimal side of the chart. Ask the students to use their knowledge of the whole number side of the place value column to tell what columns would follow ten thousandths on the decimal side.
2. Have the students create several decimal numbers (at least 4) and write them on paper in standard form. Pair each student with a partner and have them swap papers. The students should convert each number they were given in standard form into written form. This will force them to know the correct use of the word "and" in mathematics (as discussed in **Lesson 121**).
3. Prior to the lesson, make large flashcards which contain decimal numbers through the ten thousandths' column. Divide the class into two teams. Take turns asking the students to read the numbers on the cards. Pay close attention to the use of the word "and" and the ending "ths" to make sure the students are distinguishing between the whole number and decimal side of the place value chart when they are pronouncing each number. If the student correctly pronounces the number displayed on the card,

his team receives one point. If the student mispronounces the number on the card, the other team has a chance to "steal" that point by correctly pronouncing the number.

4. The students should be able to complete **Lesson 123-1** independently.

"For I know the plans I have for you," declares the Lord, "plans to prosper you and not to harm you, plans to give you hope and a future."
Jeremiah 29:11

Lesson 124

Concepts:

Compare and order decimals, decimals—tenths, hundredths and thousandths, mystery number, division of money, fraction of a number, multiplication terms, multiplication facts

Objectives:

1. The student will be able to compare and order decimals.
2. The student will be able to identify and write decimals through the thousandths' place.
3. The student will be able to identify and write decimals through the hundredths' and tenths' place.
4. The student will be able to convert percents to fractions and fractions to percents.
5. The student will be able to divide money.
6. The student will be able to find the fractional portion of a number.
7. The student will be able to identify multiplication terms and complete multiplication facts.

Teaching Tips:

Materials, Supplies, and Equipment:

1. Place value charts (for reference only)
2. *Worksheet 67*

Activities:

1. Read **Lesson 124 Explanation** together.
   Look at the batting averages shown in the example box. Have each student write these batting averages on a place value chart. Follow the steps outlined in the explanation of **Lesson 124** and compare the numbers to see which batter has the best batting average (the largest number). Once the largest number is identified, have the students find the next largest number. Follow this process until all of the numbers are ordered from the largest to the smallest. Look at the answer section to **Lesson 124 Explanation**.
   Check to make sure that each student's response is correct.
2. The students might need a review of the "greater than," "less than" signs before working **Lesson 124-1**. Once this review has been done, the students should be able to complete **Lesson 124-1** independently with little difficulty.

Now this is what the Lord Almighty says: "Give careful thought to your ways..."
Haggai 1:5

Lesson 125

Concepts:

Rounding decimals, comparing and ordering decimals, decimals — thousandths, hundredths and tenths, division with one-digit divisors and three-digit quotients, two-digit multiplication, multiplication of fractions, addition

Objectives:

1. The student will be able to round decimals.
2. The student will be able to compare and order decimals.
3. The student will be able to identify and write decimals through the thousandths' place.
4. The student will be able to identify and write decimals through the hundredths' and tenths' place.
5. The student will be able to complete division problems that contain a one-digit divisor and a three-digit quotient.
6. The student will be able to complete two-digit multiplication problems.
7. The student will be able to multiply fractions.
8. The student will be able to complete addition problems.

Teaching Tips:

Review the rounding of whole numbers before beginning **Lesson 125**.

Materials, Supplies, and Equipment:

1. Dry erase board or laminated posterboard
2. Dry erase markers or overhead markers
3. Play money (coins)
4. *Worksheet 67*

Activities:

1. Read **Lesson 125 Explanation** together.
   Have each student draw a number line on his paper. Draw a number line on the dry erase board (or laminated posterboard) for the students to see. Remind them that when rounding numbers you are deciding whether a given number is closer to the number just above it or below it in numerical sequence. Have the students look at the example number line and the steps involved in the rounding process. Remind them that the magic number in rounding is five. Anything below five rounds down. Anything five or above rounds up. This should not be a difficult concept because the students have done this with whole numbers.
2. If the students need additional examples, use the play money. Place $0.62 cents on a student's desk. Ask the student if that amount of money is closer to having zero cents or having a dollar. (The student should respond that it is closer to a dollar.) Make a money number line on the dry erase board just like the number line drawn in **Activity 1**. Place *0.62* on the number line to show that it is more than halfway and larger than 0.50. For this reason it is rounded up to a dollar. You may wish to show several other money examples, if it helps the students.
3. The student should be able to complete **Lesson 125-1** independently.

If anyone would come after me, he must deny himself
and take up his cross daily and follow me.
Luke 9:23

Lesson 126

Concepts:

Estimation of decimals (addition and subtraction), rounding decimals, comparing and ordering decimals, decimals—thousandths, multiplication of mixed numbers, three-digit multiplication, division terms, division facts

Objectives:

1. The student will be able to estimate decimal addition problems and subtraction problems.
2. The student will be able to round decimals.
3. The student will be able to compare and order decimals.
4. The student will be able to identify and write decimals through the thousandths' place.
5. The student will be able to multiply mixed numbers.
6. The student will be able to multiply three-digit numbers.
7. The student will be able to identify division terms and complete division facts.

Teaching Tips:

Estimating decimals is simply the combination of rounding decimals and then adding or subtracting them. If you present it that way to the students, they will usually see it as a simple task.

Materials, Supplies, and Equipment:

1. Dry erase board and markers

Activities:

1. Review **Lesson 125** on rounding.
   Write several decimal numbers on the dry erase board and ask the students to round them to the nearest whole number. Draw a number line on the dry erase board, if necessary, to emphasize what the students learned in **Lesson 125**.
2. Read **Lesson 126 Explanation** together.
   Look at the estimated and actual answers shown in the example.
   Use the numbers from **Activity 1** and create addition and subtraction problems out of them. Have the students find the estimated answer to these addition and subtraction equations.
3. Have the students complete **Lesson 126-1** independently.
   If any students need additional assistance, work with them individually.

Then Jesus said to them, "Whoever welcomes this little child in my name welcomes me; and whoever welcomes me welcomes the one who sent me. For he who is least among you all—he is the greatest."
Luke 9:48

Lesson 127

Concepts:

Addition of decimals, estimation of decimals (addition and subtraction), rounding decimals, comparing and ordering decimals, division of money, estimating quotients, estimating products, multiplication of mixed and whole numbers

Objectives:
1. The student will be able to add decimals.
2. The student will be able to estimate decimal addition and subtraction problems.
3. The student will be able to round decimals.
4. The student will be able to compare and order decimals.
5. The student will be able to complete problems that requires the division of money and contains a two-digit divisor.
6. The student will be able to estimate division problems that contain a one-digit divisor.
7. The student will be able to estimate products.
8. The student will be able to multiply mixed and whole numbers.

Teaching Tips:

Materials, Supplies, and Equipment:
1. Place value chart
2. Graph paper or lined paper

Activities:
1. Read **Lesson 127 Explanation** together.
   Have the student write the sample problem down on their place value chart or on the graph paper (lined paper). This will help them to keep the columns straight. Have them bring the decimal down first and then add or subtract the numbers. Remind them that adding decimals is exactly like adding or subtracting other numbers; the only difference is the presence of the decimal.
2. The student should be able to complete **Lesson 127 Practice** independently.

"Praise be to the name of God for ever and ever; wisdom and power are his.
He changes times and seasons; he sets up kings and deposes them.
He gives wisdom to the wise and knowledge to the discerning."
Daniel 2:20-21

Lesson 128

Concepts:

Subtraction of decimals, addition of decimals, estimation of decimals (addition and subtraction), rounding decimals, divisibility, multiplication equations, division of fractions

Objectives:

1. The student will be able to subtract decimals.
2. The student will be able to add decimals.
3. The student will be able to estimate decimal addition problems and subtraction problems.
4. The student will be able to round decimals.
5. The student will be able to use divisibility rules to identify the divisibility of a given number.
6. The student will be able to calculate percentage discounts and sales tax on given transactions.
7. The student will be able to complete multiplication equations.
8. The student will be able to divide fractions.

Teaching Tips:

Review **Lesson 127** before beginning **Lesson 128**.

Materials, Supplies, and Equipment:

1. Place value chart (if necessary)
2. Graph paper or lined paper (if necessary)
3. *Worksheet 68*

Activities:

1. Read **Lesson 128 Explanation** together.

    Complete the example problem together by having the student write the problem on his graph paper or place value chart if necessary. The students should have little difficulty with this lesson. If problems arise, monitor the student to see what the problem is. More than likely it is a lack of the subtraction process (borrowing) than anything to do with the decimal information.

2. The student should be able to complete **Lesson 128-1** independently.

"...fear and reverence the God of Daniel. For he is the living God and he endures forever; his kingdom will not be destroyed, his dominions will never end."
Daniel 6:26

Lesson 129

Concepts:

Decimals in word problems, subtraction of decimals, addition of decimals, estimation of decimals (addition and subtraction), time equivalents, averaging with remainders, exponents, missing addends

Objectives:

1. The student will be able to solve word problems that contain decimal information.
2. The student will be able to subtract decimals.
3. The student will be able to add decimals.
4. The student will be able to estimate decimal addition problems and subtraction problems.
5. The student will be able to identify time equivalents.
6. The student will be able to average a set of numbers and correctly round the remainders.
7. The student will be able to identify and calculate the value of exponents.
8. The student will be able to solve for missing addends.

Teaching Tips:

Students are successful at problem solving if they understand the four steps to a solution.

Materials, Supplies, and Equipment:

Activities:

1. Direct the student to **Lesson 129**. Explanation and read orally.
2. Have the student write the four steps to a solution on their own paper.
3. Read the first problem in **Lesson 129-1** orally.
   Work the problem following each step of the process carefully.
4. Students should be able to complete **Lesson 129-1** independently.

Blessed are they whose transgressions are forgiven, whose sins are covered.
Blessed is the man whose sin the Lord will never count against him.
Romans 4:7-8

Lesson 130

Concepts:

Problem solving—working backwards, decimals in word problems, subtraction of decimals, addition of decimals, giving change, triangles, problem solving-using more than one operation

Objectives:

1. The student will be able to work problem solving equations by working backwards.
2. The student will be able to solve word problems which contain decimal information.
3. The student will be able to subtract decimals.
4. The student will be able to add decimals.
5. The student will be able to calculate the change due from a given transaction or purchase.
6. The student will be able to identify and label different types of triangles.
7. The student will be able to solve problems that require the use of more than one operation to reach the answer.

Teaching Tips:

Any additional logic problems that can be supplemented, on a daily basis, will help the students with tasks like working backwards.

Materials, Supplies, and Equipment

Activities:

1. Read **Lesson 130 Explanation** orally.
   Discuss which mathematical operations "undo" each other.
   Work through the example problem together, explaining each step orally.
2. Work problem #1 on **Lesson 130-1** together orally.
3. Have the students complete **Lesson 130-1** independently.

Test:

1. Test 13 covers Lessons 116-125.
2. Administer Test 13, allowing the students 30-40 minutes to complete the test.

Therefore do not let sin reign in your mortal body so that you obey its evil desires.
Romans 6:12

Lesson 131

Concepts:

Decimal times a whole number, subtracting decimals, word problems with decimals, adding decimals, triangles, LCD

Objectives:

1. The student will be able to multiply a decimal by a whole number.
2. The student will be able to find the difference between two decimals.
3. The student will be able to solve word problems involving decimals.
4. The student will be able to add decimals.
5. The student will be able to draw three types of triangles: isosceles, equilateral, and scalene.
6. The student will be able to find the least common denominator.

Teaching Tips:

Allow the students many opportunities to work with concrete examples before they solve written problems.

Materials, Supplies, and Equipment:

1. Base 10 blocks
2. *Worksheet 69*

Activities:

1. Use a 100 tile to begin this lesson.
   a. We know that multiplication is repeated addition, so 0.67 x 3 = 0.67 + 0.67 + 0.67

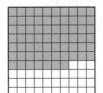 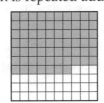

   b. If we add the number of individual tiles in each of these hundred tiles, we find the sum is 2.01.
   c. If we multiply,   0.67   the product is 2.01.

$$\begin{array}{r} 0.67 \\ \times\quad 3 \\ \hline 2.01 \end{array}$$

2. Ask the students, **"When we multiply, how do we know where to put the decimal point?"**
   a. Show them these examples, and see if they can eventually determine where the decimal point will go. See if they can generalize and come up with a rule. **(In each example, the number of decimal places in the product is equal to the number of places in the decimal factor.)**

$$\begin{array}{r} 0.9 \\ \times\quad 1 \\ \hline 0.9 \end{array} \qquad \begin{array}{r} 0.13 \\ \times\quad 3 \\ \hline 0.39 \end{array} \qquad \begin{array}{r} 0.22 \\ \times\quad 2 \\ \hline 0.44 \end{array} \qquad \begin{array}{r} 5.1 \\ \times\quad 4 \\ \hline 20.4 \end{array} \qquad \begin{array}{r} 0.31 \\ \times\quad 6 \\ \hline 1.86 \end{array}$$

3. Read **Lesson 131 Explanation** with the students.
4. The students will be able to complete **Lesson 131 Practice** independently.

Cast all of your anxiety on Him for he cares for you.

1 Peter 5:7

Lesson 132

Concepts:

Multiplying two decimals, decimal times a whole number, subtracting decimals, protractor, place value, multiplying mixed numbers, addition of equations

Objectives:

1. The student will be able to multiply two decimals.
2. The student will be able to multiply a decimal by a whole number.
3. The student will be able to find the sum or difference of a decimal.
4. The student will be able to find the measure of angles with a protractor.
5. The student will be able to demonstrate knowledge of place value by putting letters in place value categories to solve a riddle.
6. The student will be able to multiply mixed numbers.
7. The student will be able to solve an addition equation.

Teaching Tips:

Students often start counting the decimal places from the left instead of the right.

Materials, Supplies, and Equipment:

1. *Worksheet 70*

Activities:

1. Tell the students: **"Today we are going to multiply a decimal by a decimal. Watch as I work these problems and see if you can figure out how I know where to put the decimal place. (In each example, the number of decimal places in the product is equal to the number of places in both factors.)"**

2. a.

4.2	12.2	0.16
x 0.2	x 3.4	x 0.01
8 4	488	016
00	366	000
8.4	41.48	000
		0.0016

3. Read **Lesson 132 Explanation** with the students.
4. The students will be able to complete **Lesson 132 Practice** independently.

In Him was life, and the life was the light of men.
John 1:4

Lesson 133

Concepts:

Dividing decimals, dividing fractions, quadrilaterals, parallelograms, and polygons, multiplying two decimals, decimal times a whole number, place value

Objectives:

1. The student will be able to divide a decimal by a whole number.
2. The student will be able to divide fractions.
3. The student will be able to identify the following: quadrilaterals, parallelograms, squares and polygons.
4. The student will be able to find the product of two decimals.
5. The student will be able to multiply a decimal by a whole number and place the answers in a crossword puzzle.
6. The student will be able to find numbers written in standard form.

Teaching Tips:

Encourage the students to place the decimal point in the quotient BEFORE they begin the division process.

Materials, Supplies, and Equipment:

Activities:

1. Read **Lesson 133 Explanation** with the students.
   Remind the students that the decimal point in the quotient is to be placed directly above the decimal point in the dividend.
2. Work the following example problems with the students before they begin working independently.

$$5\overline{)85.75} = 17.15 \qquad 7\overline{)174.86} = 24.98 \qquad 9\overline{)613.08} = 68.12$$

3. The students will be able to complete **Lesson 133 Practice** independently.

Bear one another's burdens, and so fulfill the law of Christ.
Galatians 6:2

Lesson 134

Concepts:

Dividing decimals with zeros, dividing decimals, multiplying decimals, decimals times whole numbers, dividing by a two-digit divisor, ordering whole numbers

Objectives:

1. The student will be able to divide decimals working with zeros in the dividend.
2. The student will be able to divide a decimal by a whole number.
3. The student will be able to multiply two decimals and find the products in a word search.
4. The student will be able to multiply a decimal by a whole number.
5. The student will be able to divide by a two-digit divisor.
6. The student will be able to write numbers in standard form and order them from least to greatest.

Teaching Tips:

Encourage the students to place the decimal point in the quotient BEFORE they begin the division process.

Materials, Supplies, and Equipment:

1. *Worksheet 71*

Activities:

1. Read **Lesson 134 Explanation** with the students.
2. Work the following example problems with the students before they begin working independently.

$$4\overline{)39.62} = 9.905 \qquad 6\overline{)36.45} = 6.075$$

3. The students will be able to complete **Lesson 134 Practice** independently.

Do not be deceived; God is not mocked, for whatever a man sows, that he will also reap.
Galatians 6:7

Lesson 135

Concepts:

Understanding percent, dividing decimals, decimal times a whole number, multiplying fractions, ordering decimals

Objectives:

1. The student will be able to find equivalent ratios, fractions, and percents.
2. The student will be able to divide a decimal by a whole number.
3. The student will be able to multiply a decimal by a whole number.
4. The student will be able to color a hundreds chart to show the value of given percents.
5. The student will be able to multiply two fractions and connect the points to create a circle design.
6. The student will be able to order decimals from largest to smallest.

Teaching Tips:

Materials, Supplies, and Equipment:

Base ten blocks, scratch paper

Activities:

1. Read **Lesson 135 Explanation** with the students.
2. Distribute the following base ten blocks to each student: 1 one hundred tile, 9 rods of ten and 9 cubes.
3. Have the students use the base ten blocks to represent the decimal 0.44.
   (Place the following on top of the one hundred tile: 4 rods of ten and 4 ones.)
4. Ask the students to write the decimal as a percent on their scratch paper **(44%)**.
5. Play the following decimal game:
   a. A student goes to the board and writes a decimal or a percent. Then challenge the students to use the base ten blocks to represent the number. The student calls on another student to share their answer. The first student with the right answer takes the place of the person at the board.
6. The students will be able to complete **Lesson 135 Practice** independently.

Set your mind on things above, not on things that are on earth.
Colossians 3:2

Lesson 136

Concepts:

Percents and decimals, understanding percent, ratios, dividing decimals, multiplying decimals, ordering decimals, rounding to thousands', finding products by estimating

Objectives:

1. Given a percent, the student will be able to find an equivalent decimal.
2. Given a decimal, the student will be able to find an equivalent percent.
3. Given a ratio, the student will be able to find an equivalent decimal, percent, and fraction.
4. The student will be able to divide decimals working with zeros in the dividend.
5. The student will be able to divide a decimal by a whole number.
6. The student will be able to multiply two decimals and order the products from least to greatest to solve a riddle.
7. The student will be able to round numbers to the nearest 1,000.
8. The student will be able to estimate the product of two decimals.

Teaching Tips:

Materials, Supplies, and Equipment:

Activities:

1. Read **Lesson 136 Explanation** with the students.
2. Play a game with the students at the chalkboard to reinforce these concepts.
   a. Divide the class into two equal teams.
   b. Call one person from each team to the board. Give them a decimal and have them write the equivalent percent on the board or give them a percent and have them write and equivalent decimal on the board.
   c. Each team with a correct answer gets one point.
   d. The team with the correct answer first gets one point.
3. The students will be able to complete **Lesson 136 Practice** independently.

May grace and peace be multiplied to you in the knowledge
of God and of Jesus our Lord.
2 Peter 1:2

Lesson 137

Concepts:

Percent as a fraction, percent as a decimal, ratio as a percent, percent as a ratio, dividing decimals, rounding to the nearest 100, dividing money

Objectives:

1. Given a percent, the student will be able to find the equivalent fraction and reduce it to lowest terms.
2. Given a percent, the student will be able to find the equivalent decimal.
3. The student will be able to color a hundreds chart to show the value of given ratios.
4. The student will be able to divide a decimal by a whole number.
5. The student will be able to round numbers to the nearest 100 and place them in acrossword puzzle.
6. The student will be able to divide a decimal by a two-digit divisor.

Teaching Tips:

The students have worked with renaming fractions extensively. This activity gives them the opportunity to apply this information to another type of problem.

Materials, Supplies, and Equipment:

Activities:

1. Read **Lesson 137 Explanation** with the students.
2. The students will be able to complete **Lesson 137 Practice** independently.

And in the morning, a great while before day, he (Jesus) rose
and went out to a lonely place, and there he prayed.
Mark 1:35

Lesson 138

Concepts:

Fraction as a percent, percent as a fraction, percent as a decimal, percent as a ratio, adding mixed numbers, adding decimals

Objectives:

1. Given a fraction, the student will be able find an equivalent percent.
2. Given a percent, the student will be able to find the equivalent fraction and reduce it to lowest terms.
3. Given a percent, the student will be able to find equivalent decimals and order them from least to greatest. The student will be able to find their way through a decimal maze.
4. The student will be able to write percents as ratios.
5. The student will be able to add mixed numbers.
6. The student will be able to find the sum and difference of two decimals.

Teaching Tips:

The students have worked with equivalent fractions. This allows them to apply the information they know to another type of problem. Students should grasp this concept easily.

Materials, Supplies, and Equipment:

1. *Worksheet 72*

Activities:

1. Read **Lesson 138 Explanation** with the students.
2. The students will be able to complete **Lesson 138 Practice** independently.

...but their plot became known to Saul. And they were also watching the gates day and night so that they might put him to death; but his disciples took him by night, and let him down through an opening in the wall, lowering him in a basket.
Acts 9:24, 25

Lesson 139

Concepts:
Finding a percent of a number, changing fractions into percents using a calculator, finding equivalent fractions, percents, decimals and ratios, adding mixed numbers, ordering fractions and decimals, divisibility

Objectives:
1. The student will be able to find the percent of a number.
2. The student will be able to use a calculator to change a fraction into a percent.
3. The student will be able to change a fraction to a percent.
4. The student will be able to find an equivalent decimal, percent ,ratio, and fraction.
5. The student will be able to subtract two mixed numbers.
6. The student will be able to order fractions and decimals.
7. The student will be able to decide if a number is divisible by 2, 3, 5 and 10.

Teaching Tips:
Bring in newspapers and let the students find sale items. Show them how to determine the amount of their savings.

Materials, Supplies, and Equipment:
1. newspapers and catalogues
2. *Worksheet 73*

Activities:
1. Read **Lesson 139 Explanation** with the students.
2. Point out to the students that we use this concept every day when shopping for bargains.
3. Have the students work in teams and develop a sales brochure for a major toy store, deducting 15% off the products. They may draw pictures of the toys or clip pictures from catalogues. Tell them to give each item a retail price and a sale price based on the 15% discount.
4. Taking it Further: Have the students bring in sales receipts from stores. Ask them to determine how much a senior citizen would save on the total bill before tax if they got a 5% discount.
5. The students will be able to complete **Lesson 139 Practice** independently.

This is my beloved son, listen to him.
Mark 9:7

Lesson 140

Concepts:

Problem solving using decimals, percent of a number, fractions to percents, percents to fractions, divisibility, comparing decimals

Objectives:

1. The student will be able to solve word problems using percents.
2. The student will be able to find the percent of a number.
3. Given a fraction, the student will be able find an equivalent percent.
4. Given a percent, the student will be able to find the equivalent fraction and reduce it to lowest terms.
5. The student will be able to shade numbers in a table that are divisible by 2.
6. The student will be able to compare decimals using >, < , or =.

Teaching Tips:

Materials, Supplies, and Equipment:

Activities:

1. Read **Lesson 140 Explanation** with the students.
2. The students will be able to complete **Lesson 140 Practice** independently.

Test:

1. Test 14 covers Lessons 126-135.
2. Administer Test 14, allowing the students 30-40 minutes to complete the test.

And now these three remain: faith, hope, and love. And the greatest of these is love.
1 Corinthians 13:13

Lesson 141

Concepts:

Standard measure to ⅛ inch, addition of decimals, multiplication of fractions, addition of fractions with unlike denominators, division — two-digit divisor and one-digit quotient, addition of four-, five-, and six-digit numbers, addition terms and facts

Objectives:

1. The student will be able to identify, measure, read, write and label given items using Standard (Customary) measurements of inches, half inches, quarter inches and eighth inches.
2. The student will be able to add decimals.
3. The student will be able to multiply fractions.
4. The student will be able to add fractions with unlike denominators.
5. The student will be able to complete division problems which contain a two-digit divisor and yield a one-digit quotient.
6. The student will be able to add four- and five-digit numbers.
7. The student will be able to identify addition terms and complete addition facts.

Teaching Tips:

Some students may still be using portions of the Metric System and the Standard (Customary) System. They may not realize that Metric and Standard (Customary) Units of measurement are *not* the same. Explain that Standard measurements were originally developed by an English king. For this reason, the Customary system does not have a base unit (like the Metric System). A "foot" was the length of the king's foot. A "yard" is the distance from the king's nose to the tip of his outstretched arm. Needless to say, this accounted for the random nature of this system. The Metric system has a base unit of 10. The students should remember this from their previous studies, but may need a reminder.

Materials, Supplies, and Equipment:

1. 12 inch rulers (with ½, ¼, and ⅛ inch markings)
2. Measuring tapes (retractable metal)

Activities:

1. Pass out the rulers and measuring tapes so that every child, or at least every two children have a ruler, or tape. Have the students examine the markings between the 1 inch and 2 inch markings on the ruler or tape. Discuss the ½ inch line and the ¼ inch line, which the students should have little difficulty pointing out due to prior experience. Then, point out that there are several smaller markings between the ½ and ¼ inch lines. Explain that these are ⅛ inch markings. Have the student count the number of these lines (remember to include the ½ and ¼ lines, too) and see how many of these ⅛ lines are present between the 1 inch and 2 inch marking. **Seven lines will be present, including the ½ and ¼ markings.** Discuss that the ⅛ markings are used just like the ¼ and ½ inch markings. They are to give more accurate measurements.

2. Read **Lesson 141 Explanation** together and have the students look at the ruler examples. Remind the students that the diagrams in the book may not be drawn to scale; they are drawn for easy reference. Have the students measure several small items around the room. Pencils, paper clips, book widths, shoe lengths, and finger lengths are all handy items for the students to use. (Remind the students, if necessary, that we sometimes refer to the ¼ measurement as "quarter." This is because it is a quarter of the whole inch — just like in fractions ¼ is a quarter of the whole shape.) Practice reading several measurements to the ⅛th by measuring these objects around the room. Encourage the students to find objects in the room that measure to ⅛ of an inch. Make sure to emphasize the appropriate way to pronounce measurements such as "4 and ⅝" or "2 and ⅜."

3. Have the student complete **Lesson 141-1** independently. Again, remember that the pictures in the book may not be drawn to scale. Do not have the student use an actual ruler to measure the diagrammed nails, have them use the pictured ruler. This exercise is designed to assess the student's ability to read each measurement.

4. As part of the lesson, either at the beginning or at the end, review all of the standard measurements and their equivalents (inches, feet, yards, and miles). If an extra activity is needed for this review, divide the students into small groups. Have them measure these items as a group and record the results: the person in each group who has the farthest long jump, the person in the group with the longest arm span from fingertip to fingertip with arms stretched out, the person with the largest hand span from thumb tip to pinkie tip, etc. Try to be creative and think of any other measurements which can be taken in inches, feet, or yards.

Oh, the depth of the riches of the wisdom and knowledge of God! How unsearchable his judgments, and his paths beyond tracing out!
Romans 11:33

Lesson 142

Concepts:
> Standard weight, Standard measure to ⅛ inch, subtraction of decimals, division –
> two-digit divisor and two-digit quotient, subtraction of fractions
> with unlike denominators, addition terms and facts

Objectives:
1. The student will be able to identify, measure, read, write and label given items using Standard (Customary) measurement units of weight.
2. The student will be able to identify, measure, read, write and label given items using Standard (Customary) measurements of inches, half inches, quarter inches and eighth inches.
3. The student will be able to subtract decimals.
4. The student will be able to complete division problems containing a two-digit divisor and yielding a two-digit quotient.
5. The student will be able to subtract fractions with unlike denominators.
6. The student will be able to identify addition terms and complete addition facts.

Teaching Tips:

Materials, Supplies, and Equipment:
1. Various boxes, cans, and bottles that weigh varied amounts
2. Scales
3. Ounce and pound weights

Activities:
1. Explain that the students are going to study the units of weight in the Customary System. Have them look over the boxes, cans, scales and weights. It would be a good idea to have uncooked rice, dry beans, unpopped popcorn or some other dry product to use for measurement, pre-measured into plastic sandwich bags in varying weights. This will allow the students to see and feel the different amounts of weight using different dry products. It would be a good idea to set this up at different centers and allow the students several minutes at each center to experiment with each of the items.
2. Read **Lesson 142 Explanation** orally. Point out the different weight amounts shown (the cheese, butter and pickup truck full of watermelons). Remind the students of the various weight amounts they felt at the centers. Ask the students, **"Can you name any other objects that would weigh about 1 pound? Can you name any other objects that would weight about an ounce? Can you name any other objects that would weigh about a ton?"**
   Listen to the student answers and respond accordingly.
3. Assign the students to complete **Lesson 142-1** independently.
   They should have little difficulty with this concept.

The Lord is my rock, my fortress and my deliverer; my God is my rock, in whom I take refuge. He is my shield and the horn of my salvation, my stronghold.
Psalm 18: 1-2

Lesson 143

Concepts:
Standard liquid measure, Standard weight, Standard measure to feet, multiplication of decimals, addition of mixed numbers, place value through billions' place, subtraction

Objectives:
1. The student will be able to identify, measure, read, write, and label given items using Standard (Customary) measurement units of liquid measure.
2. The student will be able to identify, measure, read, write and label given items using Standard (Customary) measurement units of weight.
3. The student will be able to identify, measure, read, write and label given items using Standard (Customary) measurements of feet, yards and miles.
4. The student will be able to multiply decimals.
5. The student will be able to add mixed numbers.
6. The student will be able to identify place value through the billions' place.
7. The student will be able to complete subtraction problems.

Teaching Tips:
If possible, prior to the lesson have several centers set up with various ounce, cup, quart and gallon containers. Also have a gallon of liquid (water) at each center. Allow the students to experiment with the various liquid measurements by pouring the water from one container into another and comparing the amounts.

Materials, Supplies, and Equipment:
1. Measuring containers in the following sizes: cups, pints, quarts and gallons.
2. Access to water, or some non-staining liquid.
3. *Worksheet 74*

Activities:
1. Read **Lesson 143 Explanation** together. Discuss the different measuring containers and allow the students to compare them by passing them around the room. (This can be omitted if centers have already been established and visited as described in the Teaching Tip above). Demonstrate how four quarts is the same amount of liquid as one gallon by using a quart container to fill up a gallon container. Have four students come up one at a time and each one pour a quart container of water into the gallon container. After the fourth student has done this, the gallon container should be full. Complete the example problems in **Lesson 143 Explanation** by using the measuring containers to prove they are correct.
2. If space and equipment allow, have the students divide into groups and demonstrate how many pints are needed to fill one quart, how many cups are needed to fill one pint and how many cups are needed to fill one quart. If time, space, or equipment do not allow this activity, conduct it as a whole class demonstration with as much student participation as possible.
3. The students should be able to complete **Lesson 143-1** independently. Allow them to use the liquid containers if a manipulative is necessary to enable students' understanding of this exercise.

I do not hide your righteousness in my heart; I do not conceal your love and your truth from the great assembly. Do not withhold your mercy from me, O Lord, may your love and your truth always protect me.
Psalm 40:10-11

Lesson 144

Concepts:

Standard (Fahrenheit) temperature, Standard liquid measure, Standard weight, Standard measure to inch, division of decimals, place value through billions' place, subtraction of mixed numbers, equivalent fractions

Objectives:

1. The student will be able to read, and write temperatures given in Fahrenheit degrees.
2. The student will be able to identify, measure, read, write and label given items using Standard (Customary) measurement units of liquid measure.
3. The student will be able to identify, measure, read, write and label given items using Standard (Customary) measurement units of weight.
4. The student will be able to identify, measure, read, write and label given items using Standard (Customary) measurements of inches, feet, yards and miles.
5. The student will be able to divide decimals.
6. The student will be able to identify place value through the billions' place.
7. The student will be able to subtract mixed numbers.
8. The student will be able to find equivalent fractions.

Teaching Tips:

Most of the students should have no difficulty reading a thermometer using Fahrenheit degrees.

Materials, Supplies, and Equipment:

1. Weather sections of the local newspaper from the past four or five days.
2. Glass of ice water, a cup of hot coffee (or liquid), and a glass of water that has been sitting at room temperature for at least 2 hours.
3. Several *Fahrenheit* thermometers

Activities:

1. Read **Lesson 144 Explanation** together. Discuss the temperature ranges and at what temperature things would begin to get cold, or hot. Point out the reference temperatures on the thermometer picture in the book (212° boiling point, 98.6° normal body temperature, 32° freezing, and 72° comfortable room temperature).
2. Have the students break up into five small groups. Each group will need a thermometer. Give one group the ice water, one group the hot coffee or liquid, (monitor this group carefully to avoid any accidents), one group the room temperature water. The last two groups will need no additional equipment besides the thermometer. Have the groups with the ice water, the coffee and the water at room temperature place their thermometer in the liquid and monitor the temperature. Have one of the additional two groups measure the room temperature by simply laying their thermometer on a desk top and monitoring it. Have the final group measure the temperature of one of the students in the room by having him hold the thermometer in his closed fist. Allow enough time for the students to monitor these temperatures. Then come back together and discuss the data collected. Keep this data for additional use in **Lesson 148**.

3. If an extra activity is needed, have the student look over the weather sections of several papers. Ask them to notice the actual temperatures and forecast temperatures for the past several days. Then check and see if the temperatures which were forecast match to the actual temperature that was recorded.
   You might make this an ongoing activity where the students monitor the temperatures and record the changes.
   This could be easily correlated with a science unit.

4. The students should be able to complete **Lesson 144-1** independently.

Create in me a pure heart, O God, and renew a steadfast spirit within me.
Psalms 51:10

© MCMXCVIII Alpha Omega Publications, Inc.

Lesson 145

Concepts:

Metric measurement, Standard (Fahrenheit) temperature, Standard liquid measure, Standard weight, subtraction of four-, five, and six-digit numbers, renaming mixed numbers

Objectives:

1. The student will be able to identify, measure, read, write and label given items using Metric units of measurement.
2. The student will be able to read and write temperatures given in Fahrenheit degrees.
3. The student will be able to identify, measure, read, write and label given items using Standard (Customary) measurement units of liquid measure.
4. The student will be able to identify, measure, read, write and label given items using Standard (Customary) measurement units of weight.
5. The student will be able to subtract four-, five- and six-digit numbers.
6. The student will be able to rename mixed numbers.

Teaching Tips:

Before beginning the lesson remind the students of the differences between the Standard (Customary) System of measurement and the Metric System of measurement.

Have a large chart made from laminated posterboard which matches the conversion chart shown on **Lesson 145 Explanation**. Covering the chart with lamination will allow you to write on the board with a dry erase marker or overhead marker which can be erased with paper towels and water. It will make the chart reusable.

Materials, Supplies, and Equipment:

1. Centimeter ruler with millimeter markings
2. Meter stick with centimeter markings and millimeter markings.
3. Large Metric conversion chart
4. Overhead markers
5. 5" x 2" rectangles of posterboard

Activities:

1. Have enough rulers for each student to have one individually. Pass out the rulers and have the students measure something personal, i.e.: their desktop, the length of their shoe or the length of the chair leg. Discuss that these items can be measured in either centimeters or millimeters. Give examples of items which would be better to measure in millimeters and items it would be better to measure in centimeters. Try to involve the students as much as possible. The students should have little difficulty with this activity. Practice measuring items that require use of centimeters and millimeters (2 cm, 3 mm) in order to remind them of the base 10 relationship in the Metric system.
2. Ask the students to name the other Metric measurements commonly used besides millimeters and centimeters (kilometers).

3. Read **Lesson 145 Explanation** together.

   Discuss the conversion chart by using the large instructional conversion chart and overhead markers. Discuss the prefix names (Kilo, Hecto, Deka, deci, centi, and milli). You might want to make up a class acronym to help the students remember the order of the prefix columns.

   Practice several conversions as a class, using the large conversion chart.

   Allow the students to complete some example problems by using the large chart and overhead markers. Have the students make their own copy of the conversion chart. They can simply copy the chart onto a piece of notebook paper. If you wish to have an additional activity, have the students make individual conversion charts out of small pieces of posterboard approximately 5" x 2."

   They can keep these for use whenever necessary.

4. Complete all the example problems, except the last one, using the large instructional conversion chart. Have the students complete the last example on their own charts and check their answer with the book. If additional problems are necessary, have the students create their own problems and convert them together using the conversion chart. Be sure to practice converting both from smaller units to larger units and from larger units down to smaller units.

5. The students should be able to complete **Lesson 145** independently. If any students still need extra assistance, work with them on the practice problems.

For God did not give us a spirit of timidity, but a spirit
of power, of love and of self-discipline.
2 Timothy 1:7

Lesson 146

Concepts:

Metric weight, Metric measurement, Standard (Fahrenheit) temperature, Standard liquid measure, addition of mixed numbers and renaming their sums, decimal place value through thousandths, multiplication terms and facts

Objectives:

1. The student will be able to identify, measure, read, write and label given items using Metric measurement units of weight.
2. The student will be able to identify, measure, read, write and label given items using Metric units of measurement.
3. The student will be able to read, and write temperatures given in Fahrenheit degrees.
4. The student will be able to identify, measure, read, write and label given items using Standard (Customary) measurement units of liquid measure.
5. The student will be able to add mixed numbers and rename their sums, if necessary.
6. The student will be able to identify decimal place value through the thousandths.
7. The student will be able to name multiplication terms and complete given multiplication facts.

Teaching Tips:

Before starting the lesson, pass around a one kilogram weight or an object that weighs about one kilogram (a book) to give the students a sense of the unit weight. Also pass around a feather or other object which weighs about one milligram to give the students a sense of the weight difference between a kilogram and a milligram.

Materials, Supplies, and Equipment:

1. Large instructional Metric conversion chart from **Lesson 145**.
2. Individual student Metric conversion charts
3. Metric liquid containers, Metric measuring rulers and sticks and Metric weights and scales, if possible.

Activities:

1. Review **Lesson 145** by going over the Metric conversion chart.
   Discuss the three different basic units of the Metric system (grams, liters and meters). Use the Metric weights, liquid measurements, and rulers to reiterate and demonstrate the differences, if necessary. Give examples of various gram amounts (1 g is about the weight of a paper clip, etc.) and measurements by weighing items in the classroom like a paper clip, a book or a child (if you have a the proper type of Metric scale).
   You might want to allow the students to break into groups and "play" with items that are various weights in order to "feel" the different weights.
   Read **Lesson 146 Explanation** together. Complete the example problems.
2. Ask the students to brainstorm and list of any other items that weigh a kilogram, gram or milligram.
3. Stress the importance of the weight difference and equivalences explained in **Lesson 146** (1 kilogram = 1,000 grams).

4. The students should be able to complete **Lesson 146-1** independently.

In a large house there are articles not only of gold and silver, but also of wood and clay; some are for noble purposes and some for ignoble. If a man cleanses himself from the latter, he will be an instrument for noble purposes, made whole, useful to the Master and prepared to do any good work.
2 Timothy 2: 20-21

Lesson 147

Concepts:

Metric liquid measure, Metric weight, Metric measurement, Standard (Fahrenheit) and Metric (Celsius) temperature, division with two-digit divisors and three-digit quotients, subtraction of mixed numbers with unlike denominators, division terms and facts

Objectives:

1. The student will be able to identify, measure, read, write and label given items using Metric measurement units of liquid measure.
2. The student will be able to identify, measure, read, write and label given items using Metric measurement units of weight.
3. The student will be able to identify, measure, read, write and label given items using Metric units of measurement.
4. The student will be able to read, and write temperatures given in Fahrenheit and Celsius degrees.
5. The student will be able to complete division problems that contain a two-digit divisor and yield a three-digit quotient.
6. The student will be able to subtract mixed numbers with unlike denominators.
7. The student will be able to identify division terms and complete division facts.

Teaching Tips:

Have as many examples of various liquid weight measurements as possible.
Some suggestions are liter soda bottles, soda cans, soup cans, juice boxes or any other packaged container with a metric measurement printed on the label.

Materials, Supplies, and Equipment:

1. Large instructional Metric conversion chart from **Lesson 145**.
2. Individual student Metric conversion charts
3. Metric liquid containers (liter container and milliliter container or dropper)
4. *Worksheet 75*

Activities:

1. Review **Lesson 145** by going over the conversion chart.
   Discuss the three different basic units of the Metric system (grams, liters and meters) again. Use the liquid containers and the rulers to demonstrate the differences if necessary. Give examples of various liquid amounts and measurements. You might want to allow the students to break into groups and "play" with these items. If you prefer, you can set them up in centers with water as was done in **Lesson 143** (on Standard liquid measure) and have the students use these containers prior to the actual lesson.
2. Read **Lesson 147 Explanation** together and complete the example problems.
3. The students should be able to complete **Lesson 147-1** independently.

Praise be to the God and Father of our Lord Jesus Christ! In his great mercy he has given us new birth into a living hope through the resurrection of Jesus Christ from the dead, and into an inheritance that can never perish, spoil or fade—kept in heaven for you...
1 Peter 1:3-4

Lesson 148

Concepts:

Metric (Celsius) temperature, Metric liquid measure, Metric weight, Metric measurement, division with two-digit divisors and a zero in the quotient, division with one-digit divisor and two-digit quotient, least common multiple, division terms and facts

Objectives:

1. The student will be able to read and write temperatures given in Celsius degrees.
2. The student will be able to identify, measure, read, write and label given items using Metric measurement units of liquid measure.
3. The student will be able to measure, read, write and label given items using Metric measurement units of weight.
4. The student will be able to identify, measure, read, write and label given items using Metric units of measurement.
5. The student will be able to complete division problems that contain a two-digit divisor and a zero in the quotient.
6. The student will be able to complete division problems which contain a one-digit divisor and yield a two-digit quotient.
7. The student will be able to find the least common multiple when given two numbers.
8. The student will be able to identify division terms and complete division facts.

Teaching Tips:

Materials, Supplies, and Equipment:

1. Several Celsius thermometers
2. Glass of ice water, a cup of hot coffee, and a glass of water which has been sitting at room temperature for at least 2 hours.
3. The weather section from the newspaper for the past several days.
4. *Worksheet 76*

Activities:

1. Remind the students that the Fahrenheit scale is used in Customary (Standard) measurement. Today's lesson will cover the Metric temperature measurement of Celsius degrees. Look at the example thermometer in **Lesson 148 Explanation** and point out the reference temperatures (0° freezing, 100° boiling point, and 37° body temperature). Compare these to the Fahrenheit temperatures discussed in **Lesson 144** so that the student can see the difference in the two scales.
2. Have the students conduct the same exercises that they did in **Lesson 144 Activity #1**. This time use the Celsius thermometers. After the students have measured the temperatures and you have discussed them as a class, graph the temperature differences between the Fahrenheit readings taken in **Lesson 144** and the Celsius readings taken today of the same items.
3. If an additional exercise is needed, have the students complete the same newspaper exercise done in **Lesson 144 Activity #3**.
4. The students should be able to complete **Lesson 148-1** independently.

This is the confidence we have in approaching God; that if we ask anything according to his will, he hears us. And if we know that he hears us—whatever we ask—we know that we have what we asked of him.
1 John 5: 14-15

Lesson 149

Concepts:
Problem solving with measurement data, Metric (Celsius) temperature, Metric liquid measure, triangles, divisibility, division of money with a one-digit divisor, multiplication of larger decimal numbers, missing addends

Objectives:
1. The student will be able to complete a given mathematical problem that requires the use of measurement data to solve the equation.
2. The student will be able to read and write temperatures given in Celsius degrees.
3. The student will be able to identify, measure, read, write and label given items using Metric measurement units of liquid measure.
4. The student will be able to identify and label scalene, isosceles, equilateral and right triangles, as well as calculate measurements of missing angles on each triangle.
5. The student will be able to apply the divisibility rules for two, three, five and ten.
6. The student will be able to divide dollar amounts that contain a one-digit divisor.
7. The student will be able to multiply larger decimals.
8. The student will be able to solve for missing addends.

Teaching Tips:

Materials, Supplies, and Equipment:

Activities:
1. Read **Lesson 149 Explanation** together and discuss the **4-Step Plan** for solving word problems. Explain that all of the problems in this lesson will deal with measurement.
2. Complete the example problem together. Remind the students that some measurement unit conversions may need to be made in the data provided in the problem before any mathematical process can be performed.
3. The student should be able to complete **Lesson 149-1** independently.

...build yourselves up in your most holy faith and pray in the Holy Spirit.
Keep yourselves in God's love as you wait for the mercy of
our Lord Jesus Christ to bring you to eternal life.
Jude 20-21

Lesson 150

Concepts:

Problem solving by drawing a picture, problem solving with measurement data, using a compass to draw circles, metric liquid measurement, division with a one-digit divisor and a three-digit quotient, division or larger decimal numbers, using data contained in a chart, identifying Celsius and Fahrenheit temperatures

Objectives:

1. The student will be able to complete a given mathematical problem using the problem solving strategy of drawing a picture.
2. The student will be able to complete given mathematical problem that requires the use of measurement data to solve the equation.
3. The student will be able to use a compass to draw a circle and label the radius, diameter, and name of the circle.
4. The student will be able to identify, measure, read, write and label given items using Metric measurement units of liquid measure.
5. The student will be able to complete division problem that contains a one-digit divisor and yield a three-digit quotient.
6. The student will be able to divide larger decimal numbers.
7. The student will be able to answer questions by using data contained in a chart.
8. The student will be able to identify temperatures in both Fahrenheit and Celsius degrees.

Teaching Tips:

Explain to the students that "a picture is always worth a thousand words"! Drawing pictures on difficult problems can make things much clearer.

Materials, Supplies, and Equipment:

1. Paper and pencil

Activities:

1. Read **Lesson 150 Explanation** together.
   Discuss the different ways this problem may be solved.
   Look at both example solutions (24 + 24 + 35 + 35 = 118) and (24 x 2) + (35 x 2) = 118 and explain why they arrive at the same answer by using different mathematical strategies based on a knowledge of mathematical rules and information.
2. Complete **Lesson 150-1 problem #1** together and check the students' answers together.
   Assist any students that need further assistance.
3. The student should be able to complete the rest of **Lesson 150-1** independently.

Test:

1. Test 15 covers Lessons 136-145.
2. Administer Test 15, allowing the students 30-40 minutes to complete the test.

Lesson 151

Concepts:

Bar graphs, multiplication of decimals, fractional portion of a number, averaging without remainders, factor trees, four-, five- and six-digit addition, problem solving using more than one operation

Objectives:

1. The student will be able to read and interpret information using both vertical and horizontal bar graphs.
2. The student will be able to multiply decimals.
3. The student will be able to find the fractional portion of a number.
4. The student will be able to average a given set of numbers.
5. The student will be able to complete factor trees.
6. The student will be able to add four-, five- and six-digit numbers.
7. The student will be able to complete word problems which require the use of more than one operation to solve the problem.

Teaching Tips:

The next nine lessons are all on constructing and interpreting graphs. This can be a very exciting unit of study for the students if you use a little creativity. Taking surveys either within the classroom, or by visiting other classrooms can make activities more fun. Having the students survey their families at home, or at church, might be a creative way to make the unit of study more interesting. Try to be creative for your students!

Materials, Supplies, and Equipment:

1. Rulers
2. Colored pencils or crayons
3. Paper (lined notebook paper is fine)

Activities:

1. Read **Lesson 151 Explanation** together.
   Go over the first graph. Discuss the parts of the graph: the dollar amounts on the side of the graph, the times listed on the bottom of the graph and the corresponding bar lines.
   Discuss the proper way to read a graph: for example, the bar for pony rides is halfway between the $250 and the $300 line. Halfway between $250 and $300 is $275. This means that the total amount made on pony rides is $275.

2. Conduct a survey within the classroom. Survey the students on their favorite ice cream flavor. Give them four or five choices and vote on each choice. Once this data is compiled, ask the students to make two bar graphs to show this information; one horizontal bar graph and one vertical bar graph. The students need to use rulers to draw all lines straight. They also need to neatly color the bars.
3. The students should be able to complete **Lesson 151-1** independently.

For nothing is impossible with God.
Luke 1:37

© MCMXCVIII Alpha Omega Publications, Inc.

Lesson 152

Concepts:

Line graphs, bar graphs, multiplication of larger decimals, averaging with remainders, prime & composite numbers, multiplication of fractions, addition equations

Objectives:

1. The student will be able to read and interpret information presented in a line graph.
2. The student will be able to read and interpret information using both vertical and horizontal bar graphs.
3. The student will be able to multiply larger decimal numbers.
4. The student will be able to average a set of numbers which yield a remainder.
5. The student will be able to identify prime and composite numbers.
6. The student will be able to multiply fractions.
7. The student will be able to complete addition equations.

Teaching Tips:

Explain that line graphs are good for showing change over a period of time.
Double line graphs are good for comparing this type of information.

Materials, Supplies, and Equipment:

1. Rulers
2. One centimeter graph paper
3. Colored pencils or crayons
4. *Worksheet 77*

Activities:

1. Read **Lesson 152 Explanation** together.
   Discuss the fact that line graphs are good at showing changes over a period of time.
2. Choose one subject area where you can give the students several test scores or daily homework grades. Have the students make a line graph, using the one centimeter graph paper, to show this information. This makes each graph personalized for each student. If you would rather have each child create the same graph, give the students a set of grades and have them create a graph.
   The student needs to use the rulers and colored pencils to create a neat graph.
3. Once the student has created a graph to show the test scores (Activity #2) have them swap test scores with another student, or give them another set of test scores (in case swapping test scores could be embarrassing or uncomfortable for some students). Have the students create a double line graph to compare these two sets of data.
4. The student should be able to complete **Lesson 152-1** independently.

…I tell you the truth, if you have faith as small as a mustard seed,
you can say to this mountain, "Move from here to there,"
and it will move. Nothing will be impossible for you.
Matthew 17:20b

Lesson 153

Concepts:

Pictographs, line graphs, division of decimals, multiplication of mixed numbers, three-digit times one-digit multiplication, column additions, subtraction equations

Objectives:

1. The student will be able to read and interpret information presented in pictographs.
2. The student will be able to read and interpret information presented in a line graph.
3. The student will be able to divide decimal numbers.
4. The student will be able to multiply mixed numbers.
5. The student will be able to complete three-digit by one-digit multiplication problems.
6. The student will be able to complete column addition.
7. The student will be able to complete subtraction equations.

Teaching Tips:

Pictographs can be great fun. Try to think of different pictures to use for the graphic on the pictograph. Most students will enjoy drawing these pictures.

Materials, Supplies, and Equipment:

1. Colored pencils or crayons
2. Rulers

Activities:

1. Read **Lesson 153 Explanation** together.
   Answer the example problems together.
   Create a class pictograph which shows the number of students in your class that have pets. Have the students use one stick person as the unit of measurement. One whole stick person should equal two students. If you would like to show the number of pets owned by the students in your class, or type of pets owned by the students in your class, this would also work. If you choose to do this, have the students use one cat picture (dog, fish, etc.) to represent 2 animals. Have the student use the rulers and colored pencils/crayons to create a neatly colored and straight graph. Stress that pictographs, and all graphs, need to be neat so that there is no difficulty interpreting the information contained in the graph.
2. The students should be able to complete **Lesson 153-1** independently.

Thou shalt have no other gods before me.
Exodus 20:3

Lesson 154

Concepts:

Circle (pie) graphs, pictographs, cross products, multiplication of mixed and whole numbers, multiplication by 10, 100, and 1,000, two- and three-digit subtraction, place value through billions'

Objectives:

1. The student will be able to read and interpret information presented in a circle (or pie) graph.
2. The student will be able to read and interpret information presented in pictographs.
3. The student will be able to calculate cross products.
4. The student will be able to multiply mixed and whole numbers.
5. The student will be able to multiply by 10, 100, and 1,000.
6. The student will be able to subtract two- and three-digit numbers.
7. The student will be able to identity place value through the billions' place.

Teaching Tips:

Pie, or circle, graphs can be shown either with numbers in each slice of the pie or as percentages in the slices of the pie. Make sure the students understand that all the sections of the graph must add up to 100 if using whole numbers, or 100% if using percentages. If the pie graph shows fractions, then all fractions should add up to one whole. (Remind them that there should never be a percentage total more than 100%, or a fraction total larger than one whole.) Also remember that pie graphs can show breakdowns on numbers which are larger than 100 or smaller than 100. If this is the case, they must be able to convert this information to percentages or fractions, if needed. This concept may be difficult for some students to comprehend, but may will understand it by this point due to their prior studies with fractions, decimals, and whole numbers.

Materials, Supplies, and Equipment:

1. Compass
2. Ruler
3. Colored pencils or crayons.
4. *Worksheet 78*

Activities:

1. Read **Lesson 154 Explanation** together.

   Discuss the proportions of the pie graph and how each "pie slice" size needs to be accurate to the number proportions of the pie. For example: The pie graphs below show an incorrect number/slice proportion and a correct number/slice proportion.

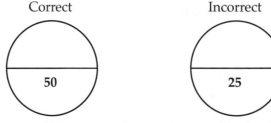

If the pie graph is supposed to total to 100 then half of the pie graph should total to 50 not 25. If the graph needs to show 50%, or ½, then the pie slice should be half of the circle.

2. Have the students draw a circle using their compasses. Instruct the students to make a circle graph which shows the following information: Title: "Favorite Bible Stories of 200 Students" Data: David & Goliath — 125, Daniel and the Lions' Den — 50, Shadrach, Meshach, and Abednego (Fiery Furnace) — 12, Joseph and the Coat of Many Colors — 13. Remind the students that each pie slice should be proportioned according to the number in the slice. The finished graph should look similar to the one below. The easiest way to do this is to have the students make a pie graph showing the actual numbers which correspond to each category. If you would like to have them convert this information to percentages or fractions, the answers are provided below. This might be an activity better suited for your advanced students because these fractions and percentages are not easily converted with this data.

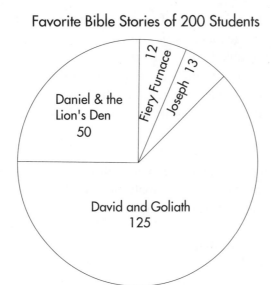

Favorite Bible Stories of 200 Students

If percentages are used the answers are as follows: David — 62.5%, Daniel — 25%, Joseph — 6.5%, Furnace — 6% (all added together = 100%).

If fractions are used the answers are as follows: David — ⅝, Daniel — ¼, Joseph — ¹³⁄₂₀₀, Furnace — ³⁄₅₀.

Have the students neatly color each pie slice a different color.

3. The student should be able to complete **Lesson 154 Practice** independently.

Worship the Lord your God, and serve Him only.
Matthew 4:10

Lesson 155

Concepts:

Coordinate graphs, circle (pie) graphs, decimal place value through thousandths', division of fractions, two-digit times two-digit multiplication, four-, five-, and six-digit subtraction, place value through billions'

Objectives:

1. The student will be able to read and interpret information presented in a coordinate graph.
2. The student will be able to read and interpret information presented in a circle (or pie) graph.
3. The student will be able to identify place value through the thousandths place on the decimal side of the place value chart.
4. The student will be able to divide fractions.
5. The student will be able to multiply two-digit numbers by two-digit numbers.
6. The student will be able to subtract four-, five-, and six-digit numbers.
7. The student will be able to identify place value through the billions' place.

Teaching Tips:

Many fun coordinate picture books may be found at your local teachers' supply store. The students will enjoy plotting coordinates to reveal various pictures. Many teaching magazines also offer these type of activities.

Materials, Supplies, and Equipment:

One centimeter graph paper

Activities:

1. Read **Lesson 155 Explanation** together.
   Have the students use the centimeter graph paper to plot the following coordinates: (4, 1), (5, 5), and (2, 5). Connect the coordinates in the order they were given. Ask the students what shape is made by connecting these coordinates.
   It should reveal a triangle. Most students should have no difficulty with this lesson due to prior experience with coordinate graphs and graphing.
2. The students should be able to complete **Lesson 155-1** independently.
3. Have the students create their own coordinate picture on a piece of graph paper and write down the coordinates on an index card. Collect these and use them as a student center in the room during your study of graphs. The students will enjoy doing these during their spare time.
4. Try to find some multi-level coordinate pictures to keep on hand for extra work. These take a lot of time to complete and the students can work on them in their spare time.

Oft a heart bowed in grief
Looks to Jesus for relief,
Seeks the Savior's loving care,
Learns to have more faith in prayer.
— Donaghy

Lesson 156

Concepts:

Range, mean, coordinate graphs, calculating the percent of a number, subtraction of mixed numbers with common denominator, three-digit multiplication, addition and subtraction of money, compare/order whole numbers

Objectives:

1. The student will be able to calculate the range of a given set of numbers.
2. The student will be able to calculate the mean of a given set of numbers.
3. The student will be able to read and interpret information presented in a coordinate graph.
4. The student will be able to calculate a given percent of a given number.
5. The student will be able to subtract mixed numbers with a common denominator.
6. The student will be able to multiply three-digit numbers by three-digit numbers.
7. The student will be able to add and subtract monetary amounts.
8. The student will be able to compare and order whole numbers.

Teaching Tips:

"Mean," "range," "median," and "mode" are all statistical terms that the students have probably never heard of. Calculating a mean is no different than calculating an average. You may want to review averaging (and averaging with remainders) before beginning the lesson. The students, however, should have no difficulty with this lesson.

Materials, Supplies, and Equipment:

Calculator

Activities:

1. Read **Lesson 156 Explanation** together.
   Go over the definitions of "range" and "mean" orally. Have the students calculate the range and mean of the following data: 90, 100, 105, 107, 88, and 92.
   Range — 19.   Mean — 97.
2. For additional practice you may give the students a set of their grades from one subject area and have the students calculate the range and mean of them.
3. The student should be able to complete **Lesson 156-1** independently.

God's way is the best way, though I may not see
Why sorrows and trials oft gather 'round me;
He ever is seeking my gold to refine,
So humbly I trust Him, my Savior divine.
— Leech

Lesson 157

Concepts:
Range, mode, mean, converting percents to decimals, subtraction of mixed numbers with unlike denominators, parallel, perpendicular, and intersecting lines, space figures, estimating products, compare/order whole numbers

Objectives:
1. The student will be able to calculate the range of a given set of numbers.
2. The student will be able to calculate the mode of a given set of numbers.
3. The student will be able to calculate the mean of a given set of numbers.
4. The student will be able to convert a given percent into a decimal.
5. The student will be able to subtract mixed numbers with unlike denominators.
6. The student will be able to identify parallel, perpendicular, and intersecting lines.
7. The student will be able to draw and label given space figures.
8. The student will be able to estimate products.
9. The student will be able to compare and order whole numbers.

Teaching Tips:

Materials, Supplies, and Equipment:
Calculator

Activities:
1. Have the students look at the first 10 books of the Old Testament.
   How many chapters are in each book?
   This data is shown below:

Genesis - 50	Joshua - 24
Exodus - 40	Judges - 21
Leviticus - 27	Ruth - 4
Numbers - 36 1 Samuel - 31	
Deuteronomy - 34	2 Samuel - 24

   Ask the students which books have the same number of chapters?
   Joshua and 2 Samuel both have 24. Explain that if we are looking at this information as a set of data, 24 would be the mode.
2. Read **Lesson 157 Explanation** together.
   Explain that the mode is simply the number that appears *most frequently* in a set of data. Stress that there will not always be a mode. The second example problem illustrates this. There may also be several numbers that appear more than once, but you are looking for the number that appears *the most*.
3. Have the students calculate the mode of the following data:
   89, 23, 75, 45, 98, 65, 89, 75, 17, 75.   Mode — 75
4. Have the students calculate the range and mean of the same set of data:
   Range — 81,   Mean — 65.
5. Have the students complete **Lesson 157-1** independently.

The Lord knows those who are His.
2 Timothy 2:19

Lesson 158

Concepts:

Range, median, mode, mean, converting percents to fractions, addition and subtraction of whole numbers and mixed numbers, rays and angles, multiplication equations, rounding to the nearest 10, 100 and 1,000

Objectives:

1. The student will be able to calculate the range of a given set of numbers.
2. The student will be able to calculate the median number of a given set of numbers.
3. The student will be able to calculate the mode of a given set of numbers.
4. The student will be able to calculate the mean of a given set of numbers.
5. The student will be able to convert a fraction to a percent.
6. The student will be able to add and subtract whole numbers and mixed numbers.
7. The student will be able to draw, identify, and label rays and angles.
8. The student will be able to solve multiplication equations.
9. The student will be able to round numbers to the nearest 10, 100 and 1,000.

Teaching Tips:

Review "range," "mean," and "mode" before beginning the lesson.
You may also want to review comparing and ordering whole numbers.

Materials, Supplies, and Equipment:

1. Calculator
2. *Worksheet 79*

Activities:

1. Read **Lesson 158 Explanation** orally.
2. Practice finding the median number using the data below:

Genesis - 50	Joshua - 24
Exodus - 40	Judges - 21
Leviticus - 27	Ruth - 4
Numbers - 36 1 Samuel - 31	
Deuteronomy - 34	2 Samuel - 24

Begin by putting all of the numbers in order from either the smallest to the largest or the largest to the smallest (it really makes no difference). 4, 21, 24, 24, 27, 31, 34, 36, 40, 50. Have the students put their left index finger on the first number and their right index finger on the last number. Simultaneously move both fingers one number at a time until the student reaches the middle number. With this data there will be two numbers left in the middle. As explained, have the students calculate the mean of these two numbers to get the median number.

3. If additional practice is still needed, give the students a set of their grades, or use the same grades given to them in **Lesson 157**, and have them calculate the median number.

4. The student should be able to complete **Lesson 158-1** independently.

See that you do not look down on one of these little ones. For I tell you that their angels in heaven always see the face of my Father in heaven.
Matthew 18:10

Lesson 159

Concepts:

Probability, range, median, mode, and mean; discounts and sales tax, addition of fractions with unlike denominators, exponents, rounding to the nearest 10, 100 and 1,000

Objectives:

1. The student will be able to find the probability of a simple event.
2. The student will be able to calculate the range of a given set of numbers.
3. The student will be able to calculate the median number of a given set of numbers.
4. The student will be able to calculate the mode of a given set of numbers.
5. The student will be able to calculate the mean of a given set of numbers.
6. The student will be able to calculate a given discount on a sales item and calculate sales tax on the same item.
7. The student will be able to add fractions with unlike denominators.
8. The student will be able to give the value of an exponential number.
9. The student will be able to round numbers to the nearest 10, 100 and 1,000.

Teaching Tips:

Materials, Supplies, and Equipment:

1. Marbles — two red, one white, one green, and one blue (or any other colors as long as there are 2 of the same color and all of the rest are different)
2. Cup
3. Box or hat

Activities:

1. Show the students the four different colored marbles. Put the four marbles into the cup. Ask the students to tell you what color marble could you pull out if you reach in and grab one. Allow time for student response. Remind them that there are only four marbles in the cup. Ask them your chances of pulling out a blue one (¼). Ask them the chances of pulling out a red marble (¼). Explain that probability of pulling out a red marble is the same as pulling out a blue marble (and the rest of the colors as well) because there is only one of each color.
2. Add the additional red marble into the cup and ask the students to tell you the chance (probability) of pulling out a red marble (⅖). The odds have just increased because you now have two red ones instead of one.
3. Read **Lesson 159 Explanation** orally. Discuss each example problem carefully.
4. If additional practice is needed, conduct this same example exercise in your room. Instead of giving the "privilege of playing the symbols," give some type of treat: have the students write their name on an index card, or small piece of paper. Place all of the names in a hat or box. Have each student calculate their chance or probability, of winning. Draw one out, or have a student draw one out.
5. The student should be able to complete **Lesson 159-1** independently.

The angel of the Lord encamps around those who fear Him, and he delivers them.
Psalm 34:7

Lesson 160

Concepts:

Probability, median, mode, mean, triangles, estimating quotients with a one-digit divisor, problem solving

Objectives:

1. The student will be able to write the probability of an event as a fraction renamed to lowest terms.
2. The student will be able to calculate the median number of a given set of numbers.
3. The student will be able to calculate the mode of a given set of numbers.
4. The student will be able to calculate the mean of a given set of numbers.
5. The student will be able to draw and identify isosceles, scalene, equilateral and right triangles.
6. The student will be able to estimate division problems which contain a one-digit divisor.
7. The student will be able to work problem solving equations with data obtained from a chart.
8. The student will be able to create a pie graph from a give set of data.

Teaching Tips:

Review **Lesson 159** before beginning this lesson.

Materials, Supplies, and Equipment:

1. Deck of cards
2. *Worksheet 80*

Activities:

1. Repeat the "name in the box" activity from Lesson 159.
   This time choose only six names (four boys and two girls). Write these six names on the board and ask the students what the probability is that a girl's name will be drawn ($\frac{2}{6} = \frac{1}{3}$).
   Then 'ss' name will be drawn ($\frac{4}{6} = \frac{2}{3}$).
2. Read **Lesson 160 Explanation** orally.
3. Take the deck of playing cards and have the students tell you the probability of drawing various cards from the deck. For example, ask what the probability is that a jack will be drawn ($\frac{4}{52}$). Then ask the probability of drawing a jack of spades ($\frac{1}{52}$). Do this a few times to make sure that the students grasp the concept of probability with several variables.
4. Assign **Lesson 160-1** as an independent assignment.

Tests:
1. Test 16 covers Lessons 146-155.
2. Administer Test 16, allowing the students 30-40 minutes to complete the test.
3. Quarter Test 4 covers Lessons 121-160.
4. Administer Quarter Test 4, allowing the students 40-60 minutes to complete the test.
5. Final Exam covers Lessons 1-160.
6. Administer the Final Exam, allowing the students 60-120 minutes to complete the test.

I will praise you forever for what you have done; in your name I will hope, for your name is good. I will praise you in the presence of your saints.
Psalm 52:9

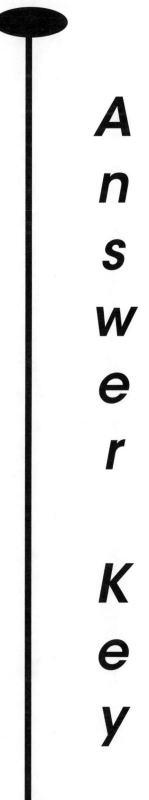

Answer Key

Lesson 1

1. 4 = addend
    9 = addend
    13 = sum;   9   15   5   11
    14;   13;   17;   8;   10;   11
     9;   10;   11;   18;   8;   11
    12;   8;   6

2. 7 + (1 + 4) = (7 + 1) + 4 -- Grouping Property of Addition
    3 + 5 = 8 so 5 + 3 = 8 -- Order Property of Addition
    3 + 0 = 3 -- Zero Property of Addition

3. 1. $\frac{3}{7}$ 2. $\frac{2}{5}$ 3. $\frac{3}{4}$

    4. $\frac{5}{9}$ 5. $\frac{7}{9}$ 6. 1

    7. $\frac{9}{17}$ 8. $\frac{2}{3}$ 9. $\frac{1}{3}$

    10. $\frac{4}{7}$ 11. $\frac{8}{9}$

4. parallel;   perpendicular;   intersecting

5. 7753.10;   85332.10;   99772.1

Lesson 2

1. 14 = minuend
    – 7 = subtrahend
     7 = difference;   9;   6;   4;   3
     6;   11;   1;   0;   1;   3
     5;   4;   1;   11;   2;   1
    10;   8;   2

2. 0;   10;   12;   0
    8
    9
    7
    9

3. 0145.78;   01244.57;   13467.8

4. one-fifth   — $\frac{1}{5}$

    five-eighths   — $\frac{5}{8}$

    two-thirds   — $\frac{2}{3}$

    eleven-twelfths   — $\frac{11}{12}$

    two-ninths   — $\frac{2}{9}$

    one-fourth   — $\frac{1}{4}$

5. *a* ‖ *b*
    r⊥*a* or *r*⊥*b*
    Any two:
    m & *a*;   *m* & *b*;   *r* & *a*;   *b* & *r*

6. $\frac{1}{2}$ 1 $\frac{5}{6}$ $\frac{2}{3}$

    $\frac{3}{4}$ $\frac{1}{3}$ $\frac{9}{14}$ $\frac{17}{30}$

    $\frac{1}{3}$ $\frac{7}{9}$ $\frac{5}{8}$

    BUILT ON ROCK

Lesson 3

1. 8 = multiplicand
    x 9 = multiplier
    72 = product   6;   27;   28;   18;   7
    49;   21;   63;   24;   42;   9
    14;   35;   12;   15;   56;   0
    GREAT!

2. 24;   24;   30;   30
    0;   0;   5;   23;   0;   231

3. ray AB   –

    right angle   –

    acute angle   –

    obtuse angle   –

4. 9; 11;   16;   15;   8
   3;   6;   0;   9;   7

5. 2;   2;   4
   1;   8;   1
   2;   2;   2

6. ⑧   10;   15;   ⑮   ⑩
   ⑥   ⑧   ④   9;   ⑨
   ⑩   6;   ⑩   12;   ⑯

   ALWAYS PASS

7. The number shaded should read 170.

Lesson 4

1. 8;   6;   4;   5;   2;   1
   9;   3;   10;   5;   11;   3
   9;   2;   7;   9;

2. 7, 7;   5, 5
   1,   5,   1,   10,   0
   It is impossible to divide any number
   by 0.

3. $\frac{2}{3}$; $\frac{5}{6}$; $\frac{4}{7}$; $\frac{5}{8}$; $\frac{1}{4}$

4. right angle
   obtuse angle
   acute angle
   right angle
   acute angle

5. MATH

Lesson 5

1. 13;   8
   13;   7

2. 12;   2;   5;   10;   10

3. 9 = multiplicand
   x 9 = multiplier
   81 = product
                63; 56; 20; 12; 32; 54
   12; 28; 12;   4; 20; 63; 18; 30

4. $1.68
   $7.75
   $3.34
   $4.50

5. 7;   4;   5;   9;   6
   5;   5;   4;   4;   3

6. Starting at top in clockwise direction:
   14;   17;   16;   12
   11;   12;   14;   15

7. 6;   36;   24
   7;   18;   72

8. triangle;   hexagon;   pentagon
   square;   decagon

Lesson 6

1. 5;   23;   0
   84;   11;   7
   56;   12;   14

2. (35 ÷ 7) + 49 = 54
   4 x (8 + 12) = 80
   (15 – 7) x 2 = 16
   (29 + 3) ÷ 4 = 8
   17 + (18 – 5) = 30 or (17 + 18) – 5 = 30
   (16 – 6) + 4 = 14

3. 8;   15;   14

4. 4 = divisor
    3 = quotient
   12 = dividend;   3;   9;   4;   9
                      7;   8;   4;   8;   5

5. 9 = multiplicand
   x 4 = multiplier
   36 = product   63;   18;   81;   72
                   9;   54;   0;   45;   90

6. 10;   45;   10;   42;   16

7. octagon;   hexagon;   pentagon;
   decagon;   square

8. $\overleftrightarrow{AB}$

   $\overline{AB}$

   $\overrightarrow{AB}$

Lesson 7

1. $n = 10$ Check: $10 + 39 = 49$
   $n = 133$ Check: $133 + 41 = 174$
   $n = 24$ Check: $24 + 73 = 97$
   $n = 76$ Check: $76 + 15 = 91$
   $n = 83$ Check: $83 + 96 = 179$
   $n = 11$ Check: $11 + 38 = 49$

2. 3;   40;   4
   91;   40;   9   A CLOCK

3. 27;   6;   14

4. 8;   7;   2;   6
   7;   8;   7;   5

5. $\frac{1}{2}$; $\frac{1}{2}$; $\frac{2}{7}$; $\frac{1}{3}$

   $\frac{1}{2}$; $\frac{1}{2}$; $\frac{5}{9}$; $\frac{7}{9}$

6. similar: b and h;   c and f
   congruent: a and e;   d and g

7. 2 gallons;   5 pints;   10 pints
   8 pints;   1 gallon;   12 quarts

Lesson 8

1. $n = 89$ Check: $89 - 11 = 78$
   $n = 212$ Check: $212 - 31 = 181$
   $n = 190$ Check: $190 - 3 = 187$
   $n = 106$ Check: $106 - 75 = 31$
   $n = 145$ Check: $145 - 126 = 19$
   $n = 337$ Check: $337 - 238 = 99$

2. $n = 65$; $n = 865$; $n = 1$ $n = 306$

3. $(45 \div 9) + 4 = 9$; $2 \times (8 + 16) = 48$
   $(34 - 2) \times 2 = 64$; $(9 + 3) \div 4 = 3$
   $7 + (20 - 5) = 22$; $(46 - 24) + 6 = 28$
   or $(7 + 20) - 5 = 22$

4. 53;   33;   27

5. $\frac{1}{2}$; $\frac{1}{3}$; $\frac{1}{3}$; $\frac{1}{5}$; $\frac{1}{4}$

   $\frac{1}{10}$; $\frac{1}{7}$; $\frac{1}{2}$; $\frac{3}{8}$; $\frac{1}{4}$

RATTLESNAKE

6. Answers will vary.

7. 2;   3;   4
   72;   3,520;   72

Lesson 9

1. 1. 20 miles
   2. 3,520 miles
   3. 3,100 miles
   4. 168 miles

2. $n = 98$ $n = 50$ $n = 21$ $n = 573$

3. $n = 151$ $n = 408$ $n = 227$ $n = 482$

4. 10, 12, 14
   3, 7, 2
   16, 32, 64

5. $\frac{1}{16}$, $\frac{2}{16}$, $\frac{3}{16}$, $\frac{4}{16}$, $\frac{9}{16}$,

   $\frac{12}{16}$, $\frac{16}{16}$

6. Answers will vary.

Lesson 10

1. 1. 6 days   2. 50 minutes
   3. 3 miles   4. 50 minutes

2. $n = 91$; $n = 25$; $n = 103$ $n = 49$
   $n = 97$; $n = 47$; $n = 747$ $n = 515$

3. 1. Palo Verde Trail
   2. Palo Verde Trail, Horton Creek
   3. Highline Trail, Palo Verde Trail, Horton Creek Trail, and Dan's Trail
   4. Six Shooter Canyon

4. Numbers with lines of symmetry are: 3, 8, and 0.

5. 6, 36, 7
   13, 21, 34

6. $\frac{4}{5}$; $\frac{2}{5}$; $\frac{3}{5}$; $\frac{5}{5}$

   $\frac{2}{5}$; $\frac{3}{5}$; $\frac{4}{5}$; $\frac{5}{5}$

Lesson 11

1. Six thousand, three
   Two thousand, one hundred forty-nine
   Four thousand, nine hundred seventy-six
   Three thousand, forty-one

2. 6;   10;   13;   75

3. $\frac{19}{5}$; $\frac{22}{8}$; $\frac{4}{3}$; $\frac{33}{4}$

4. 18 days
   270 miles

5. Mr. Smith's Answers:
   Pencils $0.25 ea.,
   Notebook paper $1.75 per pack,
   Crayons $0.88 per box.

   Mrs. Calloway's Answers:
   Pencils $0.30 ea.,
   Notebook paper $1.50 per pack,
   Crayons $0.80 per box.

   Pencils are cheaper at Mr. Smith's, Notebook paper is cheaper at Mrs. Calloway's, Crayons are cheaper at Mrs. Calloway's

6. teacher check labeling
   CD is the <u>radius</u> of the circle.
   AB is the <u>diameter</u> of the circle.

7. 101.1;   130.8;   150.7

Lesson 12

1. Six million, four hundred fifty-nine thousand, twenty-one
   Five million, eight hundred thirty thousand, four hundred twelve

2. 630 inches
   12 sheets

3. (2 x $1.33) + ($2.49 ÷ 3) + ($1.29 x 4) + ($1.45 x 2) = $2.66 + $0.83 + $5.16 + $2.90 = $11.55
   2,024 meters

4. symbol = CROSS

5. Circle 3 has all required items.

6.
8.59	3.80	4.68
+ 2.37	+ 2.35	+ 7.5
10.96	6.15	12.18

7. $3.60
   $7.47
   $50.16

Lesson 13

1. 8,254,215,754
   9,433,602,091
   20,096,000,051

2. 20 friends
   65 coins

3. $5\frac{5}{8}$;   9; $4\frac{2}{3}$, $6\frac{1}{5}$; $2\frac{1}{8}$

4. cone;   sphere;   rectangular pyramid
   triangular pyramid;   cylinder;   cube

5. 4.17;   2.82;   0.03;   0.88;   11.25

6. Total bill = $75.49
   Money shown = $383.00

7. Yellow boxes are: 24, 88, 2, 12, 50, 6
symbol = CROSS

Lesson 14

1. 50,000 + 6,000 + 200 + 40 + 3
Fifty-six thousand, two hundred forty-three

   200 + 40 + 5; Two hundred forty-five

   1,000 + 80 + 9 or 1,000 + 0 + 80 + 9
One thousand, eighty-nine

   900,000 + 80,000 + 1,000 + 300 + 40 + 1
Nine hundred eighty-one thousand, three
hundred forty-one

2. 500,064,233,902
10,000,065,789

3. $2\frac{1}{10}$ – $\frac{21}{10}$

   $9\frac{3}{4}$ – $\frac{39}{4}$

   $1\frac{3}{4}$ – $\frac{7}{4}$

   $3\frac{7}{10}$ – $\frac{37}{10}$

4.

   rectangular   triangular   cone
   pyramid   prism

5. Hot chocolate = 172°
Swimming pool = 78°
Soda = 45°

6.   59   a. addend
     + 47   b. addend
      106   c. sum;   95; 88; 163; 143

7. 27;   8;   10;   20;   42;   56
   40;   36;   81;   6;   0;   28

Lesson 15

1. CC XL III;   D LXX I
   XXX IV;   VIII

---

2. 296   – Two hundred ninety-six
   2,096   – Two thousand, ninety-six
   296,000   – 200,000 + 90,000 + 6,000
   2,960   – Two thousand, nine hundred sixty
   200,960   – 200,000 + 900 + 60

3.

1	0	0	0	6	0	0	0	0	0
1	5	3	1	0	5	7	9	2	4
4	7	6	3	8	4	5	1	3	1
7	4	0	4	8	9	9	1	4	0
5	0	0	0	4	5	0	4	7	9
9	3	5	9	8	2	1	8	2	5
0	4	0	0	7	2	5	5	3	7
0	6	5	9	8	0	0	9	6	8
9	8	8	1	8	3	2	0	1	4
6	5	2	3	5	6	1	0	4	9

4. $8\frac{4}{8} = 8\frac{1}{2}$

   $7\frac{5}{5} = 8$

   $32\frac{15}{21} = 32\frac{5}{7}$

   $28\frac{2}{3}$

5. P = (25 m + 25 m) + (20 m + 20 m) = 90 m
P = (15 cm + 15 cm) + (3 cm + 3 cm) = 36 cm
P = 20 cm + 10 cm + 8 cm + 6 cm + 9 cm = 53 cm

6. 11;   10;   10;   10;   14;   14
    8;   7;   9;   4;   5;   11

7. >;   <;   =
   >;   <;   =

Lesson 16

1. 3,742;   7,612;   12,655
   2,779;   19,682;   284,643

2. 24; Twenty-four; 20 + 4
   42; Forty-two; 40 + 2
   115; One hundred fifteen; 100 + 10 + 5
   1,620; One thousand, six hundred twenty;
              1,000 + 600 + 20

3. 44,716,225; 6,710,855; 735,320,310,004

4. $4\frac{2}{6} + 5\frac{3}{6}$ – $9\frac{5}{6}$

   $6\frac{5}{8} + 9\frac{2}{8}$ – $15\frac{7}{8}$

   $3\frac{5}{8} + 2\frac{2}{8}$ – $5\frac{7}{8}$

   $22\frac{3}{6} + 15\frac{2}{6}$ – $37\frac{5}{6}$

5. P = 26 m; P = 16 cm
   P = 70 cm; P = 72 m

6. 11; 1; 3; 1; 8; 2
   3; 4; 5; 0; 0; 10

Lesson 17

1. 87 is closer to 90
   352 is closer to 350
   5,793 is rounded to 5,790
   missing number is 5,800.
   61 = 60
   82 = 80
   38 = 40
   56 = 60

2. REPENTANCE

3. XXXIV; LVI; III; XVII; CXXV; M

4. 1,060 = One thousand, sixty; 1,000 + 60
   1,006 = One thousand, six; 1,000 + 6
   1,600 = One thousand, six hundred; 1,000 + 600

5. $2\frac{3}{10}$; $1\frac{1}{3}$; $2\frac{6}{25}$; 1; $9\frac{1}{5}$

6. Area = 25 cm^2; Area = 60 cm^2

7.

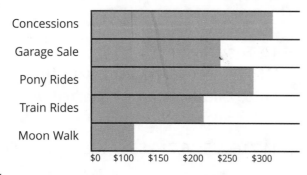

8. 3; 2; 5; 0; 5

Lesson 18

1. 2,580; 6,890; 460
   5,900; 1,100; 3,900
   4,000; 3,000; 3,000

2. 23; 517; 691; 731; 762; 8,090; 24,500;
   503,002; 513,902; 698,233
   ETERNAL JOY

3. 22; 65; 900; 4; 90

4. $2\frac{2}{3}$; $1\frac{6}{11}$; $7\frac{2}{14} = 7\frac{1}{7}$; $17\frac{6}{20} = 17\frac{3}{10}$

5. $3.99 x 3 = $11.97
   teacher check

6. Larger square = 750 m^2
   Smaller square = 25 m^2
   725 m^2 area of larger square NOT
      INCLUDING blue area.
   Total area of rectangle =
      540 m^2 ÷ 2 = 270 m^2

7. Cooking
   News
   7; 27
   Home/Decor – 16 + Cooking – 7 = 23
   News-27 – Sports – 25 = 2 more

8. 40; 22; 54; 42; 72; 15

Lesson 19

1. Yes
   No
   Yes
   Yes
   No

2. 320; 8,730; 209,330
   43,800; 6,800; 7,600
   874,000; 3,000; 1,000

3. < ; > ; <

4. $\frac{1}{2}$; $\frac{10}{17}$; $\frac{1}{3}$; $\frac{2}{9}$

   Crown

5. Answers will vary.

6.

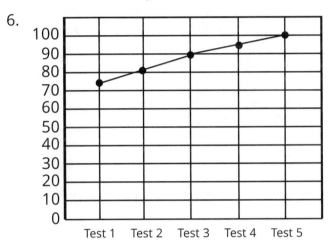

7. 69;   450;   390;   180;   276

Lesson 20

1. Profit/Loss   2015 – ($11,144);
                 2016 – $996,305;
                 2017 – $2,008,031

2. 1. $3.00 more
   2. $28.00
   3. 5 paperback books – $5.00 more;
   4. cannot answer from data given.

3. 451,210; 2,130; 8,550; 5,470; 123,210
   451,200; 2,100; 8,500; 5,500; 123,200
   451,000; 2,000; 9,000; 5,000; 123,000

4. 987,384;   943,000;   781,908
   564,038;   546,999

5. $n = 4$; $n = 44$; $n = 37$; $n = 60$; $n = 13$

6. Monday – 3 cell phones, Tuesday – 2 1/2
   cell phones, Wednesday – 3 cell phones,
   Thursday – 3 1/2 cell phones, Friday – 6
   cell phones, Saturday – 7 1/2 cell phones

7. 8;   9;   9;   9;   8

Lesson 21

1. 64;   100;   976;   1,199;   690;   254

2. $\frac{5}{10} = \frac{1}{2}$; $\frac{5}{8}$; $\frac{11}{12}$; $\frac{18}{21} = \frac{6}{7}$

3. 1 five dollar bill   – $5.98
   3 quarters
   2 dimes
   3 pennies

   1 five dollar bill   – $5.71
   2 quarters
   2 dimes
   1 penny

   1 five dollar bill   – $5.46
   1 quarter
   2 dimes
   1 penny

4. Jersey $330.00 ÷ 15 = $22.00
   Pants $375.00 ÷ 15 = $25.00

   $500.00 – $200.00 = $300.00 Balance
   to be split.
   $300.00 ÷ 15 = $20.00 per player for
   league fees

5. V = 5 m x 3 m x 5 m = 75 m³
   V = 15 cm x 4 cm x 5 cm = 300 cm³

6. __5__ thousands   __5__ hundred millions
    __9__ hundreds   __6__ billions
    __2__ ten thousands   __8__ tens
    __0__ ten millions   __2__ hundred billions

7. $n = 17$; $n = 418$; $n = 118$; $n = 65$
   $n = 14$

Lesson 22

1. 3,294;   5,359;   2,695;   1,292;   609

2.   137   279   56
      + 23   + 106   + 33
      ─────   ─────   ─────
       160   385   89

3. 1 – twenty dollar bill, 1 – five dollar bill
   3 – quarters, 2 – dimes, 3 – pennies

   1 – fifty dollar bill, 3 – one dollar bills
   1 – quarter, 2 – pennies

   1 – ten dollar bill, 1 – five dollar bill
   1 – quarter, 1 – nickel, 3 – pennies

   1 – five dollar bill, 3 – one dollar bills
   3 – quarters, 2 – dimes, 4 – pennies

4. 1. $90.00
   2. $35.00
   3. $125.00

5. V = 7 m x 5 m x 6 m = 210 m³
   V = 5 m x 10 m x 4 m = 200 m³

6. Answers will vary.

7. 3;   0;   8;   2;   7

Lesson 23

1. 79;   32;   111;   29
   51;   73;   149;   223

2. 3,141;   89,553;   921;   889
   LOST

3. Color: $\frac{13}{10}$; $\frac{35}{12}$; $\frac{35}{4}$; $\frac{16}{3}$; $\frac{34}{9}$; $\frac{32}{5}$
   FISH

4. $12 + $3 + $10 = $25
   25 x $1.00 = $25.00

   $3.00 + $5.25 = $8.25
   $20.00 – $8.25 = $11.75

5. 15,928;   15,298;   12,441;   12,144
   21,854;   21,548;   21,282;   12,540

6. trapezoid   rhombus   square
   parallelogram   rectangle
   quadrilaterals

Lesson 24

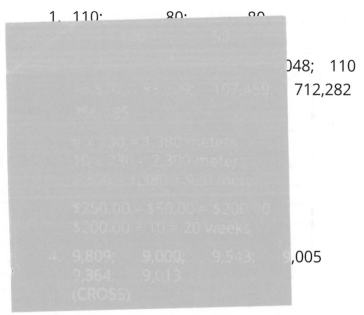

1. 110;   80;   80

   048;   110
   712,282

4. 9,809;   9,000;   9,543,   9,005
   9,364;   9,013
   (CROSS)

5. 3,346;   138.94;   26,190

6. Teacher check

Lesson 25

1. 22;   29;   24;   14
   139;   168;   226;   571

2. 100;   200;   100;   600

3. 6,240;   7,695;   619,557;   9,493
   914,450
   860,513;   1,219;   93,927;   810
   2,650
   Answer: GOD IS MY ROCK

4. 72;   76;   88;   92
   105;   88;   147;   155

5. 20;   800;   1,000
   60;   500;   3,000
   100;   200;   5,000

6. *n* = 24   Check: 8 + 24 = 32
   n = 46   Check: 46 + 9 = 55
   n = 20   Check: 22 + 20 = 42
   n = 20   Check: 20 + 15 = 35

Lesson 26

1. 4,388;   407,946;   781;   737
    6,163;   6,607;   41,049; 468,081

2. 124;   639;   273;   476
    470;   125;   778;   163

3. 400;   400;   1,100;   1,000;   7,000

4. 80;   250;   150

5.   12 = addend
    + 9 = addend
     21 = sum
            10;   25;   38;   36

6. 15;   6;   4;   2;   5

Lesson 27

1. 30;   40;   70
    300;   800;   1,200
    6,000;   6,000;   1,000

2. 215;   1,108;   133;   13,766;   97,693

3. 600;   2,400;   2,200
    5,000;   4,000;   2,000

4. $n = 3$; $n = 5$; $n = 5$; $n = 70$

5.   17 = minuend
    – 10 = subtrahend
      7 = difference
            10;   10;   4;   5

6.  – Hexagonal prism

    – Triangular pyramid

    – Hexagonal pyramid

    – Rectangular prism

    – Triangular prism

    – Rectangular pyramid

Lesson 28

1. $52.65; $428.92; $291.49; $165.46
    $9.16; $22.79; $6.19; $12.77

2. 30;   50;   10
    100;   100;   800
    2,000;   3,000;   0;   10,000

3. 99,551;   175,963; 161,060; 175,801
    8,098;   14,888; 288

4. 111;   16;   324;   106
    322;   250;   9;   7
    3;   13
    CORNERSTONE

5. 15 = minuend
    n = subtrahend
    6 = difference

    $n = 9$

    $n = 10$

    $n = 9$

    $n = 50$

6.

    Triangular Prism   Triangular Pyramid   Rectangular Prism

    Rectangular Pyramid   Hexagonal Prism   Hexagonal Pyramid

Lesson 29

1. 1. $6.50
    2. 12 – 3 = 9 + 4 = 13
    3. $3.50 + $4.00 = $7.50 $10.00 – $7.50
        = $2.50

2. $9.16; $8.62; $19.53; $31.49

3. 3,500;   56,300;   300;   400;   200

4. 4;   9;   6;   4

5. *n* = 2;   *n* = 4;   *n* = 2;   *n* = 4

6. – Hexagonal prism

 – Cone

 – Sphere

– Cylinder

 – Rectangular Pyramid

– Triangular Prism

Lesson 30

1. 1. 1 more
   2. 36 students in all
   3. 2 more
   4. 23 people

2. $114.77; $747.27; $67.11; $417.18

3. 10; 40; 40; 140; 70; 120

4. BLESSED BE THE ROCK

5. 32;   31

6. Teacher check

Lesson 31

1.

x	0	1	2	3	4	5	6	7	8	9	10
0	0	0	0	0	0	0	0	0	0	0	0
1	0	1	2	3	4	5	6	7	8	9	10
2	0	2	4	6	8	10	12	14	16	18	20
3	0	3	6	9	12	15	18	21	24	27	30
4	0	4	8	12	16	20	24	28	32	36	40
5	0	5	10	15	20	25	30	35	40	45	50
6	0	6	12	18	24	30	36	42	48	54	60
7	0	7	14	21	28	35	42	49	56	63	70
8	0	8	16	24	32	40	48	56	64	72	80
9	0	9	18	27	36	45	54	63	72	81	90
10	0	10	20	30	40	50	60	70	80	90	100

2. 4; 8; 12;16;20;24;28; 32
   36; 40

   5;   10; 15; 20; 25; 30; 35; 40
   45; 50

   9, 5;   9, 9;   2, 2
   14;   35;   16

3. 0.1   P
   0.02   R
   0.13   I
   0.99   N
   0.70   C
   2.05   E
   PRINCE

4. 35,450;   131,860;   76,110
   109,100;   62,114

5. 229;   257
   253;   317

6. 3 = divisor
   27 = dividend
   9 = quotient
   9;   8;   9;   3;   8
   9;   7;   3;   3

7. 1. 30 minutes – division
   2. $5.50 – subtraction
   3. $72.00 – multiplication
   4. $10.70 – addition

Lesson 32

1. 5;   4;   8;   5;   4
   1, 16; 4, 4; 2, 8   1, 20; 2, 10; 4, 5

2.

x	0	1	2	3	4	5	6	7	8	9	10
0	0	0	0	0	0	0	0	0	0	0	0
1	0	1	2	3	4	5	6	7	8	9	10
2	0	2	4	6	8	10	12	14	16	18	20
3	0	3	6	9	12	15	18	21	24	27	30

3. 171;   948;   833;   758
   603;   978;   154;   828
   UPRIGHT

© MCMXCVIII Alpha Omega Publications, Inc.

4. 17.93
    77.39

5. 9 = divisor
    36 = dividend
    4 = quotient
    6;   5;   8;   5;   10
    3;   4;   7;   2

6. 69,985;   79,146;   190,120
    55,787

Lesson 33

1. 6, 2, 3;   2, 5;   3, 5

2.

x	2	3	4	5	6	7	8
5	10	15	20	25	30	35	40
6	12	18	24	30	36	42	48
7	14	21	28	35	42	49	56
8	16	24	32	40	48	56	64

3. 1. liters
    2. grams
    3. meters
    4. grams
    5. liters
    6. meters

4. 3,856;   7,347;   10,432;   8,410
    12,683;   9,578;   9,821;   1,974
    2,903

    WATERS

5. 8;   8;   3;   5;   6

6. 1,000,000,091   – one billion, ninety-one

    34,000,000   – thirty-four million

    34,000,000,000   – thirty-four billion

    1,000,091   – one million, ninety-one

    3,400,000   – three million
                        four hundred thousand

Lesson 34

1. 4,158;   3,652;   2,799;   10,368
    25,950

2. green candy $\frac{2}{5}$;   orange balloons $\frac{3}{4}$

    blue candy $\frac{3}{5}$;   pink balloons $\frac{1}{4}$

3. 164;   87;   5,923
    GOD IS ABLE

4. 330,780;   324,000;   323,012
    60,545;   60,456
    PEACE

5. 108: 2, 3
    903: 3
    310: 2, 5, 10
    345: 3, 5

6. 32 = 8, 2, 2, 4, 2, 2, 2
    18 = 2, 3, 3
    14 = 2, 7

7.

1	2	3	4	5	6	7	8	9	10
11	12	13	14	15	16	17	18	19	20
21	22	23	24	25	26	27	28	29	30
31	32	33	34	35	36	37	38	39	40
41	42	43	44	45	46	47	48	49	50

Lesson 35

1. 1. 7 x 300 = 2,100 The cost is $2,100.
    2. 3 x 1,000 = 3,000 The cost is $3,000.
    3. 34 x 10 = 340 The cost is $340.
       2 x 50 = 100 The cost is $100.
       (Best Deal – rent by the day)
    4. 14 x 200 = 2,800 The cost is $2,800.

2. 60;   600;   6,000
    80;   800;   8,000
    420;   4,200;   42,000
    270;   2,700;   27,000

3. 452;   711;   848;   745;   3,808

4. pkgs: 2; 3; 4; 5
   buns: 16; 24; 32; 40; 48

5. 157   T
   219   A
   1,049   K
   49,002   E
   591,000   O
   600,012   F
   625,000   F
   TAKEOFF

6. Prime numbers: 2; 5; 43; 31; 37; 7; 5; 3;
   3; 47; 11; 11; 5; 13; 13; 17; 23; 13; 11; 29;
   41; 13; 19; 3; 3; 17; 19   YES

7. 81 = 9, 3, 3   3, 3
   42 = 7, 2, 3
   21 = 3, 7

Lesson 36

1. 1,323; 1,287; 2,492; 8,288; 6,876

2. 8;   8;   3;   2;   5

3. 18;   13;   7
   100;   20;   7
   (3 x 9) + 5 = 32;   8 x (13 - 4) = 72
   (12 ÷ 3) + 8 = 12

4. 30;   300;   3,000
   210;   2,100;   21,000
   4,620;   46,200;   462,000
   2,760;   27,600;   276,000

5. 36 = 6, 2, 3 2, 3
   45 = 9   3, 3
   25 = 5, 5

6. Prime numbers: 5; 37; 29; 11; 7; 19; 17
   WATCHDOG

7. 2,415;   2,836;   660;   4,764

Lesson 37

1. 67,640;   76,680;   305,805
   125,222;   79,272   (DOUGH)

2. 2,205; 4,307; 1,440; 513;   1,372

3. 48,979;   493,215;   1,022,441
   80,477

4. 6 = addend
   + 7 = addend
    13 = sum
    12;   15;   18;   14;   10;   11

5. 4,032; 1,664; 2,799; 2,368; 950

6. 15;   150;   1,500;   15,000;
      1,500   15,000;   150,000

7. 1. 3 x 3   – A
   2. 2 x 2 x 3 – N
   3. 2 x 2 x 5 – E
   4. 3 x 7   – E
   5. 2 x 3 x 3 – D
   6. 2 x 3 x 5 – L
   7. 3 x 5   – E
   A NEEDLE

Lesson 38

1. 1,800;   490;   4,000;   1,000
   500;   1,600;   15,000;   36,000

2. 12; 120; 1,200; 12,000; 1,200;
   12,000; 120,000

3. 13,680   54,560   384,373
   92,214   83,352   4,371
   936   4,680   816
   1,050   162   441
   225   58   75
   AND YE SHALL KNOW THE TRUTH
   AND THE TRUTH SHALL MAKE
   YOU FREE.

4. 16 = minuend
    – 7 = subtrahend
     9 = difference
   8;   9;   10;   8;   6;   3;   7

5. 22,818 A;   10,101 N;   20,046 G
   1,359 E;   348 L;   193 S
   ANGELS

6. $n = 42$ Check: $42 + 33 = 75$
   $n = 46$ Check: $46 + 53 = 99$
   $n = 129$ Check: $129 + 68 = 197$
   $n = 87$ Check: $87 + 44 = 131$
   $n = 102$ Check: $102 + 27 = 129$
   $n = 133$ Check: $133 + 113 = 246$

Lesson 39

1. $n = 9$ Check: $9 \times 9 = 81$
   $n = 8$ Check: $8 \times 7 = 56$
   $n = 12$ Check: $12 \times 3 = 36$
   $n = 8$ Check: $8 \times 9 = 72$
   $n = 9$ Check: $9 \times 10 = 90$
   $n = 6$ Check: $6 \times 6 = 36$

2. 4,200;   1,800;   1,200;   200
   2,000;   300;   35,000;   60,000

3. octagon;   square;   hexagon
   pentagon;   decagon

4. $n = 100$ Check: $100 - 31 = 69$
   $n = 187$ Check: $187 - 83 = 104$
   $n = 165$ Check: $165 - 68 = 97$
   $n = 45$ Check: $45 - 14 = 31$
   $n = 105$ Check: $105 - 26 = 79$
   $n = 79$ Check: $79 - 33 = 46$

5. $2 \times 0 = 0$; $1 \times 1 = 1$; $2 \times 1 = 2$
   $3 \times 1 = 3$; $2 \times 2 = 4$; $5 \times 1 = 5$
   $3 \times 2 = 6$; $4 \times 2 = 8$; $9 \times 1 = 9$
   $2 \times 5 = 10$; $3 \times 4 = 12$; $7 \times 2 = 14$
   $3 \times 5 = 15$; $8 \times 2 = 16$; $6 \times 3 = 18$
   $4 \times 5 = 20$; $7 \times 3 = 21$; $11 \times 2 = 22$
   $6 \times 4 = 24$; $5 \times 5 = 25$; $9 \times 3 = 27$
   $6 \times 5 = 30$; $8 \times 4 = 32$; $11 \times 3 = 33$
   $9 \times 4 = 36$; $8 \times 5 = 40$

6. 3,510 = L;   3,040 = A;   1,316 = A
   3,551 = D;   2,044 = B;   71,610 = A
   332,088 = E;   117,273 = G;   50,176 = E
   288,610 = L;   A BALD EAGLE

Lesson 40

1. 10x10;   100;   2; 2
   10x10x10;   1,000;   3; 3
   10x10x10x10;   10,000;   4; 4
   10x10x10x10x10;   100,000;   5; 5
   10x10x10x10x10x10;   1,000,000;   6; 6

2. $n = 8$ Check: $8 \times 5 = 40$
   $n = 8$ Check: $8 \times 7 = 56$
   $n = 6$ Check: $6 \times 9 = 54$

3. 800;   900;   2,400;   200
   900;   1,600;   54,000;   20,000

4. Cone: This figure has curved sides.
              The base is not a polygon.

   Cylinder: 2 parallel bases that are not
              polygons; curved sides.

   Pyramid: All faces are triangles that
              meet at a point.

   Sphere: All points are the same
              distance from the center.

   Prism: All faces are rectangles with
              two parallel polygon bases.

5. 15,124;   87,205;   50,250;
   96,099;   89,996

6.

x	5	6
3	15	18
4	20	24
5	25	30

x	5	9
0	0	0
1	5	9
7	35	63

x	2	3
5	10	15
6	12	18
7	14	21

7. Prime numbers are:
   37; 3; 11; 5; 47; 41; 7; 5; 3; 17; 41
   31; 7; 43; 19; 5; 11; 43
   19; 13; 3; 17; 11; 7; 7; 41
   17; 11; 17; 13; 2; 5; 5
   5; 23; 29; 2; 7; 11; 3; 3; 3
   CRAB

Lesson 41

1. 4 R1;   6 R2;   4 R1;   6 R2;   6 R2

2. 54;   811;   104;   559;   1,093;   35

3. 3, 7;   4, 4; 2, 2; 2, 2   3, 5

4. bus = 12 <u>tons</u>
   turkey = 9 <u>pounds</u>
   can = 12 <u>ounces</u>

5. water freezes = 32°
   body temperature = 98.6°
   water boils = 212°

6. 19th century
   20th century
   10th century
   13th century
   16th century.

7. $\begin{array}{r} 5 \\ \underline{\times\,6} \\ 30 \end{array}$ = multiplicand
   = multiplier
   = product   28;   6;   45;
                 20;   48;   56

Lesson 42

1. 18 R1;   13 R3;   17 R1;   16 R4

2. 9 R8;   6 R2;   6 R1;   8 R1
   5 R2;   2 R3;   8 R3;   3 R3

3. 74;   129;   422;   51;   445;   552
   938;   84;   134;   811;   777;   784

4. 48 = 6, 8; 2, 3; 2, 4; 2, 2
   35 = 7, 5
   26 = 2, 13
   21 = 7, 3
   54 = 9, 6; 3, 3; 2, 3

5. room = feet
   ceiling = feet
   house = miles
   football field = yards
   6 yd = <u>18ft</u>;   2 miles = <u>3,520 yd</u>
   24yd = <u>72 ft</u>;   220 yd = <u>660 ft</u>
   24 ft = <u>8 yd</u>

6. century
   B.C.
   decade
   A.D.
   millennium

7. 30 = dividend
   5 = divisor
   6 = quotient;   6;   7;   6;   8;   9

Lesson 43

1. $0.08; $1.08; $2.03; $0.80

2. 27 R5;   10 R3;   34 R7;   9 R1;   8 R3

3. 499,896;   13,978;   4,338;   3,546
   319,789

4. yellow numbers: 71
   brown numbers: 11, 5, 13, 7
   green numbers: 72, 12, 9, 10, 36, 4, 24
   62, 6, 21, 8, 75, 15, 78, 55

5. 3 gal = 12 qt   4 pt = 2 qt
   4 c = 1 qt $\frac{1}{2}$ pt = 1 c

6. 5;   15;   23;   20;   13;   45

7. 9;   16;   25;   8;   100

Lesson 44

1. $n = 27$ Check: 3 x 9 = 27   27 ÷ 3 = 9
   $n = 25$ Check: 5 x 5 = 25   25 ÷ 5 = 5
   $n = 35$ Check: 5 x 7 = 35   35 ÷ 7 = 5
   $n = 20$ Check: 4 x 5 = 20   20 ÷ 4 = 5
   $n = 45$ Check: 5 x 9 = 45   45 ÷ 5 = 9
   $n = 72$ Check: 8 x 9 = 72   72 ÷ 8 = 9

2. $1.45; $6.16; $6.40; $2.02

3. 65 R4;   69 R4;   79 R1;   30 R3

4. 406 x 7 = 2,842
   361 x 3 = 1,083

263 x 4 = 1,052
729 x 8 = 5,832

5.
536,250	582,731	80,342
+236,695	+48,046	+19,517
772,945	630,777	99,859

6. <u>5</u> Thousands
   <u>9</u> Hundreds
   <u>2</u> Ten thousands
   <u>0</u> Ten millions
   <u>5</u> Hundred millions
   <u>2</u> Hundred billions
   <u>8</u> Tens
   <u>6</u> Billions

7. 8;   7;   9;   5;   21
   10; 13; 25; 50; 75
   ALPHA OMEGA

Lesson 45

1. 340 R5;   460 R3;   697 R1

2. 285 x 4 = 1,140
    475 x 6 = 2,850
    319 x 9 = 2,871
    562 x 3 = 1,686

3. $0.61; $4.26; $5.97
    $11.00; $0.42

4. 34 R3;   56 R2;   27 R5;   78 R4

5. 72 C;   58 A;   45 R;   524 E;   23 G
    GRACE

6. 764,533,322
    122,355,789
    655,433,281

7. 1. 2016 – 200 + 350 + 250 + 300 = 1,100
        2017 – 350 + 500 + 500 + 400 = 1,750
        Difference – 1,750 – 1,100 = 650

    2. 300 – 200 = 100
        400 – 350 = 50

    3. Week 1 –   350 – 200 = 150
        Week 2 –   500 – 350 = 150

Week 3 –   500 – 250 = 250
Week 4 –   400 – 300 = 100

Lesson 46

1. 40 R3;   50 R6;   40;   105
    50 R4;   150;   110 R1;   102

2. 453 R3;   789 R2;   389 R2

3. 2,491;   2,652;   6,364;   2,475;   3,534

4. $0.88 $5.97 $4.71 $4.26

5. 22 E;   30 L;   71 E;   39 F;   25 E
    85 R;   62 I;   61 S;   63 S;   42 T
    RESIST & FLEE

6. $67.98 + 15.78 + 1.00 = $84.76
    $100.00 – 84.76 = $15.24 in change

    725 + 75 + 60 + 150 = 1,010
    1,010 x 3 =3,030 people

Lesson 47

1. 50;   80;   400;   700

2. 301 R1;   10 R4;   160 R5
    109 R4;   406
    104 R1;   305 R1

3. 2;   0;   4

4. 52;   77;   573;   363;   14

5. 36;   8;   1,000;   64;   9

6. n = addend;   25 = addend   50 = sum;
    n = 25 n = 25; n = 75; n = 5

7. 7,439;   7,101;   7,006;   6,973;   6,849
    6,513;   6,023;   5,990;   5,842;   5,680

Lesson 48

1. 24;   30

    5;   21
    30;   8

2. 50;   30;   50;   90;   800

3. clockwise from top
   104 R0;   90 R5;   120 R6
   110 R1;   72 R0;   107 R6

4. 137 R4;   122 R3;   238 R2;   455

5. 4,313;   3,267;   14,597;   102,335
   124,392   JESUS

6. 99,186;   276,790;   306,720
   258,060;   101,682

7. $n = 15$; $n = 45$; $n = 15$; $n = 33$

8. 2;   2;   22;   5;   6;   11
   1;   14;   45;   3;   5;   5

Lesson 49

1. 36 R3 $(\frac{3}{4})$ = 36.75 = 37
      51 R3 $(\frac{3}{5})$ = 51.6 = 52

2. 46 R2 $(\frac{2}{4})$ = 46.5 = 47
      42 R3 $(\frac{3}{6})$ = 42.5 = 43
              59

3. 800;   300;   90;   90

4. 0, 32;   2, 2;   6, 4, 4

5. 3;   6;   6;   0;   1;   2
   9;   7;   7;   9;   7;   4

6. 29,108 – 27,790 = 1,318 feet
   29,064 – 27,890 = 1,174 feet
   29,108 + 29,064 = 58,172 feet

   Kanchenjunga & K2 = 856 ft.
   difference is greater than 44 ft.
   difference between Everest & K2.

7. 50;   70;   190
   300;   700;   1,600
   13,000; 7,000; 2,000

8. $n = 9$; $n = 15$; $n = 18$
   $n = 50$; $n = 25$; $n = 3$

Lesson 50

1. $9.32 R2 ($9.326) is the exact answer.
   2 people will pay $9.33 and one will
   pay $9.32

   24 flowers will go in five arrangements
   and 25 flowers will go in one.

2. 43 R $(\frac{2}{3})$ = 44;   92 R $(\frac{4}{5})$ = 93
                    11;4

3. 90;   50;   20;   800
   900;   400;   60;   700

4. 10 x 10 x 10;   3;   3
   10^4;   10,000;   4;   4
   10^5;   100,000;   5;   5
   10 x 10 x 10 x 10 x 10 x 10; 6;   6

5. $n = 45$; $n = 161$; $n = 24$; $n = 4$

6. $n = 6$ Check: 9 x 6 = 54
   $n = 7$ Check: 7 x 7 = 49
   $n = 5$ Check: 3 x 5 = 15
   $n = 9$ Check: 5 x 9 = 45
   $n = 10$ Check: 10 x 10 = 100
   $n = 7$ Check: 7 x 6 = 42

Lesson 51

1. 3;   7;   2 R7;   4 R15;   6 R18
   7 R55; 6 R39; 9 R5; 8 R10; 7 R8

2. 9, 2, 3, 3, 3;   9, 3, 3;   7, 3

3. 5, 9, 6;   6, 12, 8;   8, 18, 12

4. 1. 9
   2. 13

3. 3, 9
4. 7, 32

5. 1. liters
   2. meters
   3. grams

6. first figure   –   square
   second figure   –   dodecagon
   third figure   –   pentagon
   fourth figure   –   octagon
   fifth figure   –   hexagon

7. | 28 | 72 | 56 | 27 | 14 |
   |----|----|----|----|----|
   | 18 | 25 | 24 | 8 | 81 |
   | 20 | 54 | 64 | 5 | 0 |

   MUSSELS

Lesson 52

1. 2 R17;   2 R12;   2 R30;   5 R7
   2 R49;   6 R15;   2 R29;   7 R63

2. Ravens: 16 R1, 7 R1, 9 R1, 6 R1
   Clouds: 2 R3, 4 R3, 5 R3, 2 R3, 9 R3
   Barn: 9 R2, 6 R2, 9 R2, 33 R2
   Field: 9 R4, 5 R4, 5 R4, 6 R4, 9 R4

3. /6, 4, 3, 2, 2, 2/   /3, 4, 2, 2/   /5, 4, 2, 2/
   Order of numbers may vary.

4. 4, 6, 4;   5, 8, 5;   6, 12, 8

5. 2, 5, 10
   2, 5, 10, 3
   3
   2, 3

6. $\frac{3}{4}$ inch   3 inches

7. 3 = Divisor   4   4   4
   15 = Dividend   3   6   7   4
   5 = Quotient   9   7   6   4

Lesson 53

1. 11 R30;   12 R26;   21 R4
   33 R18;   72 R4;   87 R14

2. | 7 R8; | 42 R1; | 24 R9; | 79 R9; |
   |-------|--------|--------|--------|
   | 14 R24; | 5 R6; | 26 R16; | 19 R3; |
   | 8 R2; | 9 R4; | 63 R11; | 35 R12; |
   | 7 R5; | 14 R10; | 4 R7; | 6 R13 |

   DOVE

3. 6;   9;   7;   9;   9

4. 5, 7, 11, 2, 23, 3, 19, 29, 37, 31, 5, 23
   41, 3, 13

5. 2, 5, 10
   2, 5, 10, 3
   3
   2, 3

6. paper clip = 1 inch
   crayon = 3 inches

Lesson 54

1. 7 R2;   5 R64;   8 R4;   8 R58;   7 R29

2. 5 R20;   6 R20;   3 R16;   9 R6;   7 R72

3. 1. composite;   2, 2, 3
   2. prime
   3. composite;   3, 3
   4. composite;   5, 5
   5. composite;   2, 2, 2, 3
   6. prime
   7. composite;   2, 2, 2, 5
   8. composite;   5, 11

4. ? = 12;   ? = 25

5. 26,092;   59,640;   64,271
   42,215

6. 1. $70
   2. Cake Walk
   3. $330
   4. Moon Walk
   5. Darts
   6. 100
   7. $20 less
   8. Darts

© MCMXCVIII Alpha Omega Publications, Inc.

7. $\frac{2}{10}$

$\frac{1}{10}$; $\frac{1}{10}$

$\frac{2}{10}$

Lesson 55

1. 132 R12;   132 R6;   175 R27
   641 R20;   155 R17;   193 R9
   114 R12;   135 R4

2. 21;   48;   574;   90;   147
   5,584; 6,363; 89,343; 4,764; 8,054

2	1		5	5	8	4	
	4		7		0		
4	7	6	4		5		
				4	8		
				9	0		
				3			
				4			
		6	3	6	3		

3. 5;   1;   9;   4;   6, 9

4. 71 R4;   35 R10;   19 R36   13 R67

5. 433;   172;   489;   489

6.

3	1	0	9	5	2	9	6	3
M	A	J	K	N	N	O	Y	R
	5	7	0	0	0	0	0	2
T	U	N	C	S	E	R	I	S
3	2	1	5	1	8	1	0	2
F	H	S	U	E	J	A	L	T
2	9	9	6	0	0	0	8	8
F	B	C	T	W	D	A	W	L
2	0	0	1	1	0	6	9	8
O	T	E	H	O	U	S	E	O
8	1	7	1	0	0	0	0	0
F	R	E	S	H	K	L	I	P
9	0	0	0	0	0	0	1	0
T	D	R	W	A	L	K	E	R

A SEA HORSE

Lesson 56

1. 180;   407;   208;   190
   108;   402;   609;   140

2. 236;   307;   253;   242;   133

3. 3 R1;   7 R60;   18
   9 R8;   19 R36;   66 R39

4. 54,000,000   –   fifty-four million
   126,000   –   one hundred twenty-six thousand
   100,026   –   one hundred thousand twenty-six
   126,000,000 –   one hundred twenty-six million
   540,000   –   five hundred forty thousand
   5,400   –   five thousand four hundred

5. 11;   19;   60
   47;   52;   75

6. 81;   36;   36;   8;   16;   3;   42
   14;   9;   48;   32;   25;   8;   42
   72;   12;   18;   63;   12;   20;   64
   24;   42;   28;   30;   21;   56;   18
   54;   15;   49;   80;   33;   18;   35
   I WILL PRAY AS LONG AS I BREATHE

7. 352
   266
   4,984
   600
   600
   504
   832
   A MUSSEL

Lesson 57

1. 400 ÷ 50 = 8;   900 ÷ 30 = 30
   4000 ÷ 80 = 50;   60,000 ÷ 30 = 2,000

2. 5 R4;   130;   20 R39;   340 R9

3. 11;   16;   18;   10;   12
   18;   5;   7;   8
   9;   15;   14
   WATCH TIME FLY

4. 345 –   C
   809 –   H
   1,900 –   E
   5,000 –   E
   8,900 –   T
   98,000 –   A
   890,000 – H
   CHEETAH

5. 949 R7;   764 R3;   789 R44
   1,350 R32

6. 5 + (6 x 4) = 29;   2 + (8 – 6) = 4 or
                          (2 + 8) – 6 = 4
   (25 – 5) + 7 = 27;   56 – (9 x 2) = 38
   (12 x 12) – 12 = 132; (30 ÷ 2) x 3 = 45

7. $n = 3$; $n = 5$; $n = 9$; $n = 7$
   $n = 10$; $n = 8$; $n = 6$; $n = 3$

Lesson 58

1. $2.03; $3.04; $14.00
   $0.91; $0.79; $0.56

2. 6 x 6 = 36;   7 x 7 x 7 = 343
   10 x 10 x 10 x 10 x 10 = 100,000
   2 x 2 x 2 x 2 = 16

3. 404 R4;   300;   209;   68

4. $n = 36$; $n = 41$; $n = 79$
   $n = 57$; $n = 50$; $n = 113$

5. sums colored red:
   <u>by 10:</u>   2 + 8 = 10;   4 + 6 = 10;
   12 + 8 = 20;   13 + 7 = 20

   sums colored blue:
   <u>by 3</u>   22 + 5 = 27;   12 + 9 = 21;
   1 + 2 = 3;   12 + 3 = 15

   sums colored green:
   <u>by 2:</u>   6 + 8 = 14;   17 + 7 = 24;
   15 + 9 = 24;   5 + 3 = 8

6. 1,000,002   –   one million, two
   456,900   –   four hundred fifty-six
                   thousand, nine hundred

   3,890   –   three thousand, eight
                   hundred ninety
   1,002   –   one thousand, two
   389,000   –   three hundred eighty-
                   nine thousand
   4,569,000   –   four million, five
                   hundred sixty-nine
                   thousand

7. 18   2   <u>5</u>
   1   <u>7</u>   <u>17</u>
   6   16   <u>3</u>

Lesson 59

1. 2, 5, 10
   2, 5, 10, 3
   2, 5, 10, 3
   2, 3

2. $12.00; $19.36; $12.13; $17.56

3. $479.29; $523.70; $1,598.93
   $689.59; $80.27; $220.82; $790.42
   $78.29

4. $n = 3$ $n = 87$ $n = 4$
   $n = 51$ $n = 52$ $n = 163$

5. 24;   31
   5;   21
   28;   8

6. 29 + 37 = 66   A
   78 + 51 = 129   S
   76 + 89 = 165   W
   37 + 111 = 148   A
   28 + 234 = 262   L
   134 + 167 = 301   L
   347 + 489 = 836   O
   514 + 619 = 1,133   W
   A SWALLOW

© MCMXCVIII Alpha Omega Publications, Inc.

Lesson 60

1. 1. <u>He purchased a watch for $12.95.</u>
      lunch cost = $3.45

   2. lunch cost = $4.65

   3. <u>he spent $6.95 on Wednesday.</u>
      spent $3.85 more on Friday than on Tuesday

   4. $6.00 each day

2. $4.25;　　$8.95;　　$1.23;　　$12.32

3. 5;　　6;　　2;　　3;　　3;　　11
   8;　　9;　　7;　　1;　　8;　　1

4. $n = 91$　　　Check:　91 – 22 = 69
   $n = 177$　　Check:　177 – 73 = 104
   $n = 135$　　Check:　135 – 38 = 97
   $n = 82$　　　Check:　82 – 11 = 71
   $n = 91$　　　Check:　91 – 21 = 70
   $n = 119$　　Check:　119 – 13 = 106

5. divisible by 2:　4, 20, 14, 60, 54, 10, 76,
   　　　　　　　　　98, 8, 44, 22, 4, 26, 28
   divisible by 3:　3, 15, 45, 9, 60, 54, 39,
   　　　　　　　　　33, 69, 57, 75, 93
   prime numbers:　47, 67, 23, 31, 7, 5,
   　　　　　　　　　43, 13, 11, 17, 41, 19

6. round up　–　18
   round up　–　49

7. round to　31　T
   round to　29　E
   round to　71　A
   round to　64　C
   round to　213　H

Lesson 61

1. decade
   centuries
   millennium
   A.D.
   B.C.

2. 6 R2;　　3 R2;　　2 R1;　　4 R1;　　3 R3
3. 501;　　　6,020

4. decagon;　　　pentagon
   hexagon
   octagon　　　heptagon

5. 24　=　2,　2,　3, 2
   15　=　3, 5
   　8　=　2, 4,　2, 2

6. $n = 21$;　　　　$n = 10$;　　　　$n = 33$
   $n = 5$;　　　　$n = 9$;　　　　　$n = 4$

7. 　3　=　Multiplicand
   　5　=　Multiplier
   15　=　product
   100;　　　48;　　　54
   40;　　　28;　　　45

Lesson 62

1. A.M., P.M., A.M., P.M

2. <u>triangular prism</u>:
   5　faces
   6　vertices
   9　edges

   <u>hexagonal prism</u>:
   8　faces
   12　vertices
   18　edges

   <u>rectangular prism</u>:
   6　faces
   8　vertices
   12　edges

   <u>cylinder</u>:
   2　faces
   0　vertices
   2　edges

   <u>cone</u>:
   1　faces
   1　vertices
   1　edges

   <u>rectangular pyramid</u>:
   5　faces
   5　vertices
   8　edges

3. Wednesday

Monday and Sunday both had 54°F

5°F

4. 13 R6;   15 R2;   19 R2;   80;   37

5. 72 = 9, 4, 2, 3, 3, 2, 2
   12 = 6, 3, 2
   36 = 6, 3, 2 3, 2

6.

4	9	1	3
$\times\,5$	$\times\,7$	$\times\,9$	$\times\,5$
20	63	9	15

7. $n = 6$; $n = 10$; $n = 5$; $n = 4$

Lesson 63

1. 14th
   15th
   20th
   18th
   23rd
   10th

2. Right; Obtuse; Obtuse; Acute   Acute

3. 25
   computers – 140 more
   Total of all items = 200
   40

4. 6;   2;   5
      3;   4
   POWER

5. JAMES: 6 + 1 + 6 + 5 + 7 = 25
   JOHN: 6 + 8 + 8 + 7 = 29
   ANDREW: 1 + 7 + 4 + 9 + 5 + 6 = 32
   SIMON PETER: 7 + 9 + 6 + 8 + 7 + 7 + 5
   + 6 + 5 + 9 = 69

   JOHN has a numerical value that is a
   prime number – 29

6. ? = 2, quotient = 8
   quotient = 3
   ? = 5, quotient = 5
   ? = 5, quotient = 5

Lesson 64

1. 1 hour   –   C. 60 minutes
   90 seconds   –   E. 1½ minutes
   24 hours   –   F. 1 day
   72 hours   –   B. 3 days
   120 minutes   –   D. 2 hours
   5 minutes   –   A. 300 seconds

2. 401
   107
   220 R1
   190 R1

3.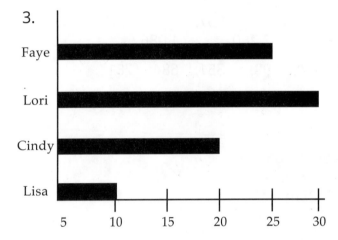

4. P = 102 m;   P = 37 cm

5. 9;   8;   2;   7
   EVIL

6. LOVE   FAITH   PATIENCE
   JOY   PEACE   KINDNESS
   GOODNESS   GENTLENESS
   SELF-CONTROL

7. ☐   –   Square

    ▭   –   Rectangle

    ▱   –   Rhombus

    ▱   –   Parallelogram

    ⏢   –   Trapezoid

Lesson 65

1. 5:15;   7:55;   11:25;   8:00;   9:55

2. 3 minutes   –   180 seconds
   2 days   –   48 hours
   1 hour   –   60 minutes
   60 seconds   –   1 minute

3. $9 \times 8 = 72$ mm^2
   12 mm $\times 20$ mm $= 240$ mm^2
   240 mm$^2 - 72$ mm$^2 = 168$ mm^2

4. 32.5 = 33;   54.1 = 54;   44.

5. 2,832;   957;   2,810
            2,280   1,086

6. 92;   93;   351;   684;   781

7. $n = 605$; $n = 32$; $n = 97$; $n = 27$

Lesson 66

1. 28th
   15
   26
   520
   1,200
   7
   369 days
   2 days

2. No
   3 hours 5 minutes
   2 hours 25 minutes
   7 hours 35 minutes

3. 180;   Not applicable
   60;   Not applicable
   86,400;   1
   48;   172,800
   120;   Not applicable

4. 64.75 = 65;   36.66 = 37;   6.5 = 7

5. Across: 1. 8,400;   2. 6,192
   Down: 3. 13,981;   4. 5,075

6. 873,263;   1,278,667;   67,896   5,123

7. 4;   1, 9;   6

Lesson 67

1. Pacific
   Central
   7:00 P.M
   9:00 A.M.

2. 3 weeks
   15 school days
   January, February, March, April, May,
   June, July, August, Sept., Oct., Nov.,
   Dec.
   February, April, June, Sept., & Nov.

3. 2½ hours
   150 min.
   by 4:30 P.M at the latest
   8 hours

4. 4 R7;   Check: 40 x 4 + 7 = 167
   4 R10;   Check: 20 x 4 + 10 = 90
   3 R63;   Check: 70 x 3 + 63 = 273
   5 R2;   Check: 33 x 5 + 2 = 167

5. 359,934;   13,080;   138,752
   613,571;   66,256

6. $8.50 $\times$ 4 = $34.00 per day
   $34.00 $\times$ 4 = $136.00 per week
   $136.00 $\times$ 4 = $544.00 per month salary

   $6.00 $\times$ 4 = $24.00 per day
   $24.00 $\times$ 4 = $96.00 per week
   $96.00 $\times$ 4 = $384.00 per month salary

   $544.00 – $384.00 = $160.00 more

Lesson 68

1. seven dollars and twenty-five cents

   twenty dollars and fifty cents

   ninety dollars and twenty-two cents

   fifteen dollars and ninety-eight cents

2. 37 R12;   18;   28 R24;   56

3. Pacific
   4:00
   2:00 in Salt Lake City
   12:00 noon in LA

4. 52
   365 (366 in leap year)
   12
   7
   Jan, March, May, July, August, Oct., Dec.

5. 2 hours & 30 minutes
   4:45 P.M
   9 hours & 45 minutes
   5 hours & 7 minutes

6. $n = 6$; $n = 9$; $n = 3$; $n = 3$

7. Winter 12,593 + 13,967 + 11,274
   = 37,834
   Summer 20,473 + 26,385 + 28,583
   = 75,441
   Difference 75,441 – 37,834 = 37,607

   $55.00 + $38.00 + $100.00 + $40.00 + ($5.00 x 7) = $268.00

Lesson 69

1. 1 dollar, 1 quarter, 1 penny = ($1.26)

   1 dollar, 2 quarters, 2 dimes, 1 penny = ($1.71)

   3 dollars, 2 quarters, 1 dime, 4 pennies = ($3.64)

   1 five, 2 ones, 3 quarters, 1 dime = ($7.85)

   2 ones, 3 quarters, 1 nickel, 1 penny = ($2.81)

2. $2.81
   $2.71
   $2.45

3. teacher check

4. 12
   5,200
   91
   520

5.

10^2 10 x 10	100	2	2
10^3 10 x 10 x 10	1,000	3	3
10^4 10 x 10 x 10 x 10	10,000	4	4
10^5 10 x 10 x 10 x 10 x 10	100,000	5	5
10^6 10 x 10 x 10 x 10 x 10 x 10	1,000,000	6	6

6. $4.55; $11.14; $7.47
       $6.80; $6.31

7. $n = 45$; $n = 103$; $n = 372$; $n = 379$

8. 784 R3;   469 R8;   386 R3

Lesson 70

1. No, answer is 405,547
   Yes, each knife is $11.00
   No, the movie ticket by itself is almost $19.00, she needs at least $10.00 more.
   Yes, this is the correct answer.
   No, the difference is $17.05.

2. .15¢ = 1 dime and 1 nickel

   $2.41 = 2 one dollar bills, 1 quarter 1 dime, 1 nickel, 1 penny

   $17.05 = 1 ten dollar bill, 1 five dollar bill, 2 one dollar bills, 1 nickel

   $11.35 = 1 ten dollar bill, 1 one dollar bill, 1 quarter, 1 dime

3. 11:00   5:00
   9:00   1:00
   7:00   4:00

4. numbers to be colored:
   22, 98, 30, 35, 14, 25, 50, 9, 2, 33, 15

© MCMXCVIII Alpha Omega Publications, Inc.

5. $10 \times 10 \times 10 \times 10 \times 10$
   100,000;   5;   5

   $10 \times 10 \times 10 \times 10 \times 10 \times 10$
   1,000,000;   6;   6

   $10 \times 10 \times 10 \times 10 \times 10 \times 10 \times 10$
   10,000,000;   7;   7

   $10 \times 10 \times 10 \times 10 \times 10 \times 10 \times 10 \times 10$
   100,000,000;   8;   8

6. $n = 188$; $n = 291$; $n = 602$ $n = 632$

Lesson 71

1. 1. V, Point V;   2. $\overline{AB}$, line segment AB

    3. $\overleftrightarrow{CD}$, line CD;   4. $\overrightarrow{EF}$, ray EF

    5. Plane X;   A plane is a flat surface that goes on and on in all directions.

2. mystery number = 21
    mystery number = 71

3. $\frac{7}{10}$; $\frac{4}{8} = \frac{1}{2}$; $\frac{1}{13}$; $\frac{5}{8}$

    $\frac{3}{11}$; $\frac{4}{12} = \frac{1}{3}$; $\frac{5}{12}$; $\frac{10}{20} = \frac{1}{2}$

4. 3 gallons;   3 pints
    4 quarts;   12 pints
    4 gallons;   9 quarts

5. B.C.
    decade
    millennium
    century
    answers will vary;   A.D.

6. 4;   19;   8
    21 R9;   16 R22;   23 R8

Lesson 72

1. $p \parallel q$; k intersects l; $c \perp d$

252

2. Point M;   Line AB
    Line Segment EF;   Ray XY
    Line f;   Line Segment LM

3. $\frac{3}{4}$ L; $\frac{4}{7}$ Y; $\frac{2}{3}$ D

    $\frac{1}{2}$ O; $\frac{1}{6}$ T; $\frac{3}{10}$ A

    $\frac{3}{17}$ U; $\frac{1}{3}$ R; $\frac{1}{4}$ H

    $\frac{4}{5}$ E; $\frac{13}{17}$ W; $\frac{7}{9}$ F

    $\frac{4}{11}$ G; $\frac{9}{19}$ I

YOU ARE THE LIGHT OF THE WORLD

4. 1. A.M.
    2. P.M
    3. P.M
    4. A.M.
    5. A.M.

5. 2 yards
    9 feet
    4 yards
    2 feet
    1 mile
    5,280 yards
    36
    3
    3

6. 3 R2;   3 R18;   5 R2;   3 R3
    3 R6;   6 R27

Lesson 73

1. 1. acute   5. right
    2. obtuse   6. acute
    3. right   7. obtuse
    4. acute   8. right

2. 1. acute
    2. obtuse
    3. right
    4. parallel
    5. perpendicular
    6. intersecting

3. A & B
    X & Y
    Point V
    B & Y   or   A & Y

4. 1. point   –   •D

    2. parallel   –

    3. line   –

    4. line segment –

    5. ray   –

    6. intersecting lines   –

    7. perpendicular lines   –

    8. plane –

5. 20;   21;   18
    15;   42;   2

6. 1998   –   20th century
    1289   –   13th century
    1843   –   19th century
    1509   –   16th century
    894   –   9th century

7. 180 seconds
    300 minutes
    2 days
    3 minutes
    10 hours
    120 hours

Lesson 74

1. 45°
    90°
    110°

2.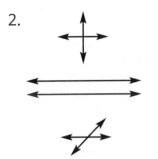

3. •K

    A   B
    R   S
    L   M
    T

4. 300 seconds
    180 minutes
    5 days
    8 minutes
    100 hours
    216 hours
    60
    60
    24
    24

5. ? = 3;   ? = 7;   ? = 2;   ? = 5

6. 8, 4, 2, 2, 2   4, 2, 2   5, 6, 3, 2

7. 25;   32;   22;   33;   31
    23;   33;   56;   78;   78
    32;   89;   33;   56

SALT OF THE EARTH

Lesson 75

1. △XYZ

    $\overline{XY}$, $\overline{XZ}$, and $\overline{YZ}$

    ∠X, ∠Y, and ∠ Z

    Scalene

    Yes

2. isosceles;   equilateral
   scalene;   isosceles
   First one is a right triangle.

3.

4. ∠R = 55°;   ∠S = 90°   ∠T = 35°
   scalene
   Yes

5. 35 minutes

   $1\frac{1}{2}$ hours

   1 hour

   $2\frac{1}{2}$ hours

6. 13 R34;   16 R35;   11 R18   5 R1

Lesson 76

1. 1.   ∠D, ∠C, ∠F, ∠E
   2. $\overline{CD}$ and $\overline{EF}$, $\overline{CE}$ and $\overline{DF}$
   3.   trapezoid;   (parallelogram)
      rhombus;   (rectangle)
      square

2. rectangle;   square;   trapezoid
   parallelogram;   rhombus

3. 1. rhombus, square, rectangle
     parallelogram
   2. square, rhombus
   3. rectangle, square
   4. trapezoid
   5. square
   6. rectangle

4. isosceles   scalene
   right   acute
   acute   obtuse
   acute   acute

5. 2,710;   7,224;   2,556
       1,462;   2,196

6. 1. three hundred sixty-five billion,
     eight hundred ninety-one million,
     twenty-seven thousand
   2. thousands
   3. 6
   4. 8
   5. 2

Lesson 77

1. 1. triangle
   2. octagon
   3. quadrilateral
   4. decagon
   5. hexagon
   6. pentagon
   7. quadrilateral
   8. regular polygon

2. teacher check drawings

triangle	3;	0
quadrilateral	4;	2
pentagon	5;	5
hexagon	6;	9
octagon	8;	20
decagon	10;	35

3. scalene;   equilateral;   isosceles

4. 1,764; 2,277; 6,942; 19,228; 29,716

5. 136° – obtuse
   45° – acute
   90° – right

6. a. 1:00 P.M
   b. 12:00 P.M
   c. 11:00 A.M.
   d. 10:00 A.M.
   e. 9:00 A.M.

Lesson 78

1. 2 cm;   10 m;   16 cm;   6 cm
   4 cm;   20 m;   32 cm;   12 cm

2. 84%
   85%
   82%
   67%

3.

  ⬚   –   rectangle

  ▱   –   rhombus

  ⬡   –   octagon

  ⬡   –   hexagon

  ⏢   –   trapezoid

  ▱   –   parallelogram

  ⬠   –   pentagon

4. 1. A, D, F, G, H, I
   2. B, C
   3. A, I, G
   4. A, D, H, I, G
   5. I, G
   6. H
   7. B
   8. C

5. 76,032;   184,008;   331,128
   548,730;   60,882

6. 7,920,000,000–G; 792,000,000–R
   972,000–A; 792,000–C; 79,002–E
   9,702–G; 7,901–I; 792–F; 92–T
   GRACE;   GIFT

7. 60

Lesson 79

1. CORN CRIB

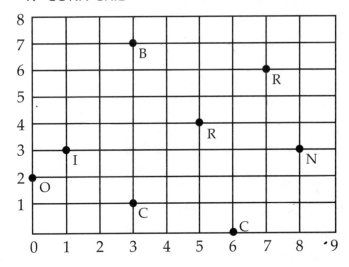

2. 1. A radius is any segment from the center to a point on the circle.
   2. A diameter is any segment containing two points on the circle and passing through the center.
   3. A chord is any line segment that begins and ends on the circle. teacher check drawing

3. square should be circled
   rectangle should be circled
   equilateral triangle should be circled

4. $n = 9$; $n = 9$; $n = 7$; $n = 6$

5. 45,000,916;   4,000,002;   27,005
   17,804;   2,722

6. 18;   14;   16;   12;   11
   17;   13;   14;   12;   14

Lesson 80

1. 1. 5 pieces of candy
   2. 8 candy bars
   3. 4 boxes

2. 1. (The drawing should have a radius of 3 cm.)
   2. (The drawing should have a diameter of 12 cm.)

3. triangle;   hexagon;   parallelogram
   trapezoid;   octagon;   pentagon
   rectangle;   rhombus

4. triangle: Polygon
   rectangle: Parallelogram,
                  Quadrilateral, Polygon
   trapezoid: Quadrilateral, Polygon
   circle: none
   rhombus: Parallelogram,
                  Quadrilateral, Polygon
   pentagon: Polygon
   hexagon: Polygon

   1. No
   2. Yes

5. 125;   64;   100;   81;   32;   625

6. 4;   4;   51;   3;   9
   8;   29;   67;   16;   16

7. 1.   60   M
   2.   40   Y
   3.   60   P
   4.   20   E
   5.   90   A
   6.   80   C
   7.   10   E
   8.   130   I
   9.   400   G
   10.   680   I
   11.   900   V
   12.   1,250   E
   13.   6,670   T
   14.   8,810   O
   15.   10,000   Y
   16.   12,780   O
   17.   16,000   U
   My peace I give to you.

Lesson 81

1. Answers will vary.

2. Answers will vary.

3. Point – Point K
   Line – DE
   Line Segment
   Ray – X Y
   Plane – A plane is a flat surface
   that goes on and on in all
   directions.

4. B.C. – Before Christ
   A.D. – Anno Domini (In the year
   of our Lord)
   decade – 10 years
   century – 100 years
   millennium – 1,000 years

5. 7 R3; 6 R2; 9 R7; 9 R3; 3 R2

6. Any 20 of the following:
   138; 87; 149; 92; 91; 133;
   98; 93; 119; 71; 81; 121;
   99; 84; 79; 111; 97; 89;
   83; 78; 124; 90; 94

7. Answers will vary.

Lesson 82

1. $\overline{AB} \cong \overline{UV}$
   $\angle PQR \cong \angle XYZ$
   $\triangle QRS \cong \triangle MNL$ $\square CDEF \cong \square LMNO$

2. yes   no   yes   no
   1   1   1   1   2   2

3. right   acute   obtuse

4. 3 hours – E
   48 months – G
   120 seconds – F
   104 weeks – B
   100 years – A
   365 days – C
   10 years – D

5. 1. 9 candy bars
   2. 5 cents a piece
   3. $7.50
   4. $190.00

6. 1. 11, 7, 4
   2. 7
   3. 11, 7, 5
   4. 12
   5. 33

Lesson 83

1.

2. Answers will vary. The pattern should
   be symmetrical.

3.

Scalene   Equilateral   Isosceles   Right

4. 437 R4   521 R4   362 R10   410 R12

5. 1. 304 bags
   2. 3 shelves
   3. $12.00
   4. $3.75 an hour

6.

2 x 2	7 x 2	3 x 7	7 x 4	3 x 4	7 x 6	7 x 7	7 x 8	2 x 5
6 x 8	3 x 1	3 x 2	3 x 3	4 x 9	9 x 9	8 x 2	5 x 5	8 x 1
5 x 6	3 x 5	5 x 2	2 x 3	1 x 7	8 x 8	3 x 6	3 x 9	2 x 6
6 x 7	7 x 5	6 x 6	5 x 4	2 x 4	8 x 9	3 x 8	9 x 7	4 x 4
5 x 8	9 x 4	5 x 1	9 x 2	4 x 8	8 x 7	9 x 5	8 x 3	8 x 5
2 x 9	6 x 5	9 x 8	1 x 1	2 x 8	9 x 1	4 x 5	8 x 4	2 x 7
6 x 3	9 x 6	8 x 1	4 x 1	9 x 3	2 x 1	8 x 6	4 x 6	4 x 7

Lesson 84

1. Triangular Prism   5 Faces
         9 Edges
         6 Vertices

   Rectangular Prism   6 Faces
         12 Edges
         8 Vertices

   Pentagonal Prism   7 Faces
         15 Edges
         10 Vertices

   Triangular Pyramid   4 Faces
         6 Edges
         4 Vertices

   Rectangular Pyramid   5 Faces
         8 Edges
         5 Vertices

   Hexagonal Pyramid   7 Faces
         12 Edges
         7 Vertices

2. 1. Congruent   2. Congruent
   3. Congruent   4. Not Congruent

3. △ABC ~ △LMN   △PQR ~ △XYZ

4. Shapes should be symmetrical.

5. Answers will vary

6. 120 ÷ 6 = 20   320 ÷ 4 = 80
   450 ÷ 9 = 50   640 ÷ 8 = 80
   3,600 ÷ 6 = 600   4,500 ÷ 5 = 900
   1,800 ÷ 6 = 300   4,000 ÷ 5 = 800

7.

					10 ÷ 5					
				4 ÷ 2	16 ÷ 4	12 ÷ 6				
			6 ÷ 3	24 ÷ 6	15 ÷ 5	12 ÷ 3	16 ÷ 8			
		2 ÷ 1	28 ÷ 7	27 ÷ 9	21 ÷ 3	12 ÷ 4	8 ÷ 2	18 ÷ 9		
	8 ÷ 4	36 ÷ 9	9 ÷ 3	14 ÷ 2	40 ÷ 4	28 ÷ 4	18 ÷ 6	20 ÷ 5	2 ÷ 1	
14 ÷ 7	4 ÷ 1	21 ÷ 7	49 ÷ 7	30 ÷ 3		60 ÷ 6	35 ÷ 5	6 ÷ 2	32 ÷ 8	6 ÷ 3

Lesson 85

1. 12 cm;   15 cm;   12 cm

2. teacher check

3. Square   –
   Rectangle   –
   Parallelogram   –
   Trapezoid   –
   Rhombus   –

4. 20 minutes
   30 minutes
   10 hours
   11 hours
   30 minutes
   24 hours
   24 hours
   168 hours

5. 7 = A;   5 = R;   4 = G
   9 = E;   8 = C
   GRACE

6.

81 ÷ 9	18 ÷ 9	8 ÷ 8	9 ÷ 3	36 ÷ 9	56 ÷ 8	12 ÷ 3	18 ÷ 3
45 ÷ 9	8 ÷ 2	12 ÷ 2	27 ÷ 9	5 ÷ 1	10 ÷ 2	20 ÷ 4	48 ÷ 8
36 ÷ 6	15 ÷ 3	64 ÷ 8	35 ÷ 7	14 ÷ 2	24 ÷ 3	30 ÷ 6	40 ÷ 8
42 ÷ 7	72 ÷ 8	25 ÷ 5	12 ÷ 2	54 ÷ 9	24 ÷ 8	16 ÷ 2	27 ÷ 3
64 ÷ 8	49 ÷ 7	5 ÷ 5	63 ÷ 9	16 ÷ 8	54 ÷ 9	40 ÷ 8	18 ÷ 2

7. Answers will vary.

Lesson 86

1. 1. 6 cm^2
   2. 3 cm^2
   3. 8 cm^2
   4. $5\frac{1}{2}$ cm^2
   5. $6\frac{1}{2}$ cm^2
   6. 4 cm^2

2. 1. 12 m
   2. 12 m
   3. 16 cm
   4. 4 m

3. cone, rectangular prism

4. Rectangular Prism 6 Faces
           12 Edges
           8 Vertices

   Square Pyramid   5 Faces
           8 Edges
           5 Vertices

   Triangular Prism   5 Faces
           9 Edges
           6 Vertices

5. 1.

   2.

   3.

   4.

6. 1,063; 1,778; 1,301; 1,132; 1,744

7. 251 R25; 411 R10; 138 R34; 121 R34

Lesson 87

1. 1. 36 cm^3
   2. 54 cm^3
   3. 72 cm^3
   4. 180 cm^3

2. 21 cm^3 4 mm^3 11 m^3
   10 cm^3 79 mm^3 37 m^3

3.

Polygon	Square	Square	Rectangle	Rectangle
Length	8 cm	10 m	11 m	12 cm
Width	8 cm	10 m	3 m	5 cm
Perimeter	32 cm	40 m	28 m	34 cm
Area	64 cm^2	100 m^2	33 m^2	60 cm^2

4. Cube   6 Faces
          12 Edges
          8 Vertices

   Triangular Pyramid 5 Faces
          9 Edges
          6 Vertices

   Pentagonal Prism   7 Faces
          15 Edges
          10 Vertices

5. 9,170 – P 1,989 – A 4,861 – L
   6,374 – O 14,132 – C 8,620 – S
   6,624 – O 8,835 – R
   CARPOOLS

6. 70

60	35	15	7	45	125	645
4	51	10	82	35	78	605
76	23	55	91	80	56	900
89	123	85	62	190	63	365
43	64	105	89	700	755	700

7. ? = 7;   ?? = 22; ? = 9
   ? = 3;   ??? = 751

Lesson 88

1. <u>first box:</u>
   Front – 300 cm^2, 600 cm^2
   Top – 100 cm^2, 200 cm^2
   Side – 300 cm^2, 600 cm^2

   Total = 1,400 cm^2

<u>second box:</u>
Front – 18 cm², 36 cm²
Top   – 24 cm², 48 cm²
Side   – 12 cm², 24 cm²

Total = 108 cm²

2. 1. 32 cm³
   2. 24 cm³
   3. 36 cm³
   4. 90 cm³

3. 4 cm x 8 cm   5 cm x 10 cm

4. Answers will vary.

5. 236   200   293   234   217   203

6. $1.33 $0.98 $8.10
   $9.36 $4.08 $0.46

7. 682,541,000,379

Lesson 89

1. 1. 6 cm
   2. 10 cm

2. Front – 50 cm², 100 cm²
   Top   – 70 cm², 140 cm²
   Side   – 35 cm², 70 cm²

   Total = 310 cm²

3. 2 cm x 4 cm
   5 cm x 1 cm
   3 cm x 3 cm = largest area

4. 1. 1 one, 3 quarters, 4 pennies
   2. 1 five, 2 ones, 3 quarters, 2 dimes
   3. 1 ten, 3 ones, 1 nickel, 2 pennies
   4. 3 ones, 2 quarters, 1 nickel,
       2 pennies
   5. 2 ones, 1 dime, 3 pennies

5. 2,498   3,868   95   261   306

6. 4 + (8 ÷ 2) = 8
   (7 x 3) – 6 = 15
   (8 ÷ 2) x 9 = 36
   76 – (3 x 8) = 52
   9 + (9 x 8) = 81

Lesson 90

1. 1. 12 possible sandwiches:

   wheat and turkey
   wheat and pastrami
   wheat and ham
   wheat and roast beef

   white and turkey
   white and pastrami
   white and ham
   white and roast beef

   rye and turkey
   rye and pastrami
   rye and ham
   rye and roast beef

   2. 12 possible combinations:
   35   39   37   59   57   97
   53   93   73   95   75   79

2. 1. 20 cm
   2. 4 cm
   3. Length = 16 cm
       Area = 64 cm²
   4. 15 cm
   5. 4 cm

3. Front – 900 cm², 1,800 cm²
   Top   – 300 cm², 600 cm²
   Side   – 300 cm², 600 cm²

   Total = 3,000 cm²

4. 1. 8 cm³
   2. 44 cm³
   3. 24 cm³
   4. 30 cm³

5. perimeter of figure A = 16 cm
   area = 15 cm²

   perimeter of figure B = 26 cm
   area = 42 cm²

6. 974   7   1,318   770   1,826   2,625

7. 1. 1,376,000 – S
   2. 1,247,581 – H
   3. 1,246,421 – O

4. 314,000   –   E
5. 14,000   –   H
6. 3,216   –   O
7. 684   –   R
8 210   –   N
SHOEHORN

Lesson 91

1. $\frac{1}{4}$ $\frac{1}{3}$

   $\frac{3}{4}$ $\frac{3}{6}$

   one-fifth   – $\frac{1}{5}$

   four-fifths   – $\frac{4}{5}$

   two-thirds   – $\frac{2}{3}$

   three-sevenths   – $\frac{3}{7}$

2. 16 R6;   29 R22;   7 R27;   13 R23

3. $\frac{1}{3}$ $\frac{3}{5}$

   one-fifth   – $\frac{1}{5}$

   seven-ninths   – $\frac{7}{9}$

   one-twelfth   – $\frac{1}{12}$

   three-fourths   – $\frac{3}{4}$

4. Answers will vary.

5. 280   850   30
   600   800   9,500
   4,000   4,000   40,000

6. $n = 95$ Check: 95 – 17 = 78
   $n = 306$ Check: 306 – 117 = 189
   $n = 264$ Check: 264 – 77 = 187
   $n = 106$ Check: 106 – 75 = 31
   $n = 267$ Check: 267 – 188 = 79
   $n = 900$ Check: 900 – 890 = 10

7. 1. •P   –   e. point P
   2. r   –   c. line r
   3. A   B   –   f. line segment $\overline{AB}$
   4.   –   a. parallel lines
   5.   –   d. perpendicular lines
   6.   –   b. intersecting lines

Lesson 92

1. $\frac{2}{6}$ $\frac{9}{12}$ $\frac{6}{10}$

   $\frac{9}{21}$ $\frac{8}{24}$ $\frac{16}{36}$

   4   25   2   27   16

   $\frac{1}{2} = \frac{2}{4},$ $\frac{3}{6},$ $\frac{4}{8}$

   $\frac{2}{7} = \frac{4}{14},$ $\frac{6}{21},$ $\frac{8}{28}$

   $\frac{1}{9} = \frac{2}{18},$ $\frac{3}{27},$ $\frac{4}{36}$

2.

   $\frac{2}{5}$ $\frac{6}{8}$ $\frac{11}{12}$ $\frac{6}{10}$

3. Answers will vary.

4. obtuse angle   right angle   acute angle

5. 2:00 P.M
   4:30 A.M.
   12:00 P.M
   1:00 A.M.
   6:00 P.M
   1. and 2.   Answers will vary.

6.

135	33	144	121	113	41	67	88	99
67	17	132	47	99	789	54	2	117
90	166	101	48	98	945	55	29	149
77	789	98	14	111	21	60	18	119
91	12	67	188	117	49	57	4	116
145	10	89	120	145	401	88	68	89

100

7. 40 R18;   54 R9;   24 R24;   43 R12

Lesson 93

1. $\underline{4}$: 1, 2, 4
   $\underline{24}$: 1, 2, 3, 4, 6, 8, 12, 24
   common factors: 1, 2, 4
   GCF: 4

   $\underline{13}$: 1, 13
   $\underline{18}$: 1, 2, 3, 6, 9, 18
   common factors: 1
   GCF: 1

   $\underline{16}$: 1, 2, 4, 8, 16
   $\underline{28}$: 1, 2, 4, 7, 14, 28
   common factors: 1, 2, 4
   GCF: 4

   $\underline{45}$: 1, 3, 5, 9, 15, 45
   $\underline{40}$: 1, 2, 4, 5, 8, 10, 20, 40
   common factors: 1, 5
   GCF: 5

   $\underline{10}$: 1, 2, 5, 10
   $\underline{20}$: 1, 2, 4, 5, 10, 20
   common factors: 1, 2, 5, 10
   GCF: 10

   $\underline{81}$: 1, 3, 9, 27, 81
   $\underline{18}$: 1, 2, 3, 6, 9, 18
   common factors: 1, 3, 9
   GCF: 9

2. $\frac{2}{18}$ $\frac{12}{21}$ $\frac{8}{18}$

   $\frac{12}{32}$ $\frac{18}{42}$ $\frac{10}{45}$

   42   35   24   36   10
   5   180   160   56   500

3. 70°   90°

4. 64 cm, octagon
   45 cm, pentagon

5. 232 R4   417   137 R40   433

6. 20th century   17th century
   13th century   21st century
   6th century   9th century
   1st century   2nd century
   1st century   15th century

7. Answers will vary.

Lesson 94

1. $\frac{3}{4}$ $\frac{1}{3}$ $\frac{1}{10}$ $\frac{2}{3}$ $\frac{2}{5}$

   $\frac{1}{8}$ $\frac{6}{89}$ $\frac{3}{13}$ $\frac{3}{4}$ $\frac{1}{4}$

2. $\underline{18}$: 1, 2, 3, 6, 9, 18
   $\underline{24}$: 1, 2, 3, 4, 6, 8, 12, 24
   common factors: 1, 2, 3, 6
   GCF: 6

   $\underline{17}$: 1, 17
   $\underline{23}$: 1, 23
   common factors: 1
   GCF: 1

   $\underline{5}$: 1, 5
   $\underline{25}$: 1, 5, 25
   common factors: 1, 5
   GCF: 5

   $\underline{25}$: 1, 5, 25
   $\underline{40}$: 1, 2, 4, 5, 8, 10, 20, 40
   common factors: 1, 5
   GCF: 5

   $\underline{54}$: 1, 2, 3, 6, 9, 18, 27, 54
   $\underline{24}$: 1, 2, 3, 4, 6, 8, 12, 24
   common factors: 1, 2, 3, 6
   GCF: 6

   $\underline{28}$: 1, 2, 4, 7, 14, 28
   $\underline{42}$: 1, 2, 3, 6, 7, 14, 21, 42
   common factors: 1, 2, 7, 14
   GCF: 14

3. 42   18   63   108   60
    15   200   270   1,400   180

4. 1. 21 cm³   2. 216 cm³
    3. 42 cm³   4. 200 cm³

5. Answers are from left to right
    and top to bottom:

    Rectangular Pyramid
    Rectangular Prism
    Hexagonal Prism
    Cylinder
    Octagonal Pyramid
    Octagonal Prism

6. A = 3;   B = 4;   C = 8;   D = 6
    E = 1;   F = 5;   G = 9;   H = 2
    I = 7

7. 38   79   17   49

8. 1. 5 days
    2. 168 hours
    3. 3 years
    4. 60 months
    5. 2 weeks
    6. 7 weeks
    7. 35 days

Lesson 95

1. <;   <;   >;   <
    =;   >;   <;   =
    >;   <;   <;   <

2. 1. $\frac{2}{9}$ 5. $\frac{1}{29}$ 9. $\frac{1}{2}$

    2. $\frac{3}{4}$ 6. $\frac{1}{12}$ 10. $\frac{7}{10}$

    3. $\frac{5}{6}$ 7. $\frac{1}{8}$ 11. 1

    4. $\frac{4}{5}$ 8. $\frac{1}{4}$

    Praise the Lord!

3. <u>16:</u> 1, 2, 4, 8, 16
   <u>28:</u> 1, 2, 4, 7, 14, 28
   common factors: 1, 2, 4
   GCF: 4

<u>11:</u> 1, 11
<u>22:</u> 1, 2, 11, 22
common factors: 1, 11
GCF: 11

<u>14:</u> 1, 2, 7, 14
<u>21:</u> 1, 3, 7, 21
common factors: 1, 7
GCF: 7

4. <u>1st house:</u>

    $\frac{5}{15}$ $\frac{3}{9}$ $\frac{4}{12}$

    $\frac{2}{6}$ $\frac{1}{3}$ $\frac{10}{30}$

    <u>2nd house:</u>

    $\frac{17}{34}$ $\frac{4}{8}$ $\frac{6}{12}$

    $\frac{10}{20}$ $\frac{1}{2}$ $\frac{45}{90}$

    <u>3rd house:</u>

    $\frac{4}{14}$ $\frac{10}{35}$ $\frac{6}{21}$

    $\frac{20}{70}$ $\frac{2}{7}$ $\frac{12}{42}$

5. Square   –
    Rectangle   –
    Parallelogram   –
    Trapezoid   –
    Rhombus   –

6. 20 m, 16 m²

    24 cm, 36 cm²

    24 m, 27 m²

7. $1.80 $2.75 $1.99 $2.57

Lesson 96

1. 1. T   2. O   3. A
    4. D   5. S   6. T

7. O   8. O   9. L
TOADSTOOL

2. <;   <;   >;   =
   <;   <;   >;   =

3.

$\frac{2}{6}$	$\frac{6}{12}$	$\frac{9}{18}$	$\frac{3}{9}$	$\frac{30}{60}$	$\frac{4}{8}$	$\frac{3}{3}$
$\frac{2}{4}$	$\frac{10}{50}$	$\frac{10}{40}$	$\frac{50}{100}$	$\frac{4}{10}$	$\frac{7}{12}$	$\frac{7}{14}$
$\frac{10}{20}$	$\frac{3}{8}$	$\frac{5}{15}$	$\frac{14}{102}$	$\frac{6}{8}$	$\frac{7}{21}$	$\frac{60}{120}$
$\frac{4}{8}$	$\frac{7}{70}$	$\frac{13}{13}$	$\frac{8}{64}$	$\frac{10}{50}$	$\frac{8}{8}$	$\frac{55}{110}$
$\frac{7}{28}$	$\frac{35}{70}$	$\frac{5}{45}$	$\frac{12}{48}$	$\frac{50}{75}$	$\frac{34}{68}$	$\frac{75}{100}$
$\frac{5}{65}$	$\frac{6}{16}$	$\frac{39}{78}$	$\frac{7}{49}$	$\frac{17}{34}$	$\frac{6}{18}$	$\frac{25}{100}$
$\frac{7}{7}$	$\frac{4}{40}$	$\frac{2}{14}$	$\frac{67}{134}$	$\frac{5}{60}$	$\frac{12}{12}$	$\frac{6}{36}$

Shape should be a HEART.

4. octagon   hexagon   pentagon

5. 2
   3
   11

6. 919   1702   955   1894
   1609   1109   1491   1332

7. 80   50   40   60
   400   700   500   900

Lesson 97

1. 1. $3\frac{1}{2}$

   2. $2\frac{1}{2}$

   3. $2\frac{7}{8}$

   $\frac{21}{5}$ $\frac{58}{7}$ $\frac{31}{8}$ $\frac{59}{6}$

   $\frac{46}{7}$ $\frac{11}{2}$ $\frac{52}{3}$ $\frac{35}{4}$

2. $\frac{4}{7}$ $\frac{2}{6} = \frac{1}{3}$ $\frac{4}{8} = \frac{1}{2}$

   $\frac{10}{15} = \frac{2}{3}$ $\frac{6}{20} = \frac{3}{10}$ $\frac{9}{10}$

3. $\frac{6}{18} = \frac{1}{3}$ $\frac{10}{14} = \frac{5}{7}$ $\frac{4}{7}$

   $\frac{2}{18} = \frac{1}{9}$ $\frac{10}{14} = \frac{5}{7}$ $\frac{13}{17}$

4. $\frac{11}{12}$ – P

   $\frac{8}{9}$ – A

   $\frac{3}{4}$ – L

   $\frac{1}{2}$ – M

   $\frac{1}{3}$ – S

   PALMS

5. $\frac{12}{16} = \frac{3}{4}$ $\frac{10}{15} = \frac{2}{3}$ $\frac{4}{32} = \frac{1}{8}$

   $\frac{10}{25} = \frac{2}{5}$ $\frac{17}{34} = \frac{1}{2}$ $\frac{7}{28} = \frac{1}{4}$

   $\frac{10}{90} = \frac{1}{9}$ $\frac{6}{36} = \frac{1}{6}$

6.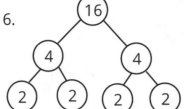

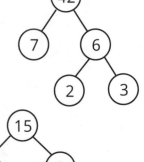

7. 108 is divisible by   –   2, 3
   476 is divisible by   –   2
   210 is divisible by   –   2, 3, 5, 10
   945 is divisible by   –   3, 5

8. San Francisco, CA – 11:00 A.M.
   Honolulu, HI – 9:00 A.M.
   Austin, TX. – 1:00 P.M.
   Juneau, AL. – 10:00 A.M.
   Denver, CO. – 12:00 P.M.

7. 189   293   90   219   109

Lesson 98

1. $3\frac{2}{5}$ 4 $4\frac{1}{7}$ $9\frac{1}{2}$

   $6\frac{3}{4}$ $4\frac{3}{9} = 4\frac{1}{3}$ 6 $8\frac{6}{9} = 8\frac{2}{3}$

   $1\frac{2}{25}$ $2\frac{18}{36} = 2\frac{1}{2}$ $5\frac{8}{14} = 5\frac{4}{7}$ 4

2. $\frac{5}{4}$, $\frac{20}{7}$, $\frac{11}{8}$, $\frac{13}{6}$,   Drawings will vary.

3. $\frac{4}{12} = \frac{1}{3}$ $\frac{1}{9}$ $\frac{3}{7}$ $\frac{4}{8} = \frac{1}{2}$

   $\frac{2}{14} = \frac{1}{7}$ $\frac{4}{6} = \frac{2}{3}$ $\frac{2}{18} = \frac{1}{9}$ $\frac{4}{32} = \frac{1}{8}$

4. $\frac{10}{12} = \frac{5}{6}$ $\frac{2}{8} = \frac{1}{4}$ $\frac{16}{16} = 1$ $\frac{5}{8}$

   $\frac{4}{15}$ $\frac{2}{10} = \frac{1}{5}$ $\frac{6}{24} = \frac{1}{4}$ $\frac{3}{15} = \frac{1}{5}$

5.

$\frac{1}{3}$	$\frac{2}{7}$	$\frac{8}{20}$	$\frac{6}{4}$	$\frac{7}{3}$	$\frac{3}{12}$	$\frac{4}{9}$	$\frac{5}{12}$
$\frac{5}{15}$	$\frac{2}{5}$	$\frac{4}{5}$	$\frac{2}{3}$	$\frac{3}{6}$	$\frac{7}{12}$	$\frac{7}{16}$	$\frac{4}{9}$
$\frac{6}{25}$	$\frac{9}{18}$	$\frac{2}{4}$	$\frac{4}{8}$	$\frac{9}{9}$	$\frac{8}{9}$	$\frac{5}{6}$	$\frac{5}{11}$
$\frac{7}{15}$	$\frac{8}{16}$	$\frac{3}{5}$	$\frac{7}{14}$	$\frac{6}{10}$	$\frac{5}{10}$	$\frac{4}{7}$	$\frac{8}{20}$
$\frac{8}{76}$	$\frac{8}{20}$	$\frac{3}{4}$	$\frac{5}{7}$	$\frac{8}{11}$	$\frac{6}{7}$	$\frac{7}{7}$	$\frac{1}{7}$
$\frac{5}{12}$	$\frac{1}{9}$	$\frac{5}{7}$	$\frac{6}{8}$	$\frac{8}{15}$	$\frac{9}{13}$	$\frac{1}{12}$	$\frac{9}{27}$
$\frac{7}{18}$	$\frac{1}{6}$	$\frac{2}{8}$	$\frac{9}{17}$	$\frac{7}{8}$	$\frac{3}{9}$	$\frac{6}{18}$	$\frac{1}{6}$

Shape should be a CRAB APPLE.

6. Prime numbers are:
   3, 5, 41, 11, 2, 7, 19, 17
   The answer is eggplant.

Lesson 99

1. 4, 8, 12
   8, 16 – LCD = 8

   3, 6, 9, 12, 15
   5, 10, 15 – LCD = 15

   8, 16, 24
   6, 12, 18, 24 – LCD = 24

   5, 10, 15, 20
   4, 8, 12, 16, 20 – LCD = 20

   7, 14, 21
   2, 4, 6, 8, 10, 12, 14 – LCD = 14

   6, 12
   4, 8, 12 – LCD = 12

   2, 4, 6
   3, 6 – LCD = 6

   8, 16, 24
   12, 24 – LCD = 24

2. $\frac{7}{7} = 1$ $\frac{2}{12} = \frac{1}{6}$ $\frac{4}{9}$

   $\frac{10}{24} = \frac{5}{12}$ $\frac{8}{32} = \frac{1}{4}$ $\frac{9}{48} = \frac{3}{16}$

3. $\frac{2}{18} = \frac{1}{9}$ $\frac{10}{16} = \frac{5}{8}$ $\frac{4}{18} = \frac{2}{9}$

   $\frac{10}{32} = \frac{5}{16}$ $\frac{12}{16} = \frac{3}{4}$ $\frac{10}{20} = \frac{1}{2}$

4. Fractions that equal to $1\frac{1}{2}$ are:

   $\frac{6}{4}$; $\frac{12}{8}$; $\frac{9}{6}$; $\frac{18}{12}$; $\frac{27}{18}$

   Answer to riddle: A BOOK

5. $\frac{7}{4}$ $\frac{27}{10}$ $\frac{41}{10}$

   $\frac{29}{7}$ $\frac{10}{3}$ $\frac{29}{5}$

   $\frac{21}{8}$ $\frac{41}{6}$ $\frac{11}{9}$

6. 2,320   3,856   4,224
    6,881   3,861   1,167

7. 45,110   51,492
    564,599   51,553

8. 1. 1,002,584; 981,456,331
    2. 99; 7,907,309
    3. 679,843; 832; 1,877; 79,476,804
    4. 222
    5. 3,576; 983,208
    6. 45,761

LESSON 100

1. 1. Flattop and Sugarloaf Mountain
    2. Lookout Mountain
    3. Elk Tooth
    4. Cracktop
    5. 5:00 A.M.

2. 5, 10, 15, 20, 25, 30
    6, 12, 18, 24, 30 – LCD = 30

    12
    2, 4, 6, 8, 10, 12 – LCD = 12

    3, 6, 9, 12, 15, 18, 21, 24
    8, 16, 24 – LCD = 24

3. $3\frac{3}{4}$ – $\frac{15}{4}$

    $7\frac{1}{4}$ – $\frac{29}{4}$

    $5\frac{1}{7}$ – $\frac{36}{7}$

    $2\frac{5}{6}$ – $\frac{17}{6}$

    $2\frac{1}{6}$ – $\frac{13}{6}$

    $1\frac{1}{4}$ – $\frac{5}{4}$

4. $\frac{6}{7}$ $\frac{2}{16} = \frac{1}{8}$ $\frac{17}{17} = 1$

    $\frac{9}{18} = \frac{1}{2}$ $\frac{8}{10} = \frac{4}{5}$ $\frac{3}{12} = \frac{1}{4}$

$\frac{20}{45} = \frac{4}{9}$ $\frac{7}{21} = \frac{1}{3}$ $\frac{4}{10} = \frac{2}{5}$

$\frac{6}{18} = \frac{1}{3}$ $\frac{20}{75} = \frac{4}{15}$ $\frac{13}{30}$

5. $n = 20$ Check: 9 x 20 = 180
    $n = 12$ Check: 7 x 12 = 84
    $n = 12$ Check: 12 x 3 = 36
    $n = 15$ Check: 15 x 9 = 135
    $n = 18$ Check: 18 x 10 = 180
    $n = 27$ Check: 27 x 6 = 162

6.

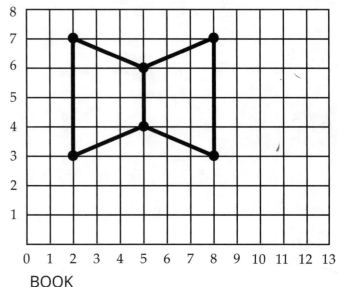

BOOK

Lesson 101

1. $\frac{3}{4}$ $\frac{3}{6} = \frac{1}{2}$ $\frac{5}{10} = \frac{1}{2}$ $\frac{7}{8}$

2. 21 is the addend and 66 is the sum
    36   24   28

3. Answers will vary.

4. Perimeter = 40 cm
    Area = 75 cm^2
    Volume = 375 cm^3

5. 6,000   2,160   10,500
    1,410   6,370   6,000

6. 6,495   6,491   6,489   6,487
    456,900   436,900   436,090   435,900

7. c ‖ d
   c ⊥ a, d ⊥ a
   point M
   point P
   segment PN

Lesson 102

1. $\frac{3}{10}$ $\frac{1}{8}$ $\frac{3}{6} = \frac{1}{2}$ $\frac{2}{9}$

2. $\frac{3}{10}$ $\frac{16}{16} = 1$ $\frac{8}{8} = 1$ $\frac{13}{24}$

3. 6   10   20   30
   12   40   24

4. Ray – B
   Right angle – C
   Acute angle – A
   Obtuse angle – D

5. 540   4,900   352   1,170   2,745

6. 10   60   130   171 = a. minuend
   200   200   600   891 = c. subtrahend
   1,000 7,000 3,000
   answer = b. difference

Lesson 103

1. $5\frac{3}{10}$ $10\frac{4}{6} = 10\frac{2}{3}$
   $22\frac{5}{6}$ $14\frac{3}{6} = 14\frac{1}{2}$

2. 3, 2; $\frac{5}{8}$ 2, 10; $\frac{5}{10} = \frac{1}{2}$

   1, 12, 12; $\frac{10}{12} = \frac{5}{6}$

   20, 5, 20; $\frac{7}{20}$

3. ∠I = 133°   △HIJ, scalene
   ∠B = 60°   △ABC, equilateral
   ∠O = 70°   △MNO, isosceles

4. 8   11   50   50   0
   25   11   33   20   80

5. 101,760   234,000   31,395
   227,360   283,128   204,417
   18,421   325,171   163,955

101,760	243,001	546,849	213,551	12,879	54,212
354,894	234,000	32,551	894,255	97,245	31,110
101,894	31,395	227,360	45,281	78,521	110,877
34,562	79,564	283,128	213,447	31,894	45,612
564,897	189,781	229,452	204,417	21,580	213,450
78,409	98,653	661,239	18,421	325,171	163,955

6. 780   12,890   210
   1,300   31,900   600
   781,000 452,000   15,000

Lesson 104

1. $15\frac{9}{12} = 15\frac{3}{4}$ $31\frac{3}{10}$ $42\frac{31}{40}$

   $\frac{5}{16}$ $9\frac{9}{12} = 9\frac{3}{4}$ $3\frac{15}{20} = 3\frac{3}{4}$

2. rows or columns colored red:
   bottom row
   far right column

3.
$$\frac{7}{10} = \frac{7}{10}$$
$$-\ \frac{1}{5} = \frac{2}{10}$$
$$\frac{5}{10} = \frac{1}{2}$$

$$\frac{1}{6} = \frac{1}{6}$$
$$+\ \frac{2}{3} = \frac{4}{6}$$
$$\frac{5}{6}$$

4. 143,000   238,000   292,500
   4,800,000 25,200

5. $4\frac{3}{4}$ gallons

6.

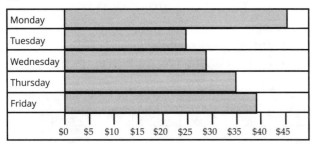

	$0	$5	$10	$15	$20	$25	$30	$35	$40	$45
Monday										
Tuesday										
Wednesday										
Thursday										
Friday										

7. trapezoid   rhombus
    square   rectangle   parallelogram

Lesson 105

1. 1   1   1   2

 $16\frac{5}{10} = 16\frac{1}{2}$ $10\frac{3}{11}$ $9\frac{2}{3}$ $4\frac{1}{6}$

2. $5\frac{7}{12}$ $18\frac{29}{35}$ $1\frac{2}{6} = 1\frac{1}{3}$

 $67\frac{1}{5}$ $47\frac{4}{10} = 47\frac{2}{5}$ $5\frac{13}{24}$

3. $n = 2$ $n = 3$ $n = 7$ $n = 10$

4. $15\frac{3}{4}$ years old

 12:30 P.M

 9 gallons

 Yes

5.

6	4	24	15	3	5	6
6	3	7	8	2	3	6
0	12	1	9	2	4	36
11	25	3	89	5	10	32
9	2	18	9	3	27	21
5	9	8	6	15	3	40
45	0	2	78	4	14	56

6. Chord = $\overline{AB}$ or $\overline{DF}$
    Diameter = $\overline{CD}$
    Radius = $\overline{CE}$, $\overline{EF}$, or $\overline{ED}$

7. 10 is the multiplicand
    7 is the multiplier
    70 is the product
    54   40   63   24   28
    12   64   4   45   21   6

Lesson 106

1. $9\frac{4}{3} = 10\frac{1}{3}$ $11\frac{11}{10} = 12\frac{1}{10}$

 $40\frac{15}{12} = 41\frac{3}{12} = 41\frac{1}{4}$

 $24\frac{46}{30} = 25\frac{16}{30} = 25\frac{8}{15}$

2. 4;   16;   3,12;   15,12,15

 $13\frac{5}{15} = 13\frac{1}{3}$

3. 5   6   7   6   9   8

4.

10 x 10 x 10	1,000	3	3
10 x 10 x 10 x 10	10,000	4	4
10 x 10 x 10 x 10 x 10	100,000	5	5
10 x 10 x 10 x 10 x 10 x 10	1,000,000	6	6

5. 4 qts = 1 gal   6 pt = 12 cups

 $\frac{1}{2}$ gal = 2 qts   8 cups = 4 pts

 5 gal = 20 qts   2 cups = 1 pt

6. 35 is the dividend
    7 is the divisor
    5 is the quotient
    5   6   9   7
    8   7   4   9

Lesson 107

1. $5\frac{5}{4} = 6\frac{1}{4}$ $4\frac{1}{3}$ $25\frac{9}{8} = 26\frac{1}{8}$

 $21\frac{7}{12}$ $44\frac{7}{10}$

 $15\frac{46}{30} = 16\frac{16}{30} = 16\frac{8}{15}$

2. $13\frac{7}{5}$ – $14\frac{2}{5}$

 $13\frac{10}{7}$ – $14\frac{3}{7}$

 $21\frac{12}{8}$ – $22\frac{1}{2}$

 $21\frac{5}{4}$ – $22\frac{1}{4}$

3. Clockwise from the top:

   $13\frac{11}{15}$ $7\frac{14}{24} = 7\frac{7}{12}$ $19\frac{7}{12}$ $14\frac{5}{6}$

4. 12 R3   10   12   11 R2   13 R2

5. 20   72   20
   16   14   12

6. $\frac{1}{4} + \frac{2}{4} = \frac{3}{4}$

   $\frac{4}{8} + \frac{6}{8} = \frac{10}{8} = 1\frac{2}{8} = 1\frac{1}{4}$

   $2\frac{1}{6} + 3\frac{1}{4} = 5\frac{5}{12}$

   $2\frac{1}{2} - 1\frac{1}{4} = 1\frac{1}{4}$

Lesson 108

1. $70\frac{3}{4}$ $19\frac{1}{2}$ $9\frac{3}{6} = 9\frac{1}{2}$

   $1\frac{3}{5}$ $1\frac{2}{8} = 1\frac{1}{4}$

2. $8\frac{3}{4}$ $32\frac{2}{3}$ $44\frac{1}{2}$

   $6\frac{1}{2}$ $8\frac{1}{6}$ $3\frac{2}{3}$

3. $11\frac{1}{3}$ $257\frac{2}{9}$ $46\frac{4}{5}$ 35

   $3\frac{2}{8} = 3\frac{1}{4}$ $898\frac{1}{3}$ $10\frac{1}{7}$ $4\frac{5}{6}$

4. $0.62 $0.89 $6.00 $1.25

5.

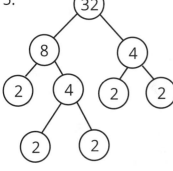
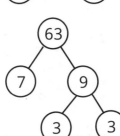

6. Across: Down:
   1. 108   1. 1,085
   2. 573   4. 587
   3. 379   5. 1,219
                        6. 77

7. 1,834   326   456   652   36

Lesson 109

1. $7\frac{5}{6}$ $2\frac{7}{8}$ $6\frac{2}{5}$

   $5\frac{13}{15}$ $46\frac{2}{11}$ $14\frac{7}{10}$

2. $12 = 11\frac{2}{2}$ $11 = 10\frac{3}{3}$

   $13 = 12\frac{8}{8}$ $45 = 44\frac{5}{5}$

   $76 = 75\frac{6}{6}$ $24 = 23\frac{1}{1}$

   $6 = 5\frac{4}{4}$ $9 = 8\frac{7}{7}$

3. Prime numbers are :
   31, 5, 11, 13, 29, 3, 2, 23, 19, 41, 17, 37, 29, 19, 3

4. $11\frac{15}{12} = 12\frac{1}{4}$ $4\frac{13}{6} = 6\frac{1}{6}$

   $22\frac{13}{10} = 23\frac{3}{10}$ $11\frac{7}{8}$

5. 4,395   10,052   78,600
   35,369   282,444

6. <u>7</u> is in the hundreds' place
   <u>9</u> is in the millions' place
   <u>6</u> is in the ones' place
   <u>2</u> is in the hundred millions' place
   <u>0</u> is in the ten thousands' place
   <u>5</u> is in the billions' place

7. $n = 6$ $n = 35$
   $n = 30$ $n = 98$

Lesson 110

1. $11\frac{5}{6}$ $40\frac{17}{12} = 41\frac{5}{12}$ $33\frac{1}{8}$

   $18\frac{3}{4}$ $6\frac{11}{10} = 7\frac{1}{10}$

2. $8\frac{19}{12}$ $15\frac{1}{2}$

   $7\frac{5}{3}$ $62\frac{1}{5}$

   $12\frac{6}{5}$ $4\frac{3}{5}$

   $4\frac{14}{10}$ $8\frac{2}{4} = 8\frac{1}{2}$

3. 49   75   114   129   63

4. $2\frac{1}{4} + 1 + 4\frac{1}{2} + 5 + 4\frac{1}{2} = 17\frac{1}{4}$

   $\frac{1}{4} + 2 + \frac{1}{4} + 2\frac{3}{4} + 1 = 6\frac{1}{4}$

   $4\frac{1}{2} + 2 + 3\frac{1}{4} = 9\frac{3}{4}$

   $1\frac{1}{2} + 4\frac{1}{4} + 0 + \frac{1}{2} + 1 = 7\frac{1}{4}$

   $4\frac{1}{2} + 0 + 2\frac{3}{4} + 5\frac{1}{4} + 0 + 4\frac{3}{4} + 2 +$

   $3\frac{1}{2} + 3\frac{1}{4} = 26$

5. Answers will vary.

6. $3.69 + $1.49 = $5.18
   $1.99 + $0.99 + $1.49 = $4.47
   Kimberly spent $0.71 more than Tom. ($5.18 – $4.47 = $0.71)
   Dinner = $24.32
   $50.00 – $24.32 = $25.68
   Jumbo beef order =
   $3.29 + $1.49 + $0.99 = $5.77
   Chicken Plate order =
   $4.99 + $0.89 = $5.88
   Answer: The jumbo beef, fries and large drink would cost $0.11 less.

Lesson 111

1. 1. 6
   2. 4
   3. 10
   4. 9

2. $7\frac{1}{8}$ $1\frac{1}{2}$ $\frac{5}{6}$ $1\frac{5}{7}$ $\frac{7}{8}$

3. $2\frac{5}{6}$ $1\frac{3}{4}$ $6\frac{2}{5}$ $3\frac{7}{10}$

   $2\frac{5}{10} = 2\frac{1}{2}$

4.

Ex:	Multiples	LCD	
$\frac{2}{3}$	3, 6, 9, 12, 15	12	C
$\frac{1}{4}$	4, 8, 12		
$\frac{1}{4}$	4, 8, 12	8	H
$\frac{3}{8}$	8, 16		
$\frac{1}{2}$	2, 4, 6, 8, 10	10	R
$\frac{1}{5}$	5, 10, 15		
$\frac{1}{4}$	4, 8, 12	12	I
$\frac{4}{6}$	6, 12, 18, 24		
$\frac{2}{8}$	8	8	S
$\frac{3}{4}$	4, 8, 12, 16, 20		
$\frac{4}{5}$	5, 10, 15	15	T
$\frac{1}{3}$	3, 6, 9, 12, 15		

CHRIST

5. $2\frac{5}{6}$ $6\frac{10}{21}$ $24\frac{7}{10}$

   $12\frac{3}{4}$ $17\frac{11}{24}$

6. 52   75   4
   150   29   7
   32   59   83

7. 722.75; 722 R6   1,274.571; 1,274 R4
   385.333̄; 385 R2   1,590.5; 1,590 R1

Lesson 112

1. $\frac{1}{8}$ $\frac{6}{24} = \frac{1}{4}$ $\frac{2}{30} = \frac{1}{15}$ $\frac{1}{21}$

   $\frac{4}{9}$ $\frac{7}{64}$ $\frac{6}{6} = 1$ $\frac{3}{16}$

2. 8   2   3   2
   10   9   6   16

3. 2 $1\frac{19}{35}$ $8\frac{4}{5}$· $9\frac{11}{18}$

   $3\frac{20}{21}$ $3\frac{5}{18}$ $2\frac{7}{8}$ $12\frac{4}{5}$

   $35\frac{13}{36}$ $28\frac{4}{10} = 28\frac{2}{5}$

4. Quotients colored in red:
   56   37   97   27
   Quotients colored in blue:
   59   42   28   19

5. equilateral   scalene   isosceles
                     right

6. 497   6,939   10,587
        39,893   12,567

7. 1. 606,892   T
   2. 547,008   I
   3. 377,962   G
   4. 98,000   E
   5. 1,000   R
   6. 977   L
   7. 917   I
   8. 97   L
   9. 7   Y
   TIGERLILY

Lesson 113

1. $\frac{20}{7} = 2\frac{6}{7}$ $\frac{63}{32} = 1\frac{31}{32}$

   $\frac{45}{16} = 2\frac{13}{16}$ $\frac{16}{3} = 5\frac{1}{3}$

   $\frac{40}{14} = 2\frac{6}{7}$ $\frac{36}{10} = 3\frac{3}{5}$

   $\frac{9}{8} = 1\frac{1}{8}$ $\frac{48}{15} = 3\frac{1}{5}$

   $\frac{39}{16} = 2\frac{7}{16}$ $\frac{275}{32} = 8\frac{19}{32}$

   $\frac{682}{50} = 13\frac{16}{25}$ $\frac{144}{56} = 2\frac{4}{7}$

2. $\frac{1}{24}$ $\frac{2}{21}$ $\frac{2}{84} = \frac{1}{42}$ $\frac{4}{35}$

   $\frac{6}{15} = \frac{2}{5}$ $\frac{42}{99} = \frac{14}{33}$ $\frac{26}{5} = 5\frac{1}{5}$ $\frac{15}{28}$

3. $3.73   3 ones, 2 quarters, 2 dimes,
            3 pennies
   $5.78   1 five, 3 quarters, 3 pennies
   $3.65   3 ones, 2 quarters, 1 dime,
            1 nickel
   $14.01   1 ten, 4 ones, 1 penny
   $10.01   1 ten, 1 penny

4. 4   7   5   9
   16   20   6   27
   12   45   10   3

5. $n = 273$ Check: 273 – 75 = 198
   $n = 267$ Check: 267 – 56 = 211
   $n = 230$ Check: 230 – 43 = 187
   $n = 116$ Check: 116 – 75 = 41
   $n = 516$ Check: 516 – 326 = 190
   $n = 301$ Check: 301 – 208 = 93

6.

135	189	113	234	512	344
B	D	R	O	K	E
199	312	117	150	250	249
G	B	G	W	L	O
176	190	211	144	117	261
O	D	S	F	T	E

DOGWOODS

7. A. 150°
   B. 35°
   C. 70°

Lesson 114

1.

		$3 \div \frac{1}{3} = 9$	$3 \times \frac{3}{1} = 9$
		$4 \div \frac{1}{2} = 8$	$4 \times \frac{2}{1} = 8$
How many halves are in three?			$3 \times \frac{2}{1} = 6$
	▥ ▥		$2 \times \frac{5}{1} = 10$
How many eighths are in two?		$2 \div \frac{1}{8} = 16$	

2. $\frac{136}{42} = 3\frac{10}{42} = 3\frac{5}{21}$ $\frac{28}{12} = 2\frac{4}{12} = 2\frac{1}{3}$

   $\frac{121}{40} = 3\frac{1}{40}$ $\frac{50}{6} = 8\frac{2}{6} = 8\frac{1}{3}$

3.

$\frac{1}{6}$	$\frac{2}{3}$	$\frac{2}{21}$	$\frac{1}{2}$	$\frac{2}{9}$
B	L	A	N	S
$\frac{2}{35}$	$\frac{3}{28}$	$\frac{3}{5}$	$\frac{1}{15}$	$\frac{1}{16}$
E	B	R	A	L
$\frac{1}{24}$	$\frac{2}{3}$	$\frac{2}{15}$	$\frac{24}{35}$	$\frac{1}{3}$
L	O	D	L	I
$\frac{6}{35}$	$\frac{1}{36}$	$\frac{8}{15}$	$\frac{1}{16}$	$\frac{5}{9}$
A	M	R	O	P
$\frac{1}{12}$	$\frac{1}{2}$	$\frac{2}{21}$	$\frac{4}{5}$	$\frac{8}{63}$
N	E	D	R	S

BASEBALL DIAMONDS

4. 33   25   11
   14   19   10

5. 945   2,688   2,706
   1,880 1,816   760

6. 4,000   2,000   1,000
   4,000   10,000   6,000
   1,000   2,000   5,000
   9,000   3,000   2,000

7. 5   9   2
    12   10   8
    4   3   11
    20   21   18
    14   33   5
    5   6   24

Lesson 115

1. $\frac{3}{21} = \frac{1}{7}$ $\frac{1}{20}$ $\frac{2}{35}$ $\frac{1}{48}$

   $\frac{4}{6} = \frac{2}{3}$ $\frac{8}{20} = \frac{2}{5}$ $\frac{10}{15} = \frac{2}{3}$ $\frac{5}{8}$

   $\frac{15}{42} = \frac{5}{14}$ $\frac{16}{10} = 1\frac{6}{10} = 1\frac{3}{5}$ $\frac{14}{15}$

   $\frac{7}{16}$

2. 18   27   0   14
   8   24   45
   TOOTHPASTE

3. $\frac{99}{16} = 6\frac{3}{16}$ $\frac{75}{16} = 4\frac{11}{16}$ $\frac{99}{56} = 1\frac{43}{56}$

   $\frac{108}{24} = 4\frac{12}{24} = 4\frac{1}{2}$ $\frac{65}{24} = 2\frac{17}{24}$

   $\frac{119}{50} = 2\frac{19}{50}$

4. $\frac{1}{21}$ $\frac{12}{77}$ $\frac{21}{32}$ $\frac{3}{6} = \frac{1}{2}$

   $\frac{8}{54} = \frac{4}{27}$ $\frac{7}{7} = 1$ $\frac{10}{3} = 3\frac{1}{3}$

   $\frac{16}{15} = 1\frac{1}{15}$

5. 25   135
   63   319

6. 43,800   189,950   49,560
    122,780   438,000   1,899,500
    495,600   1,227,800   4,380,000
    18,995,000 4,956,000   12,278,000

7. 1. 18 windows
   2. 6 curtains

Lesson 116

1. $\frac{30}{7} = 4\frac{2}{7}$ $\frac{56}{5} = 11\frac{1}{5}$

   $\frac{6}{5} = 1\frac{1}{5}$ $\frac{28}{8} = 3\frac{1}{2}$

   $\frac{8}{3} = 2\frac{2}{3}$ $\frac{32}{15} = 2\frac{2}{15}$

   $\frac{30}{10} = 3$ $\frac{20}{2} = 10$

2. $\frac{5}{42}$ A $\frac{9}{10}$ C

   $\frac{2}{35}$ O $\frac{1}{28}$ M

   $\frac{5}{24}$ B

   A COMB

3. 1. $1\frac{1}{4}$ ice cream sandwiches

   2. $\frac{3}{16}$ of a bottle

4.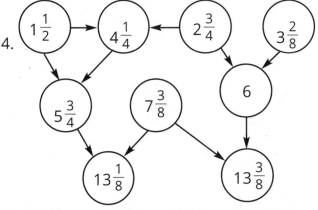

5. 8 R19   12 R24   17 R8   23 R22

6. Answers clockwise from top:
   1,080; 1,512; 1,917; 1,323

   Answers clockwise from top:
   442; 325; 234; 611

7. 8   99   4   7

Lesson 117

1. 1. 3 to 2; 3:2; $\frac{3}{2}$

   2. 3 to 1; 3:1; $\frac{3}{1}$

   3. 4 to 2; 4:2; $\frac{4}{2}$

2. 1. $\frac{2}{4}$

   2. $\frac{2}{7}$

   3. $\frac{1}{7}$

   4. $\frac{3}{7}$

   5. $\frac{1}{3}$

3. $\frac{6}{1} = 6$ $\frac{28}{1} = 28$ $\frac{18}{1} = 18$

   $\frac{84}{1} = 84$ $\frac{12}{1} = 12$ $\frac{24}{1} = 24$

   $\frac{2}{1} = 2$ $\frac{24}{1} = 24$ $\frac{15}{1} = 15$

   $\frac{8}{1} = 8$ $\frac{36}{1} = 36$ $\frac{11}{1} = 11$

4.

$\frac{2}{35}$ A	$\frac{1}{21}$ R	$\frac{1}{28}$ B	$\frac{3}{14}$ Z	$\frac{5}{28}$ M
$\frac{3}{20}$ K	$\frac{3}{4}$ W	$\frac{1}{16}$ L	$\frac{3}{8}$ I	$\frac{5}{16}$ J
3 A	$\frac{1}{18}$ E	$\frac{1}{4}$ T	$\frac{3}{4}$ C	$\frac{5}{24}$ P
$\frac{3}{42}$ H	$\frac{1}{24}$ Z	$\frac{1}{32}$ F	$\frac{5}{16}$ D	$\frac{5}{32}$ I
$\frac{3}{10}$ U	6 O	$\frac{1}{8}$ M	$\frac{3}{4}$ K	$1\frac{1}{2}$ G

A WATCH DOG

5. $\frac{6}{5} = 1\frac{1}{5}$ $\frac{8}{8} = 1$ $\frac{24}{5} = 4\frac{4}{5}$

   $\frac{12}{2} = 6$ 9 $\frac{30}{9} = 3\frac{1}{3}$

   $\frac{8}{3} = 2\frac{2}{3}$ $\frac{36}{8} = 4\frac{1}{2}$

6. 49,403   359,744   62,712
   383,990   135,660

7. 6 – N   9 – I   6 – N
   3 – E   8 – C   3 – E
   6 – N   5 – T   7 – S
   NINE CENTS

Lesson 118

1. Trucks/Wheels

1	2	3	4	5	6
18	36	54	72	90	108

   Drink Mix/Water

1	2	3	4	5
3	6	9	12	15

   Fertilizer/Trees

2	4	6	8	10	12
7	14	21	28	35	42

2. 1. $\frac{2}{4}$

   2. $\frac{4}{2}$

   3. $\frac{2}{7}$

   4. $\frac{4}{7}$

   5. $\frac{1}{2}$

   6. $\frac{1}{4}$

   7. $\frac{1}{7}$

3. $\frac{28}{7} = 4$ $\frac{28}{3} = 9\frac{1}{3}$ $\frac{30}{5} = 6$

$\frac{32}{8} = 4$ $\frac{20}{1} = 20$ $\frac{36}{7} = 5\frac{1}{7}$

$\frac{100}{20} = 5$ $\frac{35}{3} = 11\frac{2}{3}$

4. 21   72   0   70
   44   81   63   48

5. $\frac{1}{16}$ $\frac{1}{28}$

   $\frac{4}{15}$ $\frac{7}{12}$

   $\frac{19}{12} = 1\frac{7}{12}$ $\frac{7}{20}$

   $\frac{2}{18} = \frac{1}{9}$ $\frac{6}{12} = \frac{1}{2}$

   $\frac{34}{28} = 1\frac{6}{28} = 1\frac{3}{14}$ $\frac{10}{8} = 1\frac{2}{8} = 1\frac{1}{4}$

   $\frac{1}{2}$ – L

   $\frac{7}{20}$ – I

   $\frac{4}{15}$ – G

   $\frac{1}{28}$ – H

   $1\frac{1}{4}$ – T

   $1\frac{3}{14}$ – H

   $\frac{1}{16}$ – O

   $\frac{1}{9}$ – U

   $1\frac{7}{12}$ – S

   $\frac{7}{12}$ – E

   LIGHTHOUSE

6. $n = 8$ Check: 3 x 8 = 20 + 4

   $n = 12$ Check: 12 x 12 = 89 + 55

$n = 9$ Check: 4 x 9 = 33 + 3

$n = 8$ Check: 8 x 8 = 112 – 48

$n = 9$ Check: 7 x 9 = 12 + 51

$n = 11$ Check: 11 x 11 = 188 – 67

Lesson 119

1. Answers may vary

$\frac{40}{20}, \frac{20}{10}$ $\frac{7}{14}, \frac{1}{2}$

$\frac{5}{25}, \frac{1}{5}$ $\frac{72}{8}, \frac{63}{7}$

Runners/Teams

40	36	32	28	24	20
10	9	8	7	6	5

2. $\frac{4}{20} = \frac{6}{30}$ $\frac{9}{21} = \frac{12}{28}$ $\frac{8}{32} = \frac{12}{48}$

Cheese/Teams

2	4	6	8	10	12
3	6	9	12	15	18

3. 1. $4.00
   2. $5.00
   3. $1.00
   4. $1.50
   5. 6 quarts

4. 1. $\frac{1}{18}$ – R

   2. $\frac{2}{18}$ – A

   3. $\frac{2}{9} = \frac{4}{18}$ – T

   4. $\frac{1}{3} = \frac{6}{18}$ – T

   5. $\frac{4}{9} = \frac{8}{18}$ – L

   6. $\frac{9}{18}$ – E

   7. $\frac{5}{9} = \frac{10}{18}$ – S

8. $\frac{7}{9} = \frac{14}{18}$ – N

9. $\frac{15}{18}$ – A

10. $\frac{8}{9} = \frac{16}{18}$ – K

11. $\frac{17}{18}$ – E

RATTLESNAKE

5. 456   2,133   1,302   4,473   3,420
   374   2,337   1,691   1,219   3,431

6. 29 R21;   22 R1;   21 R7;   41 R16
   19 R9;   30 R10;   6 R26;   9 R16

7. 10

Lesson 120

1. yes   no
   yes   no
   yes   yes
   yes   yes

2. Peanut Butter Cups/Scoops of Ice Cream

4	6	8	10	12	14
2	3	4	5	6	7

Cookies/Scoops of Ice Cream

3	6	9	12	15	18
1	2	3	4	5	6

Eggs/Cartons

72	60	48	36	24	12
6	5	4	3	2	1

3.   16   25   9
   343   8   27
    36   100   1,000

4. Across   Down
   1. 4,856   2. 6,188
   3. 1,482   4. 8,273
   5. 8,033   6. 8,120
   7. 6,741   8. 3,871

5. <   =   <   >
   =   =   >   =
   >   =   >   =

6. $n = 6$ Check: 6 x 6 = 100 – 64

    $n = 8$ Check: 9 x 8 = 134 – 62

    $n = 4$ Check: 4 x 4 = 121 – 105

    $n = 4$ Check: 8 x 4 = 46 – 14

    $n = 3$ Check: 7 x 3 = 156 – 135

    $n = 9$ Check: 9 x 9 = 956 – 875

Lesson 121

1. 1.7 –   one and seven tenths
    0.5 –   five tenths
    3.9 –   three and nine tenths
    1.2 –   one and two tenths

2. 357.1

3. Shaded areas are:
    1 hour, 1 minute, 48 hours, 2 hours
    1 week, a fish shape

4. 422 R8;   111 R28
    152 R33;   165 R45

5. $8\frac{5}{4} = 9\frac{1}{4}$ $6\frac{25}{20} = 7\frac{1}{4}$

    $25\frac{9}{6} = 26\frac{1}{2}$ $16\frac{31}{15} = 18\frac{1}{15}$

Lesson 122

1. 1.27
    1.86
    .95

2. 3.4 –   three and four tenths
    1.4 –   one and four tenths
    5.9 –   five and nine tenths
    2.7 –   two and seven tenths

3. A.M.   P.M   P.M

4. 20th   18th   15th
    13th   17th

5. 36 R13 should be 306 R13
    320 R1 should be 302 R0
    208 R5 should be 208 R25

6. Prime numbers are:
    11, 13, 23, 7, 19
    MERCY

7. 107,092   267,605
    181,421   210,585

8. $1\frac{3}{7}$ $5\frac{2}{4} = 5\frac{1}{2}$ $10\frac{2}{15}$

    $50\frac{5}{19}$ $4\frac{6}{10} = 4\frac{3}{5}$

Lesson 123

1. six hundred nine thousandths
    four and seventy thousandths
    six and three thousandths
    thirty-one thousandths

2. 26.84

3. 12   15   12   40

4. $19.43 $11.50 $78.10 $4.60
    $71.15 $18.28 $13.75 $2.33
    $46.11 $34.59

5. $3\frac{3}{10}$ $2\frac{18}{70} = 2\frac{9}{35}$

    $11\frac{14}{30} = 11\frac{7}{15}$ $45\frac{1}{16}$

6. 1   2   0   60   1
    53   5   30   5

7.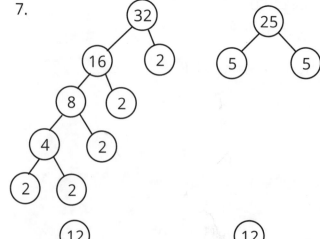

    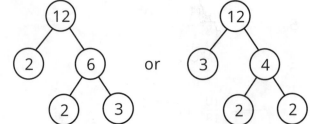

Lesson 124

1. <   >   >   >
   <   >   =

2. Shaded areas are:
   .295;   .255;   .002;

3. △   □   ○
   .372;   .309;   .218
   .309;   .204   .204
   .323;   .289

4. 2.272

5. $12.32 $2.43 $0.16 $6.41

6. 50   4   22   5

7. –   20   72   24   49   18
   24   10   14   48   63   32

Lesson 125

1. 6   18   12   9
   0.3   22.5   35.2   1.1

2. .407   .441   .559   .601
   .328   .331   .336   .342

3. Colored yellow: .421
   Colored purple: .09, 2.19, 5.39
   Colored brown: .102, 1.512, .182, .002

4. 697;   1,442 R4;   2,045   205

5. 945; 3,575; 936; 868; 1,581; 1,175

6. $\frac{1}{6}$ $\frac{2}{20} = \frac{1}{10}$ $\frac{8}{15}$ $\frac{6}{56} = \frac{3}{28}$

7. 12   10   12   10   12   7
   16   13   10   10   17   12

Lesson 126

1. 62   3   24
   5   81   85

2. 6   12   11   198   57

3. 4.4   4.2   4.0   3.6   3.4
   23.254   23.250   22.965
   21.210   21.120

4. Numbers shaded:
   45.963; 80.815; 3.584; 6.893; 9.464;
   35.695; .233; .455; 16.333; 5.504
   2.245; 65.834; .565; 3.773; 5.405
   2.884; .555; 98.123; 1.735; 56.334
   15.963; 2.784; 15.373; 49.905; 21.224
   .004; 9.555; 18.453; 1.464; 56.384
   12.005; .005; 5.664; 81.204; 98.064
   45.555; .555; 98.123; 1.735; 56.334
   2.784; 15.373; 49.905; 21.224
   JESUS

5. $\frac{63}{4} = 15\frac{3}{4}$ $\frac{27}{16} = 1\frac{11}{16}$

   $\frac{42}{8} = 5\frac{2}{8} = 5\frac{1}{4}$ $\frac{20}{15} = 1\frac{5}{15} = 1\frac{1}{3}$

6. 91,622   54,120   82,908
   63,261   67,963

7. 5 is the quotient   20 is the dividend
   4 is the divisor

   9 is the quotient   72 is the dividend
   8 is the divisor

   7 is the quotient   63 is the dividend
   9 is the divisor

   5 is the quotient   15 is the dividend
   3 is the divisor

   11 is the quotient   55 is the dividend
   5 is the divisor

   7 is the quotient   49 is the dividend
   7 is the divisor

Lesson 127

1. 6.32   43.67   62.04   38.25   83.30

2. $110 $10 $58 $0 $21

3. 5.26   5.342   5.962   5.993
   17.234   17.356   17.543   17.976

4. $0.60 $2.57 $7.06 $7.00

5. 4,800   60,000   80,000
50,000   4,000   200

  10   10   20   5   5   10

6. 22 $38\frac{2}{6} = 38\frac{1}{3}$

   $30\frac{4}{5}$ $3\frac{15}{30} = 3\frac{1}{2}$

Lesson 128

1. 5.04   3.01   51.33
29.00   4.60   17.12

2. 157.79 is the total value of the jelly beans.

3. 78
71
17
22

4. 7.9   18.5   2.4
45.65   8.13   54.55

5. Colored red: 55, 25, 10
Colored blue: 16, 32, 8
Colored yellow: 9, 3, 6

6. 8   9   6   8

7. 1   2   4   6

Lesson 129

1. 0.83 + 0.83 + 0.83 + 0.83 = 3.32 mm
the girl is taller by 1.2 cm
(139.7 cm – 138.5 cm).

2. 58.03   12.88   62.78
32.64 1761.47   333.20

3. $34 $518 $64 $227 $159 $758

4. B. 1 hour
D. 48 hours
A. 60 seconds
E. 1 day
C. 1 year

5. 32 R3 $(\frac{3}{5})$ = 32.6 = 33

  51 R1 $(\frac{1}{5})$ = 51.2 = 51

  46 R2 $(\frac{2}{4})$ = 46.5 = 47

  51 R1 $(\frac{1}{5})$ = 51.2 = 51

  70

6.

10^6 =	10 x 10 x 10 X 10 X 10 X 10	1,000,000
10^7 =	10 x 10 x 10 x 10 X 10 X 10 X 10	10,000,000
10^9 =	10 x 10 x 10 x 10 x 10 X 10 X 10 X 10 X 10	1,000,000,000
10^2 =	10 x 10	100

7. 25   45   24   72   81

Lesson 130

1. 13 years old
15 years old
228 days

2. 1.9 23.9 6.41 6.36 5.31 1.7
 U   Y   T   I   R   P
PURITY

3. 10.82 – 9.97 = .85 seconds
28.25 – 23.4 = 4.85 feet
43.65 + 43.65 = 87.30 seconds
Total team time: 37.48 seconds

4. $32.97 + $29.99 = $62.96
$62.96 – $45.25 = $17.71

  $25.00 – $3.75 = $21.25 for the swim suit + $17.00 for the shorts = $38.25 total

  14 ÷ 5 = 2 R4: (3 racks are needed)

  2 x $17.95 = $35.96
$35.96 – $16.98 =
$18.98 of the $20.00 bill was used

5. 1 dollar, 1 quarter, 1 penny, = $1.26

  1 half dollar, 1 dime, 1 nickel,
4 pennies = $0.69

2 dollars, 2 quarters, 1 dime
4 pennies = $2.64

1 dollar, 3 quarters, 1 dime, = $1.85

2 dollars, 3 quarters, 1 nickel
1 penny = $2.81

1 ten, 4 ones, 2 quarters = $14.50

6. Equilateral – 60°
   Isosceles   – 100°
   Scalene   – 20°
   Right   – 40°

Lesson 131

1. 7.4   38.4   2.4   19.17 0.98
   51.6   6.35   2.16   14.02 5.49
   170.4 17.29 44.8   104.2 30.3

2. 1. $1.44
   2. 0.65 meters
   3. 1.76 liters
   4. $3.35

3. 1. 6.25   2. 7.61   3. 9.07
   4. 8.95   5. 10.36 6. 28.37
   7. 51.44 8. 62.12 9. 21.34
   10. 29.58 11. 1,040.83 12. 106.212
   13. 5.000 14. 81.931 15. 1,132.88
   April, May and June

4. 69.91 65.71 21.1
   59.01 98.2   46.85

5.

   Isosceles   Equilateral   Scalene

6. Ex: Multiples   LCD

$\frac{2}{3}$ 3, 6, 9, 12, 15   12 A

$\frac{1}{4}$ 4, 8, 12

$\frac{1}{7}$ 7, 14, 21, 28   28 N

$\frac{3}{4}$ 4, 8, 12, 16, 20, 24, 28

$\frac{1}{2}$ 2, 4, 6, 8, 10   10 X

$\frac{1}{5}$ 5, 10, 15

$\frac{1}{8}$ 8, 16, 24   24 I

$\frac{1}{6}$ 6, 12, 18, 24

$\frac{1}{2}$ 2, 4   4 E

$\frac{3}{4}$ 4, 8, 12, 16, 20

$\frac{4}{5}$ 5, 10   10 T

$\frac{1}{2}$ 2, 4, 6, 8, 10, 12, 14

$\frac{1}{9}$ 9, 18, 27, 36   36 Y

$\frac{3}{4}$ 4, 8, 12, 16, 20, 24, 28, 32, 36

ANXIETY

Lesson 132

1. 4.37 5.44   6.65   0.52 0.1802
   0.3   0.384 0.572 6.08 7.497

2. 11.8   F
   21.5   I
   92.9   L
   230.1 C
   1.056 F
   CLIFF

3. 95.01 18.61 41 37.32 115.1
   6.155 11.39 9.63 4.45 20.57

4. 30° 150°

5. HONEYCOMB

6. $3\frac{3}{4}$ $6\frac{1}{2}$ $6\frac{22}{27}$ $7\frac{6}{7}$

7. $n = 295$
   $n = 506$
   $n = 1{,}957$
   $n = 5{,}949$

Lesson 133

1. 28.18 2.48 10.19
   21.13 0.211 21.1

2. $\frac{5}{12}$ $\frac{8}{27}$ $\frac{3}{12} = \frac{1}{4}$ $\frac{3}{12} = \frac{1}{4}$

   2   $\frac{12}{15} = \frac{4}{5}$ $\frac{54}{91}$ $\frac{63}{64}$

3. 2.943 0.3751 136.71 3,930.72

4.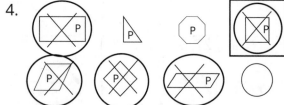

5. Across
   1. 17.4
   3. 28.5
   5. 1.92
   7. 2.73

   Down
   2. 42.1
   4. 85.2
   6. 7.13
   8. 9.73

6.

1	.	5	1	6	7	8
0	6	6	0	7	.	2
0	7	.	9	3	4	2
0	6	2	.	0	1	2
0	8	2	0	4	0	1
0	0	.	9	.	0	0
0	0	0	3	0	3	1
.	0	7	2	0	8	1
0	1	7	5	9	7	2
5	0	7	4	.	2	9
1	2	3	6	9	3	3

Lesson 134

1. 1.048 1.405 21.34 4.342
   6.405 0.076 2.09 15.706

2. 12.98 34.18 20.72 13.17 0.065

3. 0.11 3.9 5.22 1.43 0.5798
   3.57 4.828 1.554 12.02 3.468

0	.	5	7	9	8	1
4	0	.	1	1	7	.
.	1	2	3	.	9	4
8	2	2	9	5	6	3
2	.	3	.	5	7	.
8	0	3	4	4	9	4
8	2	1	1	2	4	6
7	1	2	4	0	8	8

4. 19 R1;   11 R14;   38 R21;   17 R10

5. Clockwise from the top:
   68.5, 30.65, 9.5, 129.5

© MCMXCVIII Alpha Omega Publications, Inc.

24.6, 0.8, 8.46, 0.64

32.8, 2.16, 44, 329.6

6. 1. 3,805
2. 4,012
3. 2,900,000
4. 3,000,901
5. 240,911
6. 42,009
7. 89,000,000
8. 4,000,000,017

Correct order:
3,805; 4,012; 42,009; 240,911
2,900,000; 3,000,901; 89,000,000
4,000,000,017

Lesson 135

1.

Ratio	Fraction	Percent
13 to 100	$\frac{13}{100}$	13%
50 to 100	$\frac{50}{100}$	50%
27 to 100	$\frac{27}{100}$	27%
18 to 100	$\frac{18}{100}$	18%
3 to 100	$\frac{3}{100}$	3%
39 to 100	$\frac{39}{100}$	39%
48 to 100	$\frac{48}{100}$	48%

2. 0.445   1.03   5.72   7.45

3. 38.4   68.8   3.6   7.92   2.07

4.   30%   46%

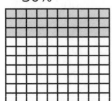   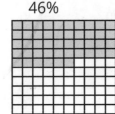

5. 1. 948.9   L
2. 948.348   Y
3. 948.08   R
4. 948.008   E

LYRE

6.

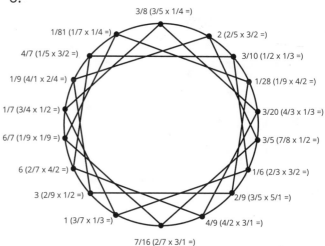

Lesson 136

1.

Fraction	Decimal	Percent
$\frac{19}{100}$	0.19	19%
$\frac{65}{100}$	0.65	65%
$\frac{3}{100}$	0.03	3%
$\frac{1}{100}$	0.01	1%
$\frac{99}{100}$	0.99	99%
$\frac{9}{100}$	0.09	9%
$\frac{12}{100}$	0.12	12%
$\frac{29}{100}$	0.29	29%
$\frac{100}{100}$	1.00	100%

2.

Free Box	0.99	50%	0.05	0.29	11%	9.9	56%	5.6	0.506	17%	Free Box
99%	0.50	0.16	$\frac{56}{100}$	30%	$\frac{99}{100}$	0.33	$\frac{17}{100}$	4%	76%	5%	0.76
40%	49%	16%	$\frac{67}{100}$	29%	$\frac{40}{100}$	1%	$\frac{5}{100}$	9%	12%	67%	Free Box
0.03	0.49	4.90	0.11	0.30	$\frac{29}{100}$	4%	0.56	12%	0.12	0.17	1.70
Free Box	0.40	2%	$\frac{3}{100}$	0.04	$\frac{11}{100}$	18%	Free Box	3%	1.12	0.67	7%

3. 1.268   38.05   7.405   0.645

4. 1.54   2.72   0.321   32.4

   0.2266   0.3516   2.09   1.482

   0.437   9.81   4.2   3.78

FOUR CANARIES

5. 1,000   10,000   9,000

   56,000   124,000   4,000

   6,000   6,000   58,000

6. 55   55.4155

   24   24.4431

   36   37.89842

   39   39.751

   30   34.96

Lesson 137

1. $\frac{1}{5}$ $\frac{7}{10}$ $\frac{1}{10}$

   $\frac{4}{5}$ $\frac{1}{4}$ $\frac{3}{4}$

   $\frac{1}{25}$ $\frac{3}{5}$ $\frac{19}{20}$

   $\frac{1}{2}$ $\frac{1}{50}$ $\frac{3}{10}$

2. 0.33   0.15   0.19

   0.06   0.60   0.27

   0.01   0.25   0.45

3.   38%   12%

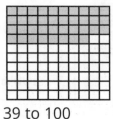

39 to 100   4 to 100   68 to 100

---

   14 to 100   11 to 100   9 to 100

4. 8.556   9.704   4.785   9.315

5. $5.96 $3.99 $8.29 $16.14

6. 92,232,700   4,600   89,700

   800   900   100

   99,512,100   1,000   18,567,300

	9	9	5	1	2	1	0	0	
		2		0		8			
		2		0		5		9	
		3			4	6	0	0	
		2				7		0	
8	9	7	0	0		3			
0		0				0			
0		0		1	0	0	0		

Lesson 138

1. 10%   40%   90%

   75%   14%   45%

   48%   50%   25%

2. 91 to 100   15 to 100   15 to 100

   89 to 100   99 to 100   12 to 100

   69 to 100   77 to 100   89 to 100

3. $\frac{1}{10}$ $\frac{1}{4}$ $\frac{1}{25}$

   $\frac{3}{20}$ $\frac{1}{5}$ $\frac{9}{50}$

   $\frac{1}{2}$ $\frac{3}{4}$ $\frac{4}{5}$

   $\frac{99}{100}$ $\frac{7}{20}$ $\frac{29}{100}$

   $\frac{7}{25}$ $\frac{97}{100}$ $\frac{1}{50}$

   $\frac{17}{25}$ $\frac{17}{100}$ $\frac{17}{20}$

4. 0.19   0.02   0.49
    0.75   0.80   0.01
    0.58   0.15   0.30
    0.66   0.61   0.27

0.11	0.12	0.49	0.58	0.61	0.80
4.5	0.99	0.30	1.4	0.66	0.75
3.3	0.89	0.27	0.13	0.11	0.2
1.0	0.15	0.19	0.75	0.01	0.73
0.01	0.02	0.32	0.99	0.07	9.8

5. 6 $6\frac{5}{8}$ $11\frac{1}{7}$ $13\frac{1}{11}$ $27\frac{1}{5}$

6. 30.33   19.22   72.912 84.39   29.04
    11.78   2.22   65.5   14.71   3.76

Lesson 139

1. 8   10   6
    28   27   50

2. 57%   82%   41%   80%
    33%   83%   22%   88%

3.

Fraction in Lowest Terms	Percent	Decimal	Ratio
$\frac{1}{4}$	25%	0.25	1 to 4
$\frac{1}{2}$	50%	0.50	1 to 2
$\frac{3}{10}$	30%	0.30	3 to 10
$\frac{13}{100}$	13%	0.13	13 to 100
$\frac{3}{20}$	15%	0.15	3 to 20
$\frac{1}{5}$	20%	0.20	1 to 5
$\frac{1}{10}$	10%	0.10	1 to 10
$\frac{6}{25}$	24%	0.24	6 to 25
$\frac{3}{4}$	75%	0.75	3 to 4

4. $5\frac{1}{2}$ $\frac{3}{8}$ 11 $3\frac{1}{5}$ $1\frac{5}{7}$

5. Fractions and letters marked with an X:

    0.10 R;   0.31 E; $\frac{1}{3}$ V;   0.09 B; $\frac{1}{7}$ R
    $\frac{2}{5}$ G; $\frac{3}{7}$ B;

    0.07 E;   0.06 H;   0.37 P

    0.09 E;   0.3 R;   0.36 G

    THIS IS MY BELOVED SON LISTEN TO HIM

6. none
    2, 5, 10
    2, 3, 5, 10
    2, 3

Lesson 140

1. 1. 53
    2. 32
    3. 21
    4. 159
    5. 159

2. 20   36   9
    32   80   64

3. 70%   80%   50%
    98%   64%   60%

4. $\frac{1}{4}$ $\frac{3}{4}$ $\frac{1}{5}$

    $\frac{7}{10}$ $\frac{11}{50}$ $\frac{3}{10}$

    $\frac{1}{25}$ $\frac{2}{5}$ $\frac{9}{100}$

    $\frac{2}{25}$ $\frac{3}{50}$ $\frac{1}{2}$

    FAITH, HOPE, AND LOVE

5.

4	7	12	44	10	91	46	29	24	59	50	200
40	73	44	13	90	67	80	15	60	57	150	61
100	61	6	17	72	55	14	9	54	63	464	68
58	51	10	99	14	19	88	11	78	53	220	51
66	13	168	8	18	5	77	66	27	21	28	98

6. >   <   >
    =   =   <
    <   >   >
    >   <   =

Lesson 141

1. $14\frac{1}{2}$

    $3\frac{1}{8}$

    $1\frac{3}{8}$

    $1\frac{1}{8}$

2. 42.90   41.20   34.91   80.80   60.21
    68.15   32.45   44.68   13.53   20.16
    83.49
    Picture should be a crown.

3. $\frac{1}{8}$ $\frac{5}{18}$ $\frac{2}{24} = \frac{1}{12}$ $\frac{6}{18} = \frac{1}{3}$

4. $\frac{7}{10}$ $\frac{5}{6}$ $\frac{19}{18} = 1\frac{1}{18}$ $\frac{7}{12}$

5. 5 R8 O; 6 R6 S;   8 R2 W
    5 R9 M; 5 R7 D; 9 R5 I
    WISDOM

6.

13,451	2,110	15,561
5,803	24,512	30,315
19,254	26,622	45,876

7. 7   17   12   10   11   1
    13   12   10   8   18   24
    problems 7 + 5 and 3 + 9
    problem 0 + 1

Lesson 142

1. Truck – 2 tons   Dog – 10 lb.
    Soup can – 12 oz.   Popcorn – 8 oz.
    Bag of potato chips – 5 lb.

2. $5\frac{1}{2}$

    $4\frac{1}{8}$

    $3\frac{5}{8}$

3. 90;   40 R9;   80 R15;   87 R3

4. 12   18   65   25   45   20
    11   12   56   10   19   12
    20 + 0 = 20
    7 + 5 = 12

5. ROCK   –   30
    DELIVERER   –   53.2
    REFUGE   –   41.3
    STRONGHOLD   –   68.1
    SHIELD   –   35.7

6.

$\frac{1}{2}$	$\frac{1}{6}$	$\frac{3}{10}$	$\frac{1}{2}$
$\frac{1}{15}$	$\frac{1}{5}$	$\frac{1}{2}$	$\frac{3}{100}$
$\frac{1}{24}$	$\frac{1}{2}$	$\frac{13}{24}$	$\frac{1}{4}$
$\frac{1}{2}$	$\frac{0}{12}$	$\frac{1}{3}$	$\frac{4}{15}$

Lesson 143

1. 16 $1\frac{1}{2}$

    $\frac{1}{2}$ 1

2. 1 ton   10 oz   12 lbs   1 lb

3. feet
    feet
    miles
    yards

4. 1. 9.2 x 9.5 = 87.4

   2. 5.0 x 4.5 = 22.5

   3. 3.5 x 2.1 = 7.35

   4. 7.2 x 3.1 = 22.32

   5. 6.1 x 5 = 30.5

   6. 4.3 x 6 = 25.8

5. $7\frac{7}{10}$ $8\frac{3}{6} = 8\frac{1}{2}$ $19\frac{9}{20}$

   $15\frac{4}{9}$ $5\frac{5}{12}$

6. Colored yellow: 3,762,000
   Colored red: 29; 8,520
   Colored blue: 2,204,000,046
                    3,891,245,001
                    3,894,451,111
                    2,897,254,019
                    2,756,433,233
                    3,104,212,891
                    2,658,543,310
                    2,784,100,310
                    3,124,567,890

7. 1   4   8   5   3   5
   17   51   11   0   3   2

Lesson 144

1. 1. C.
   2. A.
   3. D.
   4. B.

2. ounce, cup, pint, quart, gallon
   2 c   8 pt
   2 pt   2 c

3. 1. 70 lb
   2. 1 T
   3. 1 oz
   4. 50 lb
   5. 10 ft
   6. 11 in
   7. 7 mi
      2 ⅛ inch

4. Clockwise:
   11.2   2.8   22.4   5.6
   80.85   32.34   53.9   161.7

5. 1. E.
   2. C.
   3. D.
   4. A.
   5. B.

6. 3
   6
   2

7. $1\frac{3}{6} = 1\frac{1}{2}$ $7\frac{3}{10}$ $6\frac{9}{18} = 6\frac{1}{2}$

   $1\frac{23}{70}$ $7\frac{13}{66}$

Lesson 145

1. 15.5 cm   1,145 cm
   1.829 m   10,900 dm
   1,930 mm   360 mm

2. A. child with snowballs
   B. child with bat and ball
   C. child with thermometer in mouth
   D. child with water hose

3. 20 qts   15 pts
   24 fl oz   19 fl oz

4. 24,000 lbs   20 oz
   150 oz   3 tons

5. 40,000   482,030   498,701
   66,213   8,597   17,546

6. $11\frac{1}{3}$ $9\frac{3}{8}$ $31\frac{3}{11}$ $3\frac{1}{8}$ $7\frac{6}{10} = 7\frac{3}{5}$

   POWER

Lesson 146

1. 0.005 Kg   0.055 Kg   0.910 Kg
   6,000 g   75,000 g   433,000 g

2. 1. meters
   2. centimeters
   3. meters
   4. kilometers
   5. centimeters
   6. millimeters

3. thermometer readings and pictures should match the indicated temperature

4. > = > <

5. $11\frac{27}{20} = 12\frac{7}{20}$ $15\frac{7}{6} = 16\frac{1}{6}$

   $16\frac{25}{21} = 17\frac{4}{21}$ $40\frac{3}{6} = 40\frac{1}{2}$

   $33\frac{13}{10} = 34\frac{3}{10}$ $8\frac{3}{4}$

   $17\frac{4}{21}$

   CLEANSE

6. 0.139   0.193   0.236   0.326   0.329
   45.196   45.891   45.981   46.038   46.138

7.

Multiplicand	Multiplier	Product
5	5	25
7	3	21
7	9	63
6	9	54
9	8	72

Lesson 147

1. 3 L   326 ml   0.065 L
   0.520 L   9,000 ml   5,000 ml

2. a feather   -- 1 milligram
   an egg   -- 50 milligrams
   a TV set   -- 50 Kg
   a cat   -- 1 Kg
   a hamster   -- 4 g
   a hippopotamus   -- 1,000 Kg
   Mercy

3. 300 m   50 Dm
   600 m   7.5 Km

4. 3   4   2   1
   3   1   4   2

5. 187 R23;   206 R18;   907 R40
   637 R42;   776 R10

6. $2\frac{13}{24}$ $3\frac{0}{4} = 3$

   $13\frac{2}{18} = 13\frac{1}{9}$ $9\frac{8}{42} = 9\frac{4}{21}$

   $30\frac{9}{12} = 30\frac{3}{4}$ $9\frac{15}{20} = 9\frac{3}{4}$

7.

DIVIDEND	DIVISOR	QUOTIENT	REMAINDER	LETTER
15	7	2	1	Ⓟ
64	8	8	0	Ⓡ
89	9	9	8	E
27	4	6	3	N
50	7	7	1	Ⓐ
16	5	3	1	Ⓘ
8	3	2	2	Ⓢ
39	5	7	4	T
45	9	5	0	Ⓔ

   PRAISE

Lesson 148

1. 34° C   8°   10°   38° C

2. a. 15 ml
   c. 350 ml
   b. 2 L
   c. 4 L
   a. 150 ml

3. Bag 1:   226g + 3.26Kg (3,260g) + 340g
             = 4,506g = 4.506Kg

   Bag 2:   4.5Kg (4,500g) + 610g + 226g
             + 3.26Kg (3,260g) = 8,596g =
             8.596Kg

   Bag 3:   4.50Kg (4,500g) + 1,525g
             + 680g + 1,360g + 226g =
             8,291g = 8.291Kg

4. 6,500 cm   – 65 M
    3.5 cm   – 35 mm
    5,000 M   – 5 Km
    5.0 mm   – 0.50 cm
    6.0 Km   – 6,000 M

5. 206   103   108   106
    12 R3   12   12 R2   12 R4

6. 12   15   12   40
    30   20   6   6
    teacher check maze

7.

DIVIDEND	DIVISOR	QUOTIENT	REMAINDER	LETTER
20	6	3	2	(S)
13	2	6	1	(E)
19	5	3	4	M
14	4	3	2	(E)
40	7	5	5	A
17	2	8	1	(K)
16	7	2	2	(G)
64	8	8	0	(O)
89	9	9	8	E
34	5	6	4	N
50	7	7	1	(D)
16	5	3	1	(S)
9	3	3	0	(W)
49	5	9	4	T
36	5	7	1	(I)
77	8	9	5	K
52	7	7	3	(L)
45	9	5	0	(L)

SEEK GOD'S WILL

Lesson 149

1. 5.20 m = 520 cm   520 cm < 540 cm

    No. 2 qt = ½ gal.
    You will need to get more milk.

1,000 students.
Each student's arm span is 1 meter and
1,000 meters = 1 Km.

She can purchase 6 whole pounds of
bananas. 6 x 0.49 = $2.94

2.

City	High Temperature	Low Temperature	Difference
Bretton	36°	20°	16°
Brackston	35°	15°	20°
Jackson	35°	-10°	45°
Murphysville	38°	14°	24°
Louisville	40°	15°	25°
Lincoln	41°	16°	25°

3. 1. 3,780
    2. 1,420
    3. 40
    4. 6 cans

4. $0.61 $0.88 $5.97 $12.96

5. Scalene 90°   Equilateral 60°
    Isosceles 80°   Scalene 59°
    Scalene 30°

6. 1. Divisible by 5:   5, 10, 15, 20, 25, 30
       35, 40, 45, 50, 55, 60, 65, 70, 75, 80
       85, 90, 95, 100

    2. Divisible by 2:   2, 4, 6, 8, 10, 12, 14
       16, 18, 20, 22, 24, 26, 28, 30, 32, 34
       36, 38, 40, 42, 44, 46, 48, 50, 52, 54
       56, 58, 60, 62, 64, 66, 68, 70, 72, 74
       76, 78, 80, 82, 84, 86, 88, 90, 92, 94
       96, 98, 100

    3. Divisible by 10:   10, 20, 30, 40, 50,
       60, 70, 80, 90, 100

    4. Divisible by 3:   3, 6, 9, 12, 15, 18, 21
       24, 27, 30, 33, 36, 39, 42, 45, 48, 51
       54, 57, 60, 63, 66, 69, 72, 75, 78, 81
       84, 87, 90, 93, 96, 99

7. 47.144 19.40   4.20   0.048   1.91

8. 1   5   5   3   4   1

Lesson 150

1. 560 x 5 = 2,800 ft.

(112 x 2) + (56 x 2) = 336 inches

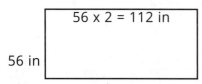

56 x 2 = 112 in

56 in

350 ÷ 2 = 175
175 + 15 = 190
350 + 175 + 190 = 715 ft

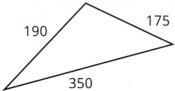

190   175

350

2. teacher check

3. a. 1.28
   b. .236
   c. .286

   a. 425
   b. 473
   c. 825

4. 25 R25;   48 R1;   122 R21;   387 R6
   10.85;   26.03;   45.95;   125.10

5. 100° C   –   B.
   37° C   –   C.
   20° C   –   E.
   -10° C   –   D.
   0° C   –   A.

6. $\frac{1}{2}$ tsp. + $\frac{1}{2}$ tsp. = 1 tsp.

   1 cup – $\frac{1}{2}$ cup = $\frac{1}{2}$ cup

   the pie mixture

   $\frac{2}{3}$ cup

   Makes two pies

New recipe:

Pie: 1 Graham Cracker Ready Crust

        $5\frac{1}{2}$ cups fresh, peeled, sliced
        cooking apples

        1 Tbs. bottled lemon juice

        $\frac{1}{4}$ cup light brown sugar, firmly
        packed

        $\frac{1}{4}$ tsp. salt

        $\frac{1}{4}$ tsp. ground nutmeg

        1 large egg yolk, slightly beaten

        $\frac{1}{2}$ cup sugar

        3 Tbs.. all-purpose flour

        $\frac{1}{2}$ tsp. ground cinnamon

Topping:

        $\frac{1}{4}$ tsp. ground nutmeg

        $\frac{1}{4}$ cup sugar

        $\frac{1}{3}$ cup butter or margarine

        $\frac{3}{4}$ cup all-purpose flour

        $\frac{1}{4}$ cup light brown sugar

Lesson 151

1. $100.00
   $200.00
   Concessions made the most money
   ($300.00) and cotton candy made the
   least ($100.00):
   $1,100.00 total sales combined

2. 0.36   18.27   2.768   39.05   0.15

3. 4
   50
   30

5
10

4. 55 28
74 29

5.

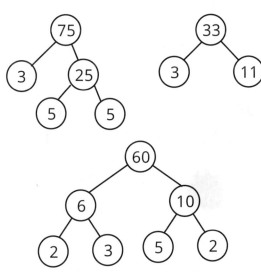

6. 10,948 969,004 971,355 75,297

7. Atlantic and Indian = 57,115,000 sq mi
Pacific and Arctic = 69,440,200 sq mi
The Pacific and Arctic are larger by
12,325,200 sq mi

Pacific Ocean = 13,215 ft &
Caribbean Sea = 8,685 ft
Difference = 4,530 ft

Oceans	Seas
Pacific	Mediterranean
Atlantic	Caribbean
Indian	South China
Arctic	Bearing

Oceans = 126,555,200 sq mi
Seas = 3,974,900 sq mi
Difference = Oceans area is larger by
122,580,300 sq mi

Lesson 152

1. Week 3
Week 1 and Week 7 both had 54°F

4°F

Week 2, Week 4, and Week 5 had a
 7° difference

Week 7 had a 2° difference

2.

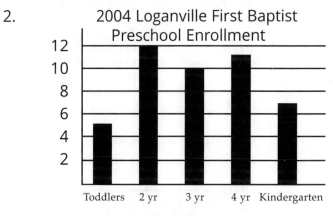

3. 2268.10 24.505 35.42
581.28 3691.2

4. 86, 51
40, 34 – 52 R3($\frac{3}{4}$) = 52.75 = 53

52, 60
15, 46 – 43 R1($\frac{1}{4}$) = 43.25 = 43

71, 36
48, 40, 16 – 42 R1($\frac{1}{5}$) = 42.2 = 42

21, 18
11, 17, 12 – 15 R4($\frac{4}{5}$) = 15.8 = 16

5. Prime numbers by row:
23, 2, 43, 37, 19, 71, 53, 23, 13
7, 61, 17, 29, 2, 37, 7
11, 17, 13, 23, 19, 23, 5, 41, 19, 5
5, 2, 31, 5, 7, 53, 67
3, 31, 2, 7, 11, 59, 61

FAITH

6. $\frac{1}{6}$ $\frac{4}{25}$ $\frac{1}{8}$ $\frac{5}{36}$

7. 28 13 30 51

Lesson 153

1. The finished product will show the
information listed. The symbol chosen
by the student might vary, but most
draw a chair.

1. (cont.)

Chairs Purchased for new Church Addition	
Fellowship Hall	(15 chairs drawn)
Room #1	(3 chairs drawn)
Room #2	(3 chairs drawn)
Room #3	(3 chairs drawn)
Room #4	(3 chairs drawn)
Office	(1 chair drawn)

(drawing of 1 chair) = 5 chairs

2.   Number of Rooms Rented at Red Mountain Inn During Summer Months

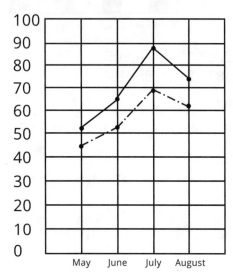

_.._.._ Rooms Rented in 2006

_____ Rooms Rented in 2007

3.

Sale Item	Amount	Cost	Unit Price
Soap	2 bars	$2.50	$1.25
	(3 bars)	$3.00	$1.00
Ground Beef	3 lbs.	$4.74	$1.58
	(5 lbs.)	$6.55	$1.31
Paper Towels	(1 roll)	$1.09	$1.09
	3 rolls	$3.30	$1.10
Breakfast Bars	(3 boxes)	$6.87	$2.29
	6 boxes	$13.86	$2.31
Soda	6 pack	$1.86	$0.31
	(12 pack)	$3.12	$0.26

4. $9\frac{1}{6}$ $11\frac{1}{4}$ $1\frac{2}{15}$ $2\frac{11}{12}$

5. 1,512   N
   1,930   O

4,689	O
858	T
932	H
1,220	E
1,990	R
4,704	G
2,262	O
1,944	D
2,394	S

NO OTHER GODS

6. 69   133   15   108   45

7. $n = 30$

   $n = 31$

   $n = 9$

   $n = 57$

Lesson 154

1. 27 + 16 + 7 + 25 + 25 = 100 students

   50 – 27 = 23 more

   There are more woodwind players

   woodwinds – 27

   brass + percussion = 16 + 7 = 23

   $50 = \frac{1}{2} = 50\%$

2. 30 min.   draw 1 TV set

   60 min.   draw 2 TV sets

   120 min.   draw 5 TV sets

   180 min   draw 9 TV sets

3. $n = 6$

   $n = 18$

   $n = 20$

   $n = 35$

   $n = 18$

4. CORRECT PROBLEMS:

   $13\frac{1}{2} \times 5 = \frac{135}{2} = 67\frac{1}{2}$

   $12\frac{3}{8} \times 7 = \frac{693}{8} = 86\frac{5}{8}$

$15\frac{3}{5} \times 9 = \frac{702}{5} = 140\frac{2}{5}$

$8\frac{4}{5} \times 12 = \frac{528}{5} = 105\frac{3}{5}$

$15\frac{1}{2} \times 2 = \frac{62}{2} = 31$

$4 \times 6\frac{1}{2} = \frac{52}{2} = 26$

$3\frac{3}{5} \times 10 = \frac{180}{5} = 36$

5. 500   800   9,000
    90   40   6,000
    20   2,000   700

6. 751   93   13
    26   182   70

7. Answers will vary.

Lesson 155

1. (2, 4)   P
    (7, 8)   R
    (1, 1)   A
    (7, 2)   Y
    (5, 1)   E
    (1, 6)   R
    PRAYER

2. 1. Corn = $\frac{1}{2}$

    Tomatoes = $\frac{1}{4}$

    Squash = $\frac{1}{8}$

    Beans = $\frac{1}{16}$

    Carrots = $\frac{1}{16}$

    2. 250 = $\frac{1}{2}$ of 500

3. 50

4. $12\frac{1}{2}$ (12.5) = $\frac{1}{8}$ of 100

5. $\frac{1}{16}$ of 1,000 = $62\frac{1}{2}$ (62.5)

3. Answers will vary.

4. Across   Down
    1. 3,404   1. 3,060
    2. 8,400   5. 5,152
    3. 5,270
    4. 6,375
    6. 2,890

5. 439,020   449,062
    557,529   1,088

6. 9
    5
    1
    0
    4

Lesson 156

1. Range: 57   Range: 200
    Mean: 59   Mean: 200

    Range: 13   Range: 28
    Mean: 23   Mean: 30

2. 18   24
    18   15
    48   25

3.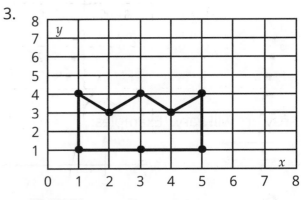

CROWN

4. 3 $6\frac{2}{3}$ 15

   $4\frac{1}{3}$ $7\frac{1}{2}$

5. 399,672   462,636   208,980
   142,848   98,559
   107,568   434,700   377,775
   186,516   204,435

399,672	398,112	451,690	209,300	186,332
462,636	208,980	142,848	130,988	377,779
399,561	466,451	98,559	434,722	298,511
459,231	613,388	107,568	434,700	356,910
890,366	516,984	106,899	377,775	186,516
255,601	215,669	434,000	186,555	204,435

6. $24.31 $76.76 $189.54

   $21.74 $42.85

   TRUST

LESSON 157

1. Range: 50   Range: $52
   Mean: 28   Mean: $50
   Mode: 28   Mode: $45

   Range: $4.75   Range: 40 m
   Mean: $5   Mean: 39 m
   Mode: no mode   Mode: 42 m

2. 15%   –   0.15
   10%   –   0.10
   5%   –   0.05
   8%   –   0.08
   100%   –   1.00
   17%   –   0.17

3. $1\frac{4}{6} = 1\frac{2}{3}$ $12\frac{5}{6}$ $2\frac{1}{6}$

   $6\frac{2}{3}$ $5\frac{1}{6}$

4. Answers will vary. Examples:

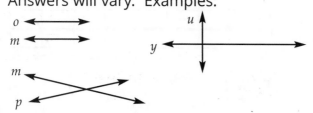

5. Sphere   Triangular Pyramid   Cone
   Rectangular Prism   Hexagonal Prism
   Rectangular Pyramid

6. 2,400   50,000   2,500,000
   18,000   4,200,000

   Largest to smallest:
   4,200,000   2,500,000   50,000
   18,000   2,400

Lesson 158

1. 1, 5, 7, 7, 18, 22, 24   10, 12, 16, 70, 70, 98
   Range: 23   Range: 88
   Mean: 12   Mean: 46
   Mode: 7   Mode: 70
   Median: 7   Median: 43

   $3, $9, $9, $22, $52   20 in, 10 in, 56 in, 14 in
   Range: $49   Range: 46 in
   Mean: $19   Mean: 25 in
   Mode: $9   Mode: no mode
   Median: $9   Median: 17

2. 5%   75%   56%   3%
   25%   50%   2%   20%

3. $36\frac{3}{4}$ $90\frac{2}{6} = 90\frac{1}{3}$ $167\frac{1}{3}$

   $3\frac{1}{4}$ $23\frac{1}{5}$

4. Acute   Obtuse   Right
   Obtuse   Right   Acute
   ∠ABC, ∠CBA, or ∠B

5. $n = 15$
   $n = 2$
   $n = 10$
   $n = 3$

6. 50   80   90
   400   900   700
   3,000   4,000   6,000

Lesson 159

1. $\frac{1}{8}$

   $\frac{2}{8} = \frac{1}{4}$

   Green = $\frac{1}{8}$ + red = $\frac{2}{8} = \frac{3}{8}$

   $\frac{1}{8}$

   Blue = $\frac{2}{8}$ + red = $\frac{2}{8}$ + green =

   $\frac{1}{8} = \frac{5}{8}$

2. 36, 41, 45, 61, 62   11, 12, 12, 17, 19, 21
   Range: 26   Range: 10
   Mean: 49   Mean: 15 R2 =

   Mode: none $15\frac{2}{6} = 15.3$
   Mean: 45   Mode: 12

                        Median: 14.5
                        (12 + 17 = 29 ÷ 2
                        = 14.5

   $37, $40, $51, $86, $86   17 L, 33 L, 46 L
   Range: $49   Range: 29 L
   Mean: $60   Mean: 32 L
   Mode: $86   Mode: none
   Median: $51   Median: 33 L

3. $45.00 $2.25 $47.25
   $29.75 $1.49 $31.24
   $63.65 $3.18 $66.83
   $100.00 $5.00 $105.00
   $22.50 $1.13 $23.63

4. $\frac{3}{30} = \frac{1}{10}$ $\frac{32}{45}$ $\frac{8}{16} = \frac{1}{2}$ $\frac{18}{21} = \frac{6}{7}$

5.

10^5	10 x 10 x 10 X 10 X 10	100,000
10^6	10 x 10 x 10 X 10 X 10 x 10	1,000,000
10^7	10 x 10 x 10 X 10 X 10 X 10 X 10	10,000,000
10^8	10 x 10 x 10 X 10 X 10 X 10 X 10 x 10	100,000,000
10^9	10 x 10 x 10 x 10 X 10 X 10 X 10 X 10 X 10	1,000,000,000

6. 90   120   6,560
   600   5,900   12,400
   46,000   133,000   946,000

Lesson 160

1. $\frac{3}{9} = \frac{1}{3}$

   $\frac{6}{9} = \frac{2}{3}$

   $\frac{0}{9}$

   $\frac{2}{9}$

   $\frac{3}{6} = \frac{1}{2}$

   $\frac{1}{6}$ $\frac{1}{6}$ $\frac{1}{6}$

   All of the outcomes are $\frac{1}{6}$ because
   they are all equally as likely.

2. 15, 36, 40, 48, 71   12, 25, 35
   Mean: 42   Mean: 24
   Median: 40   Median: 25
   Mode: none   Mode: none

   3, 6, 6, 7, 8
   Mean: 6
   Median: 6
   Mode: 6

3. 60°   70°   30°
   Set A
   4 cm _____
   4 cm _____
   4 cm _____
   Set A will form an equilateral triangle.
   The student response should
   acknowledge that an equilateral
   triangle has three sides the same
   length.

4. 75   80   100   25   500

5. 1 set of paint brushes $6.95
   2 model car kits $31.00
                              ($15.50 each)
                              $37.95
            $50.00 – 37.95 = $12.05
   $53.18 – 10.25 (needlepoint kit)
   = $42.92

5. (cont.) Woodcarving set $35.98
    Paint brushes $6.95
           = $42.92
    change   = $31.32

6. Either order:

Mandy's Book Collection
(24 total books)

Mandy's Book Collection
(24 total books)

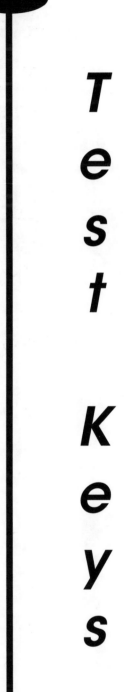

Test Keys

Test 1

1. Order Property of Addition
    Zero Property of Addition
    Grouping Property of Addition

105	66	73	21
21	18	51	90

2. 14   Minuend
    – 7   Subtrahend
     7   Difference

		7	6	13	7
20	13	1	0	1	5
12	10	0			

3. 25 x 4 = 100   5 x (4 x 0) = 0
    6 x 8 = 48

4. 5   1   can't do   25
    0   1   multiplication

5. 13   10
    12   10

Test 2

1. | | | |
    |---|---|---|
    | 9 | 23 | 2 |
    | 88 | 3 | 7 |
    | 104 | 12 | 16 |

2. | | | | |
    |---|---|---|---|
    | 6 | 10 | 9 | 5 |
    | 135 | 8 | 3 | 1 |

3. 1. 28 miles
    2. 3,255 miles
    3. 3,200 miles
    4. 5,475 miles

4. Six thousand, one hundred three

    Five thousand, one hundred forty-nine

    Four thousand, eight hundred seventy-one

    Three thousand, forty-one

    Six million, fifty-nine thousand, twenty-one

    Seven million, three hundred thirty thousand, four hundred twelve

5. | bill. | 100 mill. | 10 mill. | mill. | 100 thou. | 10 thou | thou. | hundred | ten | ones |
    |---|---|---|---|---|---|---|---|---|---|
    | 6 | 2 | 5 | 4 | 2 | 1 | 5 | 7 | 0 | 4 |
    | 9 | 4 | 3 | 3 | 2 | 0 | 2 | 0 | 9 | 1 |
    | 1 | 0 | 0 | 0 | 9 | 7 | 8 | 0 | 0 | 0 |

6. Sixteen thousand, two hundred forty-three
    10,000 + 6,000 + 200 + 40 + 3

    Five hundred forty-five
    500 + 40 + 5

    One thousand, nine
    1,000 + 0 + 9 or
    1,000 + 0 + 0 + 9 or
    1,000 + 9.

    Nine hundred eighty-one thousand, three hundred forty-one
    900,000 + 80,000 + 1,000 + 300 + 40 + 1

7. XXII
    DCCCXLII
    XIV
    CCLXXV
    XXX
    XLI

Test 3

1. | | | |
    |---|---|---|
    | 7,742 | 9,612 | 10,655 |
    | 2,774 | 19,682 | 174,643 |

2. | | | |
    |---|---|---|
    | 5,580 | 3,890 | 460 |
    | 5,900 | 2,100 | 3,800 |
    | 4,000 | 3,000 | 2,000 |

3. Not enough information.
    $26,442.00
    $410.00
    Not enough information.

4. 7,294   5,269   2,695   1,332   1,109

5. | | | | | |
    |---|---|---|---|---|
    | Estimated: | 80 | 30 | 120 | 30 |
    | Actual: | 79 | 32 | 115 | 29 |
    | Estimated: | 50 | 70 | 150 | 220 |
    | Actual: | 51 | 73 | 149 | 219 |

6.   42   19   22   34
    138   168   556   771

Test 4

1. 5,388   407,966   786   737
  3,163   16,607   40,049   468,081

2. 10   60   50
  100   600   1,300
  5,000   11,000   7,000

3. $52.75 $528.92 $291.49 $234.54
  $14.16 $27.79 $8.19 $22.77

4. 1. $8.50
  2. 11
  3. $2.50

5. Factors for
     72 are: 9 x 8   3 x 3; 2 x 4 2 x 2
     27 are: 3 x 9   3 x 3
     25 are: 5 x 5
     81 are: 9 x 9   3 x 3; 3 x 3
     42 are: 7 x 6   2 x 3
     49 are: 7 x 7

6. 1,000   18,000   2,400
  30,000   2,800,000

Test 5

1. 1,113 1,170 2,670 13,468 4,966
  519,687   297,343   140,973
  42,432   208,590

2. 1,500   210   3,200   1,200
  500   2,000   15,000   24,000

3. $n = 9$ $n = 7$ $n = 13$
  Check   Check   Check
  9 x 9 = 81   7 x 7 = 49   13 x 3 = 39
  $n = 9$ $n = 7$ $n = 8$
  Check   Check   Check
  9 x 8 = 72   7 x 10 = 70   8 x 8 = 64

4. 10 x 10 x 10 x 10   10,000   4   4
  10 x 10 x 10 x 10 x 10   5   5
               1,000,000 6   6
  10 x 10 x 10 x 10 x 10 x 10 x 10
               10,000,000 7   7

5. 17   14   140 R3   207 R1   545 R2
  437 R4 $0.98 $2.47

6. $n = 21$ $n = 25$ $n = 56$
  Check   Check   Check
  3 x 7 = 21   5 x 5 = 25   8 x 7 = 56

  $n = 48$ $n = 54$ $n = 72$
  Check   Check   Check
  4 x 12 = 48   6 x 9 = 54   8 x 9 = 72

Test 6

1. 41 R1   50 R6   50 R0   105 R1
  38 R0   147 R1   97 R5   73 R3

2. 70   90   400   700

3. 36 R1 (¼) = 36.25 = 36
  53 R3 (⅗) = 53.6 = 54
  46 R2 (²⁄₄) = 46.5 = 47
  43
  59

4. $96.56 ÷ 3 = 32.18 R2 ($32.186) is the exact answer. 2 people will pay $32.19 and one will pay $32.18.

  166 ÷ 15 = 11 R1. This means that there will be 11 people seated at 14 of the tables and the 15th table will need to seat 12.

5. 4   Check: 70 x 4 = 280
  9   Check: 50 x 9 = 450
  2 R8   Check: 40 x 2 = 80 + 8 = 88
  5 R5   Check: 50 x 5 = 250 + 5 = 255
  6 R18   Check: 80 x 6 = 480 + 18 = 498
  6 R55   Check: 70 x 6 = 420 + 55 = 475
  8 R19   Check: 40 x 8 = 320 + 19 = 339
  9 R5   Check: 80 x 9 = 720 + 5 = 725
  9 R13   Check: 20 x 9 = 180 + 13 = 193
  7 R11   Check: 90 x 7 = 630 + 11 = 641

6. 2 R59   4 R39   2 R29   9 R49
   30 R23   88 R20   87 R11

7. 4 R40   6 R36   8 R4   8 R64   7 R29
   565   442 R3   653 R8

Test 7

1. 181   408   201   193
   108      $2.03 $3.00 $14.00

2. $400 \div 50 = 8$ $900 \div 30 = 30$
   $4000 \div 80 = 50$ $60,000 \div 30 = 2,000$

3. 820   = 2, 5, 10
   9,420 = 2, 5, 10, 3
   8,000 = 2, 5, 10
   6,024 = 2, 3

4. one decade
millenniums
A.D.
B.C.

5. 1. <u>He purchased a watch for $12.95.</u>
   $7.45

   2. $22.65

   3. <u>she spent $6.95 on Wednesday.</u>
   $4.85

   4. $5.00

6. 11:20 A.M.   8:15 A.M.
    3:20 P.M.   9:27 A.M.

7. C
E
F
G
H
A
D
B

8. 4:15   8:05   11:25   10:00   10:00

Test 8

1. 4 weeks
4th week
520 weeks
1,200 months
7 weeks

2. Pacific
Central
7:00 P.M.
9:00 A.M.

3. Change due:
1 dollar, 1 quarter, 1 penny = ($1.26)

   1 dollar, 3 quarters = ($1.75)

   3 dollars, 2 quarters, 1 dime, 4 pennies
= ($3.64)

   1 ten, 3 quarters, 1 dime = ($10.85)

   2 ones, 3 quarters, 1 nickel, 1 penny
= ($2.81)

4. 1. point M
   2. line segment CB $\overline{CB}$
   3. line AD $\overleftrightarrow{AD}$
   4. ray EF $\overrightarrow{EF}$
   5. plane X

5. b || d   k intersects r   d ⊥ c

6. 1. acute   5. right
   2. obtuse   6. acute
   3. right   7. obtuse
   4. acute   8. right

7. 1. 45°
   2. 90°
   3. 160°

8. ▲ABC
$\overline{AB}$, $\overline{AC}$ and $\overline{BC}$
scalene
yes

Test 9

1. 1. (Parallelogram) (Rectangle) (Square)

   2. (Parallelogram) (Rectangle)

   3. (Parallelogram)

   4. ∠U   ∠V   ∠W   ∠X

   5. $\overline{AB}$ and $\overline{CD}$ $\overline{AC}$ and $\overline{BD}$

2. Pentagon

   Octagon

   Triangle

   Hexagon

   Decagon

3. 1. diameter
   2. 4 cm
   3. radius
   4. chord
   5. 2 cm

4. Faces = 6
   Edges = 12
   Vertices = 8

5. Pentagon

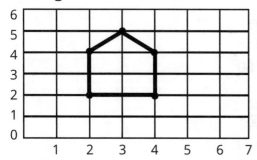

6. 1. 8 pennies
   2. 4 pizzas

7.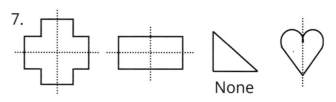

   None

8. Answers will vary.

9.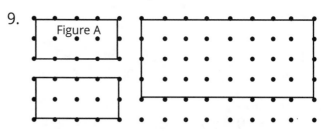

   Figure A

10.
    cone

    pyramid

    cylinder

    sphere

    prism

11. 22 cm

Test 10

1. 1. Side A = 90 cm²
   2. Side B = 18 cm²
   3. Surface area:
      Front = 90 cm² x 2 = 180 cm²
      Top   = 20 cm² x 2 = 40 cm²
      Side = 18 cm² x 2 = 36 cm²
      Total = 256 cm²

2. 1. 84 cm³
   2. 120 cm³

3. 1. 7 cm
   2. 9 cm

4. High top – red   Low top - red
   High top – brown   Low top - brown
   High top – black   Low top - black
   High top – navy   Low top – navy

5. $\frac{1}{6}$ $\frac{2}{5}$ $\frac{5}{8}$

6. $\frac{5}{9} = \frac{10}{18}$ $\frac{7}{8} = \frac{35}{40}$ $\frac{1}{10} = \frac{20}{200}$

$\frac{5}{7} = \frac{35}{49}$ $\frac{4}{9} = \frac{32}{72}$

$\frac{1}{3}, \frac{2}{6}, \frac{3}{9}, \frac{4}{12}$

$\frac{2}{5}, \frac{4}{10}, \frac{6}{15}, \frac{8}{20}$

7. **4:** 1,2,4   **9:** 1,3,9
   10: 1,2,5,10   **18:** 1,2,3,6,9,18
   common: 1,2   common: 1,3,9
   greatest: 2   greatest: 9

   14: 1,2,7,14
   28: 1,2,4,7,14,28
   common: 1,2,7,14
   greatest: 14

8. $\frac{1}{4}$ $\frac{2}{9}$ $\frac{2}{5}$ $\frac{1}{3}$ $\frac{1}{7}$

   $\frac{2}{11}$ $\frac{25}{47}$ $\frac{1}{3}$ $\frac{13}{19}$ $\frac{1}{4}$

9. $\frac{5}{7} > \frac{3}{8}$ $\frac{7}{9} < \frac{10}{11}$ $\frac{3}{7} > \frac{2}{5}$ $\frac{8}{10} > \frac{9}{12}$

Test 11

1. 1. $\frac{5}{9}$

   2. $\frac{6}{12} = \frac{1}{2}$

   3. $\frac{8}{18} = \frac{4}{9}$

   4. $\frac{7}{21} = \frac{1}{3}$

   5. $\frac{10}{25} = \frac{2}{5}$

   6. $\frac{20}{40} = \frac{1}{2}$

2. $\frac{29}{4}$ $\frac{17}{3}$ $\frac{13}{4}$ $\frac{15}{2}$

   $\frac{85}{9}$ $\frac{42}{5}$ $\frac{79}{7}$ $\frac{63}{4}$

3. 6   6 $8\frac{1}{2}$ $2\frac{5}{7}$

   $2\frac{7}{10}$ $9\frac{4}{9}$ $2\frac{1}{2}$ $8\frac{2}{3}$

4. 6   6   12   28

5. 1. 56 gumballs
   2. $1,265.92

6. $\frac{9}{14}$ $\frac{7}{9}$ $\frac{7}{10}$ $\frac{3}{4}$

7. $\frac{7}{15}$ $\frac{3}{8}$ $\frac{4}{9}$ $\frac{7}{14} = \frac{1}{2}$

8. $18\frac{3}{6} = 18\frac{1}{2}$ $16\frac{5}{9}$ $15\frac{5}{7}$ $25\frac{3}{9} = 25\frac{1}{3}$

9. $9\frac{7}{12}$ $6\frac{1}{6}$ $10\frac{7}{10}$ $9\frac{7}{15}$

10. $7\frac{5}{3} = 8\frac{2}{3}$ $16\frac{3}{2} = 17\frac{1}{2}$

    $1\frac{7}{4} = 2\frac{3}{4}$ $3\frac{6}{5} = 4\frac{1}{5}$

    $11\frac{7}{5} = 12\frac{2}{5}$ $6\frac{9}{7} = 7\frac{2}{7}$

    $8\frac{4}{3} = 9\frac{1}{3}$ $13\frac{9}{6} = 14\frac{3}{6} = 14\frac{1}{2}$

Test 12

1. $20\frac{6}{4} = 21\frac{2}{4} = 21\frac{1}{2}$ $11\frac{11}{9} = 12\frac{2}{9}$

$56\dfrac{16}{12} = 57\dfrac{4}{12} = 57\dfrac{1}{3}$ $16\dfrac{17}{12} = 17\dfrac{5}{12}$

2. $20\dfrac{7}{6} = 21\dfrac{1}{6}$ $22\dfrac{80}{56} = 23\dfrac{24}{56} = 23\dfrac{3}{7}$

$40\dfrac{48}{35} = 41\dfrac{13}{35}$ $37\dfrac{169}{99} = 38\dfrac{70}{99}$

3. $73\dfrac{3}{8}$ $18\dfrac{1}{4}$ $\dfrac{5}{6}$ $1\dfrac{7}{12}$ $6\dfrac{3}{8}$

4. $\dfrac{11}{12}$ $2\dfrac{5}{12}$ $17\dfrac{1}{5}$

$16\dfrac{5}{6}$ $32\dfrac{13}{10} = 33\dfrac{3}{10}$

5. 6   6   3   10
   9   6   4   18

6. $\dfrac{1}{56}$ $\dfrac{6}{63} = \dfrac{2}{21}$ $\dfrac{5}{12}$ $\dfrac{5}{77}$

$\dfrac{14}{16} = \dfrac{7}{8}$ $\dfrac{2}{7}$ $\dfrac{6}{7}$ $\dfrac{24}{117} = \dfrac{8}{39}$

7. $\dfrac{21}{21} = 1$ $\dfrac{18}{10} = 1\dfrac{8}{10} = 1\dfrac{4}{5}$

$\dfrac{39}{12} = 3\dfrac{3}{12} = 3\dfrac{1}{4}$ $\dfrac{33}{5} = 6\dfrac{3}{5}$

$\dfrac{36}{21} = 1\dfrac{15}{21} = 1\dfrac{5}{7}$ $\dfrac{35}{18} = 1\dfrac{17}{18}$

8. 9   77   40   20

9. $\dfrac{3}{10}$ $\dfrac{6}{28} = \dfrac{3}{14}$ $\dfrac{5}{56}$ $\dfrac{4}{21}$

$\dfrac{5}{36}$ $\dfrac{9}{20}$ $\dfrac{15}{15} = 1$ $\dfrac{7}{12}$

Test 13

1. $\dfrac{75}{7} = 10\dfrac{5}{7}$ $\dfrac{10}{3} = 3\dfrac{1}{3}$ $\dfrac{16}{7} = 2\dfrac{2}{7}$

$\dfrac{12}{25}$ $\dfrac{14}{9} = 1\dfrac{5}{9}$ $\dfrac{35}{6} = 5\dfrac{5}{6}$

$\dfrac{21}{2} = 10\dfrac{1}{2}$ $\dfrac{15}{4} = 3\dfrac{3}{4}$

2. 1 to 3; 1:3; $\dfrac{1}{3}$ 2 to 2; 2:2; $\dfrac{2}{2}$

   4 to 2; 4:2; $\dfrac{4}{2}$

3. Mittens: 2   4   6   8   10 12
   Snowmen: 1   2   3   4   5   6

   Hot Chocolate: 1   2   3   4   5
   Water: 3   6   9 12 15

4. Candy: 120 110 100 90 80 70
   Bag   12 11 10   9   8   7

   Mints: 6   5   4   3   2   1
   Roll: 36 30 24 18 12   6

5. yes   yes
   no   no
   yes   yes
   yes   no

6. 0.3   0.1
   three tenths   one tenth

   1.7   0.6
   one and seven tenths   six tenths

7. 1.32   1.06
   one and thirty-two   one and six
   hundredths   hundredths

   2.09   3.17
   two and nine   three and seventeen
   hundredths   hundredths

8. 1.639   one and six hundred
            thirty-nine thousandths

   0.030   thirty thousandths

7.008   seven and eight thousandths

0.015   fifteen thousandths

9. 4.11 $<$ 4.12   3.05 $<$ 3.50   1.05 $>$ 1.01
0.400 $>$ 0.040   4.09 $=$ 4.090   0.017 $<$ 0.170
0.250 $>$ 0.205   21.02 $<$ 21.22

10. 114   110   11   10   144
    0.9   20.5   3.7   1.3   13

Test 14

1. 82   51   27
  5   81   136

2. 3.02   19.09   93.27   68.97   134.05

3. 90.99   14.32   49.36
663.24   37.56   451.12

4. 0.8 yards
4.7 liters

5. The answer is 4, because (4 x 2) – 3 = 5
The answer is $3.98, because
$3.98 – $1.99 = $1.99

6. 46.8 29.7   19.2   17.24   32.48
156.8 16.14   0.66   70.48   30.51

7. 3.24 10.45   2.38   .0249   7.3612

8. 89.63 56.12   82.83   13.57   0.614

9. 1.56   4.05   .475   6.45

10.

Ratio	Fraction	Percent
99 to 100	$\frac{99}{100}$	99%
75 to 100	$\frac{75}{100}$	75%
21 to 100	$\frac{21}{100}$	21%
2 to 100	$\frac{2}{100}$	2%
37 to 100	$\frac{37}{100}$	37%
14 to 100	$\frac{14}{100}$	14%

Test 15

1.

Fraction	Decimal	Percent
$\frac{37}{100}$	0.37	37%
$\frac{68}{100}$	0.68	68%
$\frac{5}{100}$	0.05	5%
$\frac{9}{100}$	0.09	9%
$\frac{89}{100}$	0.89	89%
$\frac{14}{100}$	0.14	14%
$\frac{28}{100}$	0.28	28%

2. $\frac{3}{5}$ $\frac{1}{5}$ $\frac{7}{10}$

   $\frac{4}{5}$ $\frac{1}{2}$ $\frac{3}{4}$

   $\frac{2}{25}$ $\frac{1}{4}$ $\frac{9}{10}$

3. 12%   40%   70%
75%   14%   45%

4. 16   15   10
56   36   80

5. 1. 28
  2. 20
  3. 32
  4. 8
  5. Tatting, Latch-hook Rugs and
     Crochet, Knitting, Embroidery

6. $2\frac{1}{2}$ $\frac{7}{8}$ $2\frac{5}{8}$

7. 1. Tons
   2. oz
   3. lbs.

8. 32 ounces   8 cups
   8 cups   32 cups
   8 pints   48 cups

9. 10°F
   98.6°F
   32°F

Test 16

1. 0.007 Kg;   0.081 Kg;   0.478 Kg
   8,000 g;   22,000 g,   102,000 g

2. 8   546   0.012
   .017   2,000   6,000

3. 1. 38°F
   2. -18°F
   3. -4°F
   4. 78°F

4. 1. Yes.   8 oz x 8 = 64 oz
   2. 20 puppets
   3. 50 feet – 2 feet = 48 ft = 16 yards

5. 1. 59 people
   2. Vanilla and Blueberry
   3. Chocolate and Strawberry
   4. 38 people
   5. 22 people

6. 1. range = 12   mean = 94   mode = 95
   2. range = 32   mean = 88   mode = none

7.

Temp.

1. Chicago
2. Week 2
3. 51,   Weeks 3 and 4,   New York
4. 60,   Week 8,   Chicago

8. 1. 60,000,000
   2. Portugal
   3. Spain and Poland, 40,000,000

9. 1. Sleeping
   2. Piano and Homework
   3. 29%
   4. 6%
   5. 24 x 0.38 = 9.12, so Jan sleeps
      approximately 9 hours.

10.

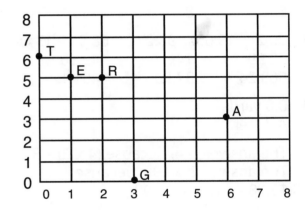

Answer: GREAT

Worksheets

Reproducible Worksheets
for use with Horizons
Mathematics 5

1 Solve the problems.

(1 + 2) + (3 + 4) = _____   (1 + 2 + 3) – 4 = _____   (4 – 3) + (2 – 1) = _____

10 + (15 + 6) – 3 = _____   (2 x 2) + 3 = _____   2 x (2 + 3) = _____

3 + (2 x 2) = _____   (3 + 2) x 2 = _____   8 + (6 ÷ 2) = _____

(14 ÷ 2) + 3 = _____   (20 ÷ 4) + 6 = _____   20 ÷ (4 + 6) = _____

(6 x 7) ÷ 7= _____   6 x (7 ÷ 7) = _____   62 – (4 x 2) = _____

(5 x 5) – 5 = _____   (62 – 4) x 2 = _____   10 x (10 – 10) = _____

2 Add parentheses to make each statement true.

27 + 3 ÷ 5 = 6   64 – 4 x 2 = 56   15 – 5 + 3 = 13

3 x 7 + 11 = 54   9 x 5 x 4 = 180   30 + 4 ÷ 17 = 2

36 ÷ 6 + 6 = 3   35 + 63 ÷ 7 = 44   43 + 5 – 15 = 33

13 – 13 x 4 = 0   48 – 24 + 6 = 18   8 x 8 x 1 = 64

14 + 81 ÷ 9 = 23   15 – 5 + 3 = 7   7 x 3 + 12 = 33

16 – 7 + 3 = 12   64 – 4 x 2 = 120   25 ÷ 5 + 5 = 10

(1) **Find the missing number.** Tell what mathematics operation you used on both sides of the equation to find the missing number.
The first two are done for you.

$8 + 3 = N$ _____ Add 8 and 3 on the left side.
__11__ $= N$

$N + 6 = 15$ _____ Subtract 6. N = 9
$N =$____

$9 + N = 17$ _____
$N =$____

$N + 3 = 8$ _____
$N =$____

$9 + N = 13$ _____
$N =$____

$N + 3 = 7$ _____
____ $= N$

$8 + N = 14$ _____
____ $= N$

$N + 5 = 12$ _____
$N =$____

$2 + N = 9$ _____
$N =$____

$N + 3 = 6$ _____
____ $= N$

$8 + N = 16$ _____
____ $= N$

$N + 6 = 11$ _____
$N =$____

$2 + N = 5$ _____
$N =$____

$5 + N = 10$ _____
$N =$____

(1) **Find the missing number.** Tell what mathematics operation you used on both sides of the equation to find the missing number.
Some problems require two steps when N is being subtracted.

$N - 6 = 7$
$\underline{13} = N$ _____ Add 6. _____

$15 - N = 6$
$15 = 6 + N$ _____ Add N to both sides of equation.
$\underline{} = N$ _____ Subtract 6.   N = 9 _____

$N - 6 = 6$
$\underline{} = N$

$N - 4 = 6$
$N = \underline{}$

$N - 2 = 6$
$N = \underline{}$

$14 - N = 8$

$\underline{} = N$

$N - 7 = 5$
$\underline{} = N$

$N - 4 = 5$
$N = \underline{}$

$14 - N = 5$

$\underline{} = N$

$16 - N = 8$

$\underline{} = N$

$N - 8 = 4$
$\underline{} = N$

$N - 4 = 2$
$N = \underline{}$

Worksheet 8

1) Complete the place value chart.

	Billions			Millions			Thousands			Units		
	hun-dreds	tens	ones	hun-dreds	tens	ones	hun-dreds	tens	ones	hun-dreds	tens	ones
43,702,000,120		4	3	7	0	2	0	0	0	1	2	0
6,750,100												
300,008,946												
250,665,000,000												
7,000,000,000												
600,200,800,100												
625,480,750												
3,500,000,000												
525,000,000,525												
72,000,000,000												
450,000,608												
_____						4	4	2	8	0	0	0
_____				2	8	3	0	0	0	0	0	0
_____				2	7	5	0	0	0	0	8	0
_____			1	0	2	1	6	5	0	0	2	3
_____				4	9	5	2	0	0	5	0	0
_____				5	3	7	0	0	0	6	5	0
_____	4	2	8	0	0	0	0	0	0	0	0	0
_____		1	7	5	0	0	0	0	0	0	0	0
_____	2	5	6	4	3	3	5	2	5	7	8	1
_____		9	0	0	0	0	5	0	0	0	0	0

(1) **Expand each number as shown in the example.**

73,286 = (7 x 10,000) + (3 x 1,000) + (2 x 100) + (8 x 10) + (6 x 1)

a. 7,248,643 = _____

_____

_____

b. 95,607,217,842 = _____

_____

_____

c. 486,273,000,000 = _____

_____

_____

d. 658,426,300 = _____

_____

_____

e. 750,500,428,000 = _____

_____

_____

f. 425,685 = _____

_____

_____

g. 52,769,208 = _____

_____

_____

h. 68,072,029,032 = _____

_____

_____

1 **Round each 2-digit number to the nearest ten.**

68 → _____   13 → _____

97 → _____   44 → _____

75 → _____   91 → _____

18 → _____   26 → _____

43 → _____   77 → _____

35 → _____   66 → _____

52 → _____   13 → _____

2 **Round each 3-digit number to the nearest hundred.**

485 → _____   632 → _____

553 → _____   848 → _____

182 → _____   361 → _____

434 → _____   775 → _____

630 → _____   265 → _____

458 → _____   334 → _____

940 → _____   125 → _____

3 **Round each 4-digit number to the nearest thousand.**

9,558 → _____   4,682 → _____

1,349 → _____   7,250 → _____

5,744 → _____   2,738 → _____

8,672 → _____   3,525 → _____

2,900 → _____   6,441 → _____

4,480 → _____   3,420 → _____

7,623 → _____   2,738 → _____

① **Find each sum.**

7,382 + 6,285	2,481 + 6,296	5,249 + 7,321	8,556 + 3,472
1,478 + 2,649	9,240 + 3,785	5,480 + 8,266	7,548 + 9,362
23,487 + 16,256	73,112 + 15,983	44,289 + 37,674	52,487 + 43,672
35,366 + 56,482	19,776 + 71,849	82,680 + 71,420	69,543 + 27,416
148,250 + 829,769	352,635 + 948,269	782,427 + 363,273	257,433 + 840,676

317

(1) **Write the correct answer.**

☐
24
35
+ 62

☐
12
46
+ 38

☐
23
17
+ 44

☐
72
14
+ 25

☐
68
24
+ 12

☐
83
25
+ 14

☐
56
42
+ 23

☐
34
43
+ 55

☐
33
42
+ 58

☐
88
42
+ 21

☐
65
24
+ 32

☐
43
34
+ 45

☐
432
123
+ 336

☐
523
128
+ 212

☐
632
127
+ 223

☐
541
238
+ 115

☐
127
223
+ 632

☐☐
542
343
+ 156

☐☐
445
276
+ 121

☐☐
356
283
+ 194

☐☐
641
342
+ 159

☐☐
346
152
+ 237

☐☐
544
267
+ 211

☐☐
365
238
+ 149

① **Find each difference.**

648 − 216	829 − 437	747 − 392	535 − 460
700 − 325	250 − 75	600 − 278	256 − 29
2,682 − 735	6,000 − 550	9,000 − 759	4,685 − 856
7,000 − 2,486	4,578 − 2,625	4,000 − 1,392	7,405 − 3,882
6,482 − 3,748	7,500 − 2,799	4,650 − 1,945	5,280 − 2,672
40,758 − 6,592	78,950 − 9,785	32,672 − 4,388	44,250 − 9,376
50,000 − 2,782	70,000 − 9,675	60,000 − 6,482	20,000 − 3,749
32,485 − 13,672	45,382 − 28,425	24,706 − 15,972	53,677 − 32,978
704,328 − 123,730	450,000 − 32,785	348,250 − 192,752	100,000 − 32,680

ESTIMATING SUBTRACTION PROBLEMS

REMEMBER:
Round 2-digit number to nearest ten.
Round 3-digit number to nearest hundred.
Round 4-digit number to nearest thousand.
Round 5-digit number to nearest ten thousand.

① Find the estimated answer and the exact answer.

96 _____	
− 42 − _____	

72 _____	
− 35 − _____	

58 _____	
− 39 − _____	

456 _____	
− 142 − _____	

672 _____	
− 328 − _____	

946 _____	
− 538 − _____	

7,384 _____	
− 2,672 − _____	

4,741 _____	
− 1,593 − _____	

69,458 _____	
− 35,280 − _____	

93,269 _____	
− 58,442 − _____	

ADD MONEY.

① Write each correct answer in dollar notation.

$2.38 + 4.69	$9.68 + 3.23	$7.00 + 4.62	$5.50 + 2.75

$62.35 + 28.20	$45.30 + 18.28	$50.00 + 46.72	$69.75 + 23.90

$124.62 + 75.69	$245.16 + 306.15	$758.52 + 69.34	$258.91 + 135.47

$1.52 3.68 + 5.22	$16.48 32.06 + 75.30	$46.08 22.50 + 34.82	$123.68 270.00 + 386.25

SUBTRACT MONEY.

② Write each correct answer in dollar notation.

$6.23 – 4.30	$8.52 – 3.28	$7.50 – 2.45	$5.68 – 3.42

$17.48 – 9.26	$19.88 – 8.95	$15.75 – 8.32	$14.66 – 6.89

$46.85 – 32.68	$55.72 – 25.35	$98.57 – 49.69	$74.08 – 61.59

$112.62 – 98.47	$224.89 – 139.25	$350.75 – 175.25	$589.70 – 349.35

① Prime factor each number using a factor tree.

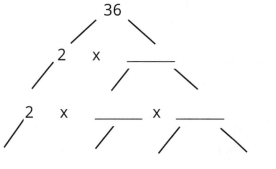

36

2 x _____

2 x _____ x _____

2 x _____ x _____ x _____

36 = _____

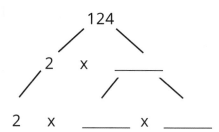

124

2 x _____

2 x _____ x _____

124 = _____

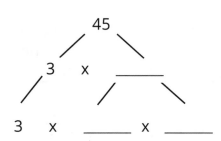

45

3 x _____

3 x _____ x _____

45 = _____

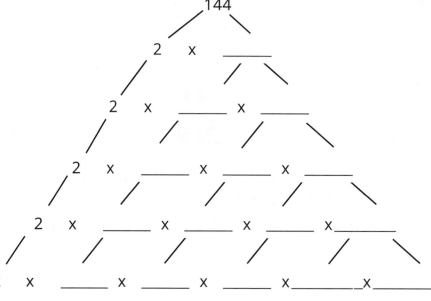

144

2 x _____

2 x _____ x _____

2 x _____ x _____ x _____

2 x _____ x _____ x _____ x _____

2 x _____ x _____ x _____ x _____ x _____

144 = _____

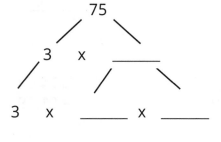

75

3 x _____

3 x _____ x _____

75 = _____

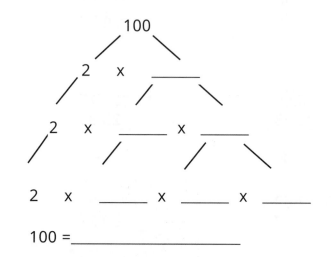

100

2 x _____

2 x _____ x _____

2 x _____ x _____ x _____

100 = _____

(1) **This game will let you find all the prime numbers less than 100.**
(1 is crossed out because prime numbers are greater than 1.)

✗	2	3	4	5	6	7	8	9	10
11	12	13	14	15	16	17	18	19	20
21	22	23	24	25	26	27	28	29	30
31	32	33	34	35	36	37	38	39	40
41	42	43	44	45	46	47	48	49	50
51	52	53	54	55	56	57	58	59	60
61	62	63	64	65	66	67	68	69	70
71	72	73	74	75	76	77	78	79	80
81	82	83	84	85	86	87	88	89	90
91	92	93	94	95	96	97	98	99	100

Follow these rules.

1. Draw a line through every number greater than 2 that is divisible by 2 (use divisibility rule).
2. Draw a line through every number that is left that is greater than 5 and that is divisible by 5 (use divisibility rule).
3. Draw a line through every number that is left that is greater than 3 and that is divisible by 3 (use divisibility rule).
4. Draw a line through every number that is left that is greater than 7 and that is divisible by 7 (divide by 7).

You should have twenty-five prime numbers that are not crossed out.

(2) **Write *prime* or *composite* by the following numbers.**

13 _____   67 _____   76 _____   91 _____

39 _____   47 _____   49 _____   53 _____

31 _____   51 _____   23 _____   81 _____

Prime number chart.

2	3	5	7	11
13	17	19	23	29
31	37	41	43	47
53	59	61	67	71
73	79	83	89	97

(1) **Write the product by adding zeros.**

16 x 10 = _____   2,385 x 1,000 = _____

43 x 100 = _____   6,792 x 10 = _____

25 x 1,000 = _____   4,350 x 1,000 = _____

8 x 1,000 = _____   1,228 x 100 = _____

59 x 10 = _____   52 x 10 = _____

60 x 100 = _____   98 x 100 = _____

93 x 100 = _____   246 x 1,000 = _____

74 x 1,000 = _____   6,285 x 100 = _____

69 x 10 = _____   200 x 10 = _____

84 x 100 = _____   50 x 1,000 = _____

35 x 1,000 = _____   4,280 x 100 = _____

68 x 100 = _____   5,000 x 1,000 = _____

72 x 1,000 = _____

48 x 100 = _____

140 x 10 = _____

236 x 100 = _____

782 x 1,000 = _____

655 x 100 = _____

982 x 10 = _____

475 x 10 = _____

Study this example.

```
              38
           x  25
           _____
             190
             760
           _____
             950
```

Add the answers together.

Answer = 950

Work two small problems

```
    4                      1
   38                     38
  x  5                   x 20
  _____                  _____
   190                    760
```

Multiply by 5.

Add one zero for ten and then multiply by 2.

(1) Write the correct answers.

24	46	53
x 32	x 12	x 22

71	16	42
x 34	x 45	x 13

82	61	35
x 51	x 16	x 26

46	58	17
x 23	x 13	x 21

34	63	39
x 15	x 44	x 14

248
x 324

Add the
answers
together.

992
4960
74400
80,352

Work three small problems

13
248
x 4
992

Multiply
by 4.

1
248
x 20
4,960

Add one zero
for ten and
then multiply
by 2.

12
248
x 300
74,400

Add two zeros
and then
multiply
by 3.

① **Write the correct answers.**

440	320	735
x 243	x 137	x 623

223	162	415
x 436	x 325	x 231

632	118	523
x 425	x 931	x 234

630	410	243
x 652	x 283	x 452

716	424	515
x 324	x 261	x 326

① **Find the missing number.**
Tell what mathematics operation you used on both sides of the equation to find the missing number.

N x 4 = 12   <u>   Divide by 4.   </u>
       <u> 12 </u> = N

2 x N = 10   <u>   Divide by 2.   </u>
         N = <u> 5 </u>

N x 5 = 20   <u>   </u>
         N = <u>   </u>

N x 7 = 49   <u>   </u>
      <u>   </u> = N

5 x N = 45   <u>   </u>
         N = <u>   </u>

N x 2 = 16   <u>   </u>
         N = <u>   </u>

7 x N = 21   <u>   </u>
      <u>   </u> = N

N x 5 = 30   <u>   </u>
         N = <u>   </u>

4 x N = 32   <u>   </u>
         N = <u>   </u>

N x 8 = 16   <u>   </u>
      <u>   </u> = N

N x 7 = 21   <u>   </u>
         N = <u>   </u>

7 x N = 56   <u>   </u>
         N = <u>   </u>

N x 9 = 27   <u>   </u>
         N = <u>   </u>

(1) **For each problem** a. name the base b. name the exponent c. write
the problem in exponential notation d. name the product.
Read the example.

	Base	Exponent	Exponential Notation	Product
4 x 4	4	2	4^2	16
2 x 2 x 2				
6 x 6				
4 x 4 x 4				
5 x 5 x 5 x 5				
2 x 2 x 2 x 2				
7 x 7				
3 x 3 x 3				
5 x 5				
8 x 8 x 8				
2 x 2				
7 x 7 x 7				
3 x 3				
2 x 2 x 2 x 2 x 2				
6 x 6 x 6				
4 x 4 x 4 x 4				
5 x 5 x 5				
6 x 6 x 6 x 6				
3 x 3 x 3 x 3				

MULTIPLY MONEY.

(1) **Write each correct answer in dollar notation.**

$.72	$.65	$.50	$.98
x 4	x 2	x 2	x 3

$1.69	$2.75	$3.50	$7.52
x 5	x 4	x 2	x 3

Write how you would read each answer.

Answer to the first one on row one _____

Answer to the first one on row two _____

DIVIDE MONEY.

(2) **Write each correct answer in dollar notation.**

$4)\overline{\$6.48}$ $2)\overline{\$3.58}$ $3)\overline{\$1.53}$ $5)\overline{\$5.75}$

$2)\overline{\$4.64}$ $3)\overline{\$5.67}$ $4)\overline{\$8.84}$ $2)\overline{\$9.50}$

Write how you would read each answer.

Answer to the first one on row one _____

Answer to the first one on row two _____

① **Find the missing number.** Tell what mathematics operation you used on both sides of the equation to find the missing number.

N ÷ 5 = 7   _____ Multiply both sides by 5
N = _35_

N ÷ 2 = 4   _____ Multiply both sides by 2
N = _8_

N ÷ 2 = 9   _____
N = _____

N ÷ 9 = 7   _____
N = _____

N ÷ 4 = 8   _____
N = _____

N ÷ 4 = 6   _____
N = _____

N ÷ 7 = 8   _____
N = _____

N ÷ 7 = 7   _____
N = _____

N ÷ 9 = 4   _____
N = _____

N ÷ 8 = 9   _____
N = _____

N ÷ 4 = 7   _____
N = _____

N ÷ 3 = 9   _____
N = _____

N ÷ 6 = 6   _____
N = _____

1. **Putting numbers into equal groups is called finding the average.**

   a. Use objects to make three piles. Put 2 objects
   in the first pile, 4 objects in the second pile, and
   6 objects in the third pile. How many objects have
   you used altogether?   _____

   b. Divide the same objects equally into 3 piles. How
   many objects do you have in each pile now?   _____

2. **Find the average number.**

   6, 8, 4   Add: _____   Count: _____   Divide: _____

   8, 9, 7   Add: _____   Count: _____   Divide: _____

   2, 3, 6, 1   Add: _____   Count: _____   Divide: _____

   5, 8, 4, 3   Add: _____   Count: _____   Divide: _____

   4, 6, 5   Add: _____   Count: _____   Divide: _____

   6, 4, 7, 3   Add: _____   Count: _____   Divide: _____

   90   84   65   71   90   74

   What is the sum of the numbers above?_____ How many

   numbers are there?_____ Divide the sum by that number.

   _____Your answer is the mean or average.

   The temperature was 70 degrees F on Tuesday, 73 degrees F on
   Wednesday and 85 degrees F on Thursday. What was the mean
   temperature?_____

   Find your grade average if you have received grades of 95, 85, 76,
   84._____

(1) **Divide. Write the correct answers.**

30 ÷ 10 = _____

41,200 ÷ 10 = _____

32,500 ÷ 10 = _____

68,200 ÷ 10 = _____

1,370 ÷ 10 = _____

4,950 ÷ 10 = _____

380 ÷ 10 = _____

700 ÷ 10 = _____

8,290 ÷ 10 = _____

41,900 ÷ 10 = _____

900 ÷ 30 = _____

45,800 ÷ 40 = _____

176,000 ÷ 80 = _____

31,500 ÷ 60 = _____

2,800 ÷ 70 = _____

31,800 ÷ 100 = _____

29,900 ÷ 10 = _____

19,000 ÷ 10 = _____

400 ÷ 100 = _____

32,800 ÷ 100 = _____

92,000 ÷ 1,000 = _____

114,000 ÷ 1,000 = _____

725,000 ÷ 1,000 = _____

400,000 ÷ 1,000 = _____

812,000 ÷ 1,000 = _____

780 ÷ 30 = _____

10,900 ÷ 100 = _____

98,000 ÷ 1,000 = _____

452,000 ÷ 100 = _____

67,000 ÷ 10 = _____

(1) **Complete these problems in two-digit division.**

$68\overline{)952}$ $\qquad$ $24\overline{)768}$

$48\overline{)1248}$ $\qquad$ $53\overline{)2597}$

$28\overline{)1512}$ $\qquad$ $35\overline{)1470}$

$23\overline{)1035}$ $\qquad$ $42\overline{)672}$

$61\overline{)2501}$ $\qquad$ $48\overline{)1632}$

① **Divide.**

$19\overline{)7,733}$ $16\overline{)3,328}$ $52\overline{)9,880}$ $56\overline{)6,048}$

$28\overline{)5,040}$ $83\overline{)33,366}$ $72\overline{)43,848}$ $95\overline{)13,300}$

$6\overline{)654}$ $4\overline{)1,224}$ $7\overline{)6,860}$ $15\overline{)10,545}$

$23\overline{)11,615}$ $47\overline{)41,360}$ $12\overline{)6,600}$ $34\overline{)27,472}$

$11\overline{)1,122}$ $22\overline{)4,488}$ $33\overline{)10,164}$ $44\overline{)18,040}$

$65\overline{)62,400}$ $45\overline{)31,050}$ $23\overline{)14,007}$ $77\overline{)69,762}$

(1) Check the appropriate column for divisibility. The first one is done for you.

	2	5	10	3
459				✔
76				
500				
84				
321				
450				
210				
685				
143				
243				
68				
305				
264				
455				
288				
462				
430				
255				
168				
4,569				

Divisibility Rules:

by 2 . . . Any number whose ones' place digit is an even number (0, 2, 4, 6, 8).

by 5 . . . Any number whose ones' place digit is 0 or 5.

by 10 . . . Any number whose ones' place digit is 0.

by 3 . . . Any number whose digits add up to a multiple of 3 (such as 3, 6, 9, or 12).

(1) **In the following sentences, write A.M. or P.M. correctly.**

Two o'clock in the morning is 2:00 _____.

It is still dark at 3:00 _____.

We ate lunch at 12:15 _____.

The wolf started to howl a little before midnight at 11:50 _____.

(2) **Answer the following questions.**

Megan and her dad walked to the store. They left the house at 9:30 A.M. The walk took them 45 minutes. What time did they arrive at the park? _____

Ben had a soccer game that started at 4:00 P.M. They played two 45-minute periods and had a 15-minute halftime break. What time did the game end if there were no timeouts called? _____

Annette and Stephen are taking Jessica to the doctor. They planned to arrive at the office at 9:05 A.M. and leave for home at 11:50 A.M. How much time will they spend at the doctor's office? _____

It takes Lisa one hour and fifteen minutes to get ready for school. What time must she begin to get ready if her bus stops by her door at 7:45 A.M.? _____

Mark needs to have some repair work done on his car. The mechanic tells him to bring it into the shop at 9:30 A.M.. It will take three hours and fifteen minutes to make the repairs. What is the earliest Mark can expect his car to be ready to drive again? _____

If a plane leaves New York at 9:05 A.M. on a trip that will arrive in Denver at 11:55 A.M. New York time, how many minutes was the plane in the air? _____

To change seconds to minutes, divide the number of seconds by 60.
To change minutes to seconds, multiply the number of minutes by 60.
To change minutes to hours, divide the number of minutes by 60.
To change hours to minutes, multiply the hours by 60.
To change hours to days, divide the number of hours by 24.
To change days to hours, multiply the number of days by 24.

① **Write the correct number to complete the following rules.**

The number of hours x _____ equals the number of minutes.

The number of days x _____ equals the number of hours.

The number of minutes ÷ _____ equals the number of hours.

The number of seconds ÷ _____ equals the number of minutes.

② **Write the correct number.**

2 hours = _____ minutes   300 seconds = _____ minutes

3 days = _____ hours   720 hours = _____ days

60 seconds = _____ minute   60 minutes = _____ hour

How many minutes are in twelve hours? _____

How many days are in 120 hours? _____

How many minutes equal 720 seconds? _____

How many seconds are in two hours? _____

3,000 seconds = _____ minutes

8 hours = _____ minutes

96 hours = _____ days

2 days = _____ hours

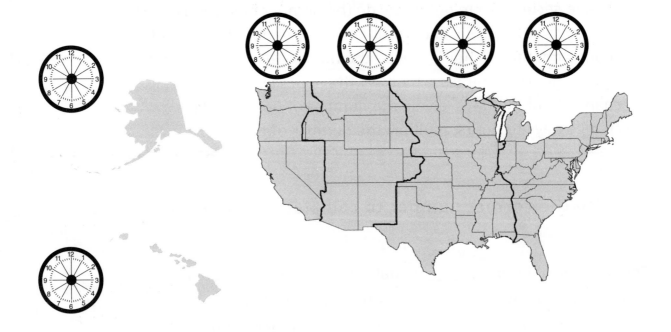

(1) **Complete the following chart.**

HAWAII	ALASKA	PACIFIC	MOUNTAIN	CENTRAL	EASTERN
10:25 A.M.	_____	_____	_____	_____	_____
_____	_____	4:35 P.M.	_____	_____	_____
_____	_____	_____	_____	_____	11:30 P.M.
_____	1:00 A.M.	_____	_____	_____	_____
_____	_____	_____	2:31 A.M.	_____	_____
_____	_____	_____	_____	1:10 P.M.	_____
_____	_____	9:46 A.M.	_____	_____	_____
6:45 P.M.	_____	_____	_____	_____	_____
_____	_____	_____	_____	12:50 A.M.	_____

① **Find the total amounts in cents of each set of coins.**

_____ ¢

_____ ¢

_____ ¢

_____ ¢

② **Write the coins that you would use. Write the dollars and coins.**

	list the coins needed for the amount	list the dollars and coins needed for the amount
$1.36	_____	_____
158¢	_____	_____
$2.41	_____	_____

③ **Write the money. Use dollar signs and decimal points.**

five dollars and fifteen cents   _____   four dollars and two cents   _____

thirteen dollars and seventy cents _____   six dollars and three cents   _____

④ **Write these cents.** Use dollar signs and decimal points. Remember to use the zero place holder. Follow the example.

6¢ is $ .06   507¢ is $5.07

54¢ is_____   60¢ is_____   192¢ is_____

307¢ is_____   5¢ is_____   42¢ is_____

1 **Write money using cent signs or dollar signs and decimal points.** Add or subtract. Label answers correctly.

_____

+ _____

_____

_____

+ _____

_____

_____

– _____

_____

_____

– _____

_____

2 ($) for dollars, (Q) for quarters, (D) for dimes, (N) for nickels, (P) for pennies. Follow the example.

Price	Amount Paid	Change	Dollars and Coins
$3.42	$5.00 – $3.42 $1.58	$1.58	1 ($), 2 (Q), 1 (N), 3 (P)
$ 2.30	$3.00	_____	_____
$ .78	$1.00	_____	_____

1 Complete the chart.

Geometry Terms	Geometry in Pictures	Geometry in Symbols	Geometry in Words
Point	• K	K	Point K
Line	D E	$\overleftrightarrow{DE}$	Line DE
Line Segment	S T	$\overline{ST}$	Line Segment
Ray	X Y	$\overrightarrow{XY}$	Ray XY Always name the end point first.
Angle	A B C	∠A, ∠ ABC, ∠CAB	Angle ABC is two rays that share a common end point.
Right Angle	M N O		A right angle measures 90˚.
Acute	R S T		An acute angle measures less than 90˚.
Obtuse	X Y Z	∠XYZ	An obtuse angle measures greater than 90˚.

2 Which ones of these drawings are lines?_____

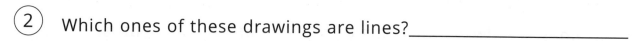

a.

b.

c.

d.

e.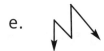

f.

① **Complete the chart.**

Geometry Terms	Geometry in Pictures	Geometry in Symbols	Geometry in Words
Intersecting Lines	l m	l intersects m	
Parallel Lines	x y	$x \parallel y$	
Perpendicular Lines	b a	$a \perp b$	

② **Complete this problem.**

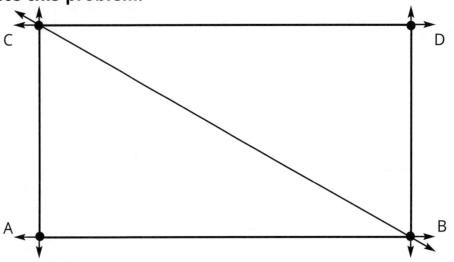

List the parallel line segments. _____

List the right angles. _____

List the lines that intersect with $\overline{CB}$. _____

③ **Match these items.**

____ lines are always the same distance apart   a. obtuse

____ an angle less than 90˚   b. parallel

____ lines that form a right angle to each other   c. rectangle

____ opposite sides equal and four right angles   d. acute

____ angle greater than 90˚   e. perpendicular

$\textcircled{1}$ **Draw angles and label them with the following names.**

ABC

R

$\textcircled{2}$ **Measure these angles using your protractor.**

∠EOD _____

∠GOB _____

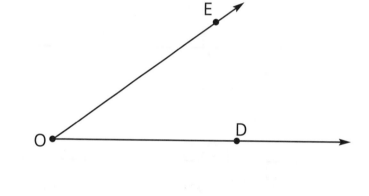

$\textcircled{3}$ **Draw an example of a right triangle. Label the angles in degrees.**

1   **Identify each triangle according to its angles.**

_____

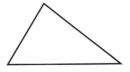

_____

_____

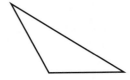

_____

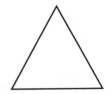

2   **Identify each triangle according to the length of its sides.**

_____

_____

_____

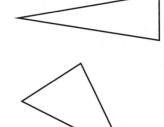

(1) **Match with the best answer.**

_____ 1. rhombus

_____ 2. rectangle

_____ 3. quadrilateral

_____ 4. parallelogram

_____ 5. square

_____ 6. trapezoid

a. Four right angles and all sides the same length.

b. Opposite sides the same length and parallel.

c. Opposite sides are parallel and all sides are the same length.

d. Has length, width, and height.

e. Only one pair of parallel sides.

f. Any figure with four sides.

g. Both pairs of sides have the same length. Four right angles.

(2) **Circle the definitions that apply to each figure.**

square   rectangle   parallelogram   quadrilateral   trapezoid   rhombus

square   rectangle   parallelogram   quadrilateral   trapezoid   rhombus

square   rectangle   parallelogram   quadrilateral   trapezoid   rhombus

square   rectangle   parallelogram   quadrilateral   trapezoid   rhombus

square   rectangle   parallelogram   quadrilateral   trapezoid   rhombus

square   rectangle   parallelogram   quadrilateral   trapezoid   rhombus

square   rectangle   parallelogram   quadrilateral   trapezoid   rhombus

1 **Match the figure to its name.**

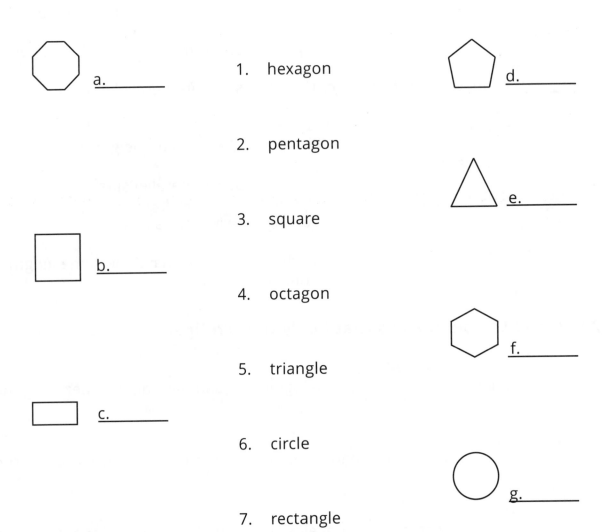

1. hexagon

2. pentagon

3. square

4. octagon

5. triangle

6. circle

7. rectangle

a. _____

b. _____

c. _____

d. _____

e. _____

f. _____

g. _____

Is each of the figures above a plane shape?   _____

Is each of the figures a closed figure?   _____

Do all the sides meet and join each other?   _____

Does each figure have three or more sides?   _____

Which ones do not?   _____

When using a compass, you may wish to back your paper with some thin cardboard so that the center point of the compass will stick in and not slide off your paper.

When drawing a circle, hold the compass at the top. Do not hold the legs of the compass, or you may change the radius of your circle.

Tip the compass slightly in the direction you are drawing so that it is not perpendicular to the paper and pull the compass through your circle. Never push the compass, because pushing may tear your paper.

1 **Construct circles with the given segment as radius and the given point as center.**

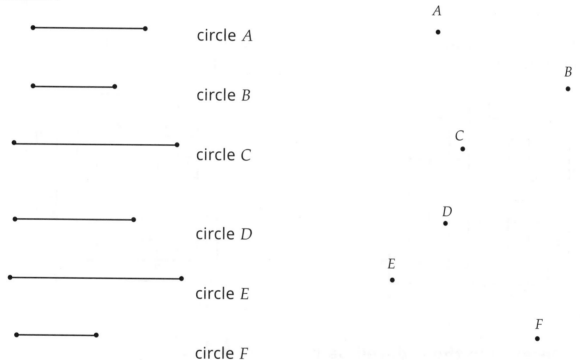

circle *A*

A
•

circle *B*

B
•

circle *C*

C
•

circle *D*

D
•

circle *E*

E
•

circle *F*

F
•

2 **Construct circles with these radii.**

1"

2 cm

$\frac{3}{4}$"

1.5 cm

$\frac{1}{2}$"

3 cm

To graph an ordered-pair number, we find the first number on the horizontal scale, then move up the graph to find the second number on the vertical scale. Remember: First number, horizontal scale; second number, vertical scale.

Locate (1, 2), (2, 3), (4, 5) on a graph

To locate (1, 2), go to 1 on the horizontal scale, then go up 2 units on the vertical scale.
Place a dot where the two come together.

(2, 3) is over 2 and up 3.
(4, 5) is "east" 4, "north" 5.

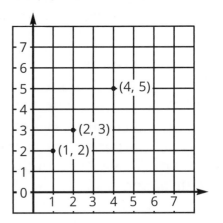

(1) **Graph the points.**
(1, 1) (2, 2) and (3, 3)

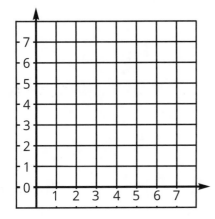

Graph the points (1, 4), (2, 3), (3, 7), (4, 6), (5, 0) and (6, 1)

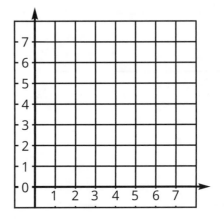

(2) **Determine the ordered-pair numbers for each letter.**

A _____

B _____

C _____

D _____

E _____

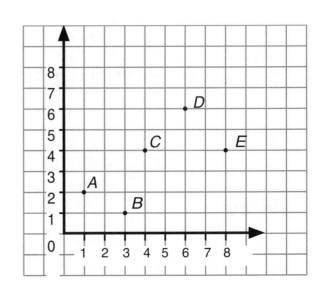

1 **Circle congruent, if the objects are exactly the same.**
Circle not congruent, if the objects are not exactly the same.

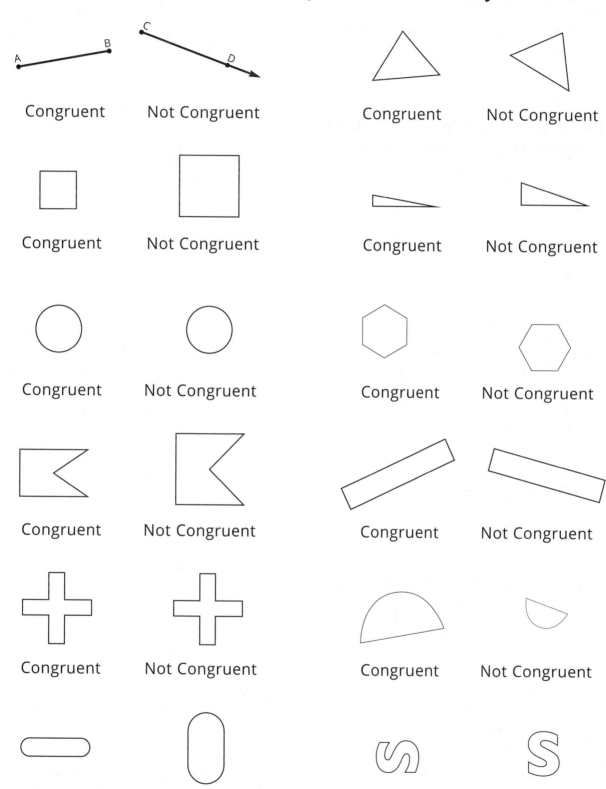

Congruent   Not Congruent   Congruent   Not Congruent

Congruent   Not Congruent   Congruent   Not Congruent

Congruent   Not Congruent   Congruent   Not Congruent

Congruent   Not Congruent   Congruent   Not Congruent

Congruent   Not Congruent   Congruent   Not Congruent

Congruent   Not Congruent   Congruent   Not Congruent

Congruent lines and shapes are exactly the same in size and shape as their congruent figures.

We use the word incongruent to describe two figures that are not congruent.

Similar shapes have the same shape but are different sizes.

① **Describe these figures as similar, congruent or not congruent.**

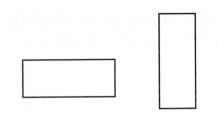

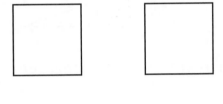

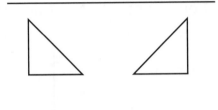

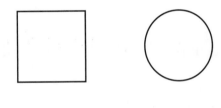

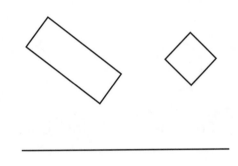

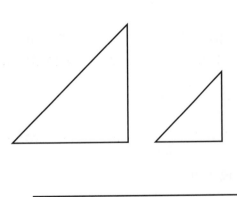

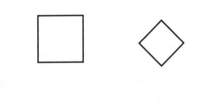

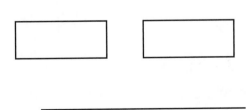

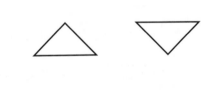

Solid shapes take up space.
Solid shapes have length, width and height. We call them 3-dimensional.
Most shapes are solid shapes.

① **Match these solid shapes to their names.**

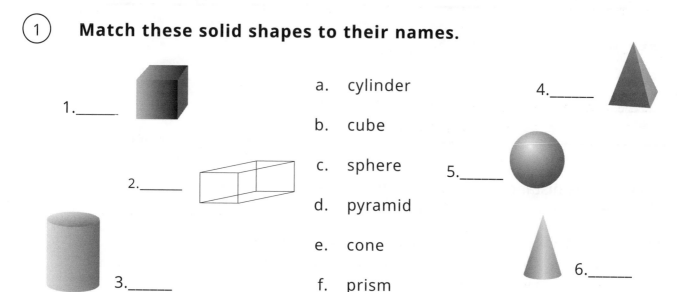

1._____

2._____

3._____

a.   cylinder

b.   cube

c.   sphere

d.   pyramid

e.   cone

f.   prism

4._____

5._____

6._____

There are many examples of solid shapes around us. Cars, lamps, refrigerators and desks are all examples of solid shapes.

② **Write the name of the solid shape by its definition.**

The bottom is round like a circle. The top is a point.

_____

This solid has six flat sides. Each side is the shape of a square. Each square is the same size. _____

The bottom may be any shape of a polygon. The top is a point. The sides must be triangles._____

This is a perfectly round shape like a ball.

_____

The top and bottom of this solid shape are circles.

_____

| $\frac{1}{4}$ | $\frac{1}{2}$ | $\frac{3}{4}$ | 1 | $\frac{1}{4}$ | $\frac{1}{2}$ | $\frac{3}{4}$ | 2 | $\frac{1}{4}$ | $\frac{1}{2}$ | $\frac{3}{4}$ | 3 | $\frac{1}{4}$ | $\frac{1}{2}$ | $\frac{3}{4}$ | 4 | $\frac{1}{4}$ | $\frac{1}{2}$ | $\frac{3}{4}$ | 5 | $\frac{1}{4}$ | $\frac{1}{2}$ | $\frac{3}{4}$ | 6 |

① **Measure the linear inches.**

_____   _____ linear inches

_____   _____ linear inches

_____   _____ linear inches

Perimeter is the distance around the outside of a plane shape.
Perimeter is measured in linear inches.

② **Measure the sides of each shape. Use your ruler.**
Use the ruler at the top of the page as a number line.
Add the inches. Find the perimeter of each shape.

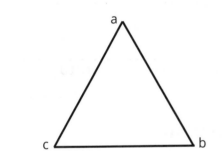

Measure from a to b. _____

Measure from b to c. _____

Measure from c to a. _____

Add.   _____ linear inches

The perimeter is _____ linear inches.

Measure from a to b. _____

Measure from b to c. _____

Measure from c to d. _____

Measure from d to a. _____

Add.   _____ linear inches

The perimeter is _____ linear inches.

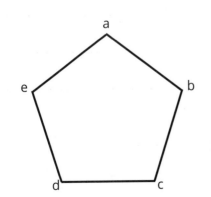

Measure from a to b. _____

Measure from b to c. _____

Measure from c to d. _____

Measure from d to e. _____

Measure from e to a. _____

Add.   _____ linear inches

The perimeter is _____ linear inches.

1 **Find the area. One unit of measurement is shown for each figure.**

1 square foot → area _____

1 square yard → area _____

2 **Find the area of each polygon. Label answers in square measurements.**

A square	side	=	7 inches	_____
A square	side	=	2 yards	_____
A rectangle	length	=	8 yards	
	width	=	4 yards	_____
A rectangle	length	=	23 inches	
	width	=	9 inches	_____
A rectangle	length	=	14 feet	
	width	=	5 feet	_____
A square	side	=	6 feet	_____
A square	side	=	9 meters	_____
A rectangle	length	=	21 centimeters	
	width	=	8 centimeters	_____
A rectangle	length	=	12 meters	
	width	=	8 meters	_____
A rectangle	length	=	16 feet	
	width	=	6 feet	_____
A square	side	=	10 miles	_____
A square	side	=	4 centimeters	_____
A square	side	=	8 kilometers	_____
A rectangle	length	=	50 kilometers	
	width	=	8 kilometers	_____
A rectangle	length	=	28 inches	
	width	=	6 inches	_____

Volume is the measurement of the space that a solid shape occupies.

The volume of a rectangle is   V = L (length) x W (width) x H (height).

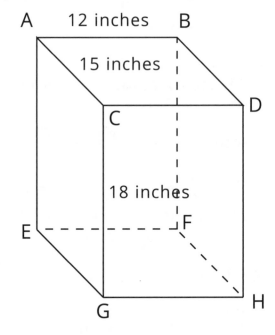

Width = 12 inches
Length = 15 inches
Height = 18 inches

Look carefully at the 3-dimensional figure.

① **Find the volume of this rectangular solid.**
Label the answer correctly.   _____

② **Using the formula of V = L x W x H, find the volume of a rectangular solid that measures.**

    a.   6 in. by 5 in. by 9 in.   _____ cubic _____

    b.   16 ft. by 14 ft. by 20 ft.   _____ cubic _____

    c.   9 yd. by 7 yd. by 11 yd.   _____ cubic _____

③ **Find the volume of a rectangular solid with dimensions of 5 feet by 6 feet by 8 feet.**   _____

④ **Find the volume of a box that measures 2 feet by 18 inches by 9 inches.**   _____

Surface area.
Look carefully at the 3-dimensional figure.

Width = 12 in.
Length = 15 in.
Height = 18 in.

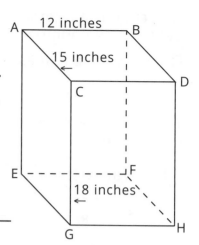

12 inches
A   B
15 inches
                    D
        C
E   F
        18 inches
                    H
    G

(1) **Find the area of rectangle ABDC.** _____

(2) **Find the area of rectangle ACGE.**
(Label correctly.) _____

(3) **Find the area of rectangle CDHG.** _____

(4) **Rectangle ABDC is congruent to rectangle** _____ .

Rectangle ACGE is congruent to rectangle _____ .

Rectangle CDHG is congruent to rectangle _____ .

(5) **Two times the area of rectangle ABDC.** _____ x 2 = _____

Two times the area of rectangle ACGE. _____ x 2 = _____

Two times the area of rectangle CDHG. _____ x 2 = _____

(6) **Add the surface area of the six sides
to find the total surface area.** _____

(7) **Find the surface area of the two boxes.**

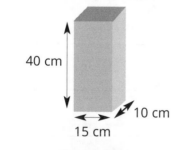

40 cm
10 cm
15 cm

Front	40 cm x 15 cm = _____ x 2 = _____
Top	15 cm x 10 cm = _____ x 2 = _____
Side	40 cm x 10 cm = _____ x 2 = _____
	Total _____

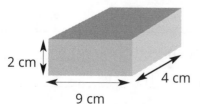

2 cm
4 cm
9 cm

Front	2 cm x 9 cm = _____ x 2 = _____
Top	9 cm x 4 cm = _____ x 2 = _____
Side	2 cm x 4 cm = _____ x 2 = _____
	Total _____

A fraction is a number that represents the parts of a whole number or a relationship between two numbers.

Fractions have names. $\dfrac{5}{6}$
5 is the numerator.
6 is the denominator.
The 5 and 6 are separated by a fraction bar.

The fraction is written and read five-sixths. A hyphen separates the numerator and denominator.

(1) **Name the part of the fraction marked with an asterisk (star).**

a. $*\dfrac{6}{8}$ _____

b. $\dfrac{14}{12}*$ _____

c. $\dfrac{2}{7}*$ _____

d. $*\dfrac{1}{9}$ _____

e. $*\dfrac{4}{11}$ _____

f. $\dfrac{13}{20}*$ _____

g. $*\dfrac{4}{12}$ _____

h. $*\dfrac{1}{10}$ _____

i. $\dfrac{6}{7}*$ _____

j. $\dfrac{2}{15}*$ _____

(2) **Write each fraction in words or numbers.**

a. $\dfrac{7}{12}$ _____

b. $\dfrac{1}{2}$ _____

c. $\dfrac{4}{7}$ _____

d. $\dfrac{2}{9}$ _____

e. $\dfrac{8}{15}$ _____

f. $\dfrac{7}{9}$ _____

g. $\dfrac{3}{8}$ _____

h. $\dfrac{2}{5}$ _____

i. one-third _____

j. four-tenths _____

k. five-eighths _____

l. one-fourth _____

m. seven-eighths _____

n. six-ninths _____

o. five-elevenths _____

Equivalent fractions are fractions that are equal to each other. Equivalent fractions may be formed by multiplying or dividing the numerator and denominator by the same number.

$$\frac{3}{4} \times \frac{2}{2} = \frac{6}{8} \qquad\qquad \frac{8}{12} \div \frac{4}{4} = \frac{2}{3}$$

The following exercises in equivalent fractions have the denominators provided for you. You will need to find the missing numerator.

Find the number that the denominator has been multiplied or divided by. Multiply or divide the numerator by the same number.

(1) a. $\dfrac{1}{2} = \dfrac{}{12}$

b. $\dfrac{2}{3} = \dfrac{}{12}$

c. $\dfrac{3}{4} = \dfrac{}{12}$

d. $\dfrac{1}{2} = \dfrac{}{8}$

e. $\dfrac{1}{3} = \dfrac{}{6}$

f. $\dfrac{3}{4} = \dfrac{}{8}$

g. $\dfrac{1}{2} = \dfrac{}{10}$

h. $\dfrac{2}{3} = \dfrac{}{15}$

i. $\dfrac{4}{5} = \dfrac{}{10}$

(2) a. $\dfrac{2}{3} = \dfrac{}{9}$

b. $\dfrac{1}{4} = \dfrac{}{16}$

c. $\dfrac{2}{5} = \dfrac{}{15}$

d. $\dfrac{3}{8} = \dfrac{}{16}$

e. $\dfrac{1}{9} = \dfrac{}{18}$

f. $\dfrac{7}{8} = \dfrac{}{16}$

g. $\dfrac{1}{5} = \dfrac{}{25}$

h. $\dfrac{5}{8} = \dfrac{}{24}$

i. $\dfrac{2}{9} = \dfrac{}{27}$

(3) a. $\dfrac{3}{9} = \dfrac{}{3}$

b. $\dfrac{2}{4} = \dfrac{}{2}$

c. $\dfrac{4}{8} = \dfrac{}{2}$

d. $\dfrac{8}{16} = \dfrac{}{2}$

e. $\dfrac{3}{12} = \dfrac{}{4}$

f. $\dfrac{4}{16} = \dfrac{}{4}$

g. $\dfrac{2}{18} = \dfrac{}{9}$

h. $\dfrac{2}{12} = \dfrac{}{6}$

i. $\dfrac{5}{10} = \dfrac{}{2}$

(4) a. $\dfrac{4}{12} = \dfrac{}{3}$

b. $\dfrac{6}{9} = \dfrac{}{3}$

c. $\dfrac{2}{10} = \dfrac{}{5}$

d. $\dfrac{10}{12} = \dfrac{}{6}$

e. $\dfrac{7}{14} = \dfrac{}{2}$

f. $\dfrac{3}{18} = \dfrac{}{6}$

g. $\dfrac{16}{18} = \dfrac{}{9}$

h. $\dfrac{7}{21} = \dfrac{}{3}$

i. $\dfrac{4}{18} = \dfrac{}{9}$

1 **Write the missing lower term.**

a. $\dfrac{3}{9} = \dfrac{}{3}$ $\left(\dfrac{3 \div}{9 \div} = \dfrac{}{3} \right)$ $\dfrac{4}{12} = \dfrac{}{3}$

b. $\dfrac{2}{4} = \dfrac{}{2}$ $\left(\dfrac{2 \div}{4 \div} = \dfrac{}{2} \right)$ $\dfrac{6}{9} = \dfrac{}{3}$

c. $\dfrac{4}{8} = \dfrac{}{2}$ $\left(\dfrac{4 \div}{8 \div} = \dfrac{}{2} \right)$ $\dfrac{2}{10} = \dfrac{}{5}$

d. $\dfrac{8}{16} = \dfrac{}{2}$ $\dfrac{7}{14} = \dfrac{}{2}$

e. $\dfrac{3}{12} = \dfrac{}{4}$ $\dfrac{3}{18} = \dfrac{}{6}$

f. $\dfrac{4}{16} = \dfrac{}{4}$ $\dfrac{16}{18} = \dfrac{}{9}$

g. $\dfrac{2}{18} = \dfrac{}{9}$ $\dfrac{7}{21} = \dfrac{}{3}$

h. $\dfrac{2}{12} = \dfrac{}{6}$ $\dfrac{12}{16} = \dfrac{}{4}$

i. $\dfrac{5}{15} = \dfrac{}{3}$ $\dfrac{4}{18} = \dfrac{}{9}$

2 **Reduce these fractions to lowest terms.**
1. Choose the greatest common factor (GCF).
2. Divide both terms by the GCF

a. $\dfrac{2}{4}$ $\dfrac{2}{10}$ $\dfrac{6}{9}$

b. $\dfrac{8}{12}$ $\dfrac{8}{16}$ $\dfrac{5}{10}$

c. $\dfrac{10}{14}$ $\dfrac{6}{8}$ $\dfrac{6}{15}$

d. $\dfrac{3}{9}$ $\dfrac{8}{20}$ $\dfrac{3}{15}$

e. $\dfrac{14}{16}$ $\dfrac{5}{15}$ $\dfrac{6}{14}$

f. $\dfrac{10}{20}$ $\dfrac{7}{14}$ $\dfrac{4}{6}$

g. $\dfrac{4}{16}$ $\dfrac{2}{12}$ $\dfrac{4}{12}$

h. $\dfrac{5}{20}$ $\dfrac{2}{14}$ $\dfrac{12}{14}$

i. $\dfrac{8}{14}$ $\dfrac{10}{12}$ $\dfrac{4}{10}$

Add or subtract. Simplify.

①

a. $\dfrac{3}{8}$
 $+ \dfrac{1}{8}$

b. $\dfrac{4}{10}$
 $+ \dfrac{2}{10}$

c. $\dfrac{3}{9}$
 $+ \dfrac{3}{9}$

d. $\dfrac{7}{21}$
 $+ \dfrac{7}{21}$

e. $\dfrac{1}{6}$
 $+ \dfrac{3}{6}$

f. $\dfrac{6}{12}$
 $+ \dfrac{3}{12}$

g. $\dfrac{5}{14}$
 $+ \dfrac{3}{14}$

h. $\dfrac{6}{16}$
 $+ \dfrac{8}{16}$

i. $\dfrac{2}{15}$
 $+ \dfrac{8}{15}$

j. $\dfrac{5}{20}$
 $+ \dfrac{10}{20}$

②

a. $\dfrac{3}{8}$
 $- \dfrac{1}{8}$

b. $\dfrac{6}{12}$
 $- \dfrac{3}{12}$

c. $\dfrac{4}{10}$
 $- \dfrac{2}{10}$

d. $\dfrac{5}{14}$
 $- \dfrac{3}{14}$

e. $\dfrac{6}{9}$
 $- \dfrac{3}{9}$

f. $\dfrac{8}{16}$
 $- \dfrac{6}{16}$

g. $\dfrac{14}{21}$
 $- \dfrac{7}{21}$

h. $\dfrac{8}{15}$
 $- \dfrac{2}{15}$

i. $\dfrac{3}{6}$
 $- \dfrac{1}{6}$

j. $\dfrac{10}{20}$
 $- \dfrac{5}{20}$

(1) Change each improper fraction to a whole number or a mixed number.

a. $\frac{5}{4}$

b. $\frac{10}{2}$

c. $\frac{7}{6}$

d. $\frac{9}{6}$

e. $\frac{15}{5}$

f. $\frac{12}{4}$

g. $\frac{13}{9}$

h. $\frac{9}{8}$

i. $\frac{12}{6}$

j. $\frac{4}{2}$

k. $\frac{5}{3}$

l. $\frac{3}{2}$

m. $\frac{6}{5}$

n. $\frac{11}{7}$

o. $\frac{15}{8}$

p. $\frac{18}{9}$

q. $\frac{14}{2}$

r. $\frac{10}{7}$

s. $\frac{12}{5}$

t. $\frac{16}{4}$

(2) Change each mixed number to an improper fraction.

a. $1\frac{1}{3}$

b. $2\frac{1}{2}$

c. $7\frac{1}{5}$

d. $4\frac{2}{3}$

e. $6\frac{1}{3}$

f. $1\frac{4}{5}$

g. $2\frac{1}{3}$

h. $7\frac{1}{2}$

i. $3\frac{2}{3}$

j. $3\frac{1}{8}$

k. $4\frac{4}{5}$

l. $1\frac{1}{6}$

m. $5\frac{2}{3}$

n. $2\frac{1}{5}$

o. $6\frac{1}{8}$

p. $5\frac{1}{3}$

q. $7\frac{2}{3}$

r. $6\frac{1}{2}$

s. $4\frac{3}{5}$

t. $3\frac{2}{5}$

① **Add unlike fractions.**

$$\frac{1}{3}$$
$$+\ \frac{1}{2}$$
_____

$$\frac{1}{4}$$
$$+\ \frac{1}{2}$$
_____

$$\frac{4}{10}$$
$$+\ \frac{1}{2}$$
_____

$$\frac{2}{4}$$
$$+\ \frac{1}{3}$$
_____

$$\frac{1}{3}$$
$$+\ \frac{1}{4}$$
_____

$$\frac{2}{5}$$
$$+\ \frac{1}{10}$$
_____

$$\frac{2}{6}$$
$$+\ \frac{1}{2}$$
_____

$$\frac{1}{7}$$
$$+\ \frac{2}{14}$$
_____

$$\frac{5}{12}$$
$$+\ \frac{1}{6}$$
_____

② **Subtract unlike fractions.**

$$\frac{7}{8}$$
$$-\ \frac{1}{2}$$
_____

$$\frac{2}{3}$$
$$-\ \frac{5}{12}$$
_____

$$\frac{1}{2}$$
$$-\ \frac{1}{10}$$
_____

$$\frac{3}{4}$$
$$-\ \frac{1}{8}$$
_____

$$\frac{1}{4}$$
$$-\ \frac{1}{16}$$
_____

$$\frac{3}{4}$$
$$-\ \frac{1}{5}$$
_____

$$\frac{4}{5}$$
$$-\ \frac{1}{2}$$
_____

$$\frac{3}{4}$$
$$-\ \frac{1}{12}$$
_____

$$\frac{1}{2}$$
$$-\ \frac{2}{7}$$
_____

1 **Add these mixed numbers. Simplify your answer. Show all work.**

$$3 \frac{4}{15} \qquad\qquad 4 \frac{4}{9} \qquad\qquad 13 \frac{1}{6}$$
$$+ \; 7 \frac{6}{15} \qquad\qquad + \; 8 \frac{2}{9} \qquad\qquad + \; 3 \frac{2}{6}$$

$$20 \frac{3}{8} \qquad\qquad 13 \frac{9}{20} \qquad\qquad 10 \frac{3}{8}$$
$$+ \; 8 \frac{3}{8} \qquad\qquad + \; 9 \frac{5}{20} \qquad\qquad + \; 4 \frac{1}{8}$$

$$3 \frac{1}{3} \qquad\qquad 5 \frac{3}{5} \qquad\qquad 2 \frac{2}{6}$$
$$+ \; 1 \frac{1}{3} \qquad\qquad + \; 4 \frac{1}{5} \qquad\qquad + \; 1 \frac{3}{6}$$

2 **Subtract these mixed numbers. Simplify your answer. Show all work.**

$$7 \frac{6}{15} \qquad\qquad 8 \frac{4}{9} \qquad\qquad 13 \frac{5}{6}$$
$$- \; 3 \frac{4}{15} \qquad\qquad - \; 4 \frac{2}{9} \qquad\qquad - \; 3 \frac{2}{6}$$

$$20 \frac{10}{16} \qquad\qquad 13 \frac{15}{20} \qquad\qquad 10 \frac{7}{8}$$
$$- \; 8 \frac{8}{16} \qquad\qquad - \; 9 \frac{9}{20} \qquad\qquad - \; 4 \frac{5}{8}$$

$$3 \frac{3}{6} \qquad\qquad 5 \frac{6}{10} \qquad\qquad 2 \frac{10}{12}$$
$$- \; 1 \frac{1}{6} \qquad\qquad - \; 4 \frac{4}{10} \qquad\qquad - \; 1 \frac{8}{12}$$

(1) **Change each improper fraction to a whole or mixed number.**

$\dfrac{11}{4}$ _____

$\dfrac{25}{7}$ _____

$\dfrac{33}{8}$ _____

$\dfrac{50}{11}$ _____

$\dfrac{26}{3}$ _____

$\dfrac{41}{5}$ _____

(2) **Complete these activities.**

Write 11 as a fraction. _____

Write $\dfrac{6}{1}$ as a whole number. _____

Write $\dfrac{32}{1}$ as a whole number. _____

Reduce $\dfrac{12}{4}$ to a whole number. _____

(3) **Write the mixed numbers.**

Change $\dfrac{7}{2}$ to a mixed number. _____

Change $\dfrac{13}{4}$ to a mixed number. _____

Change $\dfrac{31}{5}$ to a mixed number. _____

Change $\dfrac{53}{6}$ to a mixed number. _____

(4) **Write the improper fractions.**

Change $1\dfrac{1}{2}$ to an improper fraction. _____

Change $2\dfrac{2}{5}$ to an improper fraction. _____

Change $3\dfrac{4}{7}$ to an improper fraction. _____

(1) **Add these mixed numbers. Simplify your answer. Show all work.**

$$3\frac{14}{15}$$
$$+\ 7\frac{6}{15}$$

$$4\frac{4}{9}$$
$$+\ 8\frac{7}{9}$$

$$13\frac{5}{6}$$
$$+\ 3\frac{2}{6}$$

(2)

$$20\frac{5}{8}$$
$$+\ 8\frac{5}{8}$$

$$13\frac{9}{20}$$
$$+\ 9\frac{15}{20}$$

$$10\frac{7}{8}$$
$$+\ 4\frac{6}{8}$$

(3)

$$3\frac{2}{3}$$
$$+\ 1\frac{1}{3}$$

$$5\frac{3}{5}$$
$$+\ 4\frac{3}{5}$$

$$2\frac{5}{6}$$
$$+\ 1\frac{4}{6}$$

(4)

$$12\frac{8}{12}$$
$$+\ 10\frac{9}{12}$$

$$7\frac{3}{8}$$
$$+\ 4\frac{7}{8}$$

$$9\frac{2}{3}$$
$$+\ 9\frac{2}{3}$$

(5)

$$3\frac{4}{5}$$
$$+\ 2\frac{3}{5}$$

$$6\frac{17}{16}$$
$$+\ 4\frac{3}{16}$$

$$5\frac{5}{6}$$
$$+\ 3\frac{4}{6}$$

1 Add mixed numbers with unlike fractions.

$$2 \frac{1}{2}$$
$$+\ 3 \frac{2}{3}$$

$$7 \frac{2}{3}$$
$$+\ 2 \frac{1}{4}$$

$$8 \frac{1}{5}$$
$$+\ 9 \frac{1}{3}$$

$$2$$
$$5 \frac{1}{4}$$
$$+\ 6 \frac{1}{2}$$

$$4 \frac{2}{5}$$
$$+\ 8 \frac{1}{2}$$
$$6$$

$$3 \frac{2}{3}$$
$$24$$
$$+\ 7 \frac{4}{9}$$

$$1 \frac{1}{5}$$
$$+\ 4 \frac{1}{4}$$

$$2 \frac{5}{6}$$
$$+\ 9 \frac{4}{12}$$

$$9 \frac{5}{6}$$
$$+\ 9 \frac{3}{4}$$

2 Subtract mixed numbers with unlike fractions.

$$16 \frac{1}{2}$$
$$-\ 6$$

$$8 \frac{4}{8}$$
$$-\ 2 \frac{2}{4}$$

$$38 \frac{2}{3}$$
$$-\ 16 \frac{1}{4}$$

$$10 \frac{1}{6}$$
$$-\ 7$$

$$5 \frac{1}{2}$$
$$-\ 2 \frac{2}{9}$$

$$12 \frac{3}{4}$$
$$-\ 6 \frac{1}{2}$$

$$19 \frac{7}{12}$$
$$-\ 17 \frac{1}{2}$$

$$26 \frac{2}{3}$$
$$-\ 12$$

$$52 \frac{1}{6}$$
$$-\ 25 \frac{1}{9}$$

1 **Solve these problems in addition and subtraction of fractions with unlike denominators. Simplify or reduce your answer to lowest terms.**

$$45 \frac{7}{8}$$
$$- 24 \frac{3}{5}$$

$$15 \frac{6}{7}$$
$$+ 31 \frac{3}{9}$$

$$10 \frac{7}{10}$$
$$+ 8 \frac{3}{5}$$

$$11 \frac{5}{6}$$
$$- 3 \frac{2}{3}$$

$$18 \frac{3}{16}$$
$$- 7 \frac{1}{8}$$

$$35 \frac{8}{9}$$
$$- 22 \frac{7}{8}$$

$$62 \frac{4}{5}$$
$$- 5 \frac{3}{10}$$

$$6 \frac{1}{5}$$
$$+ 7 \frac{1}{3}$$

$$8 \frac{5}{6}$$
$$+ 4 \frac{1}{4}$$

$$4 \frac{1}{4}$$
$$+ 1 \frac{1}{5}$$

$$8 \frac{2}{5}$$
$$+ 4 \frac{1}{2}$$

$$16 \frac{1}{2}$$
$$- 6 \frac{2}{3}$$

$$10 \frac{1}{6}$$
$$- 7 \frac{2}{3}$$

$$5 \frac{1}{2}$$
$$- 2 \frac{4}{9}$$

$$5 \frac{5}{8}$$
$$- 1 \frac{2}{6}$$

$$24 \frac{5}{9}$$
$$+ 13 \frac{2}{3}$$

$$11 \frac{5}{11}$$
$$- 2 \frac{3}{22}$$

$$4 \frac{7}{16}$$
$$- 3 \frac{1}{4}$$

Multiply fractions by multiplying the numerators
together and the denominators together.

$\frac{3}{7} \times \frac{1}{5} = \frac{3}{35}$ or $\frac{3}{7}$ of $\frac{1}{5} = \frac{3}{35}$

Multiply to find answers.

(1) a. $\frac{3}{5} \times \frac{1}{4} = $ _____

q. $\frac{1}{4}$ of $\frac{8}{9} = $ _____

i. $\frac{4}{5}$ of $\frac{7}{9} = $ _____

b. $\frac{1}{2} \times \frac{1}{4} = $ _____

r. $\frac{6}{8} \times \frac{1}{3} = $ _____

j. $\frac{4}{5} \times \frac{8}{9} = $ _____

c. $\frac{2}{3}$ of $\frac{1}{3} = $ _____

s. $\frac{2}{5} \times \frac{3}{8} = $ _____

k. $\frac{5}{7} \times \frac{8}{7} = $ _____

d. $\frac{2}{5} \times \frac{2}{5} = $ _____

t. $\frac{2}{3}$ of $\frac{3}{4} = $ _____

l. $\frac{5}{6} \times \frac{3}{8} = $ _____

e. $\frac{7}{8} \times \frac{1}{2} = $ _____

u. $\frac{4}{2} \times \frac{4}{8} = $ _____

m. $\frac{3}{5} \times \frac{5}{5} = $ _____

f. $\frac{3}{4}$ of $\frac{5}{4} = $ _____

v. $\frac{1}{5} \times \frac{5}{8} = $ _____

n. $\frac{2}{9}$ of $\frac{6}{2} = $ _____

g. $\frac{5}{6} \times \frac{1}{3} = $ _____

w. $\frac{3}{8} \times \frac{1}{3} = $ _____

o. $\frac{7}{3} \times \frac{2}{7} = $ _____

h. $\frac{8}{9} \times \frac{2}{3} = $ _____

x. $\frac{2}{3}$ of $\frac{6}{8} = $ _____

p. $\frac{4}{3}$ of $\frac{6}{8} = $ _____

i. $\frac{1}{2} \times \frac{5}{6} = $ _____

(2) a. $\frac{5}{6} \times \frac{1}{8} = $ _____

q. $\frac{1}{16} \times \frac{4}{2} = $ _____

j. $\frac{1}{3}$ of $\frac{4}{7} = $ _____

b. $\frac{7}{9}$ of $\frac{7}{6} = $ _____

r. $\frac{3}{6} \times \frac{9}{6} = $ _____

k. $\frac{3}{5} \times \frac{7}{8} = $ _____

c. $\frac{5}{8} \times \frac{5}{7} = $ _____

s. $\frac{5}{9} \times \frac{8}{5} = $ _____

l. $\frac{1}{4} \times \frac{3}{8} = $ _____

d. $\frac{7}{9} \times \frac{2}{3} = $ _____

t. $\frac{7}{6}$ of $\frac{3}{7} = $ _____

m. $\frac{2}{3}$ of $\frac{3}{6} = $ _____

e. $\frac{4}{5}$ of $\frac{6}{5} = $ _____

u. $\frac{3}{4} \times \frac{8}{7} = $ _____

n. $\frac{7}{8} \times \frac{4}{5} = $ _____

f. $\frac{4}{5} \times \frac{7}{9} = $ _____

v. $\frac{2}{7} \times \frac{7}{5} = $ _____

o. $\frac{3}{6} \times \frac{1}{2} = $ _____

g. $\frac{7}{9} \times \frac{5}{6} = $ _____

w. $\frac{3}{7}$ of $\frac{7}{7} = $ _____

p. $\frac{1}{3} \times \frac{2}{4} = $ _____

h. $\frac{7}{8} \times \frac{9}{8} = $ _____

x. $\frac{2}{9} \times \frac{9}{4} = $ _____

1 **Multiply. Write the product in lowest terms.**

$1 \frac{2}{5} \times \frac{5}{8} =$ $2 \frac{1}{2} \times 2 \frac{1}{4} =$

$6 \times \frac{3}{4} =$ $6 \frac{1}{2} \times \frac{8}{13} =$

$7 \frac{1}{2} \times 3 \frac{1}{5} =$ $2 \times 3 \frac{2}{5} =$

$\frac{3}{8} \times 3 \frac{1}{5} =$ $6 \frac{2}{3} \times 4 =$

$2 \times 1 \frac{1}{2} =$ $6 \frac{1}{4} \times 2 \frac{2}{3} =$

$7 \frac{1}{8}$ of $2 \frac{2}{3} =$ _____ $5 \frac{2}{3} \times 3 \frac{1}{3} =$ _____

$5 \frac{2}{3} \times 4 \frac{1}{2} =$ _____ $3 \frac{5}{6}$ of $3 \frac{3}{5} =$ _____

$3 \frac{1}{5} \times 4 \frac{3}{8} =$ _____ $3 \frac{3}{4} \times 2 \frac{2}{9} =$ _____

$1 \frac{5}{7}$ of $1 \frac{1}{6} =$ _____ $4 \frac{1}{5}$ of $5 \frac{5}{7} =$ _____

$2 \frac{2}{5} \times 2 \frac{2}{4} =$ _____ $9 \frac{1}{6} \times 1 \frac{1}{11} =$ _____

If the problem contains a whole number, change the whole number to a fraction by adding a denominator of 1, invert the divisor, multiply and simplify.

$$6 \div \frac{1}{2} = \frac{6}{1} \div \frac{1}{2} = \frac{6}{1} \times \frac{2}{1} = \frac{12}{1} = 12$$

$$\frac{1}{3} \div 6 = \frac{1}{3} \div \frac{6}{1} = \frac{1}{3} \times \frac{1}{6} = \frac{1}{18}$$

Find the answer by following the division rule. Simplify the answers.

1)
a. $\frac{2}{3} \div 2 =$

b. $\frac{3}{8} \div 4 =$

c. $12 \div \frac{1}{4} =$

d. $6 \div \frac{2}{3} =$

e. $\frac{3}{5} \div 3 =$

f. $\frac{7}{8} \div 14 =$

g. $4 \div \frac{4}{9} =$

h. $\frac{3}{10} \div 9 =$

i. $\frac{5}{8} \div 5 =$

j. $\frac{4}{7} \div 8 =$

2)
a. $\frac{5}{8} \div 10 =$

b. $7 \div \frac{3}{13} =$

c. $2 \div \frac{8}{9} =$

d. $6 \div \frac{1}{3} =$

e. $\frac{3}{4} \div 6 =$

f. $8 \div \frac{4}{9} =$

g. $4 \div \frac{3}{4} =$

h. $12 \div \frac{1}{6} =$

i. $3 \div \frac{3}{7} =$

j. $9 \div \frac{4}{5} =$

A ratio is a comparison of one quantity to another.

A youth group has ten girls and fifteen boys. We say the ratio of girls to boys is 10 to 15 or 10:15. Note that we put the numbers in the ratio in the same order as the corresponding words.

There are a total number of 25 people in the youth group. The other ratios that could be considered are

number of girls to the number of people.	10:25
number of boys to the number of people.	15:25
number of boys to number of girls.	15:10

① **Answer these questions.**

If we have five bananas and seven lemons, what is the ratio of...

bananas to lemons? _____

lemons to bananas? _____

bananas to the total amount of fruit? _____

lemons to the total amount of fruit? _____

Ratios can be written as fractions. In the youth group, the ratio of girls to the total number of people can be written as 10:25 or $\frac{10}{25}$. This fraction can be reduced to $\frac{2}{5}$ or 2:5.

You have 30 marbles. 5 are red, 10 are green and 15 are black.

② **List the ratios, write as fractions and then reduce to lowest terms.**

	ratio	fraction	reduced
red marbles to green marbles	_____	_____	_____
green marbles to black marbles	_____	_____	_____
red marbles to black marbles	_____	_____	_____
red marbles to total marbles	_____	_____	_____
green marbles to total marbles	_____	_____	_____
black marbles to total marbles	_____	_____	_____

① **Divide. Write two equal ratios for each.**

$\dfrac{40}{60}$ = $\dfrac{81}{27}$ = $\dfrac{500}{625}$ = $\dfrac{16}{8}$ =

② **Multiply. Write two equal ratios for each.**

$\dfrac{1}{4}$ = $\dfrac{9}{12}$ = $\dfrac{6}{3}$ = $\dfrac{17}{5}$ =

③ **Complete the charts of equal ratios.**

Boats	1	3		7		50
Fishermen	2	6	8		22	

Students	50	40			10	
Pizzas	10		6		2	1

Eggs12		36		72	
Cartons	1		3	4	

Sundays	1	2	4	9	15	82
Weekdays	6	12				

1 Complete the chart following the examples.

	TEN THOUSANDS	THOUSANDS	HUNDREDS	TENS	UNITS AND	TENTHS	HUNDREDTHS	THOUSANDTHS	TEN THOUSANDTHS	The way it is read
375.021			3	7	5	0	2	1		Three hundred seventy-five and twenty-one thousandths
8.3										
79.6										
81.05										
1,923.17										
31.0618										
0.2561					0	2	5	6	1	Two thousand five hundred sixty-one ten thousandths
300.2										
9.009										
465										
0.410										
54.054										
0.4921										

① **Complete these activities.**

Arrange 0.3, 3, 30, 0.03, 0.003 in order from *smallest* to *largest*. _____

Arrange 0.45, 4.5, 450, 0.045, 45, 0.0045 in order from *largest* to *smallest*.

_____

Rounding is also useful when working with decimal fractions, especially in division problems. The method is the same as for whole numbers. Rounded digits must be dropped, but zeros are not used to replace them because the zeros would serve no useful purpose. They also give a false impression of accuracy.

Model: 7.04725

Rounding to the Nearest	Rounded Number
Ten thousandth	7.0473
Thousandth	7.047
Hundredth	7.05
Tenth	7.0
Unit	7

Note that when rounding to tenths, the zero is written to show that the number is accurate to the nearest tenth. As another model, rounding 45.9952 to the nearest hundredth would be written 46.00 to show that the figure is accurate to the nearest hundredth.

② **Round these numbers.**

	to nearest thousandth	to nearest hundredth	to nearest tenth	to nearest unit
27.4534	a._____	b._____	c._____	d._____
6.2047	a._____	b._____	c._____	d._____
452.9919	a._____	b._____	c._____	d._____

③ **Round these numbers to the nearest tenth.**

2.73 _____   2.79 _____   2.04 _____

9,752.34 _____   759.97 _____

1 Add or subtract.

```
  $  3.21              12.5              $  7.98
  + 14.07             + 0.38             -  2.43
```

```
   29.26               5.75               14.19
  -  5.73             26.                  6.8
                      + 7.91             + 73.52
```

```
    3.08               21                $ 11.65
   - 0.5              - 0.37                7.09
                                         + 68.42
```

```
    0.23               34.8               71.48
   65.87              - 30.9             -  0.55
  +  4.02
```

2 Add or subtract. Add zeros when necessary.

```
  32.609             0.00821            72.6948            310.73
  + 1.7316           + 3.7              -  5.3002          - 41.986
```

```
   16.634             8.4603             35.               25.63255
  372.714             0.00621           -  7.2891          -  0.00359
  +  9.063           25.31
                     + 68.
```

(1) Find the products. Multiply by whole numbers.

a.
```
    3.6
  x   5
```

b.
```
    1.4
  x  26
```

c.
```
    .48
  x  35
```

d.
```
    7.8
  x  62
```

e.
```
    2.8
  x  52
```

f.
```
    9.8
  x  31
```

g.
```
    .46
  x  28
```

h.
```
   8.82
  x  22
```

i.
```
   62.7
  x  35
```

j.
```
    7.5
  x   9
```

k.
```
    6.2
  x  45
```

l.
```
   .762
  x  25
```

m.
```
   .025
  x  62
```

n.
```
    6.3
  x   9
```

o.
```
   4.21
  x 123
```

1 **Find the correct answers.**

a.
```
    36
  x 2.5
  ─────
```

b.
```
    3.6
  x 2.8
  ─────
```

c.
```
    1.4
  x 5.2
  ─────
```

d.
```
    2.3
  x .68
  ─────
```

e.
```
  .032
  x 26
  ─────
```

f.
```
    73
  x .05
  ─────
```

g.
```
    7.8
  x 4.1
  ─────
```

h.
```
  .48
  x 3.5
  ─────
```

i.
```
  .025
  x 62
  ─────
```

j.
```
    9.8
  x 5.3
  ─────
```

k.
```
  .031
  x 16
  ─────
```

l.
```
    63
  x .04
  ─────
```

m.
```
  4.21
  x 6.3
  ─────
```

n.
```
    5.2
  x 3.7
  ─────
```

o.
```
    1.9
  x .15
  ─────
```

(1) Find the quotients. Round to the nearest 100th.

a.

5)15.610

b.

27)56.7

c.

7)58.45

d.

19)1.957

e.

8)7.216

f.

16)8.032

g.

24).048

h.

7).294

i.

9)183.87

j.

9)83.97

k.

14)57.12

l.

26)1.378

m.

8)643.52

n.

27)18.927

o.

3)23.79

① **Fill in the missing numbers.**

Fraction	Decimal	Percent
_____	.42	_____
$\frac{7}{100}$	_____	_____
_____	_____	2%

② **Suppose you have a fraction with a denominator of 10 or the decimal is in the 10ths' position. Convert the 10ths to 100ths and then write as a percent.**

Fraction	Decimal	Percent
$\frac{4}{10} = \frac{40}{100}$	.40	40%
$\frac{3}{10}$	_____	_____
$\frac{7}{10}$	_____	_____
$\frac{2}{5}$	_____	_____
$\frac{3}{4}$	_____	_____

Suppose we have 100 people in a group and 33 decide to leave early.

We could express this number as a fraction. $\frac{33}{100}$

We could express this number as a decimal. .33

We could express this number as a per cent. 33%

③ **Suppose we have 100 people in a group and 5 arrived late.**

We could express this number as a fraction. _____

We could express this number as a decimal. _____

We could express this number as a per cent. _____

(1) **Complete these items.**

14% of 76 = N

_____

45% of 20 = N

_____

25% of 100 = N

_____

72% of 25 = N

_____

68% of 25 = N

_____

27% of 6 = N

_____

45% of 5.7 = N

_____

25% of 24 = N

_____

(2) **Complete these items.**

What is 4% of 75?

_____

What is 27% of 20?

_____

What is 30% of 7?

_____

What is 21% of 200?

_____

What number is 75% of 24?

_____

What number is 5% of 6?

_____

What number is 40% of 120?

_____

What number is 17% of 2.2?

_____

(3) **Complete these items.**

What is 75% of 42?

_____

75% of 72 is what number?

_____

What number is 77% of 3?

_____

24% of 34 is what number?

_____

What is 75% of 4?

_____

80% of 175 is what number?

_____

(4) **What would be 5% sales tax on a purchase of $4.40?**

_____

1 **Write the English units of measure for the following.**

length ＿＿＿＿＿ ＿＿＿＿＿ ＿＿＿＿＿ ＿＿＿＿＿

weight ＿＿＿＿＿ ＿＿＿＿＿ ＿＿＿＿＿

liquid volume ＿＿＿＿＿ ＿＿＿＿＿ ＿＿＿＿＿ ＿＿＿＿＿

2 **Use the chart to solve the following.**

1 cup (c)	=	8 fluid ounces (fl oz)	1 quart (qt)	=	32 fluid oz
					4 cups
					2 pints
1 pint (pt)	=	2 cups	1 gallon (gal)	=	128 fluid oz
	=	16 fluid ounces			16 cups
					8 pints
					4 quarts

8 gals = ＿＿＿＿ qts   12 c = ＿＿＿＿ qts

8 pts = ＿＿＿＿ gal $\frac{1}{2}$ pt = ＿＿＿＿ c

2 pts = ＿＿＿＿ c   2 gals = ＿＿＿＿ pt

2 qts = ＿＿＿＿ pt   16 oz = ＿＿＿＿ c

＿＿＿＿ qts = 10 gals   ＿＿＿＿ pts = 12 qts 3 pts

＿＿＿＿ fl oz = 6 cups   ＿＿＿＿ fl oz = 4 cups 6 fl oz

8 cups = ＿＿＿＿ ounces   8 pts = ＿＿＿＿ cups

4 qts = ＿＿＿＿ cups   4 gals = ＿＿＿＿ cups

8 qts = ＿＿＿＿ pts   6 gals = ＿＿＿＿ cups

1 **Convert these measurements.**

1,000 millimeters = _____ meters   876 centimeters = _____ meters

1 kilometer = _____ meters   2 meters = _____ millimeters

100 centimeters = _____ meters   2 meters = _____ centimeters

2,500 millimeters = _____ meters   2 meters = _____ kilometers

4.8 kilometers = _____ meters

2 **Write the unit of measure (English or metric).**

pounds	_____	quarts	_____	feet	_____
inches	_____	liters	_____	gallons	_____
grams	_____	tons	_____	kilograms	_____
cups	_____	yards	_____	milliliters	_____
meters	_____	pints	_____	centimeters	_____
ounces	_____	miles	_____	kiloliters	_____

3 **Convert these measurements.**

1,000 ml = _____ L   625 L = _____ ml

1 ml = _____ L   2.8 L = _____ ml

43 ml = _____ L   .5 L = _____ ml

1,000 grams = _____ Kg   48 grams = _____ milligrams

1 milligram = _____ grams   16 centimeters = _____ grams

6.75 Kg = _____ grams   243 decigrams = _____ Kg

Calvin read the newspaper to get the weather report for the next day. When the newspaper reported the temperature, it gave the measurement in degrees Celsius. This confused him. He had always seen, and heard, the temperature reported in Fahrenheit degrees. What is the difference?

Celsius is a Metric unit of measurement for temperature, while Fahrenheit is a customary unit of measurement for temperature.

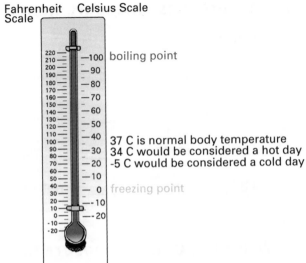

Fahrenheit Scale   Celsius Scale

100 boiling point

37 C is normal body temperature
34 C would be considered a hot day
-5 C would be considered a cold day

0 freezing point

① **Write the Celsius temperature shown.**

_____   _____   _____   _____

② **Draw the correct amount on the thermometer.**

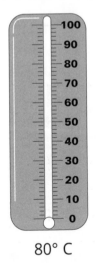   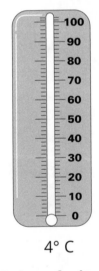

80° C   16° C   47° C   4° C

③ **Match the Celsius temperature with the approximate Fahrenheit temperature.**

95° C   A. 32° F

32° C   B. 205° F

15° C   C. 90° F

-5° C   D. 25° F

0° C   E. 60° F

(1) **Complete the sentences using the graph.**

Ashley read some books one summer about four different subjects.

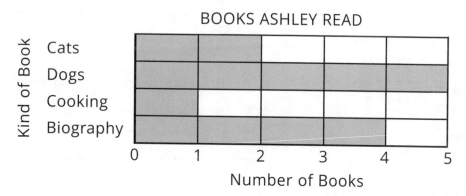

BOOKS ASHLEY READ

During the summer, Ashley read the most number of books about the subject of

_____ .

Ashley read exactly one-half as many books about cats as she read about

_____ .

The total number of books that Ashley read in the summer was _____ .

(2) **Study the graph. Answer the questions.**

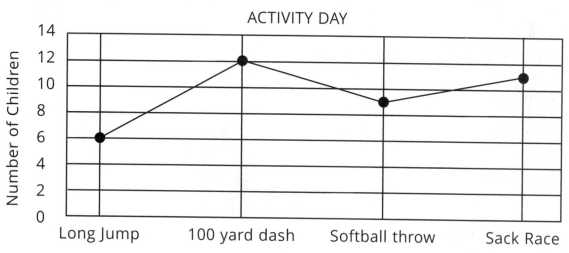

How many children took part in the sack race? _____ .

In which activity did the most children take part? _____ .

How many more children took part in the 100 yard dash than in the long jump? _____ .

What was the total number of children who took part in field day? _____ .

1 **Answer the questions using the graph.**

AGES OF CHILDREN ATTENDING SUMMER CAMP

10 years old ♀♀
11 years old ♀♀♀
12 years old ♀♀
13 years old ♀♀♀♀
14 years old ♀♀♀♀♀
15 years old ♀♀♀♀
16 years old ♀♀♀

Each ♀ stands for 10 children

How many children were 13 years old? _____

Which age group had the most number of children? _____

What was the total number of children attending summer camp? _____

What is this kind of graph called? _____

Which age groups had twenty children? _____ and _____

How many children were in the youngest three age groups? _____

2 **Study the graph. Answer** *true* **or** *false.*

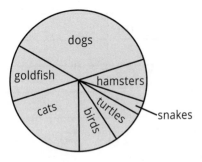

_____ More people have hamsters than dogs for pets.

_____ The number of bird pets is not as great as the number of cat pets.

_____ The goldfish outnumber the turtles.

_____ The number of snakes is small.

MEAN

The *mean* of a set of data is commonly know as the *average*. The mean is found by dividing the sum of the elements in a set of data by the number of elements in a set of data by the number of elements in the set.

(1) **Find the mean to the nearest whole number.**

22, 56, 75, 30, 38, 50

mean = _____

35, 44, 77, 68, 43, 55

mean = _____

12, 18, 17, 6, 25, 18, 22

mean = _____

17, 7, 2, 9, 8, 22, 65

mean = _____

(2) **Find the mean to the nearest tenth.**

3.2, 7.5, 9.8, 11.5, 2.9, 3.5

mean = _____

MEDIAN

Sometimes we are not interested in the sum of a set of numbers, but in how the numbers are arranged. The median is a statistical measure that relates to the arrangement of a set of numbers.

(3) **Find the median.**

22, 36, 18, 20, 19, 16, 22
median = _____

39, 46, 28, 24, 68, 73, 50
median = _____

7, 2, 9, 6, 5, 1, 15, 22
median = _____

68, 39, 46, 28, 39, 56, 48, 29
median = _____

MODE

The *mode* is the number that occurs most frequently in a list of numbers.

(4) **Find the mode.**

2, 6, 3, 2, 5, 6, 3, 2, 4, 2
mode = _____

20, 30, 35, 25, 26, 21, 20
mode = _____

10, 15, 11, 13, 30, 60, 25
mode = _____

100, 60, 90, 80, 75, 80, 90, 70, 80, 50, 95, 100, 80, 85
mode = _____

FORMULA

P = the probability of an event = $\dfrac{\text{number of possible successes}}{\text{number of possible events.}}$

(1) **Write the probabilities.**

A jar contains five balls of which two are blue and three are white. If you pick one ball out of the jar without looking, find the probabilities.

   a. P (blue) = _____

   b. P (white) = _____

A hat contains the names of seven boys and three girls. If one name is drawn from the hat at random, find the probabilities.

   a. P (boy) = _____

   b. P (girl) = _____

If the 26 letters of the alphabet are written on pieces of paper and placed in a container, what is the probability that a letter drawn at random will be a vowel?

   P (vowel) = _____

What is the probability of selecting an odd number out of the whole numbers from one to ten, inclusive?

   P (odd) = _____

What is the probability of selecting a number that is a multiple of 3 out of the whole numbers from 1 through 20?

   P (3n) = _____

(2) **If one disc is selected at random from the following group, find the probabilities.**

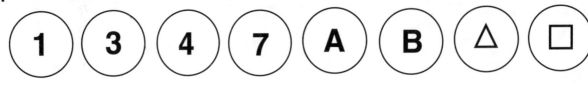

P (number) = _____

P (letter) = _____

P (shape) = _____

P (odd number) = _____

P (even number) = _____

P (vowel letter) = _____

P (square) = _____

Worksheet

Answer Key

WORKSHEET 1

9	13	18	5	11	12	10	9	16
6	13	10	12	7	11	15	10	9
14	8	7	12	10	4	15	6	8
14	14	13	5	6	16	17	11	12
9	8	7	6	8	2	5	5	4
3	3	8	1	10	9	10	7	10
2	9	4	8	4	6	11	11	7
6	12	13	13	9	15	8	13	14
10	12	6	11	15	18	14	11	12
5	12	9	10	16	16	7	14	17

WORKSHEET 2

2	8	3	1	7	2	9	4	4
6	3	7	9	5	2	3	8	5
5	5	3	4	6	2	8	3	2
6	7	5	1	4	8	4	7	6
1	3	4	0	2	5	1	2	7
3	3	5	6	6	4	0	7	9
5	5	0	5	7	7	8	8	8
1	6	4	2	1	2	3	1	3
1	2	2	3	0	5	9	1	3
4	4	0	6	8	9	7	7	6

WORKSHEET 3

9	7	8
2	3	4
12	30	1
8	5	10
27	20	18
6	40	16
24	15	35
2	4	20
10	20	30
9	21	40
25	24	3
8	6	30
45	12	10
90	36	70
20	5	60
4	14	18
24	21	28
42	48	42
35	54	60
7	6	56
49	12	70
63	30	36
56	40	8
9	72	80
72	63	54
16	48	90

WORKSHEET 4

2	3	4	2	3	5
2	6	4	7	2	5
3	8	4	2	9	2
3	2	10	5	4	7
3	8	6	4	5	9
3	7	4	6	5	8
4	7	5	9	6	4
8	5	7	9	5	8
6	7	9	6	8	7
9	7	8	9	8	9

WORKSHEET 5

1.

10	2	2
28	7	10
7	10	11
10	11	2
6	6	54
20	116	0

2. $(27 + 3) \div 5 = 6$ $64 - (4 \times 2) = 56$ $(15 - 5) + 3 = 13$
$3 \times (7 + 11) = 54$ $9 \times (5 \times 4) = 180$ $(30 + 4) \div 17 = 2$
$36 \div (6 + 6) = 3$ $35 + (63 \div 7) = 44$ $(43 + 5) - 15 = 33$
$(13 - 13) \times 4 = 0$ $48 - (24 \div 6) = 18$ $(8 \times 8) \times 1 = 64$
$14 + (81 \div 9) = 23$ $15 - (5 + 3) = 7$ $(7 \times 3) + 12 = 33$
$(16 - 7) + 3 = 12$ $(64 - 4) \times 2 = 120$ $(25 \div 5) + 5 = 10$

WORKSHEET 6

example
example
8, subtract 9
5, subtract 3
4, subtract 9
4, subtract 3
6, subtract 8
7, subtract 5
7, subtract 2
3, subtract 3
8, subtract 8
5, subtract 6
3, subtract 2
5, subtract 5

WORKSHEET 7

example
example
12, add 6
10, add 4
8, add 2
6, add N, subtract 8
12, add 7

WORKSHEET 7 (cont.)

9, add 4
9, add N, subtract 5
8, add N, subtract 8
12, add 8
6, add 4

WORKSHEET 8

Billions			Millions			Thousands			Units		
hun-dreds	tens	ones	hun-dreds	tens	ones	hun-dreds	tens	ones	hun-dreds	tens	ones
	4	3	7	0	2	0	0	0	1	2	0
					6	7	5	0	1	0	0
			3	0	0	0	0	8	9	4	6
2	5	0	6	6	5	0	0	0	0	0	0
		7	0	0	0	0	0	0	0	0	0
6	0	0	2	0	0	8	0	0	1	0	0
			6	2	5	4	8	0	7	5	0
		3	5	0	0	0	0	0	0	0	0
5	2	5	0	0	0	0	0	0	5	2	5
	7	2	0	0	0	0	0	0	0	0	0
			4	5	0	0	0	0	6	0	8

4,428,000
283,000,000
27,500,080
1,021,650,023
495,200,500
53,700,650
428,000,000,000
17,500,000,000
256,433,525,781
90,000,500,000

WORKSHEET 9

a. $= (7 \times 1,000,000) + (2 \times 100,00) + (4 \times 10,000) + (8 \times 1,000) + (6 \times 100) + (4 \times 10) + (3 \times 1)$

b. $= (9 \times 10,000,000,000) + (5 \times 1,000,000,000) + (6 \times 100,000,000) + (7 + 1,000,000) + (2 \times 100,000) + (1 \times 10,000) + (7 \times 1,000) + (8 \times 100) + (4 \times 10) + (2 \times 1)$

c. $= (4 \times 100,000,000,000) + (8 \times 10,000,000,000) + (6 \times 1,000,000,000) + (2 + 100,000,000) + (7 \times 10,000,000) + (3 \times 1,000,000)$

d. $= (6 \times 100,000,000) + (5 \times 10,000,000) + (8 \times 1,000,000) + (4 + 100,000) + (2 \times 10,000) + (6 \times 1,000) + (3 \times 100)$

e. $= (7 \times 100,000,000,000) + (5 \times 10,000,000,000) + (5 \times 100,000,000) + (4 \times 100,000) + (2 \times 10,000) + (8 \times 1,000)$

f. $= (4 \times 100,000) + (2 \times 10,000) + (5 \times 1,000) + (6 \times 100) + (8 \times 10) + (5 \times 1)$

g. $= (5 \times 10,000,000) + (2 \times 1,000,00) + (7 \times 100,000) + (6 \times 10,000) + (9 \times 1,000) + (2 \times 100) + (8 \times 1)$

h. $= (6 \times 10,000,000,000) + (8 \times 1,000,000,000) + (7 \times 10,000,000) + (2 + 1,000,000) + (2 \times 10,000) + (9 \times 1,000) + (3 \times 10) + (2 \times 1)$

WORKSHEET 10

1.
70	10
100	40
80	90
20	30
40	80
40	70
50	10

2.
500	600
600	800
200	400
400	800
600	300
500	300
900	100

3.
10,000	5,000
1,000	7,000
6,000	3,000
9,000	4,000
3,000	6,000
4,000	3,000
8,000	3,000

WORKSHEET 11

13,667	8,777	12,570	12,028
4,127	13,025	13,746	16,910
39,743	89,095	81,963	96,159
91,848	91,625	154,100	96,959
978,019	1,300,904	1,145,700	1,098,109

WORKSHEET 12

121	96	84	111
104	122	121	132
133	151	121	122
891	863	982	894
982	1,041	842	833
1,142	735	1,022	752

WORKSHEET 13

432	392	355	75
375	175	322	227
1,947	5,450	8,241	3,829
4,514	1,953	2,608	3,523
2,734	4,701	2,705	2,608
34,166	69,165	28,284	34,874
47,218	60,325	53,518	16,251
18,813	16,957	8,734	20,699
580,598	417,215	155,498	67,320

WORKSHEET 14

	100		70		60
	40		40		40
54	60	37	30	19	20

	500		700		900
	100		300		500
314	400	344	400	408	400

	7,000		5,000
	3,000		2,000
4,712	4,000	3,148	3,000

	70,000		90,000
	40,000		60,000
34,178	30,000	34,827	30,000

WORKSHEET 15

1.

$7.07	$12.91	$11.62	$8.25
$90.55	$63.58	$96.72	$93.65
$200.31	$551.31	$827.86	$394.38
$10.42	$123.84	$103.40	$779.93

2.

$1.93	$5.24	$5.05	$2.26
$8.22	$10.93	$7.43	$7.77
$14.17	$30.37	$48.88	$12.49
$14.15	$85.64	$175.50	$240.35

WORKSHEET 16

$$36 = 2, 2, 3, 3$$
$$124 = 2, 2, 31$$
$$45 = 3, 3, 5$$
$$144 = 2, 2, 2, 2, 3, 3$$
$$75 = 3, 5, 5$$
$$100 = 2, 2, 5, 5$$

WORKSHEET 17

1.

2.

prime	prime	composite	composite
composite	prime	composite	composite
prime	composite	prime	composite

WORKSHEET 18

160	2,385,000
4,300	67,920
25,000	4,350,000
8,000	122,800
590	520
6,000	9,800
9,300	246,000
74,000	628,500
690	2,000
8,400	50,000
35,000	428,000
6,800	5,000,000
72,000	
4,800	
1,400	
23,600	
782,000	
65,500	
9,820	
4,750	

WORKSHEET 19

768	552	1,166
2,414	720	546
4,182	976	910
1,058	754	357
510	2,772	546

WORKSHEET 20

106,920	43,840	457,905
97,228	52,650	95,865
268,600	109,858	122,382
410,760	116,030	109,836
231,984	110,664	167,890

WORKSHEET 21

example
example
4, divide by 5
7, divide by 7
9, divide by 5
8, divide by 2
3, divide by 7
6, divide by 5
8, divide by 4
2, divide by 8
3, divide by 7
8, divide by 7
3, divide by 9

WORKSHEET 22

example

2	3	2^3	8
6	2	6^2	36
4	3	4^3	64
5	4	5^4	625
2	4	2^4	16
7	2	7^2	49
3	3	3^3	27
5	2	5^2	25
8	3	8^3	512
2	2	2^2	4
7	3	7^3	343
3	2	3^2	9
2	5	2^5	32
6	3	6^3	216
4	4	4^4	256
5	3	5^3	125
6	4	6^4	1296
3	4	3^4	81

WORKSHEET 23

1.
$2.88	$1.30	$1.00	$2.94
$8.45	$11.00	$7.00	$22.56

two dollars and eighty-eight cents
eight dollars and forty-five cents

2.
$1.62	$1.79	$ .51	$1.15
$2.32	$1.89	$2.21	$4.75

one dollar and sixty-two cents
two dollars and thirty-two cents

WORKSHEET 24

example
example
18, multiply both sides by 2
63, multiply both sides by 9
32, multiply both sides by 4
24, multiply both sides by 4
56, multiply both sides by 7
49, multiply both sides by 7
36, multiply both sides by 9
72, multiply both sides by 8
28, multiply both sides by 4
27, multiply both sides by 3
36, multiply both sides by 6

WORKSHEET 25

1.   a.   12 objects   b.   4

2.
18	3	6
24	3	8
12	4	3
20	4	5
15	3	5
20	4	5

474, 6, 79
76°F
85

WORKSHEET 26

3
4,120
3,250
6,820
137
495
38
70
829
4,190
30
1,145
2,200
525
40
318
2,990

© MCMXCVIII Alpha Omega Publications, Inc.

1,900
4
328
92
114
725
400
812
26
109
98
4,520
6,700

WORKSHEET 27

14	32
26	49
54	42
45	16
41	34

WORKSHEET 28

407	208	190	108
180	402	609	140
109	306	980	703
505	880	550	808
102	204	308	410
960	690	609	906

WORKSHEET 29

	2	5	10	3
459				✓
76	✓			
500	✓	✓	✓	
84	✓			✓
321				✓
450	✓	✓	✓	✓
210	✓	✓	✓	✓
685		✓		
143				
243				✓
68	✓			
305		✓		
264	✓			✓
455		✓		
288	✓			✓
462	✓			✓
430	✓	✓	✓	
255		✓		✓
168	✓			✓
4,569				✓

WORKSHEET 30

1. A.M., A.M., P.M., P.M.

2. 10:15 A.M.
   5:45 P.M.
   2 hrs. 45 mins.
   6:30 A.M.
   12:45 P.M.
   170 mins.

WORKSHEET 31

1. 60, 24, 60, 60

2.
120	5
72	30
1	1
720 min.	
5 days	
12 min.	
7,200 sec.	
50	
480	
4	
48	

WORKSHEET 32

11:25 A.M., 12:25 P.M., 1:25 P.M., 2:25 P.M., 3:25 P.M.
2:35 P.M., 3:35 P.M., 5:35 P.M., 6:35 P.M., 7:35 P.M.
6:30 P.M., 7:30 P.M., 8:30 P.M., 9:30 P.M., 10:30 P.M.
12:00 A.M., 2:00 A.M., 3:00 A.M., 4:00 A.M., 5:00 A.M.
11:31 P.M., 12:31 A.M., 1:31 A.M., 3:31 A.M., 4:31 A.M.
9:10 A.M., 10:10 A.M., 11:10 A.M., 12:10 P.M., 2:10 P.M.
7:46 A.M., 8:46 A.M., 10:46 A.M., 11:46 A.M., 12:46 P.M.
7:45 P.M., 8:45 P.M., 9:45 P.M., 10:45 P.M., 11:45 P.M.
8:50 P.M., 9:50 P.M., 10:50 P.M., 11:50 P.M., 1:50 A.M.

WORKSHEET 33

1. 43¢
   29¢
   35¢
   113¢

2. 5 quarters, 1 dime, 1 penny
      1 dollar, 1 quarter, 1 dime, 1 penny
   6 quarters, 1 nickel, 3 pennies
      1 dollar, 2 quarters, 1 nickel, 3 pennies
   8 quarters, 4 dimes, 1 penny
      2 dollars, 4 dimes, 1 penny

3.
$5.15	$4. 02
$13.70	$6.03

4.
$ .54	$ .60	$1.92
$3.07	$ .05	$ .42

WORKSHEET 34

1.
$$\begin{array}{r} .57¢ \\ +\ .35¢ \\ \hline .92¢ \end{array}$$

$$\begin{array}{r} \$\ 5.60 \\ +\ \$\ 6.28 \\ \hline \$11.88 \end{array}$$

$$\begin{array}{r} \$1.29 \\ -\ \$\ .35 \\ \hline \$\ .94 \end{array}$$

$$\begin{array}{r} \$5.45 \\ -\ \$1.28 \\ \hline \$4.17 \end{array}$$

2. $.70 \qquad 2(Q), 2 (D)$
    $.22 \qquad 2(D), 2 (P)$

WORKSHEET 35

1. ∠MNO
    ∠RST

2. a, c, e, f

WORKSHEET 36

1. Line *l* intersects line m.
    Line *x* is parallel to line *y*.
    Line *a* is perpendicular to line *b*.

2. $\overline{AC}$ and $\overline{BD}$, $\overline{CD}$ and $\overline{AB}$
    ∠CAB, ∠ACD, ∠BAC, ∠DBA
    CD, AC, AB, BD

3. b
    d
    e
    c
    a

WORKSHEET 37

1.

2. 35°, 110°

3.

WORKSHEET 38

1. acute
    acute
    acute
    obtuse

2. equilateral
    isosceles
    scalene

WORKSHEET 39

1. c
    g
    f
    b
    a
    e

2. parallelogram, quadrilateral
    rectangle, parallelogram, quadrilateral
    none
    square, rectangle, parallelogram, quadrilateral
    quadrilateral, trapezoid
    parallelogram, quadrilateral, rhombus
    quadrilateral

WORKSHEET 40

1. a. 4
    b. 3
    c. 7
    d. 2
    e. 5
    f. 1
    g. 6

    yes
    yes
    yes
    no
    g-6 (circle)

WORKSHEET 41

1.

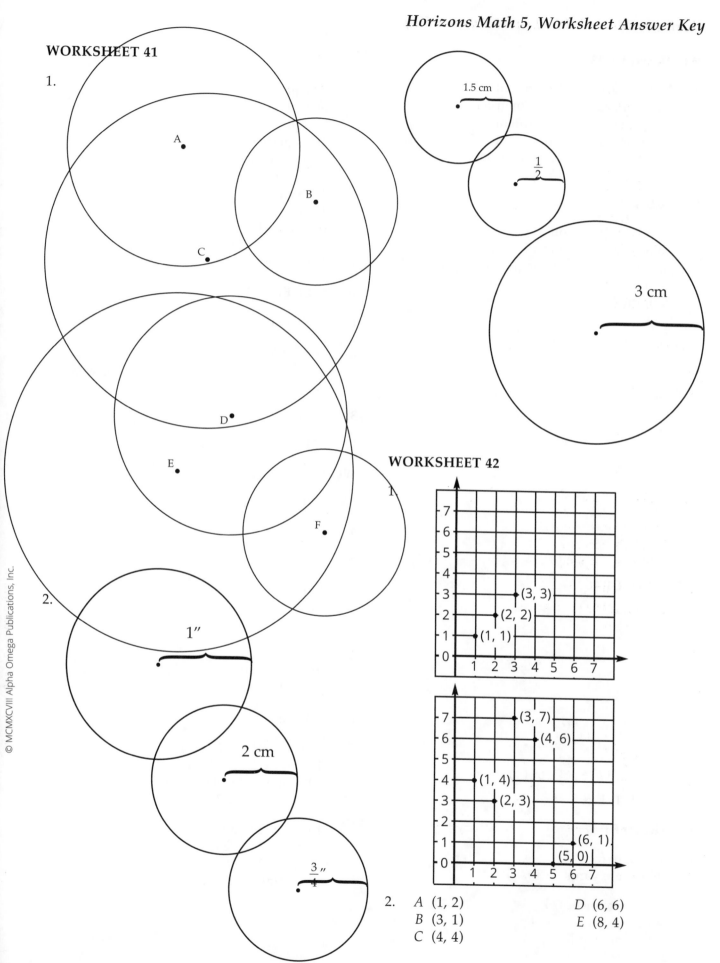

1.5 cm

$\frac{1}{2}$

3 cm

2.

1″

2 cm

$\frac{3}{4}$″

WORKSHEET 42

1.

(3, 3)
(2, 2)
(1, 1)

(3, 7)
(4, 6)
(1, 4)
(2, 3)
(6, 1)
(5, 0)

2. A (1, 2)   D (6, 6)
    B (3, 1)   E (8, 4)
    C (4, 4)

Horizons Math 5, Worksheet Answer Key

WORKSHEET 43

1. Not Congruent   Congruent
   Not Congruent   Not Congruent
   Congruent   Congruent
   Not Congruent   Congruent
   Congruent   Not Congruent
   Not Congruent   Congruent

WORKSHEET 44

1.   congruent
   congruent   congruent
   not congruent   not congruent
   similar   similar
   congruent   congruent
                 congruent

WORKSHEET 45

1. 1. b
   2. f
   3. a
   4. d
   5. c
   6. e

2. cone
   cube
   pyramid
   sphere
   cylinder

WORKSHEET 46

1. $3\frac{1}{2}$

   $1\frac{1}{4}$

   $2\frac{3}{4}$

   $1\frac{1}{2}, 1\frac{1}{2}, 1\frac{1}{2}, 4\frac{1}{2}, 4\frac{1}{2}$

   $2, 1\frac{1}{4}, 2, 1\frac{1}{4}, 6\frac{2}{4}(\frac{1}{2}), 6\frac{2}{4}(\frac{1}{2})$

   1, 1, 1, 1, 1, 5, 5

WORKSHEET 47

1. 8 square feet
   10 square yards

2. 49 square inches
   4 square yards
   32 square yards

207 square inches
70 square feet
36 square feet
81 square meters
168 square centimeters
96 square meters
96 square feet
100 square miles
16 square centimeters
64 square kilometers
400 square kilometers
168 square inches

WORKSHEET 48

1. 3,240 cubic inches

2. a. 270 cubic inches
   b. 4,480 cubic feet
   c. 693 cubic yards

3. 240 cubic feet

4. 324 cubic inches

WORKSHEET 49

1. 180 square in.

2. 270 square in.

3. 216 square in.

4. EFHG
   BDHF
   ABFE

5. 180 x 2 = 360
   270 x 2 = 540
   216 x 2 = 432

6. 1,332 inches

7. 600 cm² x 2 = 1,200 cm²
   150 cm² x 2 =   300 cm²
   400 cm² x 2 =   800 cm²
   Total   2,300 cm²

   18 cm² x 2 = 36 cm²
   36 cm² x 2 = 72 cm²
   8 cm² x 2 = 16 cm²
   Total   124 cm²

WORKSHEET 50

1. a. numerator
    b. denominator
    c. denominator
    d. numerator
    e. numerator
    f. denominator
    g. numerator
    h. numerator
    i. denominator
    j. denominator

2. a. seven-twelfths
    b. one-half
    c. four-sevenths
    d. two-ninths
    e. eight-fifteenths
    f. seven-ninths
    g. three-eighths
    h. two-fifths

    i. $\frac{1}{3}$ m. $\frac{7}{8}$

    j. $\frac{4}{10}$ n. $\frac{6}{9}$

    k. $\frac{5}{8}$ o. $\frac{5}{11}$

    l. $\frac{1}{4}$

WORKSHEET 51

1. a. 6
    b. 8
    c. 9
    d. 4
    e. 2
    f. 6
    g. 5
    h. 10
    i. 8

2. a. 6
    b. 4
    c. 6
    d. 6
    e. 2
    f. 14
    g. 5
    h. 15
    i. 6

3. a. 1
    b. 1
    c. 1
    d. 1
    e. 1
    f. 1
    g. 1
    h. 1
    i. 1

4. a. 1
    b. 2
    c. 1
    d. 5
    e. 1
    f. 1
    g. 8
    h. 1
    i. 2

WORKSHEET 52

1. a. 1   1
    b. 1   2
    c. 1   1
    d. 1   1
    e. 1   1
    f. 1   8
    g. 1   1
    h. 1   3
    j. 1   2

2. a. $\frac{1}{2}$ $\frac{1}{5}$ $\frac{2}{3}$

    b. $\frac{2}{3}$ $\frac{1}{2}$ $\frac{1}{2}$

    c. $\frac{5}{7}$ $\frac{3}{4}$ $\frac{2}{5}$

    d. $\frac{1}{3}$ $\frac{2}{5}$ $\frac{1}{5}$

    e. $\frac{7}{8}$ $\frac{1}{3}$ $\frac{3}{7}$

    f. $\frac{1}{2}$ $\frac{1}{2}$ $\frac{2}{3}$

    g. $\frac{1}{4}$ $\frac{1}{6}$ $\frac{1}{3}$

    h. $\frac{1}{4}$ $\frac{1}{7}$ $\frac{6}{7}$

    i. $\frac{4}{7}$ $\frac{5}{6}$ $\frac{2}{5}$

WORKSHEET 53

1. a. $\frac{1}{2}$ b. $\frac{3}{5}$ c. $\frac{2}{3}$

    d. $\frac{2}{3}$ e. $\frac{2}{3}$ f. $\frac{3}{4}$

    g. $\frac{4}{7}$ h. $\frac{7}{8}$

    i. $\frac{2}{3}$ j. $\frac{3}{4}$

2. a. $\frac{1}{4}$ b. $\frac{1}{4}$ c. $\frac{1}{5}$

    d. $\frac{1}{7}$ e. $\frac{1}{3}$ f. $\frac{1}{8}$

    g. $\frac{1}{3}$ h. $\frac{2}{5}$

    i. $\frac{1}{3}$ j. $\frac{1}{4}$

Horizons Math 5, Worksheet Answer Key

WORKSHEET 54

1. a. $1\frac{1}{4}$

    b. 5

    c. $1\frac{1}{6}$

    d. $1\frac{1}{2}$

    e. 3

    f. 3

    g. $1\frac{4}{9}$

    h. $1\frac{1}{8}$

    i. 2

    j. 2

    k. $1\frac{2}{3}$

    l. $1\frac{1}{2}$

    m. $1\frac{1}{5}$

    n. $1\frac{4}{7}$

    o. $1\frac{7}{8}$

    p. 2

    q. 7

    r. $1\frac{3}{7}$

    s. $2\frac{2}{5}$

    t. 4

2. a. $\frac{4}{3}$

    b. $\frac{5}{2}$

    c. $\frac{36}{5}$

    d. $\frac{14}{3}$

    e. $\frac{19}{3}$

    f. $\frac{9}{5}$

    g. $\frac{7}{3}$

    h. $\frac{15}{2}$

    i. $\frac{11}{3}$

    j. $\frac{25}{8}$

    k. $\frac{24}{5}$

    l. $\frac{7}{6}$

    m. $\frac{17}{3}$

    n. $\frac{11}{5}$

    o. $\frac{49}{8}$

    p. $\frac{16}{3}$

    q. $\frac{23}{3}$

    r. $\frac{13}{2}$

    s. $\frac{23}{5}$

    t. $\frac{17}{5}$

WORKSHEET 55

1. $\frac{5}{6}$ $\quad$ $\frac{3}{4}$ $\quad$ $\frac{9}{10}$

    $\frac{5}{6}$ $\quad$ $\frac{7}{12}$ $\quad$ $\frac{1}{2}$

    $\frac{5}{6}$ $\quad$ $\frac{2}{7}$ $\quad$ $\frac{7}{12}$

2. $\frac{3}{8}$ $\quad$ $\frac{1}{4}$ $\quad$ $\frac{2}{5}$

    $\frac{5}{8}$ $\quad$ $\frac{3}{16}$ $\quad$ $\frac{11}{20}$

    $\frac{3}{10}$ $\quad$ $\frac{2}{3}$ $\quad$ $\frac{3}{14}$

WORKSHEET 56

1. $10\frac{2}{3}$ $\quad$ $12\frac{2}{3}$ $\quad$ $16\frac{1}{2}$

    $28\frac{3}{4}$ $\quad$ $22\frac{7}{10}$ $\quad$ $14\frac{1}{2}$

    $4\frac{2}{3}$ $\quad$ $9\frac{4}{5}$ $\quad$ $3\frac{5}{6}$

2. $4\frac{2}{15}$ $\quad$ $4\frac{2}{9}$ $\quad$ $10\frac{1}{2}$

    $12\frac{1}{8}$ $\quad$ $4\frac{3}{10}$ $\quad$ $6\frac{1}{4}$

    $2\frac{1}{3}$ $\quad$ $1\frac{1}{5}$ $\quad$ $1\frac{1}{6}$

WORKSHEET 57

1. $2\frac{3}{4}$ $\quad$ $3\frac{4}{7}$ $\quad$ $4\frac{1}{8}$

    $4\frac{6}{11}$ $\quad$ $8\frac{2}{3}$ $\quad$ $8\frac{1}{5}$

2. $\frac{11}{1}$ $\quad$ 6 $\quad$ 32 $\quad$ 3

3. $3\frac{1}{2}$ $\quad$ $3\frac{1}{4}$ $\quad$ $6\frac{1}{5}$ $\quad$ $8\frac{5}{6}$

4. $\frac{3}{2}$ $\quad$ $\frac{12}{5}$ $\quad$ $\frac{25}{7}$

WORKSHEET 58

1. $11\frac{1}{3}$ $13\frac{2}{9}$ $17\frac{1}{6}$

    $29\frac{1}{4}$ $23\frac{1}{5}$ $15\frac{5}{8}$

    5 $10\frac{1}{5}$ $4\frac{1}{2}$

    $23\frac{5}{12}$ $12\frac{1}{4}$ $19\frac{1}{3}$

    $6\frac{2}{5}$ $11\frac{1}{4}$ $9\frac{1}{2}$

WORKSHEET 59

1. $6\frac{1}{6}$ $9\frac{11}{12}$ $17\frac{8}{15}$

    $13\frac{3}{4}$ $18\frac{9}{10}$ $35\frac{1}{9}$

    $5\frac{9}{20}$ $12\frac{1}{6}$ $19\frac{7}{12}$

2. $10\frac{1}{2}$ 6 $22\frac{5}{12}$

    $3\frac{1}{6}$ $3\frac{5}{18}$ $6\frac{1}{4}$

    $2\frac{1}{12}$ $14\frac{2}{3}$ $27\frac{1}{18}$

WORKSHEET 60

1. $21\frac{11}{40}$ $47\frac{4}{21}$ $19\frac{3}{10}$

    $8\frac{1}{6}$ $11\frac{1}{16}$ $13\frac{1}{72}$ $57\frac{1}{2}$

    $13\frac{8}{15}$ $13\frac{1}{12}$ $5\frac{9}{20}$ $12\frac{9}{10}$

    $9\frac{5}{6}$ $2\frac{1}{2}$ $3\frac{1}{18}$

    $4\frac{7}{24}$ $38\frac{2}{9}$ $9\frac{7}{22}$ $1\frac{3}{16}$

WORKSHEET 61

1. a. $\frac{3}{20}$ m. $\frac{1}{3}$

   b. $\frac{1}{8}$ n. $\frac{7}{10}$

   c. $\frac{2}{9}$ o. $\frac{1}{4}$

   d. $\frac{4}{25}$ p. $\frac{1}{6}$

   e. $\frac{7}{16}$ q. $\frac{2}{9}$

   f. $\frac{15}{16}$ r. $\frac{1}{4}$

   g. $\frac{5}{18}$ s. $\frac{3}{20}$

   h. $\frac{16}{27}$ t. $\frac{1}{2}$

   i. $\frac{5}{12}$ u. 1

   j. $\frac{4}{21}$ v. $\frac{1}{8}$

   k. $\frac{21}{40}$ w. $\frac{1}{8}$

   l. $\frac{3}{32}$ x. $\frac{1}{2}$

2. a. $\frac{5}{48}$ m. $\frac{3}{5}$

   b. $\frac{49}{54}$ n. $\frac{2}{3}$

   c. $\frac{25}{56}$ o. $\frac{2}{3}$

   d. $\frac{14}{27}$ p. 1

   e. $\frac{24}{25}$ q. $\frac{1}{8}$

   f. $\frac{28}{45}$ r. $\frac{3}{4}$

Horizons Math 5, Worksheet Answer Key

g. $\frac{35}{54}$

s. $\frac{8}{9}$

h. $\frac{63}{64}$

t. $\frac{1}{2}$

i. $\frac{28}{45}$

u. $\frac{6}{7}$

j. $\frac{32}{45}$

v. $\frac{2}{5}$

k. $\frac{40}{49}$

w. $\frac{3}{7}$

l. $\frac{15}{48}$

x. $\frac{1}{2}$

WORKSHEET 62

1. $\frac{7}{8}$

$5\frac{5}{8}$

$4\frac{1}{2}$

4

24

$6\frac{4}{5}$

$1\frac{1}{5}$

$26\frac{2}{3}$

3

$16\frac{2}{3}$

19

$18\frac{8}{9}$

$25\frac{1}{2}$

$13\frac{4}{5}$

14

$8\frac{1}{3}$

2

24

6

10

WORKSHEET 63

1.   a. $\frac{1}{3}$ 2.   a. $\frac{1}{16}$

b. $\frac{3}{32}$ b. $30\frac{1}{3}$

c. 48   c. $2\frac{1}{4}$

d. 9   d. 18

e. $\frac{1}{5}$ e. $\frac{1}{8}$

f. $\frac{1}{16}$ f. 18

g. 9   g. $5\frac{1}{3}$

h. $\frac{1}{30}$ h. 72

i. $\frac{1}{8}$ i. 7

j. $\frac{1}{14}$ j. $11\frac{1}{4}$

WORKSHEET 64

5:7   7:5   5:12   7:12

5:10, $\frac{5}{10}$, $\frac{1}{2}$, 1:2

10:15, $\frac{10}{15}$, $\frac{2}{3}$, 2:3

5:15, $\frac{5}{15}$, $\frac{1}{3}$, 1:3

5:30, $\frac{5}{30}$, $\frac{1}{6}$, 1:6

10:30, $\frac{10}{30}$, $\frac{1}{3}$, 1:3

15:30, $\frac{15}{30}$, $\frac{1}{2}$, 1:2

© MCMXCVIII Alpha Omega Publications, Inc.

WORKSHEET 65

Examples:

1. $\dfrac{20}{30}, \dfrac{2}{3}$ $\dfrac{27}{9}, \dfrac{9}{3}$ $\dfrac{100}{125}, \dfrac{20}{25}$ $\dfrac{8}{4}, \dfrac{2}{1}$

2. $\dfrac{2}{8}, \dfrac{4}{16}$ $\dfrac{18}{24}, \dfrac{36}{48}$ $\dfrac{12}{6}, \dfrac{24}{12}$ $\dfrac{34}{10}, \dfrac{68}{20}$

3.

4	11	
14	100	
30	20	5
8	4	
24	48	60
2	5	6
24	54	90 490

WORKSHEET 66

8.3; eight and three tenths

79.6; seventy-nine and six tenths

81.05; eighty-one and five hundredths

1,923.17; one thousand nine hundred twenty-three and seventeen hundredths

31.0618; thirty-one and six hundred eighteen ten thousandths

300.2; three hundred and two tenths

9.009; nine and nine thousandths

465; four hundred sixty-five

0.410; four hundred ten thousandths

54.054; fifty-four and fifty-four thousandths

0.4921; four thousand nine hundred twenty-one ten thousandths

WORKSHEET 67

1. 0.003, 0.03, 0.3, 3, 30

450, 45, 4.5, 0.45, 0.045,

0.0045

2. 27.4534   a. 27.453
             b. 27.45
             c. 27.5
             d. 27

    6.2047   a. 6.205
             b. 6.20
             c. 6.2
             d. 6

    452.9919   a. 452.992
             b. 452.99
             c. 453.0
             d. 453

3. 2.7   2.8   2.0
    9,752.3   760.0

WORKSHEET 68

1.

$17.28	12.88	$5.55
23.53	39.66	94.51
2.58	20.63	$87.16
70.12	3.9	70.93

2.

34.3406	3.70821	67.3946	268.744
398.411	101.77651	27.7109	25.62896

WORKSHEET 69

1.

a. 18	b. 36.4	c. 16.8
d. 483.6	e. 145.6	f. 303.8
g. 12.88	h. 194.04	i. 2194.5
j. 67.5	k. 279	l. 19.05
m. 1.55	n. 56.7	o. 517.83

WORKSHEET 70

1.

a. 90	b. 10.08	c. 7.28
d. 1.564	e. .832	f. 3.65
g. 31.98	h. 1.680	i. 1.550
j. 51.94	k. .496	l. 2.52
m. 26.523	n. 19.24	o. .285

WORKSHEET 71

1.

a. 3.122	b. 2.1	c. 8.35
d. .103	e. .902	f. .502
g. .002	h. .042	i. 20.43
j. 9.33	k. 4.08	l. .053
m. 80.44	n. .701	o. 7.93

WORKSHEET 72

1. $\frac{42}{100}$, 42%

   .07, 7%

   $\frac{2}{100}$, .02

2. .30, 30%

   .70, 70%

   .40, 40%

   .75, 75%

3. $\frac{5}{100}$ .05   5%

WORKSHEET 73

1. 10.64
   9
   25
   18
   17
   1.62
   2.565
   6

2. 3
   5.4
   2.1
   42
   18
   0.3
   48
   .374

3. 31.5
   54
   2.31
   8.16
   3
   140

4. $0.22

WORKSHEET 74

1. inch, foot, yard, mile
   pounds, ounces, tons
   cup, pint, quart, gallon

2. 32, 3
   1, 1
   4, 16
   4, 2
   40, 27
   48, 38
   64, 16
   16, 64
   16, 96

WORKSHEET 75

1. 1; 8.76; 1,000; 2,000; 1; 200; 2.500, .002; 4,800

2. English, English, English
   English, metric, English
   metric, English, metric
   English, English, metric
   metric, English, metric
   English, English, metric

3. 1; 625,000; 0.001; 2800; 0.043; 500; 1; 48,000;
   0.001;   0.16; 6750; 0.0243

WORKSHEET 76

1. 92°, 2°, 25°, 69°

2. thermometer readings and pictures
   should match the indicated
   temperature

3. 95° C   –   B.
   32° C   –   C.
   15° C   –   E.
   -5° C   –   D.
   0° C   –   A.

WORKSHEET 77

1. dogs; biography; 12

2. 11; 100 yard dash; 6; 38

WORKSHEET 78

1. 40; 14 years old; 230; picture graph;
   10 and 12; 70

2. F
   T
   T
   T

WORKSHEET 79

1. 45; 17
   54; 19

2. 6.4

3. 20; 6.5
   46; 42.5

4. 2; none or all
   20; 80

WORKSHEET 80

1. a. $\frac{2}{5}$

   b. $\frac{3}{5}$

   a. $\frac{7}{10}$

   b. $\frac{3}{10}$

   $P \text{ (vowel)} = \frac{5}{26}$

   $P \text{ (odd)} = \frac{5}{10} = \frac{1}{2}$

   $P \text{ (3n)} = \frac{6}{20} = \frac{3}{10}$

2. $\frac{4}{8} = \frac{1}{2}$

   $\frac{2}{8} = \frac{1}{4}$

   $\frac{2}{8} = \frac{1}{4}$

   $\frac{3}{8}$

   $\frac{1}{8}$

   $\frac{1}{8}$

   $\frac{1}{8}$

Unit

Tests

(1) **Correct the mismatched labels.** 10 pts.
Hint: Not all of the labels are mismatched!

25	+	14	=	39
Addend		Sum		Addend

_____   _____   _____

98	–	20	=	78
Subtrahend		Minuend		Difference

_____   _____   _____

100 – 0 = 100   15 – 0 = 15
Order Property of Subtraction

_____

4 x 5 = 20   5 x 4 = 20
Order Property of Multiplication

_____

9 x 8 = 72   72 ÷ 8 = 9
Division "Undoes" Multiplication

_____

(9 x 9) x 1 = 81   9 x (9 x 1) = 81
Order Property of Division

_____

(2) **Solve.** 6 pts.

21 – (3 x 4) = _____   15 + (50 ÷ 2) = _____   (64 ÷ 8) – 3 = _____

8 x (4 + 10) = _____   (19 – 4) + 7 = _____   (49 ÷ 7) x 3 = _____

(3) **Solve.** 8 pts.

78 + N = 95   45 − N = 23   8 x N = 64   10 x N = 100

72 ÷ N = 9   100 ÷ N = 50   N + 5 = 67   N + 16 = 30

(4) Mr. Taylor's business posted incomes of $9,893,589; $8,890,874; and $9,012,389 for the years 1995, 1996 and 1997. His expenses were $9,904,733; $6,894,569; and $4,004,358 for the same years. During which years did he make a profit and which years did he make a loss? Hint: When a company sustains losses, the amount of the loss is shown in parentheses ( ) and in red ink. 3 pts.

(5) **Write each number in standard and expanded form.** 6 pts.

One billion, two hundred million, three thousand, fifty.

    Standard:

    Expanded:

Five million, six hundred forty-three thousand, seven hundred twenty.

    Standard:

    Expanded:

Seventeen billion, six million, three.

    Standard:

    Expanded:

(6) Write the following Roman Numerals in order from the largest to the smallest. 11 pts.

XX   XVI   IX   XL

CL   CC   LM   DC

LXXXIV   MCMXCI   CDXLIX

(7) Round to the indicated place. 12 pts.

Nearest 10:   45   198   23   251

Nearest 100:   4,561   789   6,702   433

Nearest 1,000:   45,900   23,622   4,783   3,111

(8) Find the sum. 7 pts.

```
  946,205          34,013          765,197            234
+ 144,611        +  5,196        + 461,792         +  21
```

```
   405           $840.00         $4,566.00
    24             51.00          1,200.00
+  179          + 154.00        +   703.00
```

(9) Find the difference. 4 pts.

```
  123,988          453,299        $5,791.00       $2,874.00
-  41,975        - 372,006        -  567.23       - 1,352.05
```

(10) **Estimate by rounding the three-digit numbers to the nearest 10 and the four-digit numbers to the nearest 100.** 5 pts.

$$\begin{array}{r} 569 \\ + 847 \\ \hline \end{array} \qquad \begin{array}{r} 410 \\ - 218 \\ \hline \end{array} \qquad \begin{array}{r} 4,205 \\ + 7,637 \\ \hline \end{array} \qquad \begin{array}{r} 8,486 \\ - 5,128 \\ \hline \end{array} \qquad \begin{array}{r} 9,526 \\ + 4,262 \\ \hline \end{array}$$

(11) **Solve.** 4 pts.

Lisa purchased a bag of dog food, two dog bowls, and a collar. Her total cost was $17.23. If the dog food was $7.98 and the collar was $4.25, **how much** was **each dog bowl?**

Kevin purchased four new cassette tapes for $12.98. He also purchased 3 new compact discs for $36.00. **How much more** did Kevin spend on the CDs than the cassette tapes?

Molly purchased two dictionaries for $35.00 and three fictional books for $15.75. **How much** did **each dictionary** cost? **How much** did **each fictional book** cost?
Dictionaries:
Books:

(12) **Complete the factor trees.** 10 pts.

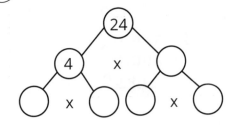 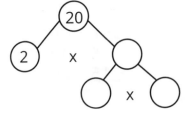 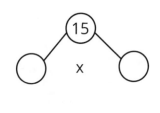

(13) **Find the product.** 5 pts.

$$\begin{array}{r} 45 \\ \times\ 2 \\ \hline \end{array} \qquad \begin{array}{r} 21 \\ \times\ 10 \\ \hline \end{array} \qquad \begin{array}{r} 100 \\ \times\ 50 \\ \hline \end{array} \qquad \begin{array}{r} 36 \\ \times\ 10 \\ \hline \end{array} \qquad \begin{array}{r} 78 \\ \times\ 3 \\ \hline \end{array}$$

① **Find the product.** 5 pts.

356	360	703	493	216
x 190	x 213	x 435	x 254	x 367

② **Estimate the products by rounding the two-digit numbers to the nearest 10 and the three-digit numbers to the nearest 100.** 6 pts.

7 x 69 =   8 x 484 =   2 x 482 =

11 x 48 =   18 x 78 =   123 x 7 =

Estimate the quotients by rounding the three-digit numbers to the nearest 10 and the four-digit numbers to the nearest 100. 3 pts.

148 ÷ 3 =   556 ÷ 7 =   2,357 ÷ 6 =

③ **Solve the equations and check.** 12 pts.

n x 9 = 81 ÷ ÷ _____ Check	n x 7 = 56 ÷ ÷ _____ Check	n x 3 = 36 ÷ ÷ _____ Check

n ÷ 4 = 5 x x _____ Check	n ÷ 5 = 9 x x _____ Check	n ÷ 8 = 9 x x _____ Check

④ **Complete the table.** 20 pts.

	Factors	Product	Exponent	Number of Zeros
10^2				
10^3				
10^4				
10^5				
10^6				

(5) Find the quotient. 8 pts.

$6\overline{)25}$ $8\overline{)98}$ $4\overline{)134}$ $8\overline{)178}$

$2\overline{)\$4.12}$ $2\overline{)\$25.00}$ $7\overline{)2,385}$ $7\overline{)3,223}$

(6) Solve. 5 pts.

Mr. Cown has several students with low homework grades. He needs to average these grades so that the mid-quarter reports can be sent to the students' parents. Average the grades below. Hint: Remember what to do with remainders!

46, 17, 34, 50   86, 24, 13, 17, 91, 27

71, 36, 64, 15   43, 26, 76, 9, 21, 80

85, 74, 28, 49

(7) Find the quotients. 12 pts.

$70\overline{)210}$ $36\overline{)89}$ $43\overline{)98}$ $68\overline{)778}$

$45\overline{)566}$ $27\overline{)\$378.00}$ $15\overline{)\$45.60}$ $15\overline{)6,105}$

$13\overline{)2,704}$ $97\overline{)13,580}$ $45\overline{)8,550}$ $23\overline{)14,763}$

(8) **Estimate by rounding the five-digit numbers to the nearest 10,000, the four-digit numbers to the nearest 1,000, the three-digit numbers to the nearest 100 and the two-digit numbers to the nearest 10.** 4 pts.

$391 \div 53 =$ $\qquad$ $782 \div 24 =$ $\qquad$ $4,241 \div 82 =$ $\qquad$ $62,899 \div 30 =$

(9) **Test each number to see if it is divisible by 2, 5, 10, or 3. Circle the correct responses.** The first one has been done for you. 5 pts.

52 is divisible by	②	5	10	3
720 is divisible by	2	5	10	3
6,531 is divisible by	2	5	10	3
4,002 is divisible by	2	5	10	3
3,025 is divisible by	2	5	10	3

(10) **Solve the problems. Underline the data that is not needed.** Some problems have information that is not needed. 6 pts.

Picture frames are on sale at 2 for $7.98. Last week the same frames were priced 2 for $13.75. If you purchase 4 frames at the sale price, how much money would you spend?

A box of 15 birthday invitations costs $3.75. The box contains 16 envelopes in case an extra one is needed. How much are you paying for each individual invitation?

Bruce's highest score on his electronic game was 95,260. This was 10 times as large as his first score on the game. He played his friend Tom and lost miserably. What was Bruce's first score?

(11)   **Match.** 11 pts.

_____ 1 hour	A. 1,000 years
_____ 90 seconds	B. 18th Century
_____ 24 hours	C. 10 years
_____ 72 hours	D. 14th Century
_____ 120 Minutes	E. $1\frac{1}{2}$ minute
_____ 5 minutes	F. 1 day
_____ 1394	G. 100 years
_____ 1788	H. 2 hours
_____ millennium	I. 60 minutes
_____ a decade	J. 3 days
_____ a century	K. 300 seconds

(12)   **Write the indicated time on each clock face. Circle A.M. or P.M. for each time, according to the event taking place.** 15 pts.

8:15	12:00	3:30	10:00	11:30
Eating breakfast	Eating lunch	Getting out of school	Going to bed	Eating a early lunch
A.M. or P.M.	A.M. or P.M.	A.M. or P.M.	A.M. or P.M.	A.M. or P.M.

If 3 hours and 45 minutes were added to each time, what time would each clock show? (Be sure to indicate A.M. or P.M. with each time.)

_____   _____   _____   _____   _____

⑬ **Label each diagram according to the specified directions.** 11 pts.

Label each time zone. Then answer the question.

If it is 12:00 P.M. in Atlanta, Georgia, what time is it in Seattle, Washington?

Use the information provided to label the calendar. Then answer the questions.

DECEMBER

S	M	T	W	T	F	S

The first day of December is on a Tuesday.
The last day of December is on a Thursday.
Christmas is on a Friday.

How many days are in the month of December?

On what day would January 1st be?

On what day would November 29th be?

⑭ **Count the change. Use the fewest coins and bills possible.**
Write the total amount due. 3 pts.

Price	Paid	Change Due
Example: $1.55	$2.00	2 dimes, 1 quarter = $0.45
$3.74	$5.00	
$8.29	$10.00	
$11.36	$15.00	

(15) **Match the figure with the appropriate name.** 11 pts.

1.

● A

2.

A   B

3.

A   B

4.

A   B

_____   _____   _____   _____

5.

A

6.

7.

D
C

8.

_____   _____   _____   _____

9.

10.
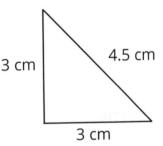

11.
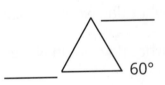

_____   _____   _____

Word Bank:

intersecting lines	right angle	point A	parallel lines
ray AB	obtuse angle	plane A	segment AB
perpendicular lines	acute angle	line AB	

---

(16) **Identify each triangle as equilateral, isosceles or scalene. Use a protractor to measure and label the missing angles. Circle the triangle that is a right triangle.**
9 pts.

1.
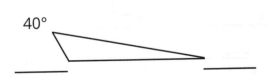
3 cm   4.5 cm
3 cm

_____

2.
60°

_____

3. 40°

_____   _____

4.
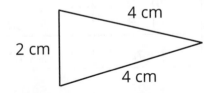
4 cm
2 cm
4 cm

_____

1 **Match the most common definition with each picture.** 10 pts.   57 points total

1. _____ Rhombus   a. ◁▷

2. _____ Square   b. ⬡

3. _____ Equilateral Triangle   c. ☐

4. _____ Scalene Triangle   d. ⬠

5. _____ Isosceles Triangle   e. ▱

6. _____ Pentagon   f. ⊖

7. _____ Hexagon   g. ⬢

8. _____ Chord   h. △

9. _____ Octagon   i. ◺

10. _____ Prism   j. ◺

2 **Find the surface area of the figure.** 9 pts.

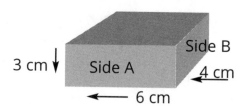

3 cm   Side A   Side B   4 cm
            6 cm

Use the above picture to answer the following questions.

1.   Find the area of Side A.

2.   Find the area of Side B.

3.   Find the surface area of the box.

Front _____   x 2 = _____

Top _____   x 2 = _____

Side _____   x 2 = _____

                    Total   _____

③ **Write the sum or difference.** 8 pts.

$3\ \dfrac{1}{4}$

$-\ 2\ \dfrac{5}{16}$
_____

$7\ \dfrac{3}{8}$

$-\ 4\ \dfrac{3}{4}$
_____

$16\ \dfrac{2}{3}$

$-\ \ 9\ \dfrac{7}{9}$
_____

$27\ \dfrac{1}{3}$

$-\ 12\ \dfrac{5}{8}$
_____

$8\ \dfrac{4}{7}$

$+\ 12\ \dfrac{2}{3}$
_____

$13\ \dfrac{6}{8}$

$+\ \ 4\ \dfrac{1}{2}$
_____

$55\ \dfrac{4}{5}$

$+\ \ 47\ \dfrac{7}{8}$
_____

$29\ \dfrac{6}{9}$

$+\ \ 99\ \dfrac{2}{3}$
_____

④ **Find the fraction of each number.** 4 pts.

$\dfrac{3}{4}$ of 28 $\dfrac{1}{7}$ of 63 $\dfrac{5}{8}$ of 32 $\dfrac{4}{9}$ of 81

⑤ **Multiply or divide. Write the answers in simplest terms.** 8 pts.

$\dfrac{2}{5}\ \times\ \dfrac{6}{7}$ $\dfrac{5}{8}\ \times\ \dfrac{5}{12}$ $1\dfrac{5}{9}\ \times\ \dfrac{2}{3}$ $2\dfrac{3}{4}\ \times\ 2\dfrac{1}{2}$

$\dfrac{1}{3}\ \div\ \dfrac{4}{7}$ $\dfrac{2}{5}\ \div\ \dfrac{1}{3}$ $6\ \div\ \dfrac{2}{3}$ $\dfrac{4}{9}\ \div\ 5$

⑥ **Use the circle to answer the following questions.** 4 pts.

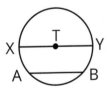

1. Name the diameter.
2. Name a chord other than the diameter.
3. Name a radius.
4. If the diameter is 6 cm, what is the radius?

(7)   **Define the figure and tell the number of faces, edges, and vertices.** You may choose from the following names: rectangular pyramid, triangular pyramid, hexagonal pyramid, triangular prism or cube. 12 pts.

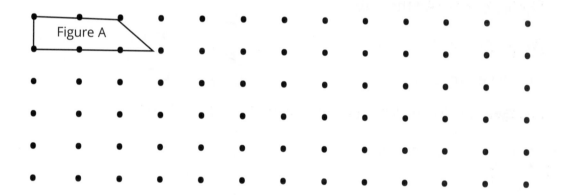

Name of Figure			
Faces			
Edges			
Vertices			

(8)   **Draw a figure that is congruent to Figure A. Draw a figure that is similar to Figure A.** 2 pts.

Figure A

① **Multiply to complete each table.** 13 pts.

Fence posts	5	10		20		
Fence row	1		3			

Water	1		3		5	
Dough Mix	3	6	9			

② **Use <, >, = to compare the decimals.** 7 pts.

One hundred and twenty hundredths   ◯   100.020

Fifteen thousands   ◯   0.15

Twenty-seven and three tenths   ◯   27.3

Two hundred and one hundredths   ◯   200.01

Fifty-seven thousandths   ◯   0.57

One and ninety-nine hundredths   ◯   1.993

Three and three tenths   ◯   3.03

③ **Round to the nearest whole number.** 5 pts.

17.099   135.901   100.5   9,002.17   577.49

Find the sum or difference. 5 pts.

73.99	94.02	823.77	211.16	100.15
+ 69.12	− 79.10	+ 663.04	− 107.05	− 94.71

Write each product. 5 pts.

8.9	0.81	1.32	12.9	21.9
x 6	x 3	x 0.5	x 4.2	x 1.4

④ **Write each quotient. Write an extra dividend in the quotient when needed.** 4 pts.

$9\overline{)262.17}$ $4\overline{)464.44}$ $5\overline{)157.8}$ $2\overline{)48.95}$

⑤ **Write each percent as a lowest term fraction.** 6 pts.

15% _____   20% _____   75% _____

10% _____   30% _____   50% _____

⑥ **Complete the table.** 10 pts.

Fraction	Decimal	Percent
$\frac{14}{100}$	0.14	14%
$\frac{62}{100}$		
		8%
	0.19	
$\frac{80}{100}$		
	0.75	

Find the percent of each number. 4 pts.

20% of 100   15% of 60   10% of 70   25% of 60

⑦ **Complete.** 6 pts.

			Basic Unit (Meter, Liter or Gram)			
Kilo	Hecto	Deka		deci	centi	milli

77 mm = _____ cm   6.89 m = _____ cm   103 cm = _____ m

141 cm = _____ m   8.14 Km = _____ dm   1.48 m = _____ mm

⑧ Write each temperature on the line provided. 4 pts.

_____ _____ _____ _____

⑨ Find the range, mean, and mode for the set of numbers. 3 pts.

88%, 92%, 100%, 78%, 97%

range _____   mean _____   mode _____

⑩ Use the chart to solve the following word problems. 4 pts.

1 cup (c) = 8 fluid ounces (fl oz)	1 quart (qt) = 32 fluid oz. 4 cups, 2 pints
1 pint (pt) = 16 fluid oz. 2 cups	1 gallon (gal) = 128 fluid oz. 16 cups, 8 pints, 4 quarts

1. Stephanie knows that it is important to drink a lot of water every day. The doctor told her to try and drink 48 ounces a day. How many cups of water is 48 ounces?

2. If Stephanie drinks a quart of water by 4:00 in the afternoon, how many ounces does she have left to drink?

3. Stephanie drank 3 pints of water on Wednesday. Was that enough to meet her goal of 48 ounces?

4. Stephanie drank 2 quarts of water on Wednesday. Was that enough to meet her goal of 48 ounces?

(11) **Place the information below in the circle graph and the bar graph.** 8 pts.
The first one has been done for you.

100 students were asked what their favorite subjects were. The answers follow:

25 Math   19 Social Studies   21 Science   23 Reading   12 Spelling

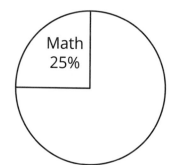

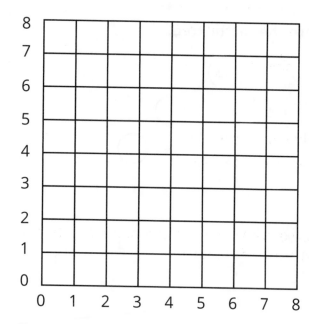

(12) **Graph the coordinates.** 5 pts.

(6, 0)

(3, 3)

(1, 4)

(2, 5)

(0, 7)

423

(1)   **Add.** 1 pt.

42,981
+ 12,873

(2)   **Subtract.** 1 pt.

$67,892
– 14,783

(3)   **Round to the nearest dollar and add.** 2 pts.

$698.25
+ 267.09

(4)   **Solve.** 1 pt.

N – (34 + 15) = 123

(5)   **Complete the factor tree.** 5 pts.

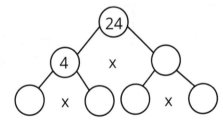

(6)   **Solve.** 1 pt.

349
x 142

(7)   **Complete the table.** 10 pts.

		Factors	Product	Exponent	Number of Zeros
10^4			10,000		
10^5		10 x 10 x 10 x 10 x 10			
10^6					

(8) **Divide.** 1 pt.

$$45\overline{)\$115.20}$$

(9) **Average.** 1 pt.

65, 98, 45, 77, 100

(10) **Tell if the numbers below are divisible by 2, 3, 5, or 10. If it is not divisible by 2, 3, 5, or 10, write *none*.** 3 pts.

6,794 =

450 =

84,593 =

(11) Chad and Larry went to the sporting goods store. They purchased a tent for $154.98, a lantern for $30.00, and a cooking set for $45.75. If they gave the cashier $300.00, how much change did they receive? 1 pt.

(12) **Estimate and compare.**   Round the two-digit numbers to the nearest 10, the three-digit numbers to the nearest 100, and the four-digit numbers to the nearest 1,000. 3 pts.

$$
\begin{array}{r}
851 \\
\times\ 21 \\
\end{array}
\quad \bigcirc \quad
\begin{array}{r}
1,907 \\
\times\ \ \ \ 5 \\
\end{array}
$$

<, >, =

Answer the following questions. 4 pts.

(13) How many hours are in two days?

(14) In what century was the year 1689?

(15) If the library opens at 9:00 A.M. and it takes Sarah 45 minutes to get there, what time will she need to leave in order to arrive at the opening?

(16) In what time zone is the state of Colorado?

(17) **Draw a pair of parallel lines to match the mathematical sentenc**e *a // b.* 1 pt.

Use the diagram below to answer the following questions. 6 pts.

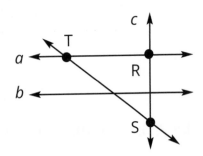

(18) Which lines are perpendicular? (write it as a mathematical sentence)

(19) Where do lines *a* and *c* intersect?

(20) Three lines intersect to form a triangle. What is the name of this triangle?

(21) What type of triangle is this? (scalene, isosceles, equilateral, or right)

(22) Is angle T of the triangle an acute or obtuse angle?

(23) If angle R of the triangle measures 90° (it is a right angle), and angle S measures 45°, what is the measurement of angle T?

(24) **Kevin worked 8 hours on Saturday, 5 hours on Monday, and 6 hours on Tuesday. If he earns $7.00 per hour, how much money did he make?** 1 pt.

(25) **Write the number below in standard, expanded, and Roman numeral forms.** 3 pts.

Three thousand, four hundred, twenty-five

Standard:

Expanded Form:

Roman Numeral Form:

㉖ **Place the correct term under each picture.** Choose from the following words: scalene triangle, equilateral triangle, or isosceles triangle. Also circle the figures that are right triangles. 4 pts.

△	◣	▷

㉗ **Find the surface area of the figure.** 9 pts.

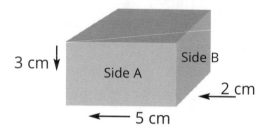

3 cm   Side B   Side A   2 cm   5 cm

Use the above picture to answer the following questions.

Find the area of Side A.

Find the area of Side B.

Find the surface area of the box.

Front _____ x 2 = _____

Top _____ x 2 = _____

Side _____ x 2 = _____

Total _____

㉘ **Add or subtract.** 4 pts.

$$5 \frac{1}{7}$$
$$+ \ 9 \frac{2}{3}$$

$$9 \frac{1}{8}$$
$$- \ 2 \frac{3}{4}$$

$$11 \frac{2}{3}$$
$$+ \ \ 8 \frac{1}{6}$$

$$47 \frac{2}{3}$$
$$- \ 32 \frac{4}{5}$$

㉙ **Find the fraction of each number.** 4 pts.

$\frac{2}{3}$ of 21

$\frac{1}{6}$ of 30

$\frac{3}{4}$ of 12

$\frac{3}{8}$ of 32

(30) **Multiply or divide. Write the answers in simplest terms.** 4 pts.

$$\frac{1}{5} \times \frac{5}{7} \qquad\qquad \frac{3}{4} \div 2 \qquad\qquad 1\frac{3}{7} \times \frac{1}{4} \qquad\qquad \frac{1}{7} \div \frac{3}{4}$$

(31) **Use <, >, = to compare the decimals.** 4 pts.

One hundred and thirty hundredths	◯	100.29
Five and four tenths	◯	5.4
Eighteen thousands	◯	0.18
Fifty-one thousandths	◯	0.51

(32) **Write each product.** 5 pts.

$$\begin{array}{r} 6.1 \\ \times\quad 9 \\ \hline \end{array} \qquad \begin{array}{r} 0.44 \\ \times\quad 8 \\ \hline \end{array} \qquad \begin{array}{r} 8.02 \\ \times\quad 0.9 \\ \hline \end{array} \qquad \begin{array}{r} 10.1 \\ \times\quad 4.5 \\ \hline \end{array} \qquad \begin{array}{r} 56.9 \\ \times\quad 1.2 \\ \hline \end{array}$$

(33) **Write each quotient. Write an extra dividend in the quotient when needed.** 4 pts.

$$9\overline{)109.53} \qquad\qquad 4\overline{)761.04} \qquad\qquad 6\overline{)907.2} \qquad\qquad 8\overline{)1,270.08}$$

(34) **Complete the table.** 10 pts.

Fraction	Decimal	Percent
$\frac{25}{100}$	0.25	25%
$\frac{69}{100}$		
		1%
	0.27	
$\frac{88}{100}$		
	0.75	

(35) **Find the range, mean, and mode for the set of numbers.** 3 pts.

1.   13, 18, 61, 11, 47, 11, 84

range _____   mean _____   mode _____

(36)

12 inches	= 1 foot	
3 feet	= 1 yard	
5,280 feet	= 1,760 yards	= 1 mile

Use the conversion chart above to answer the questions. 4 pts.

1. The length of a rectangle is 1 yard and the width is 48 inches.
   Find the perimeter.

2. Pauline ran 15,840 feet in a race. How far did she run in miles?

3. A length of a rectangle is 10 cm, and the area is 80 cm^2.
   What is the width of the rectangle?

4. Steven walked 813 yards. How many feet did he walk?

(37) **Write a percent for each fraction.** 6 pts.

$\frac{19}{100}$ _____ $\frac{1}{4}$ _____ $\frac{2}{5}$ _____

$\frac{3}{4}$ _____ $\frac{8}{50}$ _____ $\frac{3}{20}$ _____

Quarter Test 1

1. Addend   Addend   Sum
   Minuend   Subtrahend   Difference
   Zero Property of Subtraction
   Order Property of Multiplication
   Division "Undoes" Multiplication
   Grouping Property of Multiplication

2. 9   40   5
   112 22   21

3. 17   22   8   10
   8   2   62   14

4. Profit/Loss 1995 ($11,144)
                1996 $1,996,305
                1997 $5,008,031

5. <u>1,200,003,050</u>
   1,000,000,000 + 200,000,000 + 3,000 + 50

   <u>5,643,720</u>
   5,000,000 + 600,000 + 40,000 + 3,000 + 700 + 20

   <u>17,006,000,003</u>
   10,000,000,000 + 7,000,000,000 + 6,000,000 + 3

6. XL   XX   XVI   IX
   LM   DC   CC   CL
   MCMXCI   CDXLIX   LXXXIV

7. 50   200   20   250
   4,600   800   6,700 400
   46,000 24,000 5,000 3,000

8. 1,090,816   39,209   1,226,989
   255   608 $1,045.00
   $6,469.00

9. 82,013   81,293
   $5,223.77 $1,521.95

10. 1,420   190   11,800
    3,400   13,800

11. $2.50
    $23.02
    Dictionaries: $17.50
    Books: $5.25

12.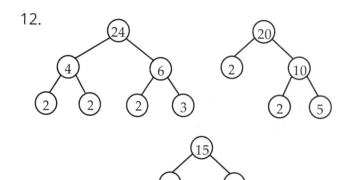

13. 90   210   5,000
    360   234

Quarter Test 2

1. 67,640   76,680   305,805
   125,222   79,272

2. 490   4,000   1,000
   500   1,600   700
   50   80   400

3. $n = 9$ Check: 9 x 9 = 81
   $n = 8$ Check: 8 x 7 = 56
   $n = 12$ Check: 12 x 3 = 36
   $n = 20$ Check: 4 x 5 = 20
   $n = 45$ Check: 5 x 9 = 45
   $n = 72$ Check: 8 x 9 = 72

4.

10^2	10 x 10	100	2	2
10^3	10 x 10 x 10	1,000	3	3
10^4	10 x 10 x 10 x 10	10,000	4	4
10^5	10 x 10 x 10 x 10 X 10	100,000	5	5
10^6	10 x 10 x 10 x 10 x 10 X 10	1,000,000	6	6

5. 4 R1;   12 R2;   33 R2;   22 R2
   $2.06; $12.50; 340 R5; 460 R3

6. 36 R3 ($\frac{3}{4}$) = 36.75 = 37

    43

    46 R2 ($\frac{2}{4}$) = 46.5 = 47

    42 R3 ($\frac{3}{6}$) = 42.5 = 43

    59

7. 3;   2 R17;   2 R12
    11 R30;   12 R26; $14.00
    $3.04   407   208
    140;   190;   641 R20

8. 400 ÷ 50 = 8
    800 ÷ 20 = 40
    4,000 ÷ 80 = 50
    60,000 ÷ 30 = 2,000

9. 720   - 2, 5, 10, 3
    6,531 - 3
    4,002 - 2, 3
    3,025 - 5

10. Last week the same frames were priced 2 for $13.75.
    $15.96
    The box contains 16 envelopes in case an extra one is needed.
    $0.25
    He played his friend Tom and lost miserably.
    9,526

11. 1 hour   - I.
    90 seconds - E.
    24 hours   - F.
    72 hours   - J.
    120 minutes - H.
    5 minutes   - K.
    1394   - D.
    1788   - B.
    millennium - A.
    a decade   - C.
    a century   - G.

12. A.M.   P.M.   P.M.   P.M.   A.M.
    12:00 P.M. 3:45 P.M.   7:15 P.M.
    1:45 A.M.   3:15 P.M.

13. 9:00 A.M.

S	M	T	W	T	F	S
		1	2	3	4	5
6	7	8	9	10	11	12
13	14	15	16	17	18	19
20	21	22	23	24	25	26
27	28	29	30	31		

31 days in December
Friday
Sunday

14. 1 dollar, 1 quarter, 1 penny = ($1.26)
    1 dollar, 2 quarters, 2 dimes, 1 penny = ($1.71)
    3 dollars, 2 quarters, 1 dime, 4 pennies = ($3.64)

15. 1. point A
    2. line segment AB
    3. line AB
    4. ray AB
    5. plane A
    6. intersecting lines
    7. perpendicular lines
    8. parallel lines
    9. right angle
    10. acute angle
    11. obtuse angle

16. 1. (isosceles)   2. equilateral – 60°60°
    3. scalene – 120°/20°   4. isosceles

Quarter Test 3

1. 1. Rhombus   - e.
    2. Square   - c.
    3. Equilateral Triangle - h.
    4. Scalene   - j.

© MCMXCVIII Alpha Omega Publications, Inc.

5. Isosceles - i.

6. Pentagon - d.

7. Hexagon - b.

8. Chord - f.

9. Octagon - g.

10. Prism - a.

2. 1. 18 cm²

   2. 12 cm²

   3. Front   <u>18 cm²</u> x 2 = <u>36 cm²</u>

      Top   <u>24 cm²</u> x 2 = <u>48 cm²</u>

      Side   <u>12 cm²</u> x 2 = <u>24 cm²</u>

                     Total 108 cm²

3. $\frac{15}{16}$ $2\frac{5}{8}$ $6\frac{8}{9}$ $14\frac{17}{24}$

   $20\frac{26}{21} = 21\frac{5}{21}$ $17\frac{10}{8} = 18\frac{2}{8} = 18\frac{1}{4}$

   $102\frac{67}{40} = 103\frac{27}{40}$

   $128\frac{12}{9} = 129\frac{3}{9} = 129\frac{1}{3}$

4. 21   9   20   36

5. $\frac{12}{35}$ $\frac{25}{96}$

   $\frac{28}{27} = 1\frac{1}{27}$ $\frac{55}{8} = 6\frac{7}{8}$

   $\frac{7}{12}$ $\frac{6}{5} = 1\frac{1}{5}$

   $\frac{18}{2} = 9$ $\frac{4}{45}$

6. 1. $\overline{XY}$

   2. $\overline{AB}$

   3. $\overline{TX}$ or $\overline{TY}$

   4. 3 cm

7.

Name of Figure	Triangular prism	Hexagonal pyramid	cube
Faces	5	7	6
Edges	9	12	12
Vertices	6	7	8

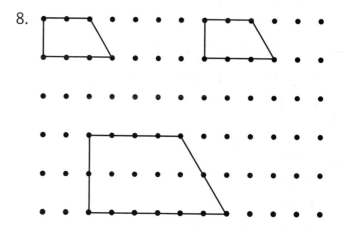

8.

Quarter Test 4

1.

Fence posts	5	10	15	20	25	30
Fence row	1	2	3	4	5	6

Water	1	2	3	4	5	6
Dough Mix	3	6	9	12	15	18

2. >

   <

   =

   =

   <

   <

   >

3. 17   136   101   9,002   577

   143.11   14.92   1486.81   104.11   5.44

   53.4   2.43   0.66   54.18   30.66

4. 29.13   116.11   31.56   24.475

5. $\frac{3}{20}$ $\frac{1}{5}$ $\frac{3}{4}$

   $\frac{1}{10}$ $\frac{3}{10}$ $\frac{1}{2}$

...on	Decimal	Percent
$\frac{14}{100}$	0.14	14%
$\frac{62}{100}$	0.62	62%
$\frac{8}{100}$	0.08	8%
$\frac{19}{100}$	0.19	19%
$\frac{80}{100}$	0.80	80%
$\frac{75}{100}$	0.75	75%

12.

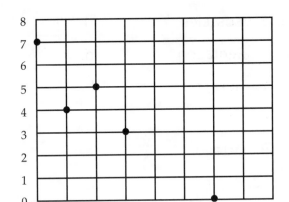

20   9   7   15

7. 7.7 cm   689 cm   1.03 m
    1.41 m   81,400 dm   1,480 mm

8. 92°   -18°
    43°   -11°

9. range   22
    mean   91
    mode   none

10.   1. 6 cups
        2. 16 ounces
        3. yes
        4. yes

11.

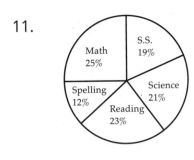

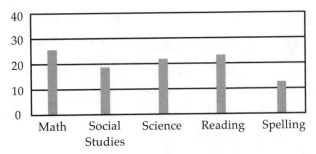

Final Exam

1. 55,854

2. $53,109

3. $965

4. N = 172

5.

6. 49,558

7.

10^4	10 x 10 x 10 x 10	10,000	4	4
10^5	10 x 10 x 10 x 10 X 10	100,000	5	5
10^6	10 x 10 x 10 x 10 X 10	1,000,000	6	6

8. $2.56

9. 77

10. 6,794 = 2
    450 = 2, 3, 5, 10
    84,593 = none

11. $69.27

12. 18,000 > 10,000

13. 48 hours

14. 17th century

15. 8:15 A.M.

16. Mountain

17. a ⟷
    b ⟷

18. a ⊥ c and b ⊥ c

19. at point R

20. TRS, SRT, or R

21. right triangle

22. acute

23. 45°

24. $133.00

25. 3,425
    3,000 + 400 + 20 + 5
    MMMCDXXV

26.

△	◺	▷
Equilateral	Scalene	Isosceles

27. 15 cm²
    6 cm²
    Front 15 cm² x 2 = 30 cm²
    Top   10 cm² x 2 = 20 cm²
    Side   6 cm²   x 2 = 12 cm²
                        Total 62 cm²

28. $14\frac{17}{21}$ $6\frac{3}{8}$ $19\frac{5}{6}$ $14\frac{13}{15}$

29. 14   5   9   12

30. $\frac{5}{35} = \frac{1}{7}$ $\frac{3}{8}$

    $\frac{10}{28} = \frac{5}{14}$ $\frac{4}{21}$

31. >
    =
    <
    <

32. 54.9   3.52   7.218
    45.45   68.28

33. 12.17   190.26   151.2   158.76

34.

Fraction	Decimal	Percent
$\frac{25}{100}$	0.25	25%
$\frac{69}{100}$	0.69	69%
$\frac{1}{100}$	0.01	1%
$\frac{27}{100}$	0.27	27%
$\frac{88}{100}$	0.88	88%
$\frac{75}{100}$	0.75	75%

35.   range = 73
        mean = 35
        mode = 11

36.   1. 168 inches
        2. 3 miles
        3. 8 cm
        4. 2,439 ft

37.   19%   25%   40%
        75%   16%   15%